*The Cooperstown Symposium on Baseball
and American Culture* 2001

ALSO IN THIS SERIES
FROM McFARLAND

*The Cooperstown Symposium on Baseball
and American Culture, 1997 (Jackie Robinson)* (2000)

*The Cooperstown Symposium on
Baseball and American Culture, 1998* (2002)

*The Cooperstown Symposium on
Baseball and American Culture, 1999* (2000)

*The Cooperstown Symposium on
Baseball and American Culture, 2000* (2001)

SERIES EDITOR: ALVIN L. HALL

The Cooperstown Symposium on Baseball and American Culture

2001

Edited with an Introduction by
William M. Simons

Series Editor: Alvin L. Hall

McFarland & Company, Inc., Publishers
Jefferson, North Carolina, and London

The Cooperstown symposium on baseball and American culture, 2001 /
edited by William M. Simons ; series editor Alvin L. Hall.

ISSN 1536-1195

ISBN 0-7864-1357-3 (illustrated case binding : 50# alkaline paper)

Cover art ©2002 Wood River Gallery

Manufactured in the United States of America

*McFarland & Company, Inc., Publishers
Box 611, Jefferson, North Carolina 28640
www.mcfarlandpub.com*

Table of Contents

PART 2: MEDIA MYTHOLOGY

Acknowledgments

Alvin L. Hall created the Cooperstown Symposium on Baseball and American Culture. Jim Gates, Tim Wiles, and their superb library staff at the National Baseball Hall of Fame and Museum provided invaluable research assistance. Hall of Fame president Dale Petrosky was again a gracious host. Sharon Corna gave much appreciated secretarial support. Colleagues and friends Thomas Beal, Mark Boshnack, Fred and Holly Bucalos, Joseph Fodero, Gerrit Gantvoort, John Hurley, Alan Levine, Armand LaPotin, Andrew Puritz, Eugene Obidinski, David Richards, Robert Russell, Dennis Shea, and Edward Wesnofske read manuscripts and offered insightful criticism. Charles Bollinger III, Jeff Cook, and Terri Weigl offered their computer expertise. State University of New York College at Oneonta Provost F. Daniel Larkin and Interim Dean Marguerite Culver contributed institutional support. Fawn Holland produced the index.

My first baseball memory is of my father running down a fly ball while playing center field for the Mohawks. He made his love of baseball mine. For this and other reasons, this book is dedicated to Shep Simons.

— *WMS*

Preface

Alvin L. Hall

The State University of New York College at Oneonta and the National Baseball Hall of Fame and Museum organized the First Cooperstown Symposium on Baseball and American Culture in June 1989. The occasion was the fiftieth anniversary of the Hall of Fame. The idea was simple: Invite scholars from around the country to come to Cooperstown during the celebration to discuss the impact of baseball on American culture. None of us knew what to expect. Had we attracted a dozen papers, we would have been satisfied. Following a single call-for-papers in *The Chronicle of Higher Education*, we received 125 abstracts from faculty members at prestigious universities, including MIT, Southern Methodist, and UCLA. Our plan was to do the Cooperstown Symposium one time and then move on to other things. The gathering proved so popular with the one hundred people who attended that they insisted that we schedule another conference the following year, and we did.

In 1990, I encountered a situation that any academic would envy. On the opening evening of the Second Cooperstown Symposium, following a keynote address by Harold Seymour, the dean of baseball historians, I found myself sitting in a rocking chair on the veranda of the Otesaga Hotel watching the sunset over Lake Otsego, James Fenimore Cooper's Glimmerglass. I had a drink in one hand and was flanked on one side by the president of a small specialty publishing company and on the other by the senior editor of the largest academic publisher in the country. Each was trying to outbid the other for the privilege of underwriting the conference in subsequent years. I began to suspect that we had stumbled upon something

1

special. The next eleven years confirmed this. The Cooperstown Symposium on Baseball and American Culture has been held every June since 1989 without any decline in interest. The papers in this volume are from the Thirteenth Cooperstown Symposium, and planning for the Fourteenth is already well underway.

We have made a discovery. Baseball, more than any other sport, has an intellectual appeal for a small, but growing, subculture on American college and university campuses; faculty enthusiasts are both passionate baseball fans and solid scholars in diverse disciplines. These academics have managed to combine their dual interests in both their teaching and their scholarship. However, on many university campuses, sport, in general, and baseball, in particular, are not considered quite as respectable for topics of research as more traditional fields. Faculty who pursue baseball are somewhat suspect. Some have encountered difficulty competing for research grants, teaching honors, and even tenure. But when they come to Cooperstown in June, they are among colleagues who think like they do and support their work. They do not need to defend what they love.

This atmosphere has been changing over time. In the 1940s, it took Harold Seymour two years to convince the history department at his university that baseball's early years provided a suitable topic for his doctoral dissertation. Now, we have several graduate students presenting papers at the Symposium each June. The future looks even better despite some of the problems that confront the game itself. The Cooperstown Symposium seems destined to flourish for years to come.

The success of the Symposium has been assured in large part because of the continuing support of the State University of New York College at Oneonta and the National Baseball Hall of Fame. For the last five years, all sessions have been held in the library of the Hall of Fame. While the idea for the conference was the dream of Tom Heitz, the former librarian, the last several years have been made especially enjoyable for the participants by the help of Jim Gates, the current librarian, and his staff. The president of the Hall, Dale Petrosky, has been especially supportive since coming on board three years ago. In the closing session of the Thirteenth Cooperstown Symposium, Petrosky told the participants that he considers the Symposium one of the most important things the Hall of Fame does each year. Somehow, that made the last thirteen years of effort worth it.

The Fourteenth Cooperstown Symposium is scheduled for June 5, 6, and 7, 2002, in the only place in the universe such a meeting could happen, the National Baseball Hall of Fame.

Alvin L. Hall
East Stroudsburg University, Pennsylvania

Introduction

William M. Simons

Literature, fantasy, and baseball form a distinctive American amalgam. As a boy, "Beat" novelist Jack Kerouac, for example, created a surreal baseball "Summer League," featuring imaginary teams, such as the Boston Fords, Pittsburgh Plymouths, and St. Louis Cadillacs. Poncho Villa and other historic personages, along with totally fictitious individuals and actual players, populated the rosters of Kerouac's fantasy baseball teams.

At our *thirteenth* gathering, the 2001 Cooperstown Symposium on Baseball and American Culture gave special attention to baseball's myths, legends, and tall tales.

Myths are the symbolic stories employed to approach our ultimate concerns; legends and tall tales are their adjuncts. "Myths," writes the acclaimed scholar Joseph Campbell, "are clues to the spiritual potentialities of the human life."[1] Humanity's archetypes — creation, the golden age, temptation, evil, sin, loss of innocence, familial strife, absent parents, leaving home, search for meaning, self-discovery, journeys, labors, trials, suffering, war, revenge, dualism, dreams, miraculous suspension of the normative laws of the universe, crossing thresholds, mysterious strangers, mentors, heroes, women as goddesses and seducers, love, redemption, homecomings, death, and immortality — provide mythology with thematic content.

Myths, asserts Campbell, concern "deep inner problems, inner mysteries, inner thresholds of passage."[2] Archetypal stories offer perspective, support, and guidance to our journey. Through myths, we seek meaning and significance in the human experience. "There is," relates Campbell,

3

"the mythology that relates you to the natural world, of which you're part. And there is the mythological that is strictly sociological, linking you to a particular society."[3] Mythology grants the world and the births, lives, and deaths of its sojourners a spiritual interpretation. The mythological transcends the empirical and the analytical. The symbolism of the sacred derives from mythology. Myth, suggests Campbell, "is the song of the imagination, inspired by the energies of the body."[4] Campbell believes,

> It would not be too much to say that myth is the secret opening through which the inexhaustible energies of the cosmos pour into human cultural manifestation. Religions, philosophies, arts, the social forms of primitive and historic man, prime discoveries in science and technology, the very dreams that blister sleep, boil up from the basic, magic ring of myth.[5]

Deanne Westbrook, professor of English at Portland State University, writes brilliantly of the pervasiveness of myth in the baseball canon. Her seminal book, *Ground Rules: Baseball & Myth*, locates the primal stories of the human experience in America's game. According to Westbrook, both the classic monomyth ("someone went on a long journey") and the American monomyth ("a stranger came to town") figure prominently in baseball lore.[6] "Baseball literature," observes Westbrook, "has the status of a functional modern mythology":[7]

> The texts are archetypal...The mythicity of baseball's texts emerge almost of necessity from a mythicity in the game itself—its rituals and rules, its characters, the tropological nature of its space and time, its "plot" (the progress and rules of play), its object (to make the circular journey from home to home), its ground (a solid stage in a shifting cosmos), and its ground rules (the principle of order within this [con]text).[8]

Westbrook's compelling content analysis illuminates the mythic structure of baseball's great texts, including Augusts Wilson's *Fences*, Mark Harris' *Bang the Drum Slowly* and *The Southpaw*, W.P. Kinsella's *The Iowa Baseball Conspiracy* and *Shoeless Joe*, Eric Rolfe Greenberg's *The Celebrant*, Jerome Charyn's *The Seventh Babe*, John Sayles' *Pride of the Bimbos*, Jay Neugeboren's *Sam's Legacy*, Bernard Malamud's *The Natural*, Philip Roth's *The Great American Novel*, and Robert Coover's *The Universal Baseball Association, Inc., J. Henry Waugh, Prop.* Oedipus and Odysseus figure prominently in Westbrook's baseball cosmology. The sacred and the profane clash. Epic journeys, passages, and homecomings provide ballast to her baseball vision. "Baseball literature," ruminates Westbrook, "has more coherence, more common themes, more familiar characters and acts, a greater tendency to approach the mysterious and the sacred, and more echoes of ancient myths than can be accounted for easily, given the secular topic and the modern setting."[9]

Westbrook's analysis of Douglas Wallop's novel *The Year the Yankees Lost the Pennant*, for example, suggests her imaginative exploration of baseball mythology. In middle age, Joe Boyd, the novel's protagonist, is flabby of body and spirit. Neither real estate sales nor his marriage to Bess elicit passion. Only the hapless Washington Senators interest him. Boyd falls prey to Applegate, the devil incarnate, exchanging his soul to bodily become Joe Hardy, a young baseball superstar, who will lead the Senators to the promised land. Westbrook observes,

> Suitably displaced Oedipal themes recur in this novel, for in undergoing his metamorphosis Joe Boyd figuratively becomes his own son, returning home as Joe Hardy, a youthful boarder in his wife's home...like Oedipus in the palace of Queen Jocasta, Joe Boyd is both son and husband, but unlike Oedipus, he is aware of the irony.[10]

Joe completes his quest. Despite the siren call of Lola, Applegate's seductive minion, Hardy, after winning the pennant for Washington, employs an escape clause to regain his life as Joe Boyd. Like Joe, Wallop's novel experienced metamorphosis, providing the basis for the classic theatrical and movie musical *Damn Yankees*.

Westbrook focuses on that part of baseball's canon that appears in printed text, but film also abounds with baseball mythology. As director and screenwriter Ron Shelton notes, "Our contemporary mythology is built around the athletic field and sports heroes. We have our white hats and our black hats, just as my generation had its Western heroes."[11]

In former times, the ancients fashioned myths from the cosmology of their deities. Modern secularists frequently fashion their myths from the popular culture — politics, literature, music, film, and sport. Cinema and baseball are fertile sources of contemporary American mythology. "There is something magical about films," observes Campbell.[12] When baseball and movies, two rich canons of American values and mores, are brought together, synergism results. Thus, the quest to explore mythology through content analysis of baseball cinema beckons.

Mythic themes punctuate many baseball films. *The Babe Ruth Story* (1948) and *The Babe* (1992), for example, embrace the legend of Ruth "calling his shot."[13] *Rookie of the Year* (1993) recounts the tall tale of 12-year-old Henry Rowengartner, whose tendons, following an arm injury, heal in a unique manner that makes it possible for him to pitch 100 mile per hour fastballs for the Chicago Cubs.[14] Likewise, *It Happens Every Spring* (1949) is a tall tale about a professor's laboratory discovery of a formula that renders baseballs elusive to bats.[15]

In *The Sandlot* (1993), a brotherhood of friends play baseball all day, and in the darkness of night, ensconced in their tree house "home," they recount their myths of the Bambino, spiritual father to all boys of the diamond, and the Beast, a voracious monster (actually a dog), who looms menacingly just beyond the sandlot's outfield fence, ready to devour lost balls and boys. During a 1962 dream cum vision, the Babe, 14 years after his apotheosis, miraculously appears, inspiring *The Sandlot*'s Benny to rescue a ball autographed by the 1927 Yankees, a quest that creates a new legend.[16]

The Natural (1984) mirrors the myth of paradise and paradise lost. The film opens with a tableau of a father and a son playing catch in a bucolic Eden, but a heart attack fells the father. Young Roy Hobbs then commences a long and arduous journey, paralleling the Arthurian legends. Roy's bat Wonderboy is a surrogate for the King's sword Excalibur. *The Natural* ends as it begun, a father and a son tossing a ball back and forth in the fields of their Edenic home. Now, however, it is Roy who is the father.[17]

The profane approaches the sacred through mythology. *Stealing Home* (1988) depicts Katie Chandler as a baseball goddess. Romantic, ethereal, and divinely mad, Katie is not bound by temporal constraints. Twice Katie saves Billy Wyatt, a baseball acolyte. When his father dies, Billy reverently entombs his baseball vestments and aspirations. In the summer that follows, Katie comforts Billy through the mysteries of sex. "When you have a goddess as the creator," observes Campbell, "it's her own body that is the universe."[18] With the authority of a goddess, Katie restores knowledge of Billy's identity: "You're a ballplayer; that's what you are." Subsequently, however, a costly fielding error and a loss of self-confidence terminate Billy's progress in the minor leagues, leaving him "lost as lost can be" for a second time. This depression festers for 14 years. But prior to committing suicide, Katie leaves instructions for Billy to dispose of her ashes. To complete the ritual, Billy recovers a baseball pendant that Katie gave him a generation ago. When he releases the goddess' ashes upon a pier from which Katie had once dreamt of ascending to meet her lover in the clouds, Billy, like Odysseus, completes his mythic journey, and, despite the advent of early middle age, is finally able to return to the family of baseball.[19]

Katie Chandler is a baseball goddess, but Annie Savoy is the game's high priestess. Annie's sacred catechism affirms her belief in the Church of Baseball. Candles sanctify her household altar, shrine to the mythic heroes of the game, whose framed photographs adorn the walls of Annie's temple/residence. *Bull Durham* (1988) casts Annie in a minor league evocation of the Oedipal myth. Crash Davis, a journeyman catcher who represents honest mediocrity, resents his primary function on the Durham Bulls, hastening the development of major league prospect Ebby LaLoosh, an undisciplined young pitcher who possesses a "million dollar arm but five-cent head." If Crash and Ebby are surrogate father and son, Annie, romantically involved with both the man and the boy, is the wife-mother in this mythic family. Crash and Annie, the symbolic parents, feud over the upbringing of their pitcher/son.

As the personification of patriarchy, Davis employs tough love to impose obedience, self-control, and respect for craft upon LaLoosh. The young pitcher/prodigal son rebels at Crash's regimen in a manner that resembles Westbrook's depiction of that "phase of Oedipal attachment to the mother, with accompanying feelings of competition, fear, and even hatred of the father." Renaming her man-child Nuke, Annie invokes instructions on breathing through eyelids, mystic incantations, bondage sacraments, and sacred garters to safeguard LaLoosh's Oedipal journey to the major leagues. And Nuke, the fictive son, incestuously shares Annie's bed. Through sexual cohabitation, the venerable priestess believes she can bestow spiritual growth and baseball advancement upon her Oedipal novitiate.[20]

Myth, writes Westbrook, also "evokes the sense of a universe where time and space may obey the laws of an unknown physics or be measured not in mechanistic terms but in human, psychological ones. There are opportunities in such a world to encounter the sacred, the numinous, the uncanny."[21] An epiphany punctuates many a baseball film. Both versions of *Angels in the Outfield* (1951, 1994), for example, feature celestial intervention on the baseball diamond.[22] The Capraseque intercession of *Mr. Destiny* allows Larry Burrows to rectify, 20 years later, "the worst moment" of his life: Larry's June 14, 1970, strikeout in the bottom of the ninth with two outs, which cost his team the all-state high school championship.[23] Obedience to the command of a mysterious voice converts an Iowa farm into a baseball park in *Field of Dreams* (1989), enabling Ray Kinsella to reconcile with his deceased father John. Joe Jackson, present in defiance of time and space, acts as muse to familial healing. *Field of Dream's* Jackson is not history's long dead exile of the sordid Black Sox scandal, but the Shoeless Joe of John Kinsella's mythology — heroic, incorruptible, incomparably talented.[24] And, in *Frequency* (2000), reverence for the "Amazing" Mets allows John Sullivan, a New York City police detective, to contact, resurrect, and share a heroic quest with his fireman father, Frank, who perished 30 years before during the 1969 World Series.[25]

Film and literature contribute significantly to baseball mythology. In addition to the shared consciousness of the popular culture, however, every baseball fundamentalist constructs a personal mythology drawn from individual experience. Those of us who invest the game with symbolism and significance frequently encounter the great archetypes on the diamond. The personal myths that I have fashioned from my baseball odyssey are not thematically unique; I present one of mine — *Mysterious Stranger* — confident that other members of the baseball fraternity harbor their own unique variations on it.

Mysterious Stranger

Late December 1993, the weather was brutal. Snow and ice rendered roads treacherous. A bone-chilling wind conquered central New York.

Still, I needed to get out. Even one full day in the great indoors induced symptoms of cabin fever. And, at 44, I was fighting the battle of the bulge, more compulsively than successfully. I had not yet retired into walking; that came soon enough. Each day I doggedly jogged, laundering the mind and torturing the knees.

The venerable Camry swerved on the way to the Bubble. Battered and frayed from age and misuse, the Bubble still stood, albeit precariously, on the campus of the State University of New York at Oneonta, its field house replacement still in the future. Unheated and possessing the charm of an abandoned warehouse, the oval shaped Bubble would, at least, shield me from the cutting wind.

Between Christmas and New Year, the Bubble would not host an army of heterogeneous runners jostling one another. Indeed, for the past several days, I had counted my laps utterly alone in the emptiness of the structure. Even without nature's assault, winter intercession always emptied the campus. At this time of the year, the Bubble was officially closed, its entrance locked. I was one of the few with a key to the facility.

Cold air assaulting my lungs, I pulled the Bubble key from my pocket. The wind at my back, I maneuvered the overhead bolt lock open and then pushed hard. The semi-circular motion of the revolving metal door pulled me out of the cold and wet. Sheltered by the Bubble, I instinctively shook my body. I was not alone, however. A surreal tableau appeared in the middle of the building.

A pitcher, a batter, and a catcher formed an ensemble totally foreign to this place at this time. They ignored my entrance and gave no acknowledgement of my presence. How did they get in? Who were they? Why in the world were they playing baseball in the frigid winter air of this ragged structure? With an eye on the mysterious baseball tableau, I went through my usual routine — removed my overcoat, sat on a bench, pulled my boots off, laced up my sneakers, stretched, and started to jog. I circled around and around the baseball pantomime. Staying in the inner lane, I was never far from the baseball apparition. Neither by voice nor body language did they display an awareness of my existence. Although I did not call out a greeting or wave, I could not avert my gaze from the epiphany.

The batter crouched to the side of a portable, rubber home plate.

Behind him, in position, the catcher made a target with the big mitt. Mask removed to speak with the pitcher, the catcher, like the batter, appeared a young man of average build in his mid-twenties. And probably fairly close to the regulation 60'6" from the plate stood a pitcher unlike any I had ever seen before.

The pitcher had flaming red hair that fell below the shoulders. Long arms. A face intense, focused, and fierce. Tall, easily over 6 feet, physically dominant over the compact batter and catcher. And this pitcher was a woman. Not a girl, a woman. A very fit woman, about 30 years old. She threw a baseball harder and faster than any woman I had ever seen. I have encountered several virtually unhittable, overpowering , underhand softball pitchers. But never had I witnessed a woman throw a baseball with such velocity. Where did this singular pitcher come from? The college and surrounding community were small enough that it seemed inconceivable that such a wondrous talent could remain incognito.

The pervasive indifference, utter obliviousness, of pitcher and company to me added to my sense of unreality. I was where expectation and habit dictated; the baseball players were not. Although we shared the same space, it was as though the baseball figures existed in another dimension. I found myself fantasizing that they could neither see nor hear me. The batter's failure to ever make contact with the ball meant that I did not have to dodge projectiles. And they did not have to shout "heads." There was absolutely no contact between me and them.

At a certain point, assessment competed with wonderment in my consciousness. The batter's tentative swing bespoke inexperience. I knew what I wanted to do. I walked toward the pitcher. She ignored my approach, but I spoke, "Would you like a real batter?"

She paused, looked at her two young companions, and answered flatly, "I don't think we have one here."

"No, I meant me."

I was middle-aged, but the pitcher did not laugh. "OK," she said. Her no nonsense tone suggested that conversation and questions were not welcome. She had a rhythm and did not want to lose it.

One of the young men handed me the bat. More out of a proprietary interest in the fragile canvas skin of the Bubble and less as an act of bravado, I quickly pulled the overhead netting around our area. Then I stepped up to the plate.

The tangible quickly replaced the surreal. Pitcher and batter, that's all there was; everything else was stripped away. Trying to get a sense of what she had, I let a few pitches go by. To get my timing, I calibrated my swing. At first, I treated it like pepper. I was getting the bat on the ball. Then, gradually, my stroke lengthened. Finally, I was ready. She had the advantage of youth and conditioning, but I had experience.

She was a bit wild, but not once did she consciously test whether an inside pitch would move me back from the plate or whether I would lunge for a ball beyond the outside corner. She threw hard but not superhard, not fast enough to throw the ball by me. She had only one pitch; it did not break or drop, and it came straight at you. No curve. No slider. No sinker. No change up. None of the repertoire that converted a good fastball from a favorite batting practice pitch into an effective weapon.

She threw some by me, but line drives jumped off my bat into the netting. I hit this pitcher well. She gave no sign of disappointment. Her determination never wavered. At length, the pitcher indicated that the session was over.

I walked over to the pitcher. "My name is Bill Simons. I teach here at the college."

Her game face disappeared into an engaging smile as she accepted my handshake. "I'm Terri Johnson. I'm night editor of *The Daily Star*." Her nocturnal hours at the local newspaper perhaps explained why I had never met her before. Terri introduced her two young male companions as friends and colleagues at the *Star*.

Sincere respect and a desire to know more made me more voluble than politically correct. "You're exceptional. I've never seen another woman throw that fast."

Terri shared her story. As a nine-year-old Little Leaguer in suburban Rochester, she caught the baseball bug. Soon little Terri knew what she wanted to do when she grew up — play in the big leagues.

Softball never filled her up. Even though organized baseball options disappeared after Little League, Terri kept hope alive on the sandlot. The passage of the years never dimmed her dream. Now a once in a lifetime opportunity beckoned. The Colorado Silver Bullets, a new woman's professional baseball team, would soon hold tryouts. For Terri, it was now or never.

Better than anyone, Terri knew her strengths and weaknesses. She had a live arm; her pitch had pop. Teri also had intelligence and determination. A lack of organized team experience and formal instruction meant that Terri, over the next two months, needed to develop the skills and techniques usually acquired over many years. Bruce Bouton, a college professor who spent his undergraduate days on the mound, worked on her pitching motion. College baseball coach Don Axtell and his men's team welcomed Terri to their practices. Her strong arm gained more precision. She conquered pain and doubt.

Terri flew out to her field of dreams in Colorado. Top women ballplayers from all over the country converged on Denver. Silver Bullets manager Phil Niekro, the Hall of Fame knuckleballer, and his pitching coach-brother, Joe, evaluated their potential daughters of the diamond. Terri did well, very well. But the competition was tough. Called out by the unforgiving umpire of fate, Terri returned to Oneonta and journalism. She married and moved on.

I never saw Terri again.

Keynote Speakers

Since its inception in 1989, the Symposium has hosted a series of outstanding keynote speakers. For example, Harold Seymour, whose 1956 Ph.D. dissertation on the early years of baseball initiated the process of legitimizing academic studies of the national pastime, made, despite age and infirmity, his last public presentation at the 1990 Symposium. In 1992, Harvard paleontologist, man of letters, and cultural guru Stephen Jay

Gould infused his presentation on legends and reality in baseball with wit and wisdom. Donald M. Fehr, executive director of the Major League Players Association, provided an insider's view of the game in 1993. Documentary filmmaker Ken Burns showed and discussed excerpts from his *Baseball* series in 1994 prior to its subsequent debut on PBS. Then, in 1996 W.P. Kinsella provided an interpretive reading of his memorable baseball fiction. To mark the fiftieth anniversary of the reintegration of Major League Baseball in 1997, historian Jules Tygiel analyzed Jackie Robinson's legacy. Eliot Asinof, author of *Eight Men Out*, the definitive account of the 1919 Black Sox scandal, added verve to the 1999 gathering. Legendary sportswriter and literary figure, Roger Kahn, acclaimed for *The Boys of Summer* and other notable works, graced the 2000 proceedings. In 2001, George Plimpton, in a memorable presentation, continued the Symposium's tradition of great keynote speakers.

George Plimpton is one of America's finest writers. Editor and writer, master of essays and books, the versatile Plimpton has produced a body of work distinguished for its substance and range. Co-founder and editor of *The Paris Review*, his own articles have appeared in *Harper's*, *Esquire*, *Sports Illustrated*, and a plethora of other journals. Plimpton's most famous works recount, with wit, insight, and literary grace, his adventures as a participant observer. He has played many roles, amongst them stunt man, bullfighter, trapeze artist, standup comic, actor, boxer, quarterback, golfer, Boston Celtic, hockey player, and, of course, baseball pitcher, in his quest for authenticity. Plimpton's many books include *Out of My League, The Bogy Man, Mad Ducks and Bears, Shadow Box, Fireworks: A History and Celebration, Women Writers at Work, Chronicles of Courage, Pete Peeves or Whatever Happened to Dr. Rawff?, The Curious Case of Sidd Finch*, and *Home Run*. Plimpton has frequently attained that state where "both writer and subject in perfect union have reached a very high level of inspired performance."[26]

Plimpton's work in general and keynote address in specific fit in well with the emphasis of this year's Symposium on baseball's myths, legends, and tall tales. In a 1985 *Sports Illustrated* article, Plimpton perpetrated a memorable hoax, recounting a tall tale, in the guise of authentic reportage, of a Tibetan monk, Sidd Finch, possessed of a 168 mile per hour fastball. And Plimpton's various odysseys into the domain of the athlete evoke the secret fantasies of Walter Mitty. Plimpton's journeys, however, as literary giant Ernest Hemingway observed, often conjure up the "dark side of Walter Mitty." The great boxer Archie Moore inflicted pain and injury upon Plimpton. Nor did the writer escape unscathed on the mound at Yankee Stadium when Mickey Mantle, Willie Mays, and their cohorts found

Plimpton's "roundhouse curve" wanting. Other forays also brought forth athletic defeat — and literary triumph. We are honored to include Plimpton's keynote address in this volume.

Structure of the Anthology

This anthology contains eclectic essays delivered in Cooperstown at the 2001 Symposium and subsequently revised for publication. By virtue of their association with Cooperstown, fictive birthplace of Abner Doubleday's apocryphal creation of baseball, all of the essays embrace mythology.

The anthology is divided into four parts: *Mythic Heroes, Media Mythology, Myth and Mystery,* and *Myths in Progress. Mythic Heroes* explores the fame and significance of baseball's eponymic figures. *Media Mythology* analyzes the role of diverse forms of communication, including cinema, novels, broadcasting, advertising, children's literature, autobiography, and poetry, in rendering baseball an American epic. *Myth and Mystery* examines baseball's symbolic rituals, unresolved questions, legends, and transcendence. *Myths in Progress* confronts shibboleths about science, race, economics, and gender. Each part contains multiple essays, related by theme and topic. A guide to the paper follows.

MYTHIC HEROES

Keynote Address by George Plimpton is quite appropriately the anthology's leadoff essay. Plimpton, one of America's preeminent writers, sets the tone for the essays that follow. A practitioner of participatory journalism, Plimpton recounts encounters with baseball's mythic heroes.

How Thomson's Shot Heard Round the World Changed My Life and Made Me a Hero by Oren Renick captures the special context that rendered Bobby Thomson's 1951 pennant-winning home run an American epiphany and the Giants slugger a mythic hero. Renick also recounts how "a grain of Thomson's magic landed on me and changed my life (sort of) and made me a hero (of sorts)." Trained in the ministry and law, Renick, an associate professor in the Department of Health Administration at Southwest Texas State College, continues to play baseball in a senior league. Former chief executive to three health care organizations, he is a frequent contributor to professional journals and conferences.

The Right Myths at the Right Time: Myth Making and Hero Worship in Post-Frontier American Society — Rube Waddell vs. Christy Mathewson by

Alan H. Levy compares two mythic pitchers of the Progressive Era, Rube Waddell and Christy Mathewson. Despite their disparate personalities, Waddell and Mathewson both "embodied ideals inherent in many of the nostalgic yearnings of Americans as they entered a new century." Professor of history at Slippery Rock University, Levy, a prolific writer, is the author of *Rube Waddell: The Zany, Brilliant Life of a Strikeout Artist* (also published by McFarland).

Baseball's Ethnic Heroes: Hank Greenberg and Joe DiMaggio by Joseph Dorinson depicts the Tiger slugger and the Yankee virtuoso as mythic heroes. The Jewish Greenberg and the Italian DiMaggio, standard bearers to their respective ethnic groups, were, according to Dorinson, "men of honor" and "baseball legends." Professor of history at Long Island University–Brooklyn campus, Dorinson is a noted authority in the field of popular culture. He writes frequently for newspapers, journals, and anthologies on sports, humor, race, and ethnicity.

Searching for Hank Greenberg: Aviva Kempner's Mythic Hero and Our Fathers by William M. Simons provides detailed analysis of director Aviva Kempner's acclaimed documentary film, *The Life and Times of Hank Greenberg*. In addition, Simons casts Greenberg as a mythic generational link between himself and his own father and between Kempner and her father. "There is an enduring recognition that Hank Greenberg," asserts Simons, "symbolized, as no one before or after, that Jews could make the American Dream their own." Chairman of the History Department at State University of New York College at Oneonta, Simons is the editor of this anthology and of *The Cooperstown Symposium on Baseball and American Culture, 2000* (also published by McFarland).

"*Your*" *Bears to "Our" Bears: Race, Memory, and Baseball in Newark, New Jersey* by Robert Cvornyek relates the return of minor league baseball to Newark in 1999 to the reshaping of community mythology. During the 1930s and 1940s, the Bears of the International League were heroes to Newark's white ethnics while the city's blacks celebrated the Eagles of the Negro National League. According to Cvornyek, supporters of the current minor league team, named for the legendary Bears, hope to field new heroes who will transcend racial divisions. Associate professor of history at Rhode Island College and coordinator of the college's Labor Studies Program, Cvornyek has written extensively about black labor history.

The House That Ruth Built, and Pop Opened: Negro League Baseball at Yankee Stadium by Lawrence D. Hogan recounts the saga of black baseball hero and Hall of Famer John Henry "Pop" Lloyd. Hogan argues that Lloyd's legendary deeds merit a plaque in Yankee Stadium's Monument Park. Professor of history at Union County College, Hogan is co-director of *Out of the Shadows*, the National Baseball Hall of Fame/ Major League Baseball study of the history of black baseball in America. He is a co-founder of the John Henry "Pop" Lloyd Committee.

Wendell Smith's Last Crusade: The Desegregation of Spring Training by Brian Carroll rescues from relative obscurity the 1961 heroics of black sportswriter Wendell Smith. Although his role in facilitating Jackie Robinson's reintegration of Organized Baseball is well known, Smith's successful 1961 campaign to integrate spring training has faded from the collective memory, a situation addressed by Carroll's study. A doctoral fellow at the University of North Carolina at Chapel Hill, Carroll, for ten years, was a sportswriter for the Greensboro *News & Record*.

MEDIA MYTHOLOGY

Baseball and Supernatural Intervention: Cinematic Reflections on the Crisis of Confidence in Post–World War II America by Ron Briley analyzes mid–twentieth century films that combine fantasy and the national pastime. "Interpreting this supernatural baseball cinema within the cultural framework of the early Cold War years," argues Briley, "may shed some light on the development of American ideology and values during this crucial time period." Assistant headmaster at Sandia Preparatory School and adjunct professor of history at the University of New Mexico, Briley received the 1999 SABR/Macmillan Research Award for his article "As American as Cherry Pie: Baseball and Reflections of Violence in the 1960s and 1970s."

The Actor as Ballplayer, the Ballplayer as Actor by George Grella considers the relationship between the magic of cinema and that of the national pastime. Evoking myth and ritual, folklore and legend, Grella illuminates the reciprocity between the arts of drama and baseball. Professor of English and film studies at the University of Rochester, he frequently writes about popular culture and literature. Grella is the film critic for *City Newspaper* in Rochester and for WXXI-FM, local affiliate of National Public Radio.

"The Curious Case of Sidd Finch" and For Love of the Game: *The Perfect Game as Mythical Literature* by Craig This evokes the magical memories and images associated with pitching perfection. Perfect games figure prominently in baseball mythology, and This examines depictions of such pitching epiphanies in baseball fiction, George Plimpton's *The Curious Case of Sidd Finch* and Michael Shaara's *For Love of the Game*. This serves as director of the Office of Research and Planning, General Council on Ministries, the United Methodist Church.

The Symbiosis Between Baseball and Broadcasting by Paul D. Staudohar "explores the relationship between broadcasting and baseball, from the early days of radio through the television age." Attuned to the mythic power of the electronic media, Staudohar examines the economic impact of broadcast revenues on owners and players. Professor of business administration at California State University at Hayward, he has published nineteen books. Staudohar is the president of the International Association of Sports Economists.

The Pitch: Baseball and Advertising in the Late Nineteenth and Early Twentieth Centuries by Roberta Newman chronicles the historic relationship between two mythic icons of the American culture: advertising and baseball. According to Newman, "Professional baseball, that most American of spectator sports, has always been intimately connected with advertising, that most American of businesses, that most American of cultural products." Professor of humanities in the General Studies Program at New York University, Newman teaches a course on baseball history.

Baseball Fiction for Youth by Pamela Barron and Gail Dickinson examines baseball books for children, published since 1950. Appreciative of the magic of children's literature, Barron and Dickinson discuss how the nature and content of baseball books for young readers has changed over time. Both Barron and Dickinson are members of the Department of Information Studies at the University of North Carolina at Greensboro; Dickinson is the coordinator of the school library media program, and Barron teaches courses in children's and young adult literature. Barron also serves on selection committees for the Caldecott and Newbery awards, two of the most prestigious accolades for children's literature.

For the Record and Lives That Mattered: American Baseball Autobiographies by Thomas L. Altherr analyzes several of the more revealing baseball autobiographies. Celebrant of the magic that pervades a well–rendered autobiography, Altherr finds that the best baseball memoirs "serve up multiple perspectives on the game's history, texturing the past in ways that statistics and passing anecdotes can not." Professor of history and American studies at Metropolitan State College of Denver, Altherr won the 2001 SABR/McFarland Research Award. His numerous publications include editorship of *The Cooperstown Symposium on Baseball and American Culture, 1998* (also published by McFarland) and *Safe by a Mile*, co-authored with Charlie Metro.

Baseball Haiku: Basho, the Babe, and the Great Japanese-American Trade by Edward J. Rielly analyzes "one of the great cultural trades," the introduction of baseball into Japan from the United States and haiku into the United States from Japan. Linking the magic of sports and poetry, Rielly notes, "Harmony is an important element of haiku. It also is a long-lived effect of baseball, uniting past and present, young and old, country and country." Reilly chairs the English Department at Saint Joseph's College of Maine. His publications include *Baseball: An Encyclopedia of Popular Culture* and eight books of poetry.

MYTH AND MYSTERY

Baseball and Freemasonry in American Culture by Charles DeMotte compares the rituals, imbued with mysterious symbolism, of sport and the fraternal lodge. It is, notes DeMotte, no mere coincidence that Alexander Cartwright, one of baseball's patriarchs, found "the ritualized patterns of Freemasonry" congenial. A member of the faculty at Empire State College, DeMotte teaches courses in religious studies and history, including one entitled "American Culture and the National Pastime." His book, *The Inner Side of History*, reflects his interest in occultism.

Claude Hendrix: Scapegoat or the Ninth Man Out? by George M. Platt relates the saga of an outstanding pitcher, who, "according to a number of posthumous assessments, merits inclusion amongst baseball's outcasts." Platt offers an answer to an enduring mystery: "was Hendrix's fall from grace the fruit of history or of mythology?" Associate professor emeritus in the Hugo Wall School of Urban and Public Affairs at Wichita State University, Platt coordinated the university's centennial and writes about local history. He has served as an advisor to local governments in Pakistan and Bangladesh, ranches and fishes in the Black Hills, and goes to baseball games.

Baseball, Transcendence, and the Return to Life by Phil Oliver relates the national pastime to the mystery of personal transcendence. Drawing upon the ideals of psychologist and philosopher William James, Oliver observes, "The mythic imagination largely has to do with how we attach ourselves to cultural meanings, entities, and stories bigger than ourselves. Baseball serves nicely to illustrate many anthropological generalizations about us." A freelance writer, Oliver is the author of *William James's "Springs of Delight:" The Return to Life* (Vanderbilt University Press, 2001).

MYTHS IN PROGRESS

From Scientific Baseball to Sabermetrics: Professional Baseball as a Reflection of Engineering and Management in Society by Richard J. Puerzer discusses baseball's "application of engineering and management practices for the improvement of both on-the-field and business performance."

"From the advent of scientific baseball in the late 1800s to the use of sabermetrics and strict pitching regimens today," Puerzer documents a symbiotic relationship between industrial engineering and our mythic national pastime. Assistant professor of industrial engineering at Hofstra University, Puerser has contributed articles to *Fan Magazine* and *The Cooperstown Symposium on Baseball and American Culture, 2000*. He hopes that Casey, his young son, will root for either the Yankees or the Phillies.

Youth Select Baseball in the Midwest by David C. Ogden separates myth from reality in his examination of African-American participation in youth baseball. Focusing on the Midwest, Ogden investigates the decline of young blacks in competitive baseball and efforts to increase minority participation. An assistant professor of communications at the University of Nebraska at Omaha, Ogden formerly taught mass communication at Nebraska's Wayne State College. He has been published in *Nine: A Journal of Baseball History and Culture*.

Labor Rights and the Restructuring of Major League Baseball, 1969–1992: A Case Study of Franchise Performance and the Myth of Baseball Management by Robert H. Jackson depicts the conventional wisdom that free agency transformed labor-management relations as mythology. Drawing upon the performance of the Oakland Athletics franchise, Jackson argues that players still face a hostile labor environment. Jackson, a scholar of Latin American history and a labor relations specialist, is the author of nine books and more than 40 journal articles. A fan of the Oakland Athletics and the San Francisco Giants, he possesses an impressive baseball card collection.

Establishing Women's Professional Baseball by Elizabeth Tempesta discusses and advocates for women baseball players. Dismissing genetically-ordained male supremacy in baseball as a myth, Tempesta argues that "one cannot adequately compare the baseball abilities of men and women because women have not been given the same opportunities to develop and enhance their bodies." Tempesta is a graduate student in education and English at Boston College. She works as a web consultant for Boston College and the John F. Kennedy School of Government at Harvard University. Summer finds Tempesta on the playing fields of the New England Women's Baseball League.

Notes

1. Joseph Campbell with Bill Moyers, *The Power of Myth*, ed. Betty Sue Flowers (New York: Doubleday, 1988), 5.
2. Ibid., 4.

3. Ibid., 15.

4. Ibid., 22.

5. Joseph Campbell, *The Hero with a Thousand Faces* (Princeton: Princeton University Press, 1949), 3.

6. Deanne Westbrook, *Ground Rules: Baseball & Myth* (Urbana and Chicago: University of Illinois Press, 1996), 76.

7. Ibid., 9.

8. Ibid., 9-10.

9. Ibid., 1.

10. Ibid., 70.

11. Mack McCallum, "Reel Sports," *Sports Illustrated*, 5 February 2001, 95.

12. Campbell with Moyers, 15.

13. *The Babe Ruth Story.* Directed by Roy Del Ruth. Allied Artists, 1948; and The Babe. Directed by Arthur Hiller. Universal Pictures, 1992.

14. *Rookie of the Year.* Directed by Daniel Stern. Twentieth-Century Fox, 1993.

15. *It Happens Every Spring.* Directed by Lloyd Bacon. Twentieth-Century Fox, 1949.

16. *The Sandlot.* Directed by David Mickey Evans. Twentieth-Century Fox, 1993.

17. *The Natural.* Directed by Barry Levinson. Tri-Star Fox, 1984.

18. Campbell with Moyers, 167.

19. *Stealing Home.* Directed by Steven Kampmann and Will Aldis. Warner Brothers, 1988.

20. *Bull Durham.* Directed by Ron Shelton. Orion Picture Corporation, 1988.

21. Westbrook, 2-3.

22. *Angels in the Outfield.* Directed by Clarence Brown. MGM, 1951; and *Angels in the Outfield.* Directed by William Dear. Walt Disney, 1994.

23. *Mr. Destiny.* Directed by James Orr. Touchstone Pictures, 1990.

24. *Field of Dreams.* Directed by Phil Alden Robinson. Universal City Studios, 1989.

25. *Frequency.* Directed by Gregory Hoblit. New Line Cinema, 2000.

26. George Plimpton, "Introduction," in *Home Run*, ed. George Plimpton (New York: Harcourt, 2001), xx.

Part 1

MYTHIC HEROES

Keynote Address

George Plimpton

Perhaps I should admit at the outset that I'm a Red Sox fan. Two years ago the Yankees won the pennant, and they had a great celebration in New York. The mayor's office telephoned and asked if I would come down and join the celebration. I said "no."·I was a Red Sox fan, and I wouldn't think of becoming part of the Yankees' celebration.

Nonetheless, it was an absolutely beautiful day, and I went downtown to sort of hang around on the periphery of things at City Hall. A young woman came running up and said, "You're late; you're supposed to be in the parade." I said, "Oh, no, no. I'm not supposed to be in the parade. I told you people yesterday." She said, "No, no. You *are* in the parade." She had Mayor's Office written on the back of the tunic, and she was looking at a clipboard. She said, "No, you're supposed to be in it. We've got to get you down to where the parade starts." She commandeered a police car, and I got into the back, where prisoners sit, a wire mesh in front of me. I sat there and was taken down at absolutely top speed to the Battery, down the East River Drive, the siren going, the light flashing on top of the car. I began to get into the spirit of all this.

When we got to the Battery where the parade was being formed, I got out and I said to a man with a clipboard, "Where's my float?" He looked at the clipboard and said, "You're not on one of the floats, but you are supposed to be in one of the cars." He took me over to a small classic MG, yellow. I sat in the back and joined the parade through the Canyon of Heroes. I immediately followed the Yankee float. Schools had been let out, the people six and ten deep behind these police barricades. I came along in my little MG and, of course, they had no idea who I was. These choruses would go up behind the police barricades, "Who are you? Who are you?" Occasionally I would motion with my left arm as if I were a pitcher from the ancient days.

It was an extraordinary thing — the tickertape coming down amidst the roar of this crowd. I got out finally from the yellow MG when we reached the end of the parade route and went home absolutely exhilarated. Think of the people who have gone through the Canyon of Heroes and Wall Street — Charles Lindbergh, Dwight Eisenhower, Douglas MacArthur. I was really pepped up. I wrote a piece about this, which appeared on the op-ed page of *The New York Times*— about a Red Sox fan in the Yankee Parade. It caused the most enormous amount of enmity. On the radio the next day, Mr. Imus, a man whom I have never met, spent almost an hour going after me with fangs bared. Not only that, but a letter appeared in *The New York Times* about two days later from somebody from Medfield, Massachusetts who wrote: "If the Red Sox win the pennant next year, which they're going to, and the World Series, we're not having Plimpton in *our* parade." So I've talked it over with my wife, and we may have to move to Hartford, half way between these two teams. I've disgraced myself with both.

At any rate, baseball has been a great love. When I was very young and the Fourth of July came along, you could, in those days, buy your own fireworks, which included cherry bombs or M-80s. I had ordered a device in a catalog. Sort of looked like a kicking tee. You could put the kicking tee on the ground and put a rubber ball on top of the kicking tee. Then you would light the fuse of the cherry bomb, and it would shoot this rubber ball higher than you can believe. Much higher than you could hit it with a tennis racket — just a tiny speck in the sky. My brother and my sister and I would settle under it, wearing baseball gloves. In our imaginations, it was the last of the ninth, the Giants playing the Dodgers, and this ball would come down and usually an error resulted. This was an extraordinary game, very loud. It always drove the family cat under the piano. But it was one of the first of the baseball games that I remember.

In my early days of baseball, I used to pitch. I was tall for my age, had long fingers, and absolutely loved the whole sensation of standing on the pitcher's mound and hurling the ball towards the plate. I used to throw a big roundhouse curveball, and in a seven-inning game, I struck out 23 people. I say 23 because the catchers couldn't handle the third strikes and so very often a hitter who had struck out would end up on first. But a roundhouse curveball when you were 11 or 12 was something most of the batters had never seen before. They would leap out of the batter's box as this great sidearm curveball would sweep across. It was one of the great satisfactions of life to throw this thing.

Many of you may have seen Ken Burns' documentary on baseball. He asked me to be one of the commentators. At one point, Burns asked me to describe a memory of baseball. I was able to recall with absolute clarity a game in which I was pitching, at the age of 12, against a school in New Jersey. The score was tied 2 to 2. With runners on second and third, a fly ball was hit out to left field, to a fellow standing out there named Charlie Lee. Charlie Lee was perhaps ten. He wandered around under this ball, and he dropped it. The other team scored two runs and won the game. I described this scene to Ken Burns and his cameras. I didn't really think much about it, but in Far Hills, New Jersey, when the documentary showed on public television, Charlie Lee was sitting with his family around him in a comfortable home. He'd gone on to become an extremely successful investment counselor. Immediately after the broadcast of this description of him dropping a ball sometime in the late 1930s, his phone suddenly began to ring. People were calling up to ask, "Are you the Charlie Lee who dropped the ball?" His entire life was changed by this. I heard about it, of course, from Charlie Lee himself. He wrote me this plaintive letter describing how his life had been changed, and how people had kept calling him for weeks saying, "Are you the Charlie Lee who dropped the ball." The Ken Burns' documentary was not only extremely successful, but people bought the tapes, and it was played over and over again.

So I wrote Charlie Lee a letter. I'm not sure my letter didn't discourage him more. I wrote him that in baseball particularly, perhaps even in life, the mistakes are recorded, and you're never ever allowed to forget them. Fred Snodgrass, center fielder for the New York Giants in 1912, muffed a fly ball, and it cost the Giants the World Series. Fred Snodgrass went on to be an extremely successful man. He became the Mayor of Oxnard County in California. Distinguished career. Made a fortune. Lived a long life. Yet *The New York Times* obituary read, "Fred Snodgrass, 83, Dies, Muffed Fly Ball in 1912." So I wrote this to Charlie Lee, in the hope that at his passing the obituary would not read, "Charles Lee, Distinguished Banker Dies, Muffed Fly in 1939."

Baseball was a huge love. James Thurber wrote that 95 percent of American men put themselves to sleep at night, striking out the batting order of the New York Yankees. I don't know whether that's true, but it is true for me, to this day, as a Red Sox fan. Sometimes of course it turns into a nightmare, my big roundhouse curveball misbehaving.

When I began working for *Sports Illustrated*, I wondered if it would be possible to do some participatory journalism. My great predecessor in this particular field was Paul Gallico, a famous sportswriter during the 1920s and 1930s. Gallico's idea was that if you were going to write about sports, you really ought to know, first hand, about athletic skills at their very best. It wasn't fair to write about someone striking out in the bottom of the ninth with the bases loaded in the World Series, unless you yourself had seen how a major league curveball behaves. So Paul Gallico climbed down out of the press box, and he created for himself a number of these participatory exercises.

He caught Herb Pennock's curveball, Pennock a famous pitcher with the Red Sox and then the Yankees. He played tennis against Vinny Richards, who was one of Bill Tilden's great rivals. He got into the ring at Saratoga Springs against Jack Dempsey, who was training for the Firpo fight. Dempsey was a man who did not like to find other people in the ring with him. So Gallico, although a good athlete, was in there for about 43 seconds. He had very little to write about the next day. He couldn't remember very much, though he did write a wonderful description of what it's like to be knocked out in a book called *Farewell to Sport*…that the ring goes around one way, and then it goes around the other way, a perfect description of being clobbered and lying there on the canvas.

He later gave up sportswriting completely, going on to become a distinguished novelist. He wrote the *Poseidon Adventure*; the *Mrs. Harris* stories, and the *Snow Goose*—a famous parable about the Second World War. But in *Farewell to Sport*, dedicated to his fellow sportswriters, there is a famous chapter called "The Feel." It is about these various adventures of his. I was always fascinated by the two things that scared Gallico more than anything else; one of them was standing on the 15-meter board above an Olympic swimming pool. Scared of heights, he couldn't imagine that someone would stand on that board and go off. His other great fear was riding in the cab of a locomotive going through the switchyards of Gary, Indiana. Amidst that great maelstrom of tracks, he simply couldn't believe a locomotive going 60 miles an hour was not going to run off the tracks.

Anyway, I read *Farewell to Sport*, particularly this chapter "The Feel," and I began to wonder if it wasn't possible to do this same sort of thing, but actually get more involved, not only catch a major league curveball, but actually becoming a member of a team and participate in a game.

I went to my editors at *Sports Illustrated*, and they said, "Well you know this sort of thing has been done before, but we'll try to arrange it for you." They arranged it so that I could pitch in a post-season All-Star game between the Willie Mays All-Stars and the Mickey Mantle All-Stars. The year before, Mays' New York Giants had gone to the West Coast. As a sort of a promotion stunt, somebody arranged Mays' return to New York with these All-Stars, and there was a big crowd on hand at Yankee Stadium. I was allowed to go to the pitchers mound and try out my roundhouse curve on major leaguers.

I wrote about this in a book called *Out of My League*, which is a fairly representative title of what happened. The first batter I pitched to was Richie Ashburn, the Phillies center fielder, followed by the great Willie Mays. I got both of these future Hall of Famers out. The first pitch I threw to Richie Ashburn went right at his head, inadvertently, of course. Ashburn collapsed in the batter's box. I ran off the pitcher's mound toward him, shouting, "I'm sorry. I'm sorry"— something you do not often witness in the major leagues. Richie Ashburn then popped the ball up; it was caught by the shortstop.

Next, Willie Mays hit this towering fly ball; it was caught out by the monuments in Yankee Stadium's deep center field, but he was out. I thought, well now, this is what I am going to do in life. Why should I be fussing with a pen? Here I've faced these two famous batters, and I've got them out. So I began to fuss with the rosin bag, hoping there were some scouts in the stands.

Then, of course, the scales redressed themselves properly. Ernie Banks came up and hit a double by my ear, and then there were some walks. Finally, Frank Thomas, who played for the Pittsburgh Pirates, got up. He hit the ball into the third tier of Yankee Stadium, one of the longest balls I have ever seen hit. I remember Frank Thomas' home run and Charlie Lee's dropped fly with equal clarity. Thomas hit the ball so far that my own reaction was that I had somehow *helped*, with quite a considerable engineering feat. *Look at what he and I have done together*— not the way you're supposed to feel out there on the pitcher's mound.

The whole operation gave me a sense of what it is truly like to stand on that most sacrosanct piece of turf in the American sporting scene, a pitcher's mound, and look down and see faces that I'd only seen on bubble gum cards before. I wrote about it for *Sports Illustrated* and then enlarged this into a book called *Out of My League*, which was helped considerably by an endorsement from Ernest Hemingway, terming my experience "the dark side of Walter Mitty."

The book did quite well; it led the editors of *Sports Illustrated* to let me try a lot of other things, such as playing quarterback with the Detroit Lions, goal tender with the Boston Bruins, and so forth.

I also continued to do a number of pieces about baseball. *Sports Illustrated* sent me out to follow Henry Aaron, as he approached Babe Ruth's long-standing record of 714 home runs, opening day in Cincinnati, and then down to Atlanta to see him finally hit the ball into the stands that beat Ruth's record. It was a curious game. As soon as the home run was hit in the middle innings everybody left the stadium. Then the teams between them made a total of six or seven errors. The air just went out of the balloon after this extraordinary thing happened. People could barely play the game after that; it was so dramatic that anything that followed was sort of sloppy.

To expand my articles from *Sports Illustrated* into a book, *A Matter of Record*, I spent a lot of time interviewing various people who were involved in the game. I thought it would be interesting to talk to Al Downing — he was the fellow that threw the pitch that Aaron hit out of the ballpark — to see how this affected him. I also thought it would be interesting to interview the participants in probably the most famous home run story ever, the blast that Bobby Thomson hit off Ralph Branca in 1951. Thanks to Bill Francis and other members of the Hall of Fame staff, I polled about a hundred members of the Baseball Writers of America to see how they would rank dramatic home runs. Winning in a walk (that's a funny way of putting it), Bobby Thomson's home run led by a vast majority, odd because that home run did not win a World Series; it simply won the pennant for the Giants who then went on to lose in the World Series.

What came next in the poll was Bill Mazeroski's home run for the Pirates, in 1960, which did win a World Series against the Yankees; in fact, some of the people I wrote to said that it should have been listed as the most important because it actually won a World Series, whereas Bobby Thomson's did not.

In any case, I talked to the pitcher, Ralph Branca, in Florida. At the time, he was running an insurance company, very friendly, very polite. I felt sorry for him, because here he was being asked to describe this home run, which he'd probably been asked to describe over and over again. He told me that Bobby Thomson had hooked a ball that he thought was high and wide, and this is interesting because, as many of you know, there is now a discussion about whether Bobby Thomson knew what pitch was being thrown. The Giants had a system where a fellow encamped in the scoreboard with a telescope read the catcher's signs and communicated this news to the dugout from whence it would be signaled to the man at bat what pitch was coming. Recently, there was a long article about this in *The Wall Street Journal*. Bobby Thomson has been asked about it since and said that he was not given the signal, and you have to believe him.

In any case, when the ball was hit, Branca turned around, picked up the rosin bag, threw it to the ground and began the long walk to the locker rooms in center field where steps go up to the two different locker rooms. It was a long walk; you can imagine what a horrifying walk that must have been for Branca — three hundred, four hundred feet to these steps that go up. A photograph taken of him in the locker room, with his hands over his face won the Pulitzer Prize for photography that year.

To show you what an amazing home run it was, my mother was in Grand Central Station at the time, and when word swept through the station that this home run had been hit, everybody there began leaping up and down. Hats were thrown into the air. My mother had no idea what was going on. It was a very difficult time in the history of international relations. The Russians were being especially perky. My mother told me that if the Soviet delegation to the United Nations had been in Grand Central Station at the time, they would have found out something rather seminal about the American character. Of course, there must have been some Dodger fans there, taking their hats and throwing them to the ground and stepping on them. But my mother remembers it as being a celebration.

Branca was the last man out of the locker room. He walked out to the parking lot. There was one car left. I kept thinking what a singular scene this would be visually — one car left, in which Branca's fiancée and a priest from Fordham University sat. The fiancée burst into tears when she saw Branca coming towards them. When he got into the car. Branca said to the priest, "Why me, why me, why me?" The priest gave a rather remarkable response; he made an analogy between the suffering of Branca and that of Christ. He reminded him what Christ had realized from God — He had been given the cross because he had a strong-enough faith to bear it.

It spirited Branca up. He told me over the phone that now when he walks down the street with Bobby Thomson to banquets or to the Hall of Fame, "People don't look at Thomson. They look at me, to think that I could have gone through that and survived."

One day the managing editor at *Sports Illustrated* called me in and said, "We have an issue coming out this spring and it just so happens that the date of this issue is April first. We would like you to go out and write about the pranks that baseball players, athletes play on each other."

I went on to try to do some research; I didn't think that I was doing particularly well with the assignment, wasn't getting very good stories and so forth. So I went back into the managing editor's office, and I said, "You know I'm having a hard time with this April Fool's story. I can't seem to get much material that's very funny or very good." He then looked at me and he said, "Well, do your own."

That was a remarkable thing for him to have said; he was allowing me to attempt to fool 600,000 readers with an April Fool story. I remember it was February, a freezing cold day, a sleet storm going on; I walked out into the street without my coat, unbelievably excited to be asked to do this.

It was amazing how quickly all the ingredients of this story came to mind. April, of course, is the start of the training season, and I thought of what would happen if a pitcher who could throw the ball at an astonishing speed, a hundred and seventy miles per hour, with absolute accuracy turned up at a spring training camp. The image of such a pitcher came almost instantly to mind. It could not have been anybody who grew up in America, because you would hear about this phenom at the high school level, catapulted into the public consciousness and certainly the consciousness of the baseball hierarchy. He had to be somebody else, a foreigner, and who would that somebody else be?

Well, it immediately occurred to me that he'd have to possess some of the powers of a Far Eastern mystic to be able to throw the ball that fast. Into my mind almost instantly popped an Englishman, a young Englishman, maybe 16 years old, whose father had been killed in an airplane crash in the Himalayas, who had left his school and gone to the Himalayas to look for him, lost somewhere in the vastness of the Himalayan Mountains. My character ended up in a monastery where the people worshiped St. Milarepa. I knew something about Milarepa: he was a 16th century Saint, who learned through some sort of internal heat, or *tuma*, to be able to transform himself into other things, or to make himself very light. The really good ones can turn themselves into pagodas. I don't know who would want to turn themselves into a pagoda, but it's an irresistible thought.

All this began to come to mind instantly. The fellow's name was to be Sidd Finch. Sidd with two d's, to honor Siddhartha, the Buddha. And Finch. Not long afterwards, a man sent me a letter saying, "Do you know what the sixth meaning of Finch is in the Oxford English Dictionary? Small lie." I didn't know that. So it was a perfect name for my character.

I asked my old friend Nelson Doubleday if we could work out this scheme with his team, the New York Mets. To my delight he agreed. *Sports Illustrated* sent a photographer and this gawky schoolteacher, who was the model for Finch, down to St. Petersburg. When "The Curious Case of Sidd Finch" was published, I was giving a lecture in North Carolina. I was asleep in my room at one o'clock in the morning; the phone rang; it was *The New York Times*. The caller exclaimed, "It's not true, is it?" Like an idiot I said, "Oh, you figured it out, did you!" I should have said, "What do you mean it's not true? It is true. It's in *Sports Illustrated*, isn't it? Look at all those pictures." Instead, I let the cat out of the bag.

But it was amazing how many people fell for this ruse. *Sports Illustrated* got 2,500 letters about Sidd Finch. About 20 percent of the letters were from people who took exception to being fooled. One correspondent was so angry that he wrote, "I'm not only canceling my subscription to

Sports Illustrated, but to *Time, Life*, and *Money*." He was so outraged that he swept all Luce empire magazines off the board. Many letter writers asserted that they had figured out an anagram at the top of the story. If you could decipher it, the anagram read Happy April Fools Day. But Sidd Finch, for a time, became a national figure.

Oh, I've talked much too long here, but I did want to finish by reciting a few words by Thomas Wolfe that express a love of the game that I share:

> The scene is instant, whole and wonderful. In its beauty and design that vision of the soaring stands, the pattern of forty thousand empetalled faces, the velvet and unalterable geometry of the playing field and the small lean figures of the players, set there, lonely, tense and waiting in their places, bright, desperate solitary atoms encircled by that huge wall of nameless faces, is incredible. And more than anything, it is the light, the miracle of light and shade and color-the crisp, blue light that swiftly slants out from the soaring stands and, deepening to violet, begins to march across the velvet field and towards the pitcher's box, that gives the thing its single and incomparable beauty.
>
> The batter stands swinging his bat and grimly waiting at the plate, crouched, tense, the catcher, crouched, the umpire, bent, hands clasped behind his back, and peering forward. All of them are set now in the cold blue of that slanting shadow, except the pitcher who stands out there all alone, calm, desperate, and forsaken in his isolation, with the gold-red swiftly fading light upon him, his figure legible with all the resolution, despair and lonely dignity which that slanting, somehow fatal light can give him.

Thank you all very much.

How Thomson's Shot Heard Round the World Changed My Life and Made Me A Hero

Oren Renick

I was not at the Polo Grounds in New York City on October 3, 1951...did not listen to the game on the radio or see it on television. In fact, there is no recollection of where I was or what I was doing that day as a small child when Bobby Thomson hit his "shot heard round the world." It would be a few years before I would realize that something special for baseball and America had happened that autumn afternoon the Giants defeated the Dodgers for the National League pennant. Years would pass and then events would send me scurrying back to the pages of forgotten sports journalism to seek to capture the magic of Thomson's moment. It was there in the dimly lit stacks of a university library, between the covers of a broken down book about baseball that a grain of Thomson's magic landed on me and changed my life (sort of) and made me a hero (of sorts).

This paper is dedicated to the late Robert B. Cooke. Bob Cooke served as Sports Editor and Columnist for the New York Herald Tribune.

A Flashback to '51

It was a momentous year and, in retrospect, perhaps the most significant of the 1950s. The United States was embroiled in the Korean War. United Nations troops continued to retreat and wage a faltering defensive struggle. They were reacting to a massive Chinese Communist counteroffensive, staged in North Korea, begun late in 1950. General Douglas McArthur, commander of United Nations troops in South Korea, wrote to the House Minority Leader, Joseph Martin, that in Korea "there is no substitute for victory." McArthur was commenting on President Harry Truman's plans to negotiate a truce. Truman could no longer abide the gifted McArthur's arrogance, insubordination, and lack of respect for the President as Commander-in-Chief. He sacked McArthur from command in the Far East and replaced him with General Matthew Ridgway. Returning to a hero's welcome and tickertape parade, McArthur spoke to a joint session of Congress in April, describing the urgent military situation in Korea. He urged expansion of the war against Communist China, and closed with the refrain that "old soldiers never die, they just fade away." Within a few months, this "American Caesar" faded from the international and national scenes. In July, the United States participated in truce talks between the United Nations and the Chinese Communists.[1]

Almost simultaneously with the release of McArthur's letter to Martin, husband and wife Julius and Ethel Rosenberg were sentenced to death. A federal jury found them guilty of providing top secret information on nuclear weapons to the Soviet Union.[2]

Early in 1951, the Supreme Court ruled in *Feiner v. United States* that a speaker who displayed "a clear and present danger" of incitement to riot was subject to arrest.[3] This too was part of the zeitgeist.

And the 22nd Amendment to the Constitution was ratified. The amendment stipulated, "No person shall be elected to the office of President more than twice."[4] With the two term restriction, anxious Republicans sought refuge from the ghost of their greatest nemesis, FDR.

Senator Joseph McCarthy of Wisconsin continued his postwar campaign against internal subversion. McCarthyism, a virulent witch hunt against domestic anti–Communist, trafficked in hysteria and disregard for constitutional safeguards. In keeping with the tenor of the times, in June the Supreme Court upheld the Smith Act, unfriendly to Communists in government, and also sustained a state's right to require job applicants to sign non–Communist affidavits.[5]

On the international scene, aged lion Winston Churchill, victorious in a comeback election, was once again the British Prime Minister.[6] And, in the Third World, young leaders organized against the colonial past that Churchill embodied.

Some of the lighter highlights from 1951 included the coining of the phrase "rock 'n' roll" by Cleveland disc jockey Alan Freed to describe rhythm and blues music for white audiences; the premier of *I Love Lucy* on television; publication of J. D. Salinger's *Catcher in the Rye;* the *Merriam-Webster Dictionary* made its first reference to "fast food;" [7] and San Marcos, Texas celebrated its centennial year.

And in baseball a generational passing of the torch occurred in 1951. Willie Mays and Mickey Mantle played their first Major League Baseball games, and Joe DiMaggio his last. [8] In relation to all of the events of 1951, Thomson's home run moment was not very significant. Even in comparison to the going and coming of baseball greatness in 1951, its significance dims.

Yet if we pause in its exact historical context, it was and it remains a momentous event to be celebrated. Time has not dimmed the home run; time has dimmed its historical context. Seen in that perspective, one can argue that we have underplayed rather than overplayed Thomson's shot heard round the world.

It merits repeating: 1951 was a disturbing year. As noted, the specter of Communism clouded domestic politics and international relations. Approximately five years after the end of World War II, we were again in a shooting war. This time, however, it was different. It was in Asia; it seemed to have limited objectives; it was an affront to our status as the world's great nation state; it was a hot war at the center of what we were coming to understand as our Cold War with Communism. It was a time of national anxiety and emerging self-doubt.

We had circled the wagons to fend off further attacks on our corporate psyche. In the midst of our troubles, we were emotionally rescued by a team of men known as the New York Giants. Their symbolic charge to our rescue in the summer of 1951 still evokes what was perhaps baseball's greatest pennant race. In microcosm, we saw in them our potential as a nation if we could be unified and meld as a team. If we could only get it together and hold it together, our potential was…unlimited. After all these years, the glue that holds together the metaphor of that pennant race and our potential as a nation is Bobby Thomson and the shot heard round the world.

The Giants were thirteen-and-a-half games behind in August, and then they began their streak. They won 37 of their last 44 games, and came thundering up to tie the Brooklyn Dodgers for the National League pennant. Sports fans throughout the nation were in a frenzy as a three game playoff unfolded to determine a winner. New York won the first game, Brooklyn the second. And the third game would take on the power of myth.[9]

Each team started the ace of their pitching staff that October afternoon in the Giants' Polo Grounds Stadium. Over 34,000 fans were jammed in the stands to see "Big Don" Newcombe pitch for the Dodgers and Sal "The Barber" Maglie for the Giants. Through seven tense innings, it was tied at one, but then the Dodgers got to Maglie, and jumped ahead 4–1 in the eighth. There was laughing and gloating by the Dodgers and their rooters; with one inning left, the National League pennant was firmly in their grasp. But in the bottom of the ninth, the last half inning of the last game, the Giants began to stir, and make a final run at the Dodgers. Giant fans began to plead and pray and roar in a hope born of utter desperation. For…Al Dark led off with a ground single to right field. Don Mueller followed with another single to right as Dark scampered to third. Monte Irvin fouled out to Hodges at first, but Whitey Lockman hammered a double to left, scoring Dark and sending Mueller to third — who twisted his ankle going into the bag. Mueller had to be carried off the field, and replaced by pinch runner Clint Hartung. During this brief interlude, Giants manager Leo Durocher, with one out and the young, untested Willie Mays imminently to be on deck, sensed that the entire season came down to Bobby Thomson. As Thomson, the potential winning run, headed for the plate, Durocher put his arm around him, pleading, "If you ever hit one, hit it now."[10]

Ralph Branca was brought in to pitch for Newcombe and face Bobby Thomson, a tall Scottish-born right-handed hitter. Giants rooters were on their feet, wild-eyed, beseeching.[11]

As he approached the plate, Bobby Thomson told himself, "Give yourself a chance to hit." He then repeated the hitter's core commandments, "Wait and watch." He then thought again, "Give yourself a chance. Do a good job."[12] Branca's first pitch, a fastball, froze Thomson and was a called strike. Thomson recalled, "I took the first one right over the middle of the plate. All I could rationalize was that I was waiting and waiting." The tension mounted as Branca stared down the batter. Branca's next pitch was a fastball, high and inside. "I remember getting a glimpse of it, and I was very quick with my hands inside." This time Thomson turned on it and swung — for the National League pennant, and launched into the left-field stands the game winning home run. "I got around and that was it. I thought I hit a home run. I hit the ball, and I saw the thing go up with overspin and start to sink. I thought…it's just a base hit. And then I saw the ball disappear. I never hit a ball like that in my life."[13]

Roger Kahn would write, "For seconds, which seemed like minutes, the crowd sat dumb. Then came the roar. It was a roar matched all across the country, wherever people sat at radio or television sets, a roar of delight, a roar of horror, but mostly a roar of utter shock. It was a moment when all the country roared, and when an office worker in a tall building on Wall Street, hearing a cry rise all about her, wondered if war had been declared."[14]

A moment in time captured for us by the voice of Giants' broadcaster Russ Hodges, above the roar, the chaos, the celebration, as Thomson circled the bases. "They're going crazy! The Giants win the pennant! The Giants win — the pennant! I don't believe it!"[15]

Red Barber's call of the home run was in stark contrast to that of Hodges. You would not detect that Barber was employed by the Dodgers. We pick up Red's call as follows:

> All right, so it now stands with the Giants roaring back, clawing and scratching. They have two outs remaining. They have runners at second and third, and the big one is Lockman at second base. Hartung, the pinch runner , off third, Branca pitches and Thomson takes a strike. Big Branca called on for his most important job in his baseball career. Well, everything is the most important for all of these players as we come around. Here it is. Searing hot. Branca pumps. Delivers…Swung on and belted deep out to left field. It is — a home run! And the New York Giants win the National League pennant and the Polo Grounds goes wild![16]

Barber was silent for 59 seconds while the crowd roared. Once the crowd noise went down, he went to a commercial. After that, he put the matter into perspective, mentioning that a couple hundred Americans had been killed in Korea that week. Then he said, "The Dodgers will get over this, and so will their fans."[17]

"I Remember It Well"

The Thomson home run marks the collective memory of a generation. It is one of those national moments where a great outpouring of emotion is shared. It is one of those times when people can recall the event by introducing it, thusly, "At the moment I heard (about) it or saw (for some) it, I was at "X," doing "Y," with "Z."

There were over 34,000 fans at the Polo Grounds who witnessed the home run, but what about the rest of the nation that experienced it in real time? They, of course, depended on broadcasters. The Russ Hodges' call is the one heard over and over in reliving the moment. However, in addition to Barber, Connie Desmond and Vince Scully were there for the Dodgers. Ernie Harwell did the game for television, and Harry Caray also had a microphone.[18]

Michael Miranda tells the story of his father building a coffin on October 3, 1951. Standing 5'5" and heavyset, this 31-year-old son of immigrant parents was using wood slats from vegetable crates to create a resting place for the symbolic remains of the New York Giants. Papa Miranda hurried to put the final touches on his partisan construction project in the cellar of the Brooklyn grocery store where he worked as a delivery man. Miranda planned to place the coffin on the Bay Ridge sidewalk in front of the store as soon as his heroes closed out the Giants. Then he heard the call by Russ Hodges, and his practical joke on Giants' fans was never to be. He carried his handiwork to the top of the cellar steps and then flung it down the stairs where it crashed and awaited its discard with the rest of the next day's trash.[19]

John McBride of San Marcos, Texas and Southwest Texas State University, remembers Bobby Thomson with the clarity that comes from having been an accomplished player himself. John recalls:

> I was seven years old when Bobby Thomson hit his home run. I was listening to the game in the living room of my home in Harlingen, Texas. The Giants were my favorite team, and I hated the Dodgers. My favorite players were Monte Irvin and Alvin Dark. Of course, I went nuts when Thomson hit his home run. I went running around the living room yelling and jumping on and off my mother's blue sofa and easy chair. She got quite ticked as I recall, so I just sat on the arm of the sofa ((like riding a horse) and just yelled. It took a long time to settle down.
>
> In 1962, I won a trip to New York to play in a baseball game. The Hearst newspaper chain sponsored a local game between the 'city boys' and the 'country boys' in each of the major cities that they had a newspaper. The local paper was the San Antonio Light.
>
> Each year, the Light would choose two sets of coaches...one for the city boys and one for the country boys. These coaches would hold tryouts at various places (within San Antonio for the city team and in several outlying towns for the country team) for anyone 18 and under to come to the tryout. I went to Seguin for my tryout. Each set of coaches would choose a team and then the city team and country team would play each other in old Mission Stadium in San Antonio. Scouts from all the major league teams would attend the game and vote on two players, based on performance in the game, to go to New York(site of the main Hearst paper the now defunct New York Journal-American) to be on a team from all the U.S. Hearst cities to play against a team selected by the Journal-American from the New York City area.
>
> I went three for three in the local game with a double off the left field wall, including a single that went through the center fielder's legs

that allowed me to circle the bases only to be called out for missing third base. The double was off a guy I had been unable to touch in two years in high school ball, so I guess I was due. My third hit was a ground ball to deep short that I beat out. I could actually run in those days and was mainly an outfielder. I got selected to go to New York with a catcher, Leonard Sanchez, from South San Antonio High School.

That game got me two signing offers (Mets and Astros...i.e., Colt .45's at the time), but dad said, "No, you are going to college." I believe it was the right decision, and I went to the University of Texas and played there.

Now, back to Bobby Thomson. When I got to New York, I found I was on a team with 16 other players from around the US that included Tony Conigliaro (from Boston and later of the Boston Red Sox) and Ron Swoboda (from Baltimore and later of the New York Mets). We got to work out three times in Yankee Stadium and once in the Polo Grounds. I went to the exact spot Thomson hit his home run.

On the night of the game in Yankee Stadium with the New York team, which included Matt Galante, a coach for the Astros, there was a preliminary softball game between former pro boxers and ballplayers. Bobby Thomson was one of the ball players. I wanted to meet him, so my personal press rep from the *Journal-American* calmly went and got him and brought over him to meet me. Then he took our picture together (unfortunately, I never got a copy), but what a thrill to finally see him in person. I was 18, a small town kid from Texas in New York with a personal press rep, in Yankee Stadium and the Polo Grounds...well, sometimes dreams come true.

Oh, how did the game go? We played 10 innings until 1:00 a.m., and then had the game called due to curfew. The score was 4–4, and I was 0–2 with a fly to left and a ground out check swing to the pitcher.

My most thrilling moments were that my parents flew up from Texas unannounced; the players got five swings during batting practice and on my last swing I hit one into the seats in left field; and meeting Bobby Thomson.[20]

He would become a renown clergyman, author, and theologian, but on October 3, 1951, John Claypool was thousands of miles from both fame and the Polo Grounds. A St. Louis Cardinals fan and freshman student at Baylor University in Waco, Texas, he and his roommate listened intently to the radio broadcast of every pitch, inning after inning, and then, in that instant, the game was over. Like so many others, John Claypool remembers the minute details of time, place, and surroundings in the moment of the shot heard round the world.[21]

On the afternoon before the 1982 All-Star Game in Montreal, two men sat on a sofa in a hotel lobby. The larger man speaks, "Why do you want to talk to me with all these great stars around? Look! That's Reggie Jackson. That's who you should be interviewing."

"I'd rather talk to you."

"Okay, but I still don't know why."

The smaller man, a Canadian, breaks into a recreation of Russ Hodges' broadcast of "the Giants win the pennant! The Giants win the pennant…"

"Okay," said a smiling Bobby Thomson, "I understand. I don't mind talking about it…because it seems to mean so much to so many people. People are always telling me where they were and what they were doing when I hit the home run.

"One man wrote and said he was driving along a highway in the Middle West and before he knew it, he was sitting in the middle of a cornfield and he couldn't remember how he got there. Another guy wrote and said he was a shoe salesman and he was working the ladies' department and he was just fitting a shoe when I hit the home run. He said he got up and threw the shoe against the wall — he said he couldn't help himself — and the wall was so thin that the shoe just stuck there when the heel imbedded itself in the wall."

The interviewer said, "I hope you don't mind me asking about it, but it was a special moment for me since I grew up in New York and understand all that went on between the Giants and the Dodgers. It was more than a home run. I don't think there'll ever be anything like it again."[22]

It is 1989, and it is Al Engelken's 50th birthday. His wife Betsy, Al and their college age son set out from their home in the Washington, D.C., area to visit Fordham University. Betsy has a scheduled stop on the New Jersey Turnpike to pick up some papers for a friend.

At the scheduled exit, the car pulled over, and Betsy went to get the papers. In a few minutes, she returned with a tall, silverhaired man. She crouched down by the car window and said, "Happy Birthday. This is Bobby Thomson."

As a 12 year old Giants fan, Al had seen the home run with his nose pressed against the window of a New Jersey bank that had set up a television set for the event. When Al and Betsy were married in 1966, he gave her the ultimate compliment as she came down the aisle, "You look prettier than Bobby Thomson's homer," he said. Their first dog was named Homer for the Great Event. The family license plate reads "ENG 23"— the first three letters of the family name and Bobby Thomson's uniform number.

The two men spent an hour visiting along the New Jersey Turnpike. When Al asked Bobby Thomson why he took time off from work for somebody he did not know, Thomson replied, "…if you have the chance in life to make somebody this happy, you have an obligation to do it."

Al Engelken believes he has met a genuine sports hero and found the perfect wife along the way.[23]

In the wonderful documentary film series on baseball by Ken Burns, there is a segment on the home run, appropriately titled "Fiction is Dead" borrowed from a Red Smith piece in the *New York Herald Tribune*. In tracing the impact of the home run on the lives of people, the following is a snapshot from the Burns' documentary:

- Roger Angell (Giants fan and writer)—"Everybody remembers where he was when Bobby hit the home run"…(it was) a wonderful moment, a wonderful moment."
- Stephen Jay Gould (Giants fan and paleontologist)—It was "probably the greatest moment of pure joy of my life."
- Doris Kearns Goodwin (Dodgers fan and historian)—It was "the starkest memory, in some ways, of my childhood."
- George Plimpton (Giants fan and writer)—It was "a moment of tremendous emotion … an unbelievably emotional moment."[24]

Dick Thompson, a physician, ethicist, quality guru, writer, mentor, friend, and rabid St. Louis Cardinals fan, remembers where he was when Bobby hit the home run. He was a high school senior, getting ready for football practice in the locker room of his Missouri high school. The game was blaring on a radio. When questioned further about his reaction, Dick remembered that he finished high school in 1950, not 1951. His story is a good one. Unfortunately, it did not happen. With all due respect to the great Red Smith, where Bobby Thomson's home run is concerned, even fiction is not dead.

First Impressions

It was 1955. The Joseph McCarthy era of witch hunts for domestic communists had ended the previous December with his condemnation by Senate colleagues. The Red Scare was not over, but the Cold War with Communism continued on more appropriate fronts and, reassuringly, Eisenhower was President. He participated in the first televised press conference and spoke that year about world peace while balancing such utterances with…the United States would use nuclear weapons in the event of war. Such demands contributed to his heart attack and hospitalization during September and October. The Stock Exchange had its largest single-day dollar loss, $44,000,000,000, two days after Eisenhower's hospital admission. The United States Air Force Academy accepted its first class of cadets, and the Interstate Commerce Commission banned segregation on trains and buses crossing state lines.[26]

More important to a little boy than the Cold War and the racial divide, 1955 was the year the Brooklyn Dodgers came in from the cold and won their first World Series. Thanks to Johnny Podres, Sandy Amoros, and a roster dotted with future Hall of Famers, Brooklyn's perennial wail of "wait 'til next year" came to an end. It was also the year of my inauspicious beginnings as a Little League baseball player. Finally, it was the year two adult friends, Marcelle and Fay Mulligan, gave me my first hardback book about baseball, and from it would come my first impression of the wonderful thing Bobby Thomson had wrought.

The book was *The 1955 Mutual Baseball Almanac* by Roger Kahn and Harry Wismer. Tucked away in the chapter "A Concise History of Baseball," the writers reviewed the 1951 season, calling it the greatest pennant race ever. They even quoted from Bob Cooke's poem describing the game in part as follows:

> Then the next pitch came winging...
> Bobby Thomson swung with might and main...
> But when the panting patrons
> Saw the baseball disappear...
> New York sent forth a rapturous shout...[27]

For grown men to write or quote poetry was a bit much, but it was about baseball and it gave me chills to picture the moment. Recovering from such reverie, the authors acknowledged that my beloved Yankees had won the World Series against Thomson and his Giants.

Life's Changes and the Hero's Mantle

A decade had past. It was 1965, and Lyndon Johnson, a graduate of Southwest Texas State University where I was a professor, dominated the presidency after a landslide victory over Barry Goldwater in 1964. Unfortunately, America slid into the "big muddy" of Vietnam with a decision to increase our strength there to 125,000 men. Medicare and Medicaid were enacted with Johnson signing the Medicare bill as former President Truman watched. It was such an up and down year: civil rights demonstrators were attacked in Selma, Alabama by state troopers; the Voting Rights Act was signed; and the Watts area of Los Angeles experienced a major race riot. On an up note, the mini-skirt was introduced.[28]

The Dodgers again won the World Series, but alas it was not from Brooklyn. For me, it was a time of change and transition. As a college freshman, I encountered a strong, veteran baseball team. Though one of only two freshmen to make the varsity team, I decided to stop playing because of the demands of practice, my class schedule, and very little playing time. It was a depressing phase for I mistakenly thought my days of playing on a baseball team were over.

Looking for another outlet for my competitive juices, I was invited to try out for the varsity debate team and made it. It fed my interest in some day becoming an attorney. Also, my tutor-coach was the beautiful and brilliant coed star of the entire team. Perhaps if I stayed she would take an interest in me. She would make a wonderful wife, I thought. She did and she has...

By the spring of 1965, I had risen to the top two-man intercollegiate debate team. Individual events, including extemporaneous speaking and original oratory, were also going well. We were preparing for our most important debate tournament and then disaster struck. Our coach announced that I had also been entered in the individual event of poetry reading. Only weeks to go and I had to do poetry. I did not even know a poem, much less like one.

There was no time to go through the five stages of grief. I had to go from shock to acceptance overnight. Where would I go to find a poem that I could understand enough to present? How could I avoid complete humiliation?

Calming myself, it was concluded that only a poetry reading about something for which I had a passion would work. A baseball reading was the obvious choice. How about *Casey at the Bat*? I decided it was too familiar and would have no surprise element. Wait a minute! Do I still have the book with the poem about...Bobby Thomson's homer? Going home that weekend I found it. It is just what I need. It will get me through the ordeal, but ...the reading has to be five to seven minutes long and the reprint is not the complete poem. It cannot be stretched to more than three minutes. Despair returns. Complete humiliation is inevitable. A ray of optimism emerges. Can Cooke's book with the entire poem be found?

Checking my college library, nothing turned up the book. They did not have it, could not get it through interlibrary loan, and it was out of print. No book, no poem, no solution, only lurking humiliation.

A favorite aunt was not well, and my mother, using her unmatched manipulative powers, got me to agree to give up a weekend and travel out of state to see my aunt. We arrived midday on Saturday and after spending the afternoon listening to stories about antique furniture, China patterns, and the gallbladder surgeries of people I did not know, my mind began to wander and think of some means of temporary escape and, of course, my dilemma...no poem.

Inspiration strikes! The state university is here and maybe they have the book. Citing the perfect reason to leave, I arrived outside the library a few minutes before five p.m. They have the book! Is it in the stacks? Big problem...they close at five p.m.! Somehow guided to magically use the Dewey Decimal System, I arrive at the right row and shelf. The book is there! Grab it, find a copier, it is five p.m.! The worm turned, a copy of the poem was made, and I escaped the library as its doors slammed shut behind me. Treasure in hand...the tournament is not quite two weeks away.

The next two weeks were a blur getting ready — debate, oratory, extemp, poetry; class work, extracurricular activities. My beautiful, brilliant, coed, tutor-coach helped me with the poetry reading. At least, I was enthusiastic.

Debate teams from across the southeast and parts of the Southwest and mid–South gathered for the three day tournament at a predominantly women's state university. Individual events would have two rounds of competition with the contestants drawing for their place in the round. My first poetry round came early in the tournament, and I had imagined a setting, if not a style, for its delivery. The desired setting — an early draw, follow a love poem, and a full room of listeners to gauge audience reaction.

Believe it or not, it all happened just like that. I drew the second slot, the first guy's poem was nauseatingly sweet, and the audience was palpably enthusiastic about *Bobby Thomson at the Plate*. The second round was just as exhilarating.

I received the highest rating and award for poetry reading, superior, and the poem was part of the hallway talk of the tournament. Thus, fifteen years after becoming a baseball legend, Bobby Thomson's shot changed my life by helping me find another outlet for my love of the game and made me a kind of hero as I vicariously shared his triumph with a new generation of fans.

Silver Anniversary

It had been 25 years since the "shot heard round the world," and 1976 was also the zenith of the "Big Red Machine." Sparky Anderson's Cincinnati Reds, featuring Joe Morgan, Johnny Bench, Pete Rose, and a seeming multitude of players with Hall of Fame credentials, would sweep the rejuvenated New York Yankees in the World Series.

In November, Jimmy Carter was elected President of the United States as Americans took yet another step in expunging the Watergate Era from the national scene. Even the celebration of the 200th birthday of the United States could not salvage the fortunes of our caretaker President Gerald Ford, politically wounded by his pardon of Richard Nixon. Ford further contributed to his own defeat when he insisted in a nationally televised presidential debate that there is "no Soviet domination of Eastern Europe and there never will be under a Ford administration."[29]

In 1976, inflation was high as was unemployment. Ford and the Democratic-controlled Congress battled over appropriations. He called for fiscal restraint, vetoed a bill, and then Congress overrode his veto.[30]

Also in 1976, Patricia Hearst was found guilty of armed robbery, convicted of joining her kidnappers in a series of burglaries; multi-millionaire recluse Howard Hughes died as did Mayor Richard Daley of Chicago. The Supreme Court ruled that the death penalty was not inherently in violation of the Constitution. The decision cleared the way for the execution of death row inmates.[31]

Much of my professional career has been as a dual career or bi-vocational minister. While serving as a health care executive or university professor, I have also simultaneously ministered to faith congregations. These have typically been inner-city or transition congregations. With a pulpit to command, what better theme for a sermon masterpiece in 1976 could there be than Thomson's shot...?

Entitled *Summer of '51*, I attempted to compare our apparent national disunity with the united team effort of the '51 Giants. The sermon begins as follows:

> There is an overused expression among athletes: "Getting it all together — putting it all together." They want the weather to be right, morale to be right, and everyone in top physical condition. Then, on a given afternoon — by putting it all together, there's victory. When the athlete is interviewed afterwards, he is asked: "What do you need now?" And with both childlike simplicity and wisdom he replies, "Why, you know, to keep it all together...you know." ...
>
> In 1951, one of the great baseball pennant races occurred. The New York Giants, thirteen-and-a-half games behind in August...(You know the rest of the story by now.) ...
>
> Bobby Thomson and the Giants were at the very top of their game. Bobby Thomson and the Giants had it all together....
>
> Yet we live in a time when practically everything seems to be going to pieces, when nothing seems to be together. Like most athletes, we're not able to get it together, or hold it together for long at a time.[32]

In my collection of sermons, it remains on my short list of personal favorites.

Revisionists

This year, 2001, as America celebrates the fiftieth anniversary of the "Miracle at Coogan's Bluff," many will recall where they were, what they were doing, and how they reacted to the home run. However, some stories and comments have sought to take away from the luster of that October 3rd afternoon. The revisionists have sought to diminish the home run on two major fronts. First, the old argument claims the home run was a cheap shot and barely made it into the stands. Second, the new argument claims the Giants were stealing the catcher's signs, using a telescope from their center field clubhouse. A buzzer system notified the dugout and signals were used to relay stolen signs to the batter.[33]

A general refutation of the critics is that they do not understand how difficult it is to play baseball well or produce that single most difficult and dramatic play in the game — the home run. Ask former minor league player Michael Jordan. Ask the .250 hitting utility outfielder Deion Sanders. Ask the former minor league player and current Heisman Trophy winner Chris Weinke. Baseball is a game that keeps you humble. Just when you think you have figured it out, it bites you hard.

For those who suggest it was a cheap shot, look at a film of the home run. Thomson turned on a fast ball and hit a line drive that reached the stands in a flash.[34] It is reminiscent of a Henry Aaron homer rather than the looping home runs hit by Roger Maris.

The Polo Grounds dimensions, like those of many of the older stadiums, had a romantic idiosyncrasy. This is part of the "romance" associated with many of the old baseball stadiums demolished long ago. The Polo Grounds was 279 feet down the line in left field and 257 feet down the line in right field. However, center field was a cavernous 480 feet, and the power alleys in both left and right dropped back dramatically from the foul lines.[35] From the mid–1920s to the mid–1940s, the Polo Grounds and its dimensions were the setting for many of Mel Ott's 511 home runs that he "pulled" down the 257 foot right-field line.[36] The cavern in center field was the site for the Willie Mays' catch of the Vic Wertz rocket shot in the 1954 World Series, and the Polo Grounds happened to be where Thomson launched his homer. You play the hand you have — the dimensions, the wind, the lighting, the surface, all of it. It is a neutral hand, and the same hand is dealt to every player. Winning is often determined by how a team or a player uses those neutral factors.

A second claim made by critics is that the Giants "unfairly" stole the signs of opposing catchers.[37] During the spring of the year, I would receive a graduate degree from a school of theology. I taught at a local junior college. It was affiliated with a high school, and, to remain close to the game, I helped coach its baseball team. As the first base coach, my mind would sometimes wander — look at the spectators, unsuccessfully look for a four leaf clover, identify insects. Early in the season, I realized that if I "cheated" over the coach's box toward first base, I could typically "steal" the catcher's signs to the pitcher. Boredom was relieved, and since there were no regular left-handed hitters on the team, it became a simple matter to signal the hitters — arms folded meant fastball, hands on knees meant curve, hand to face meant change up, and hands to side meant could not determine sign. The team hit well both before and after I began giving signals. The batters seemed to like getting signals, and the team won several more games than it had the previous season. How much did my sign "stealing" contribute to those additional wins? I do not know, probably some, but the team was also better than the team of the previous season.

Was I "cheating"? Yes. Was I taking advantage of high school players? No. I was taking advantage of poor coaching by the opposition and poor umpiring. No coach and only one umpire had me move back into the coach's box the entire season.

"Cheating is as much a part of the game as scorecards and hot dogs"— Billy Martin.[38]

Now, back to the telescope. Please note that the player who used it, Leonard Schenz, had previously played for the Chicago Cubs for four years. Occasionally, he had spied signals for his Cub teammates. There was a place in the Wrigley Field scoreboard, and Schenz was out there from time to time.[39] As Billy Martin said, "Cheating is as much a part of the game as..."

Was the sign stealing significant to the Giants' success in 1951? Fundamentally, how much did the Giants' hitting improve after the sign stealing allegedly began on July 20? After that date, they hit .256 at the Polo Grounds. Prior to then they had hit .266 at home and .252 in away games. After July 20, they hit .269 away. These numbers detract from the supposed advantage of knowing what pitch is coming.[40]

July 20 denoted another benchmark; on that date, manager Leo Durocher began coaching third base. Does anyone believe that the Giants won the pennant because Leo the Lip started coaching third?[41]

After July 20, the Giants were 51–18 or a winning percentage of .739, up from 47–41 and .534 prior to that date. Neither the hitting nor the coaching accounts for the turnaround. The answer lies in the pitching. The pitching staff's ERA before July 20 was 3.47 at home and 4.49 as the visiting team. From July 20 on, it was 2.90 at home and 2.93 in away games. The offense was not significantly enhanced after the July date, but the pitching was superior and led the league with an ERA of 3.48.[42]

In the two playoff games at the Polo Grounds, the Dodgers scored 14 runs and the Giants scored five, and four of those were scored in one inning.[43] Were the Giants tipping off the Dodgers rather than stealing the Dodgers' signs?

Bobby Thomson hit six home runs off Ralph Branca in 1951.[44] Make no mistake. Ralph was a good pitcher. Look at his career statistics. However, Thomson owned Branca in '51. Charlie Dressen's decision to bring him in to face Thomson with the game on the line is a classic "second guess" decision. It was the wrong pitcher, facing the wrong hitter, in the wrong situation.

Bobby Thomson at the Plate

Bob Cooke was sports editor and columnist for the *New York Herald Tribune* in 1951. He was at the Polo Grounds on October 3, 1951 and witnessed the home run. He added to sports literature with his description of the game. Cooke composed the poem, *Bobby Thomson at the Plate*, drawing freely on *Horatius at the Bridge*.[45] It appeared in the *Tribune* and was later included in the book, *Wake Up the Echoes*, which Bob edited. The poem is reprinted in its entirety through the permission and gracious generosity of his widow, Elizabeth R. Cooke.

BOBBY THOMSON AT THE PLATE

Bob Cooke

Charlie Dressen of the Dodgers
By Brooklyn gods he swore
That the great house of Flatbush
Should suffer wrong no more.
By Brooklyn gods he swore it,
And named a trysting day,
And bade that Brooklyn fans go forth,
East and west and south and north,
To honor his array.

East and west and south and north
The baseball fans do go,
And tower, town, and cottage,
Have heard the Dodgers crow.
Shame on the fan unfaithful
Who is inclined to lag,
When Dressen of the Dodgers
Is heading for the flag.

The Dodgers back in August
Were making runs amain
With many a lofty circuit clout
In many a fruitful game
By many a solid single
Which, hit by Reese or Jack,
Like a Winning sock, or timely knock,
Proclaims the Brooklyn knack.

There be one million Faithful
The loyalist in the land
Who always by Chuck Dressen
Both noon and evening stand:
Evening and noon the Faithful
Have cheered the mighty Flock
For they can hit and hit and hit
These Bums are kings of sock.

And with one voice the Faithful
Have their glad answer given,
"Go forth, go forth, Chuck Dressen,
"Go teach New York a lesson.
"Go and return in glory
"To Ebbets, your happy home,
"And slap a big defeat upon
"Durocher's shiny dome."

And now hath every patron
Sent up his battle cry
The lead is thirteen and a half
The Lip is sure to fry:
Before the gates of Ebbets
Is met the great array
A proud man was Chuck Dressen
Upon the trysting day.

But by the Bluff of Coogan
Was tumult and affright
From Stoneham down to Leo
The Giants were in flight.
To watch was such a pity,
The Lip was so concerned,
His pennant plight, a ghastly sight,
To him, whom fortune spurned.

But Spencer, Hearn, and Maglie
Were pitching in the clutch,
And fellow name of Irvin
Was hitting far too much,
Bobby Thomson down to Yvars
Were playing for the team,
And Mueller, Jones, and Jansen,
They all were on the beam.

But still it seemed so silly,
The Bums were sure to clinch,
Then Big Newk lost, and so did Preach,
The race was not a cinch.
"It can't be done," the experts said,
Chuck has too big a lead,
But Jansen won in Boston town,
He had good stuff indeed.

And nearer, fast, and nearer,
Do the New Yorkers come,
And louder still, and still more loud
Their hits and runs, they speak out loud
For many an admiring crowd,
The Giants, still they come.
And plainly and more plainly
Now through the gloom appears
A pennant hope, a pennant prayer
The thought that maybe then and there
The while the Dodgers in their lair,
A Giant might appear.

They came down to the wire
And they were necks apart,
Again New York beat Boston,
But the Dodgers did their part.
From far behind in Philly,
They came, and won a game
Frick ordered then, a play-off,
Could he a victor name?

Giants took the first one
When Hearn was quick and fast,
The Brooks, they grabbed the second,
'Cause, Labine, he pitched at last.
Then for the big finale
The Brooks were set with Don
While Leo went with his pal Sal,
Much like a favorite son.

The Polo Grounds was crowded
With fans on every side
They cheered with Brooklyn took the lead,
The fact was hard to hide.
Then came the ninth and with it,
A four-one Brooklyn lead,
Surely New York was beaten now
Why didn't it concede?

Then up spake Dark, young Alvin,
A great clutch hitter, he:
"I'll take two and hit to right,
"I'll prolong the race, you'll see."

Then up spake young Don Mueller,
A batsman brave was he,
"I'll produce a single too,
"Just you wait and see."

Then up spake Whitey Lockman,
A solid slugger, he:
"And I will hit for two," said he,
"To mar the Flatbush glee."
But meanwhile in the bull pen,
Ralph Branca's arm is warm,
And now he's plodding toward the mound,
Big Newk can't brave the storm.

But from the Giant dugout,
Bob Thomson then appears,
He takes his place up at the plate
Midst Giant hopes and fears.

Bob looked toward Staten Island,
Which he still calls his home,
Then Leo on the coaching lines,
Composed this pretty poem:

"Oh, Thomson, Bobby Thomson,
"To whom the Giants pray,
"A Giant's life, a Giant's dream,
"Take you in charge this day!"

And so Lip spake and speaking,
With Thomson at the plate,
And thousands cheering in the stands,
Awaiting Thomson's fate.

Branca throws, it is a strike
But tension sets the pace,
It couldn't have been otherwise,
Was ever such a race?
Then the next pitch came winging,
Straight down the narrow lane,
And Bobby Thomson took a cut,
He swung with might and main.

No sound of joy or sorrow
Arose from either side,
As friend and foe in dumb surprise,
With parted lips and straining eyes,
Stood staring where it sank,
But when the panting patrons
Saw the baseball disappear
New York sent forth a rapturous shout,
And even the ranks of Flatbush fans,
Could scarce forbear to cheer.

They gave him of their cheering
They gave it to him straight,
They thundered an ovation
Long 'fore he reached the plate,
And they eyed him as a monarch,
On some celestial throne,
While Bobby toured the bases
On his power alone.

Now, when Giants of the future
Prepare for their great quest,
When Durocher starts spring training,
And asks each man his best,
With weeping and with laughter.
Still is the story told,
How well Bob Thomson kept the bridge,
In the brave days of old.[46]

Reflections

Most of this story has been written from a desk in a window lit corner of my family room. It is a room my son says is dedicated to dead baseball players. On a portion of one wall I have hung an autographed photo of the Giants' celebration at home plate. Next to it is a plaque displaying my superior rating for poetry reading and close by is a copy of Bob Cooke's poem. Fifty years can be a long time, but to me that home run is timeless. It is like it happened — just a moment ago.

Notes

1. Arthur M. Schlesinger, Jr., *The Almanac of American History* (New York: Barnes & Noble, 1993), 526–529.

2. *Ibid.*, 526–528.

3. *Ibid.*, 526.

4. *Ibid.*

5. *Ibid.*, 528–530.

6. *Ibid.*, 529.

7. Rene A. Guzman, "Flashback to '51," *San Antonio Express-News,* 28 January 2001, 1H & 8H.

8. *Ibid.*

9. Oren Renick, "Summer of '51," from the manuscript of a sermon address first delivered in 1976, 1.

10. *Ibid.*, 1–2.

11. *Ibid.*, 2.

12. Ken Burns, *Baseball* (New York: Alfred A. Knopf, 1994), 322.

13. Michael Bialas, "Giants are Gone but Thomson's Homer Lives On.," *The Times-Picayune,* 1 June 1984, Sec. 3, 7–8.

14. *Ibid.*, 7.

15. Renick, 3.

16. Bob Edwards, *Fridays with Red* (New York: Simon & Schuster, 1993), 113.

17. *Ibid.*, 114.

18. *Ibid.*, 112.

19. Michael v. Miranda, "The Essence of the Game," *The Baseball Research Journal* 29 (2000): 48.

20. John McBride, described his recollections of the Bobby Thomson home run and meeting Thomson in 1962 in an interview with Oren Renick in May 2001.

21. John Claypool, described his recollections of the Bobby Thomson home run in a conversation with Oren Renick in July 1982.

22. Joe Falls, "The Thomson HR Legend Vivid as Ever," *The Sporting News*, 26 July 1982, 8.

23. Albert R. Karr, "This 50-Year-Old Sees His Idol as Last of the Sports Heroes," *The Wall Street Journal*, 27 October 1989, Reprinted in *The National Baseball Hall of Fame and Museum Newsletter*, January 1990, 3–4.

24. Ken Burns, "The Seventh Inning: The Capital of Baseball," *Baseball: A Film by Ken Burns*, PBS Home Video, 1994.

25. Dick Thompson, described his recollections of the Bobby Thomson home run in a conversation with Oren Renick in May 2001.

26. Schlesinger, 541–544.

27. Roger Kahn and Harry Wismer, *The 1995 Mutual Baseball Almanac* (Garden City, New York: Doubleday & Co., Inc., 1955), 139–141.

28. Schlesinger, 569–574.

29. *Ibid.*, 605.

30. *Ibid.*

31. *Ibid.*, 604–606.

32. Renick, 1–3.

33. Joshua Harris Prager, "Giants' 1951 Comeback, The Sport's Greatest, Wasn't All It Seemed," *The Wall Street Journal*, 31 January 2001, A1, A14.

34. Burns, "The Seventh Inning."

35. Kahn and Wismer, 243.

36. Joseph L. Reichler, Editor, *The Baseball Encyclopedia* (New York: Macmillan, 1985), 1271–1272.

37. Prager, A1 and A14.

38. Billy Martin, "Speaking of Baseball," a poster reprint of memorable baseball quotes.

39. Prager, A1, A14.

40. Paul White, "Giants Stole the Pennant? Perhaps Not," *USA Today Baseball Weekly*, 21–27 March 2001, 4.

41. *Ibid.*

42. *Ibid.*

43. Burns, 322.

44. *Ibid.*

45. Kahn and Wismer, 139.

46. Bob Cooke, *Wake Up the Echoes* (Garden City, New York: Hanover House, 1956), 61–65.

The Right Myths at the Right Time: Myth Making and Hero Worship in Post-Frontier American Society — Rube Waddell vs. Christy Mathewson

Alan H. Levy

Introduction

At the turn of the twentieth century, the nature of hero worship in America altered markedly. The age of the industrialist, the cowboy, and the gunslinger had passed. New heroes, including political reformers and athletes, appeared. This change occurred for an interconnected set of reasons that involved new outlooks on the key qualities of the nation's culture. Two baseball players, George Edward (Rube) Waddell and Christy Mathewson, figured prominently amongst the heroes to emerge in this new era. Their characters and the myths that came to surround them fit well within the new media of the day. Mathewson and Waddell also embodied ideals inherent in many of the nostalgic yearnings of Americans as they entered a new century.

One major development in America's cultural shift at the turn of the century, exhaustively-studied among historians, concerned the closing of the frontier. This was important as perception as well as fact. Public awareness about the end of a central chapter in America's saga became an important part of the nation's *fin de siècle* sensibilities, with the nature of frontier images turning ever more into elements of nostalgia and fantasy while decreasingly being points of active cultural reference. Different sets of heroes (and villains) from other regions and professions then came to occupy the new, "active" arenas of culture.

Surrounding and influencing this shift, the nation's urban centers were gaining increasing attention and displacing the frontier as a perceived "cutting edge" of a nation that saw itself destined to lead the world in the new century. Critiques of cities were nothing new. Criticism had been mounting since Jefferson's time. Arthur Schlesinger, Sr. and latter historians have often commented on the fact that for every person who traveled to the frontier there were many more who moved to a major city. This significance was known even in the heyday of the plainsman and the cowboy. But as urban centers were now increasingly regarded as central to the nation's identity, the strengths (as well as the shortcomings) of cities began to receive even keener concern.

Accompanying such developments, and their political/cultural implications, came an important transformation in the nature of the nation's media. Newspapers and magazines greatly expanded at the turn of the century. A most significant factor here concerned an outwardly mundane technological breakthrough in the 1880s. This involved the perfection of techniques to turn raw wood pulp into low-grade paper, devoid of any "rag" content. While books and other items requiring quality paper were unaffected, the newspaper business was revolutionized.

The effects of this journalistic proliferation were many. The growth of "muckraking" was the most famous, but among the other effects were changes in the nature of newspaper layouts. Among newspaper editors, Joseph Pulitzer was a leader in developing the idea of dividing a newspaper into sections, especially for his Sunday editions. Pulitzer grasped the implications of increasing leisure time among the expanding numbers of readers who could buy now inexpensive papers. Pulitzer's newspapers were the first to have identifiable "sections" with headings like Fashion, Society, Travel, Books, Art, and Sports. For each section, the burgeoning ranks of reporters began to specialize.[1] In sports and politics especially, new levels of media scrutiny further fed the appetite of Americans for villains and heroes.

The addition of photojournalism augmented the newspaper expansion. Before the 1890s, newspapers could not readily print photographs. Now they could. The photograph gave a visibility to a new generation of leaders in areas like politics and sports which was far more intense than that experienced by the leading figures of prior generations. In politics, no one gained more fame from this than did Theodore Roosevelt. TR was perfect for this era of modulation from frontier to city. A city-boy through and through, Roosevelt personified the new urban reformer in politics. Yet the President also provided a transition for Americans who, while accepting of the new age of the city, held old (or newly manufactured) frontier images with nostalgic fondness. Roosevelt had a genuine love of the West and engaged in a good show of frontier-like activities from Western-style horseback riding to big-game hunting. He hardly fit in with the real cowboys he met out West (who thought him a bit silly), but through the newspapers he was able to cultivate quite a cowboy image. When one of his political foes, Mark Hanna, cursed TR as "that damned cowboy," he could not have given the young President a greater gift, as millions of Americans tacitly responded to the curse with a bully "damned right."

Similar hero worship also came forth in sports. In the nineteenth century, there had not been many sports figures who had captured the imagination of the mass of Americans. Sports stars generally had followings within their locales. Now with greater media coverage, the dimensions of affection and familiarity were each at work in the eagerness of the public to snap up such figures and to follow their exploits both in their athletic endeavors and in their lives off the playing field.

Certain ingredients go into the making of heroes and celebrities, in sports or in other walks of life. One critical and obvious matter involves superior ability. Almost all celebrities have this. Among politicians, TR, FDR, and JFK, for example, possessed notable qualities of mind and leadership. With sports figures too, the same basic quality must be present. Real celebrity needs more, however. Mike Tyson and Ty Cobb were each the best at what they did in their sports and eras, but the public embraced neither. Real celebrity status requires additional intangibles. Convincing descriptions of these qualities can be elusive. The words that traditionally come forth, like excitement, charisma, charm, and endearment, often merely beg the question of how to define them and thus return to the point of how these qualities are commonly conceived. While the essential nature of heroes or celebrities is ultimately elusive, the nature of the chosen heroes and celebrities does show an observer some historical patterns. Heroes of one era are not always the same sorts of people as those of other times. Sometimes, the irresistible quality of a figure actually creates the mold. Sometimes heroes seem more to embody broader sensibilities of the society about them. Often a combination of the two is at work.

In the early twentieth century, the nature of the first sports heroes embodied the pulls and tugs at work in a nation shifting into a consciously new urban century. The sports world really availed the nation of but two major areas of possibility—boxing and baseball. Horse racing was also popular, but the chief "heroes" here could hardly assume the celebrity roles of human athletes, although a few horses have come close. Of note here, as well, is the fact that one of the most famous thoroughbreds of the early twentieth century was named "Honus Wagner," a further reflection of the point of baseball being a touchstone for the nation's sports world. Golf and tennis were relatively new and purviews of the wealthy. And the heyday of basketball, football, the modern Olympics, and college sports lay in the future.

Boxing had a large following by the 1900s, but its obvious violence raised caveats. Bare knuckle fighting had only recently passed from the scene. Serious injuries and deaths were still frequent. Boxing continued to face legal restrictions. Additionally, when Jack Johnson became the first African-American heavyweight champion in the early twentieth century, racial tension plagued boxing. In many states, a theater owner could actually be arrested for showing any films of Jack Johnson fighting.

Boxing, however, gave the immigrant population of the nation's burgeoning cities a way of advancement, both individually and vicariously. While this was significant in itself, it provides a further clue as to why baseball was the more popular sport, indeed the true national pastime. Baseball held a stamp of Americanization. With their vast numbers presenting a particularly severe challenge to the early twentieth-century city, many immigrants felt pressure to learn the game of baseball to prove their acculturation. Boxing had a potentially contrasting impact, as any success by an immigrant conveyed a demand that he be accepted as he was. The nature of baseball demanded a contrasting conformity to an identifiably American set of rules. The game also balanced elements of team and individual play. Learning the rules and accepting the notion of team play were absolutely necessary, hence distinct from the pure individualism of boxing. Still, the nature of baseball allowed individuality to occupy the center stage, more than in the other team sports emerging at the time. In a nation that was departing the frontier and yet regarded nineteenth-century self-reliance with affectionate nostalgia, baseball could then be a forum for stars. In particular, pitchers, the most individualistic of ballplayers, provided people with a set of images through which they could invest themselves in the notion that certain values of an older, less bureaucratic America would endure and simultaneously hold out a standard which newcomers would have to follow.

Another element in early twentieth-century baseball, beyond its American centeredness and its effective balance of team conformity and individuality, also made it stand out. Consider the many inner city ballparks built in the era — Shibe, Baker, Ebbets, Wrigley, Comiskey, Braves, Fenway, Crosley, Forbes, Sportsman's, Briggs, and Griffith. They all opened between 1901 and 1916, and gave each inner city a greenery which struck people then, and continues to strike people, as a basic point of appeal. The fact that many of the inner city arenas were called "parks," "fields," and "yards" reflected this point of resonation for people: a green oasis in the city, something that a "ring," an ice rink, a court, or certainly a "gridiron" did not convey.

While urbanites of the early twentieth-century were taken *into* the boxing arena, they preferred, as the song of the era said, to be taken "out" to the ball game. For early twentieth-century Americans, going to a ball game held elements of escape from the hubbub of urban life, while a boxing match, usually in a crowded, smoke-filled indoor arena, symbolized a more intense version of that life. Furthermore, in contrast to our contemporary game, with its TV- and narcissism-driven elongation of play, patrons of Progressive Era baseball could take but a bit more than a late lunch, hop a trolley, and watch a game. Indeed, many would go back to work after six or seven innings, which usually took about an hour.[2]

The inner city greenery was only part of baseball's escape appeal. Baseball was also the only major spectator sport of the day which, like the pre-industrial times in which it originated, did not use a clock. This was part of the sense of being taken "out" when one went to a game, as well as of "not caring if one ever got back" to the modern clock-driven world. In this context, people often giggle derisively at one of Yogi Berra's famous dugout lines. In answer to the question "what time is it?" Yogi responded, "You mean right now?" Like all Americans before 1850, real ballplayers never care what time it is. (As usual, there is a little more to a Yogism than first meets the eye.)

The Protagonists

Amidst these dynamics of culture, aspiration, and escape, there were many star players of the early twentieth century who regularly made headlines far more than in any previous era of the game. Honus Wagner, Tris Speaker, Frank Chance, Napoleon Lajoie, Walter Johnson, Ty Cobb, and Eddie Collins were all great, received significant coverage, and had wider followings than ballplayers of prior times. Two players, however, captured the imagination of the baseball public as much or more than any other. They did so with contrasting styles, and the duo touched upon the complex ways that Americans held onto values of a bygone time as they confidently entered a new age. The two players were Christy Mathewson and Rube Waddell. They were really the leading ballplayers of the first generation to have truly national followings, products of the new media and post-frontier climate that combined with the content of their characters and their great athleticism to generate stardom.

Americans have always held affectionately to a moralistic strain that is born of simple, untutored piety. This combination of the untutored and the intensely moral contributed significantly to the appeal of Mathewson and Waddell. Since they were pitchers, "gunslingers," who could single-handedly defeat any team, the two reminded nostalgic spectators of values rooted in earlier times. "It's not the way it used to be" is a familiar refrain, and maybe it never really was "the way it used to be." But nostalgia through baseball heroes enabled people to believe certain myths about the power of individuals in past times. The nostalgia most modern ball players bring forth recalls only prior eras of baseball. But Waddell and Mathewson were unusual in that the two, in very different ways, enlivened remembrances of pasts beyond the game of baseball itself.

Christy Mathewson was the embodiment of the Christian values in which Americans either believed or at least liked to believe they believed. In *Drift and Mastery* (1914), Walter Lippman wrote of how early twentieth-century Americans held many of their heroes to higher moral standards than they would be willing or able to live up to themselves; they believed these standards were necessary for the nation's political and spiritual health.[3] Mathewson was one who could embody the highest moral standards and thus vicariously make people feel a level of moral attainment that was inspirational. His surname alone, of course, declared him the son of an apostle, and the first name carried messianic implications. One of Mathewson's nicknames was "the Christian Gentleman." Few other players' nicknames in the history of the game cast this anything-but-a-slap-on-the-back aura. Furthermore, ballplayers of Matty's era were rarely well educated, but Mathewson had graduated from Bucknell with honors. In most ballplayers, such a background would invite hazing and ridicule from both teammates and opponents. Mathewson was able to override this by simple force of personality and integrity. Of course, the incredible pitching skill he exhibited from his first appearances in the majors was also a chief part of this pattern of respect and admiration. While other players drank and carried on with reckless abandon, Mathewson always conducted himself with a propriety that was never mere contrivance. This had some significant effects. Team rules against raucous behavior could be more effectively enforced, not that Giants' manager John McGraw needed Mathewson to force his will. When a newspaperman was reportedly unfaithful to his wife while traveling with the Giants, Mathewson refused to speak to him, causing the paper to displace the reporter from his assignment. (The reporter then had to go home and try to patch up his domestic matters.) Even players otherwise disposed to speak in a coarse, profane vernacular, often changed markedly whenever the name or person of Mathewson came forth. Rube Waddell was one who became respectful.

In the summer of 1901, Mathewson was in his first full season with the New York Giants. The team was heading for a series with Chicago, and reporters were chortling about a good ole' showdown in the offing. Chicago also had an excellent young pitcher who was receiving much press too. This pitcher's demeanor was, however, nothing like that of "the Christian Gentleman." The lad's name, of course, was George Edward "Rube" Waddell.

Like Christy Mathewson, Rube Waddell was an altogether endearing character. Fans loved him and loved to read of his exploits. This affection was part of what made the two pitchers stand out among the public in such a different manner than did such excellent but more dour stars as Chance, Lajoie, Speaker, and Collins. (And Ty Cobb stood out in the opposite manner, as he was utterly and unalterably villainous.) Within the bounds of this world of affection, no two people could have been more different than were Waddell and Mathewson. While Christy represented the pious, well educated Christian, Rube was just the sort his nickname implied — a hick.

One gentleman who knew Waddell in his native Butler, Pennsylvania plainly recalled many years later: "We called him 'Rube' because he was a rube."[4] Good natured, broad shouldered, 6'2", 220 pounds, often chewing a long stalk of hay, Rube was a personification of the type of character novelists regularly exploited in American literature and folklore, characters whose simplistic, protocol-ignoring ways bring smiles to the faces of people who love to see pomposity deflated, especially by one of low circumstance. Queequeg, Huck Finn, Br'er Rabbit, Paul Bunyan, John Henry, Tom Joad, Randall Patrick McMurphy, and Forrest Gump each had some of these qualities of impish or even devilish naivete. Where some of them attacked pomposity, they were endearing; where some failed to grasp artifice, their readers cried in frustration; and where they found someone or something in which they could genuinely invest their faith, they touched readers' hearts. Rube did much the same in the real world. Nonetheless, Rube self-destructed after demonstrating greatness, under the management of Connie Mack, even as he extended his legend. For Americans love to wonder "What if." What could flawed geniuses achieve were their shortcomings somehow overcome? Beyond such dreaming, failure itself underscores the elements of imperfection and tragedy that subsume much of human aspiration, matters which for Americans harken both to the Puritans, who held that people must strive for perfection yet knew they would fail, and to the belief in the spiritual growth that comes with an embrace of human frailty, a belief which subsumed Philadelphian James Michener's conviction that no great writer could have ever been a Yankee fan.

Baseball has had plenty of flawed, lovable hicks, many of whom, like Dizzy Dean and Satchel Paige, were "crazy like a fox" in their conscious sculpting of their rube images. Rube Waddell was baseball's very first such celebrated character, and he was anything but a self-contrivance. Because he had no artifice, some have had difficulty understanding him. Some have tried to cast him as mentally challenged or even insane. But Rube was not retarded, nor was he the slightest bit psychotic. He was simply never one to follow any rules that did not make sense to him. Reportedly at age two he broke the bars on his crib when he wanted to go somewhere. When a fish eluded his hook, he dove in the water after it. He wrestled alligators (and opposing players), masticated live snakes, acted on the vaudeville stage, gulped down 100 oysters in a sitting, chased fire engines, drank too much, married three times in 11 years, hit one of his wives, and assaulted his in-laws. Though baseball conventions of the era maintained strict racial segregation, Rube played ball with blacks (or with kids, or with anyone else). In 1912, when floods hit a town in Kentucky where he was staying, Southern tradition dictated that the local blacks would do the dangerous work of repairing the dikes, under white supervision. Rube joined with the blacks and hauled sandbags for days on end. (The illness he incurred from this would ultimately weaken him and cost him his life.) Endearingly, as well as frighteningly, Rube broke every convention and did so without a hint of posture. In several exhibition games, he called his fielders off and struck out the opposing side. Thus bragging and thumbing his nose at all protocol and convention, temporarily triumphing, and ultimately self-destructing, Rube was baseball's version of a true American populist.

Rube joined the majors just a few years before Mathewson. Quickly seen as an uncontrollable wild card, he knocked about several teams, frustrating the daylights out of managers, especially Pittsburgh's Fred Clarke. In 1901, Waddell was still in his vagabond stage (which ended in 1902 when Connie Mack brought him to Philadelphia), playing for Chicago in the National League (NL), a team then known, appropriately for Rube, as the "Orphans." In 1901, the Chicago Orphans and the New York Giants were terrible teams, dueling one another for the NL cellar. Rube was the only thing in which the Chicago club could take pride; meanwhile, the rookie Mathewson was about all the New Yorkers could trumpet. (The Giants' fortunes would change in 1902 when John McGraw became their manager.)

In June 1901, when the Giants and Orphans were set for a series with one another, the prospect of a Waddell-Mathewson face off was the biggest sports item in the Chicago and New York papers, if only because the rest of the teams gave reporters so little about which to write.

Reporters wrote extensively about the two pitchers as they were preparing to square off. Mathewson's Bucknell background served as a wonderful contrast to Rube, who was reported to have once attended night school. (He had actually been enrolled for one term in a small Western Pennsylvania school, Volant College, but that was only to play baseball, and Rube rarely if ever attended classes.) Amidst all the journalistic chortling, when the prospect of facing Christy Mathewson came before him, the usually whimsical Rube was remarkably measured and respectful: "I expect to go in tomorrow's game and do my very best to win, but I am not egotist enough to claim a victory until the game is won. Mathewson is a hard man to beat." (Hardly the words of someone retarded or psychotic.) Normally, however, Rube was a complete braggart. He would often prance or even turn cartwheels in front of the opposition dugout before facing them, telling them exactly what he was going to do (and he usually did it). But before facing Mathewson he was quite subdued. Such was the respect that Mathewson could command.

The first Mathewson-Waddell match (June 15, 1901) proved to be something less than the marvel many expected. Each walked four, a high figure for two of the most accurate pitchers in the history of the game. Mathewson did strike out eight, and Rube fanned ten, though three of these were of Mathewson. Meanwhile, Chicago teed off on Mathewson. They scored nine runs, with the Giants scoring but two. Round one went to Rube, though the lowly Orphans lost the rest of the series to New York. Two weeks later they squared off again. This time Rube, likely hung over, gave up nine runs in four innings, and the Giants ended up winning 14 to 1. Baseball people were disappointed with the two match-ups. But with both pitchers so young and promising, everyone fully expected there would soon be some memorable match ups. As it turned out, no rematch would ever occur.[5]

Over the next four seasons, both players certainly lived up to their promise. From 1903 through 1905, Mathewson would win 94 games. From July 1902 through 1905, Waddell would win 97 games. In 1903 and 1904, he struck out over 300 batters, in years when batters did not swing for the fences and no other pitcher struck out 200. (His 1904 mark of 349, better than half the total of any team in the league that year, would not be broken until 1965, in a longer season and in an era of home run swings.) Arguments in these years as to who was the best pitcher in baseball centered largely on these two. What gave the arguments a special heat was the fact that they could not be resolved. The 1901 contests were forgettable games with lousy teams. By 1905, each was playing for a contender. But while Mathewson stayed on with the New York Giants, Rube had switched leagues. He left the Orphans a month before the end of the 1901 season. After traveling to the Pacific coast on an off-season barnstorming tour, and destroying his first marriage in the process, Rube, long before the major leagues moved west, signed on with a Los Angeles team — the Loo-Loos. On the West Coast, Waddell played to great fan adoration during the first half of the 1902 season. In late June, however, Connie Mack was able to lure him back east to play for the Philadelphia A's. Under Mack's careful hand, Rube was marvelous — most of the time. The problem was that now the Rube and the Christian Gentleman were in different leagues, and the possibility of a match up seemed remote. With Rube winning 24 and striking out 210 from July through September of 1902, the greatest half season any pitcher ever had, the A's won the pennant, but the NL would not agree to a much-hoped-for playoff between the two league winners. (Pittsburgh won the NL pennant with Fred Clarke still managing , and ex–Pirate Rube dearly wanted to face them). In 1903, there was a World Series, but in 1904 the McGraw-managed Giants won the NL pennant and then refused to play the American League (AL) champion. (A manager with the AL Baltimore Orioles in 1901–02, McGraw had had some run-ins with league President Ban Johnson. His 1904 refusal was an intentionally arrogant slap at his old nemesis.)

Prior to the 1905 season, amidst journalistic pressure and fan outrage, the Giants and the NL acquiesced to the idea of a playoff. As the season's pennant races were working out, the baseball world was excited at the prospect of a Waddell-Mathewson match up, for New York and Philadelphia were both leading, and now the two pitchers were at their best. The rivalry had other dimensions as well. Historically, Philadelphians had seen New Yorkers as especially crude and boorish. Until the antebellum period, Philadelphia had been the nation's largest city and its financial center. The sense of being surpassed still smarted, and around Philadelphia a haughty sense of cultural superiority over the boorish clods to the northeast entrenched itself as a pose of self-compensation. Here the pitchers' images may have blurred matters a trifle, as Main Line Philadelphians could have felt more comfortable with a devout Christian hero rather than a Rube from way out in Butler County, but that was no great issue. Rube was their best hope. Besides, his character had actually linked itself to several Philadelphia landmarks — he had once stood in as a mannequin in the main window of John Wannamaker's Department Store, and he was a part of an early twentieth-century Philadelphia riddle: What are the two most popular attractions in the City of Brotherly Love, and what do they have in common? Answer: Rube Waddell and the Liberty Bell, and both are slightly cracked.

Another incident early in the '05 season added to the rivalry. On April 24, the Giants were in Philadelphia for a series with the Phillies. After the first game, as the team's trolley was leaving the ballpark, a young fan lobbed a handful of dirt and hit Giants' catcher Roger Breshnahan right in the face. Breshnahan was enraged. He jumped off the bus, chased the boy down, and slapped him hard. A mob gathered, and Breshnahan was in real peril. Fortunately the Philadelphia police intervened and saved him. The memory of this incident remained alive throughout the season, with Philadelphians speculating how the New York police would have been less than helpful under any reversed circumstances.[6]

As the season headed into September, New York and Philadelphia fans were taunting one another. Sports betting was then a widespread enterprise in the parlors on Broadway as well as on Wall Street itself. And, of course, in both cities a myriad of drinking establishments witnessed heavy betting as the Philadelphia/New York series approached. That season Mathewson compiled a record of 31 and 9 with an ERA of 1.28. Meanwhile, Rube led the AL in wins (27), winning percentage (.730), ERA (1.48), and strikeouts (287). Moreover, NL batters hit an anemic .205 against Mathewson; against Rube, the AL batted .199. With neither pitcher generous with walks, the opposition on-base percentage in both cases was also pitiful: Mathewson, .245; Waddell, .263.[7]

In August and early September, Rube pitched a record 44 consecutive scoreless innings (Walter Johnson and Don Drysdale would later top him). With Rube at the absolute peak of his fearsome game, Philadelphians were all smiling that their favorite Rube was set to humiliate Mathewson, McGraw, Breshnahan, and the rest of the hated Giants. Then, on September 8, during a trip from Boston to New York, Rube got into a bit of horseplay with a teammate. That afternoon, A's pitcher Andy Coakley (later Lou Gehrig's baseball coach at Columbia University) appeared on a train platform wearing a fancy straw hat. Early twentieth-century convention had it that after Labor Day, ballplayers (and men in general) were to stop wearing straw hats. Those who violated the custom usually found their hats swiped off their heads and punched through. Rube loved such slapsticks, of course, and when the dapper Coakley appeared so chapeau'ed Rube leapt at the chance. Seeing this unpredictable behemoth lurching toward him, Coakley swung around. As Coakley rotated, his shoulder bag, in which he'd stored his spikes, caught Rube hard on the chin. Rube was momentarily dazed, and his jovial spirit quickly soured into anger as he thought Coakley had punched him. Sensing the misunderstanding, and fearing for Coakley's safety, several teammates rushed to restrain Rube, and they all eventually tumbled over a stack of suitcases, landing, as it happened, on Rube's pitching shoulder. On the train, the matter was soon forgotten. The Pullman porter tried to get Rube and Coakley to kiss and make up. (Rube agreed to make up but said he'd be damned if he'd kiss him.) While shaving the next morning, Rube felt a click in his shoulder. In tears, he went to Connie Mack, and they checked out Rube's throwing. Sure enough, there was something seriously wrong with Rube's throwing arm. The only thing the trainer could prescribe was rest, and this was not one of Rube's strong suits.

Rube was sullen, and in such a mood he drank more than he normally did. This hardly helped his recovery. He also pestered Mack into giving him a chance to pitch. Mack knew better, but an eager Rube was hard to refuse. Mack let him try on September 27 and October 6. Both times Rube had nothing — no speed, no control. During these tedious weeks, Rube also pestered Mack to let him try a little practice throwing. When Mack acquiesced, Rube "windmilled" his arms while warming up, experiencing another snap in his shoulder. Rumors were flying about the baseball world that Rube was actually in the clutches of professional gamblers who wanted to protect their bets on the Giants. All the rumors were false, but they would not subside. Rube's reputation for drinking and general high jinks was such that people could certainly believe such stories. The stories persisted for a generation.

Rube could only sit glumly in the dugout during the World Series. Meanwhile, Mathewson hurled a shutout in game one. The A's Chief Bender returned the favor with a shutout of his own in game two. Game three was delayed a day because of rain, so McGraw was able to start Mathewson again. Coakley faced him, and when he took the mound, several New York fans stood up conspicuously wearing straw hats. Whether or not that had unnerved him, Coakley yielded nine runs, while Mathewson tossed another shutout. Before game four, McGraw's eyes nearly popped out of his head as he saw Rube trot out of the dugout to warm up before the game. Alas, Rube had nothing: no speed, no control. He was so wild that one of his warm up tosses sailed into the stands and conked a fan in the head. Mack could not use him, and he watched Joe McGinnity toss yet another shutout for the Giants. Another rain day allowed McGraw to come back with Mathewson in game five, and Christy promptly hurled his third shutout, giving McGraw and the Giants a championship, and leaving all Philadelphia snarling about what would have happened if Rube had been healthy. (With the A's batting a pathetic .151 in the Series, a healthy Rube may not have made much difference.) [8]

Though it was a tragedy to Philadelphia fans, the failure of the Waddell-Mathewson match-up to materialize left the American baseball public with an unresolved tension between the antipodes of their hero worship. Was the mature Christian hero truly the superior of the untutored Rube? Even though it would have been a wonderful duel, much like Rube's bouts with Cy Young, perhaps it was better that the matter was left in abeyance. As the frontier had passed, it has always remained a kindly, agrarian-myth type of notion that the old hicks were somehow stronger than the machines and the virtues that displaced them, the same sentiments expressed within the legends of John Henry and Paul Bunyan. And in baseball if the balance between the Christian and the rascal somehow reassured Americans as to the endurance of certain older values, why did one have to supercede the other? (Why destroy a child's belief in Santa Claus?)

The moral lessons as to the value of the two heroic types were born out in the rest of their respective careers. Mathewson continued to pitch marvelously. In 12 seasons, from 1903 to 1914, he would win an incredible 327 games. His career total of 373 would be the third best of all time, tied with Grover Cleveland Alexander and behind only Cy Young and Walter Johnson. Rube's brilliance faded much faster. He never again experienced another season comparable to those he had between 1902 and 1905. His drinking and generally undisciplined living wore him down. After the 1907 season, Mack unloaded him to the St. Louis Browns. He faded fast after one good year there. In 1910, a young right hander named Eddie Cicotte struck him with a fast ball right on the point of his throwing elbow (Rube threw left but batted right). St. Louis released him, and he recovered but to play out a few more seasons in the minors.

While their playing quality diverged after 1905, the fundamental affection each pitcher engendered never faded. Both showed enormous spiritual strength as well, coming forth in ways that led to their premature deaths. Mathewson was 36 when the U.S. entered World War I. Well past draft age, Mathewson still insisted on doing his part. The Army wanted to use him at home to try to encourage enlistments, but Mathewson insisted on being sent over to Europe. There, leaders wanted to use him to travel about France to help with morale, but Mathewson refused special treatment. In a training exercise, he suffered phosgene (poison gas) inhalation. Mathewson's lungs never fully recovered; his life grew more circumscribed. On October 7, 1925, the great Christy Mathewson, his pulmonary system in collapse, died at the age of 45. That fall, Pittsburgh faced Washington in the World Series, and in all games players from both teams wore black arm-bands in memory of the Christian Gentleman.[9] Rube was also one always willing to sacrifice himself in emergencies. His fire fighting was legendary. He used to wear red skivvies under his uniform so he could quickly strip off and head to a fire if he heard an alarm while on the ball field. This once occurred during spring training in Hickman, Kentucky when Rube was playing for the Minneapolis Millers. Rube heard the alarm, ran, and stripped off his uniform. He commandeered the first horse he could find, raced about town, and found the fire. Seeing smoke billowing from the top of the house, Rube immediately sized up the situation. He grabbed an axe, climbed up and furiously hacked off the roof. He came down beaming with pride over his accomplishments, only to be informed of two things: (1) the fire was contained completely within the chimney, so he'd destroyed the roof for no reason; and (2) he'd forgotten that the previous day he had promised his manager he would no longer wear any red skivvies under his uniform. Small-town Kentuckians of 1911 must have loved Rube's Lady Godiva act. (Even if apocryphal, the story attests to the extent to which the Rube legend had spread.)

At more serious levels, when a teammate suffered a beaning, Rube sat with him in the hospital all night applying ice to his head and perhaps saving his life. Back in Hickman in the winter of 1912–13, he pitched in mightily, joining with the local blacks to plug the sagging levies amidst a series of floods. He had done this several times before. This time he caught a severe chill, and his lungs never recovered. Bronchitis and pleurisy set in. That spring he could not pitch for the Minneapolis Millers and had to make a living playing for a bush league team in Virginia, Minnesota called the Ore Diggers. He coughed incessantly and collapsed on the mound several times. That fall his ailments would not abate. Doctors gave him creosote, and he drank an entire bottle, leaving him with chronic stomach pains. In November 1913, he was found on the streets of St. Louis, a vagrant. He had contracted tuberculosis. Unable to digest properly, his lungs deteriorated. Rube died penniless in a sanitarium on April 1, 1914 at the age of 37. (Born on Friday the 13th and died on April Fool's Day: let star gazing numerologists speculate.) [10]

Ty Cobb lived until 1961, yet few baseball people came to his funeral. Mathewson and Waddell died young, giving of themselves to others. Each was beloved, and their myths extended with the tragedies of their early deaths. One was the pure gentleman; the other was an incorrigibly engaging miscreant. Together their images encompassed the goodness that Americans believed lay in the best of their composite character, whether the roots involved intense moral discipline or unalterably undisciplined childishness. Our nation's political culture, in parallel, produced both an

Alexander Hamilton and a Thomas Jefferson. Optimistic appraisals of American history, when dealing with such contrasting figures, have regularly, if a little too conveniently, seized upon the point that a strength of America's culture has been that it was capable of producing both figures. In the cases of each pair of heroes in politics and baseball, when encountering the limits of one figure, people can simply turn their attention to the virtues of the other. That way, as with any national myth construction, especially when the object of concern involves a mere game, some inconvenient details can be glossed over. In the early twentieth century, for baseball fans and an optimistic nation, the never resolved dichotomy between a Christian and a populist rube burnished the facile assumption that America could garner the largess of conflicting traditions. Was Mathewson a complete choir boy? No, but compared to Rube he was. How can we reconcile Rube's misbehavior and occasional bouts of violence? We think instead of a Mathewson. From there, we lament about their deaths, turn to their generosity of spirit, and wonder at their athletic prowess, which, like the perfect pasture just over the next horizon, is the promised land we never quite reach but somehow know to be out there. "A land," as Langston Hughes reflected, "that never was but must be." The two images and the yearnings they symbolize remain very much alive with a nation that is not content with limits and still sees itself as a city upon a hill.

Notes

1. George Juergens, *Joseph Pulitzer and the New York World* (Princeton: Princeton University Press, 1966), 93–174; and James Wyman Barrett, *Joseph Pulitzer and His World* (New York: The Vanguard Press, 1941), 55–83.

2. Steven A. Riess, *Touching Base: Professional Baseball and American Culture in the Progressive Era* (Westport, CT: Greenwood Press, 1980), 12–48 and 221–233.

3. Walter Lippmann, *Drift and Mastery* (Englewood Cliffs, NJ: Prentice Hall, [1914] 1961), chapter 1.

4. John Dell, "Here's the 'Real' Rube Waddell Story," *Philadelphia Inquirer*, 5 May 1962, 18.

5. Alan H. Levy, *Rube Waddell: the Zany, Brilliant Life of a Strikeout Artist* (Jefferson, NC: McFarland & Co., 2000), 87–89.

6. Levy, 166.

7. John Thomas and Pete Palmer, eds., *Total Baseball: The Ultimate Encyclopedia of Baseball*, 3rd ed. (New York: HarperPerennial, 1993), 1640, 1817.

8. Harold Seymour, *Baseball: The Golden Age* (New York: Oxford University Press, 1971), 15; and A.H. Taravin, "How a Straw Hat Kept Waddell out of a World Series," *Louisville Courier-Journal*, 15 October 1943, reprinted in *Baseball Digest*, November 1943, 1–2; and Levy, 179–86.

9. Charles Alexander, *Ty Cobb* (New York: Oxford University Press, [1984] 1985), 142–143.

10. Levy, 290–298.

Baseball's Ethnic Heroes: Hank Greenberg and Joe DiMaggio

Joseph Dorinson

> The way you swung the bat
> The way you tipped your hat
> The memory of all that
> No, no! They can't take that away
> From me!

With apologies to the Gershwin brothers, this is an assessment of Hank Greenberg and Joe DiMaggio: two men of honor, two resident "brothers" in the Hall of Fame, two baseball legends, and two exemplary ethnic figures. Both DiMaggio and Greenberg were regarded as heroes during their careers. Indeed, one indeed gained iconic status while the other—the subject of only one major biographical study—slipped into obscurity. Before we scrutinize their lives—on and off the field—some observations on the role of heroes in our culture invite mention.

In his demolition derby, which poses as an objective study of Joe DiMaggio, Richard Ben Cramer offers a thickly textured but surprisingly superficial discussion of the heroic life in America.[1] Clearly, a democratic society seems uneasy in the presence of heroes because they suggest an aristocracy of sorts. Thus, throughout our nation's history, Americans seem eager to elevate the extraordinary individual, followed by a propensity to topple him/her from the pedestal. Among contemporary writers and broadcasters—mediated *mayvns* (experts)—this pattern is painfully prevalent. In short, we are prone to smash icons. Some heroes, however, may go into temporary eclipse, but their accomplishments and their traits resist our throwaway culture.[2]

Historically, the heroic life changes, like a chameleon, to meet the special needs of the social order. According to one expert, heroes project 1000 faces. Thus, in Hellenic Greece, they appeared as God-men. In medieval European society, they reemerged as God's men while some women rib-vaulted onto the pedestal with the adoration of Mary as the "eternal female." During the Renaissance, however, women were toppled from their heavenly perch as heroic men regained center stage as the well-rounded virtuosi of Baldassare Castiglione. They evolved as gentlemen in the eighteenth century, self-made men in the nineteenth, and common men in the twentieth century. Basically, aristocrats by nature if not nurture, heroes in a democratic society mercurially flash into fame and fade into obscurity — often in a single generation. One day the people's "cherce" (in Brooklynese); the next, society's discard.[3] Two for the seesaw: Phoenix rises; Orpheus descends.

Two ascendant stars: Hank Greenberg and Joe DiMaggio, I contend, defy the debunkers and compel us to contemplate their cultural roots and historical branches. Less popular perhaps than Joe D but equally heroic to his people, Henry Benjamin Greenberg was born on January 1, 1911. The son of Romanian Jewish parents, he grew up in New York City's Greenwich Village and moved to the Bronx, where he attended James Monroe High School. There, he led his team to the New York City basketball crown. In baseball, long hours of practice in Crotona Park paid off. He also received excellent instruction from Monroe coach Tom Elliffe. After high school, Hank attended New York University briefly from 1929 to 1930. His parents resented the time and energy that young *Heimele* devoted to baseball. They wanted him to pursue higher education. But he preferred athletics to academics and honed his skills in semi-pro baseball.

Athletically, not a Bernard Malamud "Natural" or a Balanchine gazelle, Hank was a diamond in the rough. A 6'4" American-Hebrew national — 215 pounds of raw power and awkward gait — he willed and worked himself up to star stature. The Tigers scouted Greenberg, and he signed a contract, worth $9,000, with Detroit.[4] Why did Hank not sign with the local team, the New York Yankees? A *Yiddisher kop* ("Jewish head" literally; genius, figuratively), Hank realized that Lou Gehrig, a fixture at first base, would be difficult, no, impossible to dislodge from the big ball orchard in the Bronx. He "paid his dues" with several minor league years in the so-called bushes. In 1931, he clubbed forty-one doubles at Evansville while hitting .331. One year later, at Beaumont of the Texas League,

Hank hammered out thirty-nine home runs and proved to teammates that Jews did not have horns protruding from their heads (re: Aviva Kempner's film). "Hankus Pankus" arrived in the "big show" in 1933. As a rookie, he hit .301 with 12 home runs and 87 RBIs.

No sophomore slump plagued the young slugger. In 1934, he hit .339, slammed twenty-six home runs and an astonishing sixty-three doubles. As the Tigers pursued the American League pennant, Greenberg faced a dilemma: to play or not to play on the Jewish High Holidays. With the help of a rabbi, Greenberg decided to play on Rosh Hashanah. On that day, he smacked two home runs, the margin of victory in a 2–1 nail biter. On Yom Kippur, a more solemn day for "atonement," Hank opted for synagogue, Shaare Zedek, where he was greeted like a conquering hero. He received more *koved* (respect) than the resident rabbis.[5] In his absence, however, the Tigers lost 5–2. The press granted national coverage to Greenberg's choices. He powered the Tigers to a pennant. In the World Series, they held a three games to two edge against the Cardinals but lost the last two in succession to the Brothers Dean: Dizzy and Daffy.

Redemption came in 1935; Greenberg swatted 46 doubles, 36 home runs, and an amazing 170 RBIs in his first MVP season. He fielding improved measurably (.992 fielding percentage). In the World Series, the Tigers defeated the Chicago Cubs despite Hank injuring his wrist in game two, forcing him to sit out the remainder of the Series. A dynasty seemed destined for Detroit when two events altered the course of Tiger history. First, Greenberg re-injured his wrist in 1936, missing all but twelve games. That same year Joe DiMaggio arrived in New York, transforming the Yankees. While Tiger fortunes faded until 1940, Greenberg continued his marvelous hitting. In 1937, he banged out 49 doubles and 40 home runs while recording a .337 average. Most impressively, he knocked in 183 runs. Only two players ever exceeded that mark : Hack Wilson (190) and Lou Gehrig (184).

Greenberg's most compelling year, 1938, featured his assault on Babe Ruth's home run record of 60 in a single season. With five games left in the season, he had slugged fifty-eight. Greenberg refused to rationalize his failure to eclipse the Babe. He denied that anti–Semitism, rife in Detroit, rampant elsewhere, had anything to do with it. His teammates, some recorded by Aviva Kempner, thought otherwise. In that year, which signaled Hitler's murderous intent against the Jews (*Kristalnacht* occurred soon after) and the creation of Superman by two Jewish artists, Greenberg smashed 58 home runs, knocked in 146 runs, and had a .315 batting average.

In 1940, Hank helped the Tigers break the Yankee *shneid* (dominance).

He led the Tigers to another pennant with hitting, 50 doubles, 41 home runs, and 150 RBIs. His .340 batting average, coupled with an impressive .670 slugging percentage mark, again garnered him MVP honors. Any doubt about Greenberg's value to the team was dispelled early that year when he voluntarily switched positions to allow the lumbering Rudy York (great hit, no field) to replace him at first base while he patrolled left field.[6] The switch certainly contributed to Tiger dominance in 1940 American League play but may have cost them the World Series (in defensive weakness) as the Reds beat them in a deciding seventh game. Greenberg, nevertheless, was the first player ever to win MVP awards at two different positions.

Greenberg's career, abbreviated by more than four years of service in the military, spanned thirteen years of stardom: a .313 lifetime batting average and 331 home runs. He captured the American League home run title four times and the RBI title four times. Greenberg led the Tigers to four pennants and two World Series triumphs.[7]

His return from service in 1945 is a yarn from which legends are spun. Ranked by author Bert Randolph Sugar as one of baseball's 50 greatest games, the contest between the St. Louis Browns and the Detroit Tigers determined the pennant on September 30, 1945. Losing 3 to 2 in the ninth inning, the Tigers rallied. With one out, men at second and third, the Browns intentionally walked Doc Cramer to get to Hank Greenberg. After taking a "scroogie" for a ball, the Bronx slugger lined a "grand salami" (as we Brooklynites used to identify a home run with the bases loaded) into the left field stands.[8] "Tigers win the pennant. Tigers win the pennant!" Greenberg derived added pleasure from this triumph when he learned how the Washington Senator players, rivals for the American League pennant, reacted. "Goddamn that dirty Jew Bastard," they whined. "He beat us again." Ironically, Hank observed, "They were calling me all kinds of names behind my back and now they had to pack up and go home, while we were going to the World Series."[9] And in that World Series, he hit another two homers to lead his team to a victory over the Chicago Cubs (whom they also beat in 1935) in seven games.

In 1946, Greenberg socked 44 home runs and knocked in 127 runs, beating Ted Williams in both categories during a September rush. His reward was a release through waivers (with the collusion of American League owners) to the Pirates of Pittsburgh (not Penzance, though they played like them) for a career capstone. Lured by Pirate owner John Galbreath with baseball's first $100,000 contract and a shortened left field fence — christened, no, koshered as "Greenberg's Garden," the American-Jewish hero switched to the senior circuit. He became a mentor to Ralph

Kiner and as a friend of Jackie Robinson; he won the approval of Major League Baseball's first African-American player in the twentieth century. After a collision at first base, Hank apologized and urged Jackie on with encouraging words: "...don't let them get you down, you're doing fine, keep it up." Later, the Brooklyn Dodger rookie told reporters that "Class tells. It sticks our all over Mr. Greenberg."[10]

Elected to the Hall of Fame in 1956, Hank Greenberg was the first Jewish-American to be so honored. He also saved $300,000 from the $447,00 he had earned in baseball as a player. Hank climbed up to the executive suite first in Cleveland and later in Chicago, subject to anti–Semitic slurs all the way. These insults intensified Greenberg's Jewish consciousness. Raised in a semi-religious household, he did not attend synagogue regularly. When confronted with defamation of his tribe, however, Greenberg rallied to its cause. As defender of the faith, he fought opponents and teammates alike. Tiger pitcher Elden Auker remembered one incident with the White Sox. A Chicago player called Greenberg "a yellow Jewish son of a bitch." After the game, Hank called into the enemy dugout and challenged the anonymous name-caller. No one moved. "He was damn lucky, " Auker opined, "because Hank would have killed him. Hank was a tough guy."[11]

The target of beer bottles as well as verbal abuse. Greenberg was pressed to the limit. Even some teammates harbored anti–Jewish feeling. Sitting on a personal powder keg, he nearly exploded:

> There was added pressure being Jewish. How the hell could you get up to home plate every day and have some son of a bitch call you a Jew bastard and a kike and a sheenie and get on your ass without feeling the pressure. If the ballplayers weren't doing it, the fans were. I used to get frustrated as hell. Sometimes, I wanted to go into the stands and beat the shit out of them.[12]

There were other incidents. During the 1935 World Series, Cub players unleashed a barrage of vile anti–Semitic insults. Umpire George Moriarty warned the venom-spinners. Because he laced his warning with profanity, Commissioner Landis — as hypocritical as he was racist —fined Moriarty. On another occasion, Hank challenged the entire Yankee bench because of their vile and vituperative references to his heritage. He also battled belligerent and bigoted teammates. Hank threatened to brain a fellow Tiger with a "bat across your thick [southern] skull." In his final year, Hank decked a fellow Pirate for his disparaging remarks.[13] Hank Greenberg uplifted Jewish fans, among them: broadcaster Marty Glickman and journalist Ira Berkow. He also inspired a young Negro athlete named Joe Black.[14] Perhaps marginality is contagious. Greenberg emerged at a time when bigotry was making a comeback in America and girdling the globe. Detroit was the epicenter of anti–Semitism in America with Radio Priest Charles Coughlin fulminating against the "International Banker Conspirator Jew." Fortified with Henry Ford sponsored Protocols, the mellifluous Coughlin polluted the airwaves. Subject to stereotype, Jews were identified with greed on one hand and cowardice on the other; moneyed power at one level; godless Communism below. Along came Hank Greenberg. With his mighty bat and his enormous strength, he transmitted a positive image which — when Hank chose to pray instead of play on Yom Kippur — popular poet Edgar Guest captured in these lines:

> We shall miss him in the infield and we shall miss him at the bat.
> But he's true to his religion — and I honor him for that.[15]

Not only did Greenberg change gentile attitudes; he also bolstered Jewish pride. Ira Berkow's uncles likened him to a beacon. As world Jewry grew less powerful by the Hitlerian minute, Greenberg powered the Tigers to pennants and provided American Jewry a heroic model. Later, Greenberg recalled,

> After all, I was representing a couple of million Jews among a hundred million gentiles and I was always in the spotlight.... I felt a responsibility. I was there every day and if I had a bad day every son of a bitch was calling me names so that I had to make good.... As time went by I came to feel that if I, as a Jew, hit a home run I was hitting one against Hitler.[16]

Thus, when war clouds swept over our country, Hank Greenberg was initially classified 4F because of flat feet. Reclassified 1A, the great Detroit slugger entered the armed service in May 1941 at the height of his career. The first American League player drafted, he took a tremendous pay cut from $55,000 annually to a $21 monthly stipend. Discharged a few days before Pearl Harbor, Hank Greenberg was also the first major leaguer to enlist subsequent to our declaration of war.[17] Greenberg attained the rank of captain in the Army Air Corps. In the Asian Theater, Greenberg contributed to the land-based bombing raids of the Japanese home islands. Thus, not only did he win four home run titles; Hank also earned four battle stars. Discharged in 1945, he became a genuine hero on and off the field. "We are in trouble," he had proclaimed at the war's onset, "and there is only one thing for me to do— return to service." Although he realized that it might end his career — indeed armed service cost him more than four prime years of baseball — he put things in proper perspective: "...All of us are confronted with a terrible task — the defense of our country and the fight for our lives."[18]

Greenberg's own experience at war and peace sparked support for and approval of Jackie Robinson. After an "errant" Pirate pitch hit Jackie, the Negro rookie trotted in pain to first base amidst catcalls of "Coal Mine." Greenberg encouraged Robinson: "Don't let them get you down. You're doing fine. Keep it up." Greenberg remembered Jackie as a "prince" with chin held high. "I had a feeling for him," Hank said, "because of the way I had been treated." Sport historian Peter Levine called Greenberg "the greatest American Jewish sports hero of all time."[19] Strangely, Greenberg has elicited only one biography, a work he began and, after his death, journalist Ira Berkow completed.

Hank Greenberg has reemerged thanks to Aviva Kempner's recent film *The Life and Times of Hank Greenberg*. This exemplary film earned rave reviews.[20] To his fans, vividly represented on the screen, Greenberg was "a messiah, "a Jewish God," "Captain Marvel...on my shoulder," "...my big brother, my *mishpocheh* (family)." Misty-eyed Dan Shapiro also remembers Greenberg as role model. "He was especially important because he wore his Jewishness on his sleeve and heart." Walter Matthau, *alov hasholem* (may he rest in peace), indicated that Greenberg proved that a Jew could aspire to higher positions than "a presser or cutter or salesman in the garment district."[21] Like many other Jews, Hank deviated from Orthodox moorings. When anti–Semitism dogged him, however, he returned to his roots as a champion.

How did Greenberg affect this writer? Let me count the ways. The 1930s was a grim decade. Hitler, Mussolini, and Franco dominated Europe. Depression gripped America. And anti–Semitism was everywhere. Jews suffered from a massive inferiority complex. When attacked, we failed to retaliate. We needed a champion. The Golem of Prague was unavailable, and Superman was only a comic strip. Enter Henry Benjamin Greenberg swinging. He hit baseballs a country mile. No player, with the possible exception of Babe Ruth, had better power numbers in a four-year period, 1937–1940, when he averaged 43 home runs and 148 RBIS. His record for extra base hits — 96 in 1934, 98 in 1935, 103 in 1937 and 99 in 1940 were phenomenal. In addition, he battled fascists abroad and bigots at home. With baseball at the center of the nation's popular culture, Hank's exploits made a difference. In a somber period, he towered like a beacon of light. For Jewish Americans like Sen. Carl Levin (D–Michigan.), Walter Matthau, Aviva Kempner, and this observer, Hank was a desperately needed dose of chlorine with which to disinfect our country of Hitlerian germs, and a welcome jolt of oxygen to re-energize the American Dream.[22]

Greenberg admired his teammate Charlie Gehringer and Yankee slugger Joe DiMaggio because of their effortless skill and natural hitting prowess. Author G. Edward White cites DiMaggio as the Italian analogue to the Jewish Greenberg. White documents the prejudice that ran rampant in baseball, a microcosm of society. He cites an editorial in *The Sporting News* (October 1923) that conveyed an entire catalogue of ethnic stereotypes in defense of careers open to talent and in response to the presence of several baseball players who alternated white-sheeted Ku Klux Klan uniforms with their baseball garb. Of course, blacks and dark-skinned Latinos were excluded from the mix favored by baseball's premier journal.[23] This tendency was the ambivalent historical context that witnessed the rise of ethnic heroes like Joe DiMaggio, a native son of San Francisco who rocketed to stardom during the 1930s. His career would also be interrupted by service to his country in time of war. Early in his career, Jolting Joe was saddled by negative stereotypes. As he became more famous, the ethnicity receded from view. Unlike the ever curious and voracious reader, Greenberg, DiMaggio preferred comic books and remained tight-lipped.[24] He never pursued a perch in the executive suite. His iconic status blossomed with a romantic but short-lived marriage to actress Marilyn Monroe. Shunning the limelight, the Yankee Clipper maintained his image, burnished by infrequent appearances at public events.[25] Jewish songwriters were stirred to sentiment in pursuit of the evanescent Joe DiMaggio.

Joe's parents discouraged their sons' baseball activity. Father Giuseppe came from the Isola delle Femmine, an island situated northwest of Palermo, where he and his family worked as fishermen for many generations. Moving to America in search of a better life, he found a haven in the Bay Area of San Francisco. Joe was born in Martinez on November 25, 1914, the eighth of nine children. Maury Allen reports that Joe's parents spoke only Italian.[26] Uneasy with his old-world parents, Joe hated fishing (perhaps in reaction to *agita* or seasickness) and would sneak out to play baseball at every chance. He also disliked school intensely as evidenced by his attendance record. He repeatedly played hooky. His father called him *lagnusu* (lazy) and a *meschinu* (good-for-nothing).[27] Following Ping Bodie and Tony Lazzeri, Joe DiMaggio became the first Italian baseball superstar. With a career that spanned thirteen seasons, Joe hit .325, socked 361 HRs, and won the MVP title three times. He also set the record least likely to be eclipse — hitting in 56 consecutive games, which captured a nation's attention and offered a much-needed diversion from war fever. Another amazing statistic is the strikeout to home run ration of 369 to 361. During his career, he led the New York Yankees to ten pennants and nine World Series wins.[28] DiMaggio's first seven years in the majors, baseball mavens concede, were his most productive offensive seasons. Only former teammate Lou Gehrig and longtime competitor Ted Williams could match this record. The Yankee record of nine world championships and ten American League pennants during the thirteen years that the Yankee Clipper played is, from a group perspective, even more impressive. Despite, or because of, these extraordinary achievements, Joe's ethnicity played a significant role, often overlooked by both sportswriters and sycophants, in the American experience.

When DiMag launched his meteoric career, Italians had arrived in political power at both ends of America with Mayors Angelo Rossi in San Francisco and Fiorello LaGuardia in New York City. The 1930s witnessed an economic depression at home and the rise of fascism abroad. Americans sought and found heroes in sports: preferring the strong, silent types, winners without bluster, achievers minus arrogance. Joe DiMaggio and the other Joe — Louis — fit these traits nicely.[29] In addition, they had to efface older stereotypes, DiMaggio more so than Louis.

To offset the strutting Caesar from Roma, DiMaggio was both strong and shy, charismatic yet self-effacing. He played baseball, which enjoyed a vast audience. This sport possessed a cleaner image than boxing, evoking the innocence of our rural past. In stark contrast to the buffoonish boxer, Primo Carnera, Joe DiMaggio exhibited an elegance in the field and high competence at the bat from a unique, spread stance. Early in his Yankee career, Joe was heavily identified with Italian traits — some less than flattering. As late as 1939, Noel F. Busch (as in bush league) wrote the following bilge in *Life*:

> Italians, bad at war, are well suited for milder competition....Although he learned Italian first, Joe speaks English without an accent, and is otherwise well adopted [sic] to most US mores. Instead of olive oil or smelly bear grease, he keeps his hair slick with water. He never reeks with garlic and prefers chicken chow-mein to spaghetti.[30]

Dan Daniel, writing in the New York *World-Telegram*, equated DiMaggio with the "spaghetti society of romantic San Francisco." And the Yankee great considered Daniel a close friend.[31] Other writers constantly referred to him as Italian. Maury Allen cites Lefty Gomez, teammate and pal of the Clipper, on the use of epithets. The Yankees called Tony Lazzeri "Big Dago"; Frank Crosetti "Little Dago," and Joe DiMaggio just "Dago."[32]

"The most significant elements that enabled DiMaggio to move into the mainstream white world," writes young scholar Charles Coletta, Jr., in an unpublished dissertation, "were his incredible abilities on the baseball field and his naturally reticent and quiet public demeanor."[33] His dominance, Coletta persuasively argues, is linked to America's preeminent team, the New York Yankees which "invested him with a status previously unavailable" to the vast majority of Italian immigrants. Photographs of him juxtaposed the large Italian family in San Francisco with his cele-brated associates in the nightclubs of New York. He exemplified the work ethic and personified the success story. DiMaggio played America's game, often in pain, with fierce intensity, conscious that "some kid may be see-ing me for the first time."[34]

When DiMaggio held out for a substantial raise in 1938, the fans booed him. Yet, he proved a commendable counter-image to Mussolini whose popularity alarmed loyal Americans. In January 1942, hounded by fears of a fascist fifth column, government officials began a process to reclassify 600,000 Italian Americans aliens as "enemies." Restrictions were placed on their ability to travel. At a Select House Committee hearing, Ital-ian attorney Chauncey Tramulto defended his people. His most persua-sive argument derived from the DiMaggio family. Technically, Joe's parents, never having attained American citizenship, were vulnerable. Tra-multo emphasized that the DiMaggio family had produced three major leaguers and of, course, focused on Joe's greatness. Evidently persuaded, on October 12, 1942, President Roosevelt rescinded the order that catego-rized the Italians as enemy aliens, thanks in no small measure to Jolting Joe DiMaggio.[35]

Enlisted in the Air Force in February 1943, the Yankee Clipper erased any doubts about dual loyalty. Military service also removed vestigial eth-nicity. If Babe Ruth, roistering and rumbling, represented and symbolized the spirit of the "Roaring Twenties," Joe DiMaggio, poised and proper, exemplified the more sobering and solemn 1930s.[36] In his post-war career, Jolting Joe jumped into the melting pot and came up solid gold. He never achieved his pre-war measurements except for a 155 RBI season in 1948. One year later, while studying for a rite of passage, my bar mitzvah, I remem-ber Joe D (my nickname too) coming off the disabled list for a crucial three game series in Boston.[37] Following Joseph Campbell's script of separation-initiation-return, Joseph Paul DiMaggio, still pained from bone spurs from his right heel, smote four home runs, knocked in nine runs, and scored five runs, leading the Yanks over the Red Sox, still smarting from "the curse of the Bambino." As Nat "King" Cole sang: "Unforgettable!"

Insightfully, author Jack Moore observes that DiMaggio, as hero, appeared both Italian and American concomitantly. Comparable to Joe Louis who coupled negritude with American identity, DiMaggio repre-sented a safe symbol. Impeccably dressed, he also served as a symbol of sartorial elegance. Though "non-intellectual" or because of it, he stayed close to his moorings: "a big-hearted, generous and relatively unchanged boy" in the striking, if not altogether accurate, assessment of historian Andrew Rolle.[38] He brought Italians in droves to Yankee Stadium. His performance on the field and his appearance (one of the best dressed men) blunted anti–Italian feeling. The Italian-American hero achieved a kind of apotheosis in the Pulitzer-Prize winning, comeback novella of Ernest Hemingway: *The Old Man in and the Sea*. Santiago, the Cuban fisherman and ancient mariner, cannot catch any fish. In fact, he is in a slump that lasts eighty-four days. Inspired by DiMaggio's father, a fellow fisherman, and by "the Great DiMaggio who does all things perfectly even with the pain of bone spur in his heel," the old man perseveres.[39] "Grace under pressure" and "heroic dignity" mark the Hemingway hero and fuse with DiMaggio's mystique. He moved away from the tribal ties to a broader framework of associates such as Toots Shor, Walter Winchell, and Marilyn Monroe. The Monroe connection came after his illustrious baseball career. It enhanced his iconic status. A noble and star-crossed lover, he torched after his ex-wife. He seemed to exude class. Maybe shilling for Mr. Coffee and the Bowery Bank somewhat tarnished that image. How could one begrudge the Clipper a chance to make an extra buck? After all, Joe D had played in an era when salaries did not rise dramatically. In his autobiography, *Lucky To Be a Yankee*, this prince in pinstripes focused on God's gift, natural talent, and the significance of luck. Did DiMag inadvertently consign hard work and self-discipline to another place, another time?

When DiMaggio died, fans, indeed idolaters like this writer, provided grist for the media mill. Joe's obituary made the front page of *The New York Times*. Fans and celebrities offered testimony. The Associated Press conducted interviews the results of which found expression in news media throughout our country. For example, former Dodgers manager Tommy Lasorda observed: "If you said to God, 'Create someone who was what a baseball player should be and all of the great attributes,' God would have created Joe DiMaggio. And he did." From President Bill Clinton came these words of praise:

> Today, America lost one of the century's most beloved heroes....This son of Italian immigrants gave every American something to believe in. He became the very symbol of American grace, power, and skill. A brilliant individual performer, he led his magnificent Yankees to the World Series 10 out of his 13 years. His electrifying 56-game hitting streak, unequaled to this day, is one of the most remarkable achievements by any athlete in any sport.[40]

I added my two cents of cracker barrel wisdom: "Joe DiMaggio was one man who truly epitomized the 'Hemingway Hero.' He confronted adversity with grace under pressure."[41] President Clinton's effusive praise of DiMaggio "as an incredibly devoted father" would soon come under critical scrutiny with Richard Ben Cramer's expose.

Earlier, Gay Talese had brought attention to DiMaggio's dark side. Uneasy with adulation, he nevertheless welcomed sycophants. He could be curt and cruel with those who failed to obey his demands. DiMaggio resisted Talese's bid for a candid interview and spurned his feeble attempt at flattery; Joe protested "I'm not great. I'm not great. I am just a man trying to get along."[42] Subsequent efforts to strip away the façade failed as David Halberstam reveals. Joe D was a hard man to decipher. He was smart enough to realize that he was not smart enough to dissemble. A loner, he hated to be alone. So he surrounded himself with cronies and hangers-on. They cordoned off the outside world, allowing their idol to be a gallant in the public eye yet fiercely private. DiMaggio was always in control of his heroic persona.[43] Robert Lipsyte looked for a "human DiMaggio under the mask." Joe, he concluded, cultivated his own celebrity when, years ago, "he put himself in a glass case." Surly and cooperative by turns, the Yankee star could remember individual games and injuries with remarkable precision, but his observations about baseball players in the 1930s and the 1940s, "when he owned the night," were shallow. Though he loved playing with a maximum of energy and emotion, he could not dispel a knot in his stomach "because he was so shy and tense."[44]

Alan Barra wrote a eulogy that appeared in the *Village Voice*. He referred to DiMaggio's private life as "an unholy mess, a riot of contradictions awaiting a tough-mind[ed] biographer to sort them out." Readers responded with letters of outrage.[45] A tough-minded writer responded with a book. Richard Ben Cramer tried to portray the real man behind the public mask.

In the tradition of Teddy Roosevelt, Cramer's DiMaggio speaks softly and carries a "big stick." The author takes a page from the book of Ida Tarbell. He's a "muckraker," a phrase coined by the first President Roosevelt. The muck unearthed by Cramer covers a wide swath of dereliction. DiMag was a lousy husband, a bad father, and a jealous brother. Moreover, he was cheap, selfish — indeed narcissistic, vain, cruel, and stupid. Despite his sexual prowess, he was a prude and a devotee of the sexual double standard. Adding injury to insult, he beat Marilyn Monroe (only when, the sex symbol conceded, she deserved it), lied about his finances, consorted with criminals ("married to the mob?"), screwed prostitutes (he preferred blonde Marilyn look-alikes on coarse cotton sheets), and never picked up a tab. All he cared about was the color of money. In various interviews, Cramer denied any animus toward his subject. The psychobiographer, I fear, protests too much. When I queried him on the Internet regarding DiMaggio's persistent popularity, he replied:

Joe, there was something about DiMaggio that did defy understanding — and that was the innate gravity and importance of the man. Everybody who ever met him remembers that meeting. They remember what he said, how he looked, what he signed for them, how he smiled, or walked away. They remember the same way people remember where they were when Kennedy was killed. With Joe, his every appearance was an event.46

Elegantly written, Cramer's response, however, slides over the base. Evidently, the author invites critical scrutiny as well. Why, for example, would a Pulitzer Prize winner for a book on American politics spend five years tracking an American sports hero? Did the lure of a big pay-off play a part? While much research and sparkling prose went into the book, it suffers from deep if not fatal flaws. Unevenly chronicled, the narrative takes us up to the early 1960s. After a nearly thirty year gap — more conspicuous than the missing eighteen minutes on Nixon's tape — we reenter DiMaggio's troubled life in 1989. Although Cramer mentions hundreds of interviews, he rarely if ever links them to a specific source. Where are the footnotes? Or endnotes? Critics have correctly pointed to a flagrant example wherein the author places DiMaggio at Toots Shor's bistro sharing a drink with jockey Eddie Arcaro. The baseball great offers the celebrated jockey advice on how to hold a baby. Allegedly, his wife Dorothy (Arnold) flashed "a cold glint of scorn" and sneered "under her breath: 'Whose baby are you going to use for teaching?'" When did Mrs. DiMaggio say it? What did she mean? How do we know Dorothy's "blue eyes" and "cold glint of scorn" were visible in the darkly lit eatery? And who, pray tell, is the source? For Joe's (DiMaggio, not McCarthy) sake, name names.47

An icon, essayist Joseph Epstein warns, begets iconoclasts. Richard Ben Cramer relishes that role just as Joe DiMaggio deserves a small religious art object in his name. Pitching aside, he excelled in all facets of the game. He could hit, hit with power, field, throw, run, and, under pressure, perform with what the Greeks called *arete* or virtuosity "in the clutch." So where did Cramer get the "dirt" on Joe's mob connections? Writer Pete Hamill speculated that low-ranking mobsters, "notorious bullshit artists," may have bent Cramer's ear. DiMaggio's admirers actively, indeed aggressively pursued him and showered the Yankee star with unsolicited — for the most part — favors according to Epstein.48 Even Cramer concedes that Joe D paid for his less affluent teammates when out on the town. He profited from those who leeched on his name, and the leeches were legion, including his attorney Morris Engelberg. Despite his alleged failure as a husband, he deserves praise as an ex-husband, especially to the troubled and tragic Marilyn Monroe. Cramer's self-assigned role, Epstein remarks, is one of moral superiority and character assassination.49

Tommy Henrich tailored a more reliable measure of DiMaggio's genius. Having played alongside of Joe D. for eleven years (longer than anyone else), Old Reliable, the Yankee right fielder, knew his subject. Without reservation, Henrich believes that his colleague in center field was the greatest player he ever saw — indeed, besides Babe Ruth — the greatest player of all time: "Joe's burning desire to win and his corresponding fear of failure were the forces that drove him."[50] Whether at bat or in the field, the Yankee center fielder impressed his teammate with outstanding play. The best catch he witnessed came off the bat of Hank Greenberg in 1939 at Yankee Stadium. Henrich recalls:

> I was playing in right field...when Greenberg hit a long fly ball into the monuments that used to be in deep center field. DiMag was off at the crack of the bat, maybe even a split second before. He set sail for the outfield wall with his back to the plate, flying over the grass and not looking back until he was almost out of room. Then he leaped, reached up, and caught the ball in the middle of an acrobatic turn. He banged into the wall but held onto the ball.[51]

Linked by this great play, Greenberg and DiMaggio constitute a noble duo. Each emerged as a representative of a particular group; yet each earned universal appeal. DiMaggio avoided controversy and shunned conflict becoming, in the process, an "Americanized Italian."[52] Greenberg could never shed his Jewish skin despite a highly secular life. My generation remembers both with fondness bordering on adulation. Where indeed have you gone Joe D and Hank G?

Today, our landscape is graffitied with celebrities instead of heroes. Daniel Boorstin has inferred that a democratic society bears an intrinsic bias against individual heroes. Perhaps that is why gifted writers like Richard Ben Cramer pull heroes from their pedestal almost as a rite of passage. Once upon a time in America, heroes operated on the frontiers of society ennobled by rugged individualism and fortified with self-reliance. Before 1880, warrior-heroes like George Washington and Andrew Jackson dominated. Later, inventors in the mold of Henry Ford and Thomas Edison gained primacy. Then something happened. We switched from idols of production to idols of consumption. In the latter category, sports served as a surrogate frontier where the athletic hero played out the role of pathfinder/pioneer. He overcame obstacles with talent and determination. Victory went to those with superior ability. If the start was equal, then the best man won.[53] Earlier, our nation's heroes arose from common origins, like Greenberg and DiMaggio, powered by good character as well as extraordinary skill. Today, however, the celebrity occupies center stage in both sports and entertainment. Indeed, morality often plays second string. Celebrities like Madonna, Alan Iverson, and Ray Lewis blur the boundaries between heroes and anti-heroes.[54]

Thus, poets touch us. With Stephen Spender, "We think continually of those who were truly great"—who, glittering on the diamond like Greenberg and DiMaggio, "...left the vivid air signed by their honor." Forever fixed in the mystic chords of memory, they summon what Abraham Lincoln also called "the better angels of our nature." In the refrain of the Brothers Gershwin—of they we sing:

> The way you played the game
> Feted in the Hall of Fame
> The records of your swat
> The memorable home run trot
> Ethnic heroes of renown
> You wear the laurel and the crown.

Notes

1. Richard Ben Cramer, *Joe DiMaggio: The Hero's Life* (New York: Simon and Schuster, 2000), 34–35, 71–72, 80–83, 100–102, 151–153, 171–172, 248–249.

2. David L. Porter, "America's Greatest Sports Figures" in *The Hero in Transition*, ed. Ray B. Browne and Marshall W. Fishwick (Bowling Green, OH: Bowling Green University/ Popular Press, 1983), 248–259.

3. *Ibid.*

4. Jeffry Rosen, "Hank Greenberg," in *The Scribner's Encyclopedia of American Lives*, vol. 2, ed. Kenneth T. Jackson (New York: Charles Scribner's Sons, 1991), 353.

5. *The Life and Times of Hank Greenberg.* Dir. Aviva Kempner, Independent, 2000.

6. Rosen, 353–355.

7. Ira Berkow, "A Kind of Beacon" in *The New York Times Book of Sports Legends*, ed. Joseph J. Vecchione (New York: Random House/ Quadrangle Books, 1991), 98–100.

8. Bert Randolph Sugar, *Baseball's 50 Greatest Games* (New York: Exeter Books, 1986), 170–172.

9. Hank Greenberg, *The Story of My Life*, ed. Ira Berkow (New York: Times Books, 1989), 155.

10. Stephen H. Norwood and Harold Brackman, "Going to Bat for Jackie Robinson: The Jewish Role in Breaking Baseball's Color Line," *Journal of Sport History* 26 (Spring 1999), 131.

11. Peter Levine, *Ellis Island to Ebbets Field: Sport and the American Jewish Experience* (New York: Oxford University Press, 1992), 139–140.

12. *Ibid.*,139; and Greenberg, 104.

13. Norwood, 128–129.

14. Maury Allen, *Jackie Robinson: A Life Remembered* (New York: Franklin Watts, 1987),188; and Marty Glickman with Stan Isaacs, *The Fastest Kid on the Block: The Marty Glickman Story* (Syracuse NY: Syracuse University Press, 1996), 87.

15. Quoted in Levine, 136.

16. Quoted in Geoffrey C. Ward and Ken Burns, *Baseball: An Illustrated History* (New York: Alfred A. Knopf, 1994), 250–251.

17. G. Edward White, *Creating the National Pastime: Baseball Transforms Itself* (Princeton: Princeton University Press, 1996), 264.

18. Ward and Burns, 275–276.

19. Levine, 131–132.

20. Richard Sandomir, "He Batted for the Tigers, Himself and American Jews," *The New York Times*, 9 January 2000, AE38.

21. Sandomir, AE38.

22. Joseph Dorinson, "Hammerin' Hank is Back," *The Long Island Jewish Week*, 21–27 January 2000, 4, 32; and Joseph Dorinson, "My Hero, Hank," *New York Daily News*, 15 January 2000, 17.

23. White, 245–247.

24. Stephen Fox, *Big Leagues...* (New York: William Morrow, 1994), 374–375.

25. White, 260, 266–274, 374–375.

26. Maury Allen, *Where Have You Gone, Joe DiMaggio* (New York: New American Library Signet,1976), 8.

27. Carmelo Bazzano, "The Italian American Sporting Experience" in *Ethnicity and Sport in North American History and Culture*, ed. George Eisen and David K. Wiggins (Westport CT: Praeger, 1995), 111; and Jack B. Moore, "Understanding Joe DiMaggio As an Italian American Hero" in *Italian Americans Celebrate Life: The Arts and Popular Culture*, ed. Paola A. Sensi Isolani and Anthony Julian Tamburri (San Francisco: American Italian Historical Association, 1990), 169–178.

28. Donald Dewey and Nicholas Acocella, *The Biographical History of Baseball* (New York: Carroll & Graf Publishers, 1995), 113–115.

29. Moore, 171.

30. Quoted in Roy Blount, Jr., "Legend: How DiMaggio Made It Look Easy" in *The Ultimate Baseball Book*, ed. Daniel Okrent and Harris Lewine (Boston: Houghton-Mifflin Hilltown,1984), 209.

31. Moore, 177.

32. Allen, 25.

33. Charles A. Coletta, Jr., *Gangsters, Guidos, and Grandmas: Italian Americans in Twentieth Century American Popular Culture* (May 2000) Unpublished dissertation, 83–84.

34. *Ibid.*, 84.

35. Moore, 75–176; and John P. Diggins, *Mussolini and Fascism: The View from America* (Princeton NJ: Princeton University Press, 1972), 400.

36. Joseph Durso, *DiMaggio: The Last American Knight* (Boston: Little Brown, 1995), 260.

37. Ward and Burns, 315.

38. Moore, 177–178; and Coletta, 85.

39. Rudolf K. Haerle, Jr., "The Athlete as 'Moral' Leader," *Journal of Popular Culture* 8 (Fall 1974), 395.

40. *The Washington Post* , 9 March 1999, D5. From *http://www.angelfire.com/ok2/dimaggio/statements.html*

41. *Ibid.*

42. Gay Talese, "The Silent Season of a Hero," in *The Best Sports Writing of the Century*, ed. David Halberstam and Glenn Stout (Boston: Houghton Mifflin, 1999), 7.

43. Halberstam, xxi–xxiii.

44. Robert Lipsyte, "Finding a Human DiMaggio Under the Mask," *The New York Times*, 27 September 1998, SP 15.

45. Cited in Allen Barra, "Joe Cruel" Salon.com Books, 1. See *http://www.salon .com.books/feature/2000/10/19/dimaggio/.*

46. *http://discuss.washingtonpost.com/zforum/00/10180_dimaggio.htm.*

47. Biographer Steve Weinberg raises these salient points. See *http://www.iron-minds.com/ironminds/issues/001024/bookshelf3.*

48. Joseph Epstein, "Where'd He Go, Joe DiMaggio," *Commentary*, June 1999, 44–48.

49. *Ibid.* 48–49.

50. Tom Henrich with Richard Nikas, "The Last Yankee" *The National Pastime: A Review of Baseball History* (1999), 3.

51. *Ibid.* 4.

52. Coletta, 87.

53. Roderick Nash, *The Nervous Generation: American Thought, 1917–1930* (Chicago: Rand McNally, 1970), 126–137.

54. Daniel Boorstin, "From Hero to Celebrity: Human Pseudo-Event" in *Heroes and Anti-Heroes*, ed. Harold Lubin (San Francisco: Chandler, 1969), 325–340. For a devastating portrait of this controversial singer-actress, see Steve Allen, "Madonna," *Journal of Popular Culture* 27:1 (Summer 1993), 1–11.

Searching for Hank Greenberg: Aviva Kempner's Mythic Hero and Our Fathers

William M. Simons

My Father and Hank

On Sunday January 16, 2000, I drove with Rich Cohen, a physician, Little League umpire, and friend, several hours over winter roads from central New York to Manhattan. Our destination was the Film Forum, an "artsy" 181-seat theater, on Houston Street in the South Village. Aviva Kempner's documentary film, *The Life and Times of Hank Greenberg*, which had made its New York debut only four days before, was playing.

A singular combination of earnestness, tribalism, folksiness, and intellectualism defined those lined up outside the cinema awaiting entrance. Intense conversation related to Hank Greenberg dominated. An elderly man, who acknowledged that he had little interest in baseball, bitterly recalled the anti–Semitic tirades of Father Charles Coughlin. Nodding in assent, another senior citizen, stated that he had grown up in Detroit. A few men wore yarmulkes. A middle-aged man, accompanied by a boy, said he wanted his son to "know." Someone else identified himself as the physician to Joe Greenberg, Hank's younger brother. Then, in a deliberate voice, he asked me, "Why did you come?"

In the winter of 1960, Shep bought his eleven year old son a set of weights. Three evenings a week, in the basement, Shep would instruct the boy in technique and monitor his progress. And, between sets, they talked.

Over 40 years have come and gone, but those talks with my father remain vivid. Frequently Dad spoke about Hank Greenberg, the Detroit Tigers slugger of the Depression years. As my father came of age, anti–Semitism plagued the United States and Germany. In his youth, my father sought a Jewish history that leavened defeat and discrimination with victories and heroes. At the library, he read of Judah Maccabee and Bar Kokhba, but no Jewish hero loomed larger in young Shep's imagination than a contemporary, Hank Greenberg.

My father, Shepherd Simons, was born in 1923. He grew up in Lynn, Massachusetts, an old industrial city, then a manufacturing center for shoes. His parents were Jewish immigrants from Russia. Sport has threaded its way through Shep's entire life. He loved the competitiveness, comradeship, and excitement of sport. So much of my father's life and his relationship to me relates directly and indirectly to baseball. For us, the game and its memories, associations, and artifacts possess symbolism. I played on the Little League team, appropriately named for Greenberg's Tigers, that my father managed to a championship.

My father attended the Lynn Hebrew School several afternoons a week until his bar mitzvah. He resented the time spent at Hebrew School. The teachers taught Hebrew by rote, providing little sense of the meaning behind the words. Nor did Shep's Hebrew teachers have much patience for the restless energy of American boys who wanted to play baseball like Hank Greenberg. One of the teachers, the father of the boxer Abe Wasserman, hit his pupils on the head and pulled their ears to encourage greater attentiveness.

By early adolescence, Shep found Jewish theology largely irrelevant. He believed in a supreme being but found it difficult to accept that any mortal could tell him more about God than he felt. Yet young Shep identified strongly with the ethnic component of Judaism. And Hank Greenberg was central to that ethnic component.

Hank Greenberg always provided the starting point for our discussions of my father's formative experiences. For my father, Greenberg — big, strong, courageous, athletic, smart, proud of his background, and patriotic — personified the best in American Jewry. Hank, asserted Shep, "proved Jews could take it." Shep intently followed, game by game, Greenberg's 1938 assault on Babe Ruth's home run record. Decades later, my father could still dramatically recount, sometimes with poetic license, Hank's power hitting.

In his mid-teens, Shep joined Lynn AZA (Aleph Zadik Aleph), a Jewish fraternal group with a strong athletic component. Save for his military service, Shep remained active in the organization for the next twenty-seven years, first as a member and then as an advisor. Within a year after Pearl Harbor, every eligible member of Lynn AZA entered the military; three died in the service of their country. AZA's contributions to the war effort were linked, my father implied, to Hank Greenberg's example as the first major leaguer to enlist in the armed services during World War II, a counter to claims of Jewish cowardice and draft dodging. Shep contended that Hank's four and one-half years of military service cost him close to 200 career home runs. Shep, like virtually every American Jew of his generation, knew a variation of the following apocryphal story:

> A big fellow is weaving his way around a World War II embarkation point, saying in a loud voice, "Is there anybody here named Ginsberg or Goldberg? I'll kick the living daylights out of him." A soldier stands up and says, "My name's Hank Greenberg, buddy." The drunk looks him up and down and replied, "I didn't say Greenberg. I said Ginsberg or Goldberg."[1]

After four years in the Army Air Force, Shep was discharged in 1946. An Army buddy visited him in Boston that summer, and they went to Fenway Park to see a Red Sox–Tigers game. The friend told Shep that he had gone to James Monroe, Greenberg's Bronx high school and that he would get them in the Tigers clubhouse after the game. For nine innings, Shep anticipated meeting his hero, but it did not happen. When they were rebuffed at the clubhouse door, the Army buddy claimed there was some sort of mix up. More that a half-century later, my father still regretted not meeting Hank Greenberg. At age sixty, my father "appropriated" a huge blown up photograph of Greenberg from a Catskill hotel.

Within my father's Greenberg tales, I came to understand, resided something important about the relationship between fathers and sons and the struggle to reconcile Jewish and American identities. Consciously and unconsciously, I have spent much of my life coming to terms with my father's values. Separated by a generation, he and I both served as Aleph Godol (president) of Lynn AZA, the only father and son to so do. In young manhood, Shep was a counselor at a Jewish summer camp; so was I. I can match his 20-plus years as an advisor to a Jewish youth group. My father dreamed of escaping the family business to teach; I did that. Yet it is the search for Hank Greenberg, the Jewish standard bearer of our shared mythology, that has always shaped the dialogue between my father and myself.

As a bar mitzvah present, Dad gave me a copy of *The Jew in American Sports* by Harold Ribalow. The volume was organized around profiles of prominent Jewish-American athletes. I never tired of rereading it. From the vantage point of academic scholarship, the book has a modest data base and cursory analysis, but I still fondly recall the warmth, passion, and inspiration my adolescent self found in Ribalow's prose. The essential message of the book was that athletic standard bearers ought to engender pride and confidence in all American Jews.

My favorite section was Ribalow's chapter on Hank Greenberg. His portrait of Greenberg paralleled, in tone if not content, my father's account. Ribalow's confirmation of Greenberg's importance to American Jewry somehow validated my father's stories about Hammerin' Hank. Terming him a credit "to America and to Jewry,"[2] Ribalow, like my father, invested Greenberg with a mythic stature:

> When in 1945, I found myself in Ceylon, serving with the Air Force, I listened to every World Series game on the radio. And when the boys got together and heard that Hank Greenberg was still walloping homers, they felt better because they knew that 'home' was still the same. Greenberg was part of American life...[3]

Whenever I got a new baseball book, I would immediately search the text and the index, if there was one, for any reference to Hank Greenberg. Those pages dealing with Hammerin' Hank were always the first that I read. Any Greenberg anecdote or information — the 63 doubles in 1934, DiMaggio's great catch on a long drive by the Detroit slugger, the grand slam in the final game of the 1945 season that gave the Tigers another pennant — was immediately shared with my father. Dad would always listen with interest and typically add his own embellishment.

The years passed, but my search for Hank Greenberg continued. Intellectual development and graduate degrees in history only provided me with new tools. Reading evolved into formal research. Through travel and interlibrary loan, I dug deeply into general circulation and Jewish-American newspapers of decades past for additional material about Hank Greenberg and his era. A 1977 faculty appointment to the State University of New York College at Oneonta, only 22 miles from Cooperstown, prompted visits to the incomparable research library of the National Baseball Hall of Fame and Museum. I consulted all materials related to Greenberg, including his files and every issue of *The Sporting News* published between 1933–1947. I interviewed second baseman Charlie Gehringer, the aged sportswriter Fred Lieb, and other Greenberg contemporaries.

Hammerin' Hank himself corresponded with me, an exchange circumscribed by the old slugger's brief replies to my queries. Despite Greenberg's discrete responses, necessitated he explained by his own autobiographical project, I took joy in showing my father a letter written in Hank Greenberg's own hand that graciously indicated that I knew more about certain parts of his baseball career than he did.

The spring 1982 issue of *Jewish Social Studies,* a respected quarterly founded in 1933, featured my first professional article, "The Athlete as Jewish Standard Bearer: Media Images of Hank Greenberg." It was the first sports related study to appear in *Jewish Social Studies.* "The Athlete as Jewish Standard Bearer" placed Greenberg's baseball career in social-historical perspective. The article analyzed the struggle of second generation American Jewry to resolve the tension between ethnic and host society expectations amidst strident anti–Semitism:

> The assimilationist implications of Greenberg's press image coincided with aspirations harbored by many Jewish Americans during the Depression era. As progeny of immigrant parents, many Jews of this period belonged to the second generation. The second generation, ambivalent about its religious heritage, eager to acquire middle-class respectability, and anxious about the opinion of the gentile community, found Greenberg an appropriate standard bearer. Unlike the often flamboyant, braggadocious, poorly educated, financially imprudent Jewish boxers, who flaunted their ethnicity with the Star of David emblazoned on their trunks, engaged in nocturnal adventures with *shiksas,* and carried the ambience of ghetto pugnacity with them, "modest," "retiring," "clean-living," Hank Greenberg, as portrayed by the press, was an Americanized *mensch.* The Greenberg of the media, who eschewed calling attention to his private religious beliefs, offered fellow Jews an example of an upwardly mobile lifestyle that attracted relatively little animosity from gentile neighbors. The New York *Evening Post* in 1934, for example, linked Greenberg's personal success with the movement of Jews from the Lower East Side ghetto: "The last time Detroit got into the October set of games there were not nearly as many Greenbergs in the Bronx as there are now." Newspaper photographs of the articulate Greenberg, who had attended New York University for a year, often displayed a neat, immaculate gentleman, dressed in tie and jacket with a newspaper in hand and resembling a young professional or businessman more than he did a baseball player.[4]

Response to "The Athlete as Jewish Standard Bearer" was favorable. Eric Jacobson, formerly an apprentice journalist affiliated with *The Economist* and *The Wall Street Journal,* subsequently termed it the first commentary on Greenberg presented in accord with the canons of academic scholarship.[5] A revised version of the article won the Meckler Award. In the early stages of her own Greenberg project, filmmaker Aviva Kempner read "The Athlete as Jewish Standard Bearer," writing that it "really helped me in my thinking about the film."[6] Yet, my initial Greenberg article missed the mark with its intended audience, my father. Despite pride in publication of the Greenberg article, my father had difficulty with its scholarly presentation, academic language, and analysis, distancing him from the epic myth we shared.

So the search for Hank Greenberg continued. I published subsequent articles on other topics, but I was not finished with Hank Greenberg. Professional conferences and my sport history course gave me forums to try out different approaches to the Greenberg saga. Ongoing research and new perspectives kept the quest vital. Then I began to speak about Greenberg in various settings beyond academia. Synagogue, Jewish Community Center, Hillel, Little League, library, museum, and service group gatherings encouraged me to rediscover the narrative and mythic dimension of the Greenberg story. At one lecture reception, kosher hot dogs and cracker-jacks were served. Often older members of the audience, typically Jewish, related their own Greenberg vignettes. After a Cortland, New York lecture, a professor told me that her uncle, Herb Greenberg, a tall man who bore some resemblance to the old slugger, would make reservations to elite Manhattan restaurants under the name Hank Greenberg and find himself the recipient of treatment normally accorded only to celebrities.

Unfortunately, time and circumstance long precluded my father's attendance at any of my public lectures. Then, I invited him to attend a baseball talk that I was to give at The Norman Rockwell Museum in Stockbridge, Massachusetts on August 20, 1995. Twenty-four hours before I was to speak at the Rockwell Museum, however, a spike tore through my calf while climbing on the rocks of a promontory. Contrary to medical advice, refusing pain killers that might dull my senses, and driving a considerable distance, I spoke at the Rockwell Museum the next day with my father and son in attendance. Although my father enjoyed hearing me speak, I wished the lecture, entitled "American Exceptionalism and the National Pastime" had made more than fleeting mention of Greenberg.

Although cancer felled Greenberg in his seventy-fifth year, the great Jewish slugger remained a touchstone for the relationship between my father and me. I regretted never having met Hank Greenberg in person. Then, in the summer of 1999, I lamented that I had not even seen a game in the park where Greenberg played, Tiger Stadium, scheduled for demolition at the end of the 1999 season. My old college friend Al Levine, my son Joe, and I drove to Detroit. On August 14, 1999, we arrived well before the start of the Tigers-Angels game. From the stands, we walked the perimeter of Greenberg's ballpark. I recalled my father's stories of Greenberg's baseball heroics and half expected to catch a glimpse of the departed Jewish slugger. I bought my father a memento, a cup with a photograph emblazoned upon it of the stadium when it was called Navin Field during the prime of Hank Greenberg.

In 2000, my father and I separately saw *The Life and Times of Hank Greenberg.* We recognized the Hank Greenberg of our shared mythology in Aviva Kempner's film.

During his scholar's odyssey, Joseph Campbell provided profound and prolific insight into the mythic hero. "When a person becomes a model for other people's lives," observes Campbell, "he has moved into the sphere of being mythologized."[7] As the title of one of Campbell's monumental studies proclaims, the mythic hero has worn "a thousand faces."[8] And one of those faces is that of baseball player. Joseph Dorinson, Long Island University sport historian, observes, with a nod to Campbell, that a hero follows "a certain behavior pattern — initiation, separation and return — and that works symbolically with baseball."[9] Baseball heroes differ. According to biographer Marshall Smelser, "In Ruth's time baseball's holy hero was Christy Mathewson, the tricky hero was Ty Cobb, and the muscular hero was Babe Ruth."[10] In the time that shaped the mythology of my father and her father, Aviva Kempner's Hank Greenberg was the Jewish hero.

Aviva's Father and Hank

The Life and Times of Hank Greenberg, a documentary film by Aviva Kempner, is an ambitious work. In addition to chronicling the personal life and baseball exploits of the Jewish first baseman-outfielder, the 95-minute film explores Greenberg's place in American cultural and ethnic history. A number of co-religionists preceded the original Hammerin' Hank in the major leagues, but Greenberg was baseball's first Jewish superstar.

As the film makes clear, Greenberg was a great baseball player. Aside from a final season with the Pittsburgh Pirates, Greenberg's major league career (1930, 1933–1941, 1946–1947) was spent with the Detroit Tigers. Greenberg won four home run and four RBI titles. His 183 RBIs in 1937 fell only one short of Lou Gehrig's American League record, and no right-handed batter exceeded his 1938 total of 58 home runs until 1998. Only four players have higher lifetime slugging percentages than Greenberg's .605. Twice he received the American League's Most Valuable Player award. Despite injuries and four and one-half years lost to World War II military service, Greenberg augmented his .313 lifetime average with 331 career home runs and 1,276 RBI's, ensuring his election to the Baseball Hall of Fame.

The Life and Times of Hank Greenberg is not, however, about baseball statistics. The film examines Greenberg from the vantage point of culture and American Jewry. The September 1934 controversy concerning Greenberg's competing obligations to the Detroit Tigers, fighting for an American League pennant, and his Jewish heritage, which required

observance of the High Holidays, is central to Kempner's film. After ago-
nizing soul searching, heightened by conflicting advice from secular and
religious authorities, Greenberg played on Rosh Hashanah; his two home
runs paced the Tigers to a 2–1 victory. With the pennant all but assured,
Greenberg did not play on Yom Kippur. Folk poet Edgar Guest paid tribute to Greenberg's observance of the Day of Atonement, commending the
Tiger slugger for "remaining true to his religion."[11]

Aviva Kempner inhabits *The Life and Times of Hank Greenberg*. She
wrote, directed, and produced the film. And the documentary honors
Harold (Chaim) Kempner, Aviva's late father, as much as it does Hank
Greenberg.

In 1925, Harold Kempner, a Lithuanian immigrant, arrived in the
United States. Finding the American Dream elusive in Pittsburgh, New
York City, and Philadelphia, Harold "faced a lot of domestic anti–Semitism."[12] Kempner "couldn't get into medical school because he was Jewish."[13] Participating in the crusade against Hitler, Kempner served in the
American Army that liberated Europe. While stationed in Germany as a
translator, he married a Holocaust survivor. Their daughter Aviva
recounts,

> Upon liberation my mother had met my ... father who was writing a
> story for the U.S. Army newspaper about her being reunited with her
> brother. My father's mother had been rounded up and shot by the
> Nazis. The U.S. soldier married the Polish survivor and upon birth (on
> December 23, 1946) I was anointed the first American-Jewish child in
> Berlin. We all came by boat to America in 1950 and settled in Detroit.[14]

Identification with Greenberg had facilitated Harold Kempner's
Americanization. For Harold, "baseball was a ritual of American assimilation and Greenberg a symbol."[15] "Watching Greenberg made it easier for
my father, an immigrant Jew, to identify with his newly adopted land,"
Aviva reflects.[16] The ballpark more than the night school resonated with
the true American vernacular.

Harold shared Greenberg lore with Aviva and her brother Jonathan.
"It was," remembers Aviva, "like you have the Grimm's Fairy Tale that
most kids grow up on. To me, hearing about Hank Greenberg was the
fairy tale my dad would always tell us."[17] "I thought Hank Greenberg,"
remembers Aviva, "was part of the Kol Nidre liturgy:"[18]

> Every Yom Kippur I attended services with my father in Detroit and
> heard the story of how Hank Greenberg had gone to shul on this holy
> day in 1934 instead of playing baseball for the Detroit Tigers. My father
> revered Greenberg and instilled in my brother and me a deep appre-
> ciation for his hitting feats. He never let us forget how in 1938 this

Jewish player fell just two runs short of matching Babe Ruth's record of 60 home runs.[19]

Kempner transmitted his passion for Greenberg to his children. "One of the great things to do was to go to a baseball game," recalls Aviva, "and almost every time it would evoke the story of Hank Greenberg from my father."[20] Even at the dinner table, Harold Kempner told "tales of the old Tigers."[21] Her father and Hank Greenberg gave Aviva Kempner a counterbalance to the canards that Jews were timid, weak, and physically inept.

And it was the filmmaker's mother, Helen Ciesla Kempner Covensky, who inspired her first film, *Partisans of Vilna*, a documentary chronicling Jewish resistance to the Nazis. Aviva Kempner ruminates upon her mother" life: ""She was blond and green-eyed and managed to pass as a Polish Catholic after obtaining false papers."[22] Helen thus survived the Holocaust by posing as a gentile, but Auschwitz consumed the lives of her parents, sister, and other loved ones. Aviva reflects,

> I was brought up in a seemingly normal Midwest family. Except that my brother and I did not have any grandparents and our parents spoke with accents — and often about the old country and lost relatives. My mother tried to protect her children, and spared us the detailed horror stories of her war experiences. But one knows that our legacy was full of pain and losses.[23]

Kempner's Ciesla Foundation, a public, tax exempt, educational vehicle for her films carries a special legacy: "My mother's family was wiped out in the Holocaust, so I named the Foundation after her family name in order to perpetuate it."[24] As Aviva Kempner prepared for the Los Angeles opening of *Partisans of Vilna*, Hank Greenberg, a few miles away, died hard. "As soon as I heard that Hank had died," recalls Kempner, "I knew he would be my next film."[25] For Kempner, the heroic Jewish freedom fighters of her mother's Europe and the heroic Jewish baseball player of her father's America were linked chapters in a larger story:

> The Ciesla Foundation continues to be devoted to countering negative screen images of Jews. Typically, Jews are portrayed by the suicidal female Holocaust survivor, the nebbishy Jewish male, or the domineering Jewish mother. The Foundation is committed to making documentaries which counter these negative portrayals by showing non-stereotypical images of Jews. *Partisans of Vilna* ...examined the unexplored themes of Jewish resistance against the Nazis...*The Life and Times of Hank Greenberg*...focuses on an athlete who emerged when Jewish Americans faced anti–Semitism in social and economic arenas, a subject rarely documented on film. In both works, the Ciesla Foundation looks at the role and inner workings of Jewish 'heroes,' from

those facing life or death situations, to those fighting to gain approval in American popular culture.[26]

Kempner's Greenberg, viewing his home runs as weapons against Hitler, epitomizes a muscular Judaism that provides emancipation from stereotypes.

The Life and Times of Hank Greenberg provides ample historical context. The anti–Semitism encountered by Greenberg reflected the ethnic biases of the 1930s. During the Great Depression, anti–Semitism intensified with Jews serving as scapegoats for economic distress. Detroit harbored two of the era's most notorious purveyors of bigotry, automobile manufacturer Henry Ford and Father Charles Coughlin, the radio priest. In addition, Jewish-American concern with the Nazi menace abroad fueled anti–Semitism in isolationist America. Kempner emphasizes that Greenberg was an ethnic standard bearer at a time of great difficulty for American Jewry. The filmmaker demonstrates "how insidious anti–Semitism is, what we always identify with the horrible ultimate manifestations in Nazi-era Europe. Hopefully, this film has given awareness to how bad it was in this country, and how people rise above the limits of it."[27] Greenberg, prior to the emergence of modern Israel, was a tough Jew when the only other tough Jews recognized by American popular culture were disreputable boxers and gangsters

Although the film rescues Greenberg from relative neglect, neither Kempner's data nor interpretation will prove novel for specialists. The analysis and information presented are derivative. The great strength of The Life and Times of Hank Greenberg rests with its ability to convey a mood. This film superbly captures the consciousness and conversations of that generation of Jewish Americans who came of age with Hank Greenberg. Although Kempner utilizes 1983 and 1984 television interviews with Greenberg as well as extensive autobiographical remarks he recorded on a Dictaphone, the Detroit slugger is not the voice of the film. The true voice of the film is the Jewish fan writ large, and to his daughter, Harold Kempner personified the Jewish fan. Aviva confides, "I wanted my Dad's voice."[28]

Several prominent Jewish Americans appear in the documentary, discussing the profound and personal impact Greenberg had on their lives. Terming Greenberg "the single most important Jew to live in the 1930s," high profile attorney Alan Dershowitz says of Greenberg, "He is what 'they' said we could never be." "As a kid," muses Dershowitz, "I always thought Hank Greenberg would be the first Jewish president." For Michigan Senator Carl Levin, Greenberg "validated that his was the land of opportunity: look we could even play baseball." Coming of age in the 1930s, second generation Jewish-Americans, the children of East European immigrants, viewed Greenberg as the apotheosis of the American Dream. The late actor Walter Matthau acknowledged a visceral attachment to Greenberg, "He was part of my dreams, part of my aspirations. I wanted to be Hank Greenberg."[29]

Even more evocative than the observations of celebrities are the words and emotions, captured by Kempner, of those American Jews who are not famous. For many ordinary American Jews, Hank Greenberg assumed mythic proportions. Bert Gordon, a fan, remembers the powerful impact of Greenberg's physical presence: "Six feet four! My God, nobody had ever seen a Jew that big. Everybody was five feet five, five feet six!" On Yom Kippur 1934, the congregation applauded when the Tiger slugger entered the Shaarey Zedek synagogue. Jewish fans transformed Greenberg's 1938 assault on Babe Ruth's then record of 60 home runs in a season into a legendary epic. Greenberg, according to retired oral surgeon Don Shapiro, symbolically challenged restrictions against Jews: "They could deny Jewish boys the right to swim in a pool, but they couldn't deny the fact that a Jewish boy was close to breaking Babe Ruth's record." Young Harriet Colman tirelessly wrote Greenberg of her unrequited admiration; Zelig-like, she even managed to appear in a photograph of Hammerin' Hank without his knowledge. Reeve Breener, later a rabbi, found empowerment through his identification with Greenberg: "I had this Captain Marvel on my shoulder."[30]

The Life and Times of Hank Greenberg effectively synthesizes vintage newsreel footage, telling photographs, period music, Hollywood film clips, excerpts from numerous interviews, observations in Greenberg's own voice, and Hammerin' Hank, accompanied by Groucho Marx and Bing Crosby, singing *Goodbye, Mr. Ball, Goodbye*. Yiddish renditions of *Take Me Out to the Ballgame* frame the film. Beyond commentary from celebrities and ordinary Jewish correspondents, Kempner's ubiquitous interviews embrace sportswriters, baseball players, fans, and Greenberg family members.

Nonetheless, the inclusion of certain materials and the absence of others in the film elicits caveats. Kempner offers little analysis of how Greenberg's experience in the national pastime differed from that of contemporary co-religionists or from those Jewish major leaguers who preceded and followed him. A comparison of Hank Greenberg's 1934 High Holiday dilemma to that of Sandy Koufax in 1965 would have added texture to the presentation. Nor does the filmmaker compare Greenberg as an ethnic standard bearer to his contemporary, Joe DiMaggio, the great Italian-American icon. And a revealing 1980 interview with Greenberg, conducted by Elli Wohlgelernter for the William E. Wiener Oral History Collection, was not utilized.

Kempner might also have displayed a visual image of *Homage to Hank Greenberg*, a magnificent oil painting by the gifted folk artist Malach Zeldis. In this autobiographical work, Zeldis depicts Greenberg towering like a colossus high above Detroit's Navin Field, linked by an oversized radio to a Jewish household. A number of dualisms — a public school opposite a yeshiva, an American flag juxtaposed to a Star of David, a sculpture of a thinker balanced by a statue of a figure on horseback — populate Zeldis' richly detailed canvas. Zeldis' telling nuance dramatizes Greenberg's mythic status to co-religionists, struggling to reconcile Jewish and American identities.[31]

Conversely, it is not readily apparent why Kempner included certain materials, including movie excerpts from *Woman of the Year* and *The Stratton Story*. *The Life and Times of Hank Greenberg* employs commentary from Caral Gimbel, the department store heiress who was Greenberg's first wife and the mother of his three children. Yet the documentary eschews examination of marital difficulty between Caral and Hank Greenberg and their subsequent divorce. The second Mrs. Greenberg, actress Mary Jo Tarola, whose twenty-year marriage thrived until the slugger's 1986 death, does not appear in the documentary. Indeed, the film makes scant reference to Mary Jo Tarola or Greenberg's second marriage. Although omission of significant biographical details distorts a life portrait, *The Life and Times of Hank Greenberg* offers detailed coverage of its subject only through his first thirty-six years. Many matters central to the life of Hank Greenberg are given cursory mention, if any, in a written epilogue, presented in the form of a scroll. In addition to relative silence about Greenberg's divorce and remarriage, minimal attention to the second half of his life limits treatment of his years as a front office executive for the Cleveland Indians and Chicago White Sox, his collaboration with maverick baseball entrepreneur Bill Veeck, Hank's testimony in the Curt Flood case, relations with his own children, the continuing evolution of his Jewish identity, and Greenberg's thoughts about Israel.

One might argue that there is a legitimate rationale for abbreviated biographical treatment of Greenberg after 1947. His playing career ended that year. Moreover, by 1947 the chronological distance from the era of mass immigration and the appearance of the third generation lessened the need for a Jewish standard bearer. After World War II, America and its national pastime increasingly viewed minority group dynamics from a racial rather than an ethnic perspective. As Kempner emphasizes, it is significant that Greenberg's last year as a major leaguer was Jackie Robinson's first. The film depicts the veteran Jewish star offering strong encouragement to the embattled black pioneer.

The Life and Times of Hank Greenberg is an exemplary film. Kempner's documentary gives new life to an important passage in American ethnic and sport history. *The Life and Times of Hank Greenberg* is interesting, insightful, warm, and even, at times, humorous. Kempner reminds us that sports in the United States have historically related to status, self-image, inter-group dynamics, discrimination, social mobility, generational relations, assimilation, and the American Dream itself. Although *Sports Century*, a creation of ESPN *Classic*, subsequently produced an engaging and informative Greenberg documentary that addressed several of Kempner's omissions, *The Life and Times of Hank Greenberg* possesses singular aesthetic and emotional power.[32]

Due to financial exigencies, it took thirteen years, as long as Greenberg's major league career, to complete the film. Several times the imperative of raising money forced Kempner to halt production. Frustration baited but did not defeat her. A large hooked rug emblazoned with a depiction of Hank Greenberg served as Kempner's totem: "Many a night, I'd just go into the living room and turn the lights low. I'd look at Hank and say: 'I'm going to do it. It's going to get done.' And I'd pray to my Dad."[33]

"The gray ghost of Hank Greenberg has always inhabited filmmaker Aviva Kempner's life."[34] Not as a wife or mother but as the daughter of a baseball acolyte, Aviva Kempner proclaims, "The reason I decided to do this was to honor my father's hero." [35] Recipient of degrees from the University of Michigan and Antioch, Kempner possesses expertise in urban planning, psychology, and law. Her failure to pass the District of Columbia bar exam, however, fortuitously, allowed her love of film to evolve into a career. Kempner's passion for the cinema is requited by multifaceted talents as a film critic, consultant, screenwriter, director, and producer. Awarded the 1996 Guggenheim Fellowship for Cinema, Kempner was founder and first administrator of the Washington Jewish Arts Film Festival. Forever searching for her father's hero, Aviva Kempner was destined to create *The Life and Times of Hank Greenberg*.

Financial restraints initially allowed for only seven prints of *The Life and Times of Hank Greenberg*, but Kempner's brilliant campaign of film festival screenings and local premiers rendered the documentary a popular and critical phenomenon. An active web site and creative marketing of memorabilia, including posters and baseball hats trumpeting *The Life and Times of Hank Greenberg* logo, contributed to the film's visibility.[36] And Kempner traveled tirelessly, promoting the film through interviews and attendance at screenings. For a documentary, *The Life and Times of Hank Greenberg* generated impressive revenues.

Critical commentary on the documentary was extensive and overwhelmingly laudatory. National Public Radio's *All Things Considered* burnished the film's intellectual merit, and *Time* magazine widened the popular appeal of this "lovely addition to the annals of the Greatest Generation."[37] Representing the sports fraternity, *Baseball Weekly* hailed the "fascinating documentary from accomplished filmmaker Aviva Kempner."[38] The tabloid *New York Post* touted "Kempner's moving film" while the august *New York Times* proclaimed *The Life and Times of Hank Greenberg* "valuable as history."[39] The reviewer for *The New Yorker*, emblematic of cultural sophistication, acknowledged, "I will admit...that I had to wipe away a tear or two."[40] "You simply must see" Kempner's movie, exhorted *The Washington Times*, and the rival *Washington Post* called the film "adroit."[41] From Maine to California, movie reviewers, cultural commentators, Jewish literati, and sportswriters lavished praise on *The Life and Times of Hank Greenberg*.

Critical and popular acclaim brought *The Life and Times of Hank Greenberg* many awards. Perhaps the most coveted honor garnered by the film was selection by the prestigious National Board of Review of Motion Pictures as the best documentary of the year 2000. "Upon hearing of the award," Aviva Kempner "had tears of joy. After 14 years it's sheer joy to hear such great news." Kempner confessed, "I feel like a cinema Cinderella."[42]

In her mid–50s, Kempner, after years of struggle, savors the triumph of her tribute to Hank Greenberg. The rewards are personal as well as professional. "Kempner has created a long-playing, genuine salon worthy of movie versions of Paris in the '20s," reports *The Washington Post*:

> Kempner's parties, which she throws together almost weekly...steam on till 2...people break out of their little worlds and do the unexpected.
> This is not Kempner's intent, but it happens because she drifts in and out of subcultures as few of us do, sometimes because she's brassy enough to poke her way in, sometimes because she's just following her interests...The German actor Armin Mueller-Stahl comes whenever he's in town-drawn by the conversation and the people. "There's an Aviva in every city," he says, "but there's only one Aviva."[43]

Many of Kempner's guests are cited in the credits of her film as financial contributors to *The Life and Times of Hank Greenberg*.

Kempner's most important audience did not live to see her film. Divorced, Aviva's father, Harold, moved to Israel in 1973, telling her there were two things he would miss — "his kids and baseball."[44] Harold died in 1976. Through Harold's hero, Aviva preserved a powerful pathway to her father. When Aviva presented *The Life and Times of Hank Greenberg* at the Baseball Hall of Fame on Father's Day 2000, it evoked Barbra Streissand's poignant "Poppa, can you hear me?" Aviva Kempner confides, "I think my father's up there in heaven now, *kvelling* with Hank Greenberg, saying, 'You know we got your story told.'"[45]

Hank and I

Late winter 2001, I traveled to Florida for a visit with my parents and to lecture on Hank Greenberg. My parents spend the winter months in a condominium community in Lake Worth. I spoke about Greenberg on March 4, 2001, at Pete's restaurant in Boca Raton. Since the sponsoring group for my lecture was the Florida snowbird contingent of greater Lynn's Jewish Federation of the North Shore, natives of the city of my birth dominated the audience. I have made presentations about Hank Greenberg before audiences at prestigious colleges, museums, and libraries, but this gathering of 100 or so was special. These were my parents' friends, most of whom I have known in my youth.

Working the room before my talk, I was greeted by warmth, good cheer, well told vignettes, and spirited questions. One gentleman named his all-time, Jewish all-star team for me; another genially challenged me to name the three Jewish pitcher-catcher batteries to appear in the World Series. Retired businessman Ted Adelson, a wartime Navy intelligence officer, reminded me of third baseman Marv Owen's importance to Greenberg's Tigers. Several enthusiasts told me they enjoyed Aviva Kempner's film, especially footage from old newsreels showing Hank, looking like a colossus, swinging three bats in the on-deck circle and hitting towering home runs. And they preceded to tell me their own Hank Greenberg stories. Then I delivered my lecture:

> It is with humility and admiration that I stand before you. Tom Brokaw aptly called you, the men and women who came of age during the Great Depression and World War II, *The Greatest Generation.* You are the Jewish component of *The Greatest Generation.*
>
> For your generation of American Jews, Hank Greenberg exemplified Horatio Algerism, the belief that no matter what one's origins success beckoned for the industrious. Greenberg did not grow up in poverty, but he was baseball's Jewish Horatio Alger. Although nature imbued Hank with size and strength, he was not a natural ballplayer. My father idolizes Hammerin' Hank, but Dad told me repeatedly that Greenberg achieved greatness through hard work, not natural talent. Slow, flat footed, awkward, Hank was a self-made athlete.
>
> Dad, I remember you telling me how Hank Greenberg hired knothole gang kids and ushers to shag fly balls so he could take extra batting practice, pushing himself until bloody blisters covered his hands. For the good of the team, Hank, my father recounted, moved to left

field in 1940 to make way for lumbering Rudy York's bat at first base. Through endless practice, Greenberg mastered fly balls and line drives caroming off the wall and hitting the cut off man. No one ever mistook Greenberg for the balletic Joe DiMaggio, but Hank was the first player to win Most Valuable Player awards at two different positions. And my father related how Greenberg, wrapped in enough trainer's tape to cover a mummy, punished his body, aching from age and nearly a half decade of military service, to mount a triumphant comeback to baseball in 1945. Looking at this audience, comprised of those who in the Lynn of their youth cheered Hank as their Jewish standard bearer and followed him to war, it is easy to imagine a connection between the meaningful, productive lives you have built and the example set by Hank Greenberg.

Tonight you are gathered to support the Jewish Federation, and I salute your worthy endeavor. Your Jewishness, however, differs from that of the world of your fathers. For your generation in particular, reconciling American and Jewish identities was not easy. Given his mythic stature, Hank Greenberg's struggle to synthesize his Jewish and American selves was symbolically your struggle.

In 1934, conflicted over whether to play baseball on the High Holidays, Hank Greenberg, at 23 years old, was not comfortable in the role of Jewish standard bearer. Indeed when influential members of Detroit's Jewish community suggested holding a testimonial dinner for their Hank, the Tiger slugger rejected the idea, asserting that "the triumph of the Tigers is not the concern of any one group or of several groups. It is a community affair."[46] Yet his courageous resolve when assaulted by abusive taunts of "kike" and "dirty Jew," his Yom Kippur observance, and enlistment in the crusade against Hitler dramatized Greenberg's Jewish consciousness.

The Judaism of the private Hank Greenberg was far more complex than that attributed to the slugger by our tribe, his Jewish celebrants. Truth be told, Hank Greenberg was not, in a theological sense, a religious Jew. He did not provide his own children — Glenn, Stephen, and Alva — with even a rudimentary Jewish education. Glenn has no memory of his father attending a synagogue service. When a newspaper reporter assumed that the son of Hank Greenberg was obviously Jewish, Glenn retorted, "I don't know."[47] "It was embarrassing to me," acknowledged Alva, "when I realized that my father was a Jewish hero and I didn't even know what anything meant. Why, for example, he didn't play on Yom Kippur."[48]

Hank Greenberg faced pressures as the symbolic hero of the anti–Semitic 1930s. Greenberg wished to spar his children the pain that he had endured. Despite or perhaps because of the attention given to his ethnicity, Hank Greenberg's own identification with Judaism was ambivalent, particularly toward organized religion.

On Yom Kippur 1959, this ambivalence manifested itself. The Greenberg children, still oblivious to Yom Kippur's meaning, were kept out of school and taken to the Hayden Planetarium. Remembering the Greenberg family's Day of Atonement visit to the Planetarium, Stephen says of his father, "He took us someplace that was obviously special. Someplace that maybe represented the vast unknown; someplace he hadn't been to for a long, long time. It was for him a reaching out halfway or three quarters of the way back to something, but he couldn't go all the way."[49]

I am a father as well as a son. I am also a teacher. There are times when, for many of us, it seems like we have more influence on other people's children than our own. Perhaps that feeling was not unknown to Hank Greenberg.

Hank Greenberg loved his children, and they loved him. The three Greenberg children, unlike the offspring of many celebrities, all turned out well. Glenn, a Yale graduate, managed a mutual fund. A Kenyon College alumni, Alva purchased controlling interest in a Connecticut newspaper. As captain of the Yale baseball team, Stephen agonized over whether to take the field during the spring 1970 campus strike. Stephen later earned a law degree from UCLA and played minor league baseball. Subsequently Stephen Greenberg served as deputy commissioner of baseball.

And all of you have also turned out well. In a sense, my father and everyone else in this audience is a symbolic child of Hank Greenberg. In his latter years, Greenberg came to treasure his connection with you, the generation of Jewish Americans that came of age in his baseball prime. An older Hank Greenberg confided, "I realize now more than I used to how important a part I played in the lives of a generation of Jewish kids who grew up in the Thirties...It's a strange thing. When I was playing, I used to resent being singled out as a Jewish ballplayer. I wanted to be known as a great ballplayer period. I'm not sure why or when I changed, because I'm still not a particularly religious person. Lately, though, I find myself wanting to be remembered not only as a great ballplayer, but ever more as a great Jewish ballplayer."[50]

The audience was wonderful — laughing, nodding, sighing, and applauding in all the right places. Amidst overly generous accolades for my talk, I listened to still more of their Hank Greenberg vignettes.

Part of the current receptivity to celebrating Hank Greenberg, whether in Aviva Kempner's acclaimed film or my more modest endeavors, is undoubtedly, in part, an exercise in nostalgia by older Jews recalling their salad days. It is, however, much more than that. There is an enduring recognition that Hank Greenberg symbolized, as no one before or after, that Jews could make the American Dream their own. For his fellow Jews, Greenberg dramatized the promise of American life. Baseball player and patriot, Greenberg, by example, encouraged other Jews to build confident and successful lives in America amidst the fierce anti–Semitism of the Great Depression and World War II. Hammerin' Hank was a beacon for the children of Jewish immigrants. Hank Greenberg paved the way for Miss America Bess Myerson, movie star Kirk Douglas, pitcher Sandy Koufax, Secretary of State Henry Kissinger, astronaut Judith Resnick, outfielder Shawn Green, vice presidential candidate Joe Lieberman, my father and his friends, and Harold Kempner and the celebrants of his daughter's film. Screen legend Walter Matthau best summed up Greenberg's significance: "(Hank served notice that) I didn't have to wind up as a presser, cutter, or salesman in the garment center."[51]

While in Florida, my father and I took in a Red Sox–Expos spring training game in Jupiter. We had a great time. During the seventh inning stretch, my father placed his hand on my shoulder and said, "Your Hank Greenberg talk gave me real *naches*. But why didn't you use my story about the 550-foot home run Hank slammed out of Fenway Park?"

Notes

1. Ed Goldstein, "The Story of a Mature Man," *The SABR Review of Baseball Literary Opinion* 4 (1989), 73.

2. Harold U. Ribalow, *The Jew in American Sports*, rev. ed. (New York: Bloch Publishing Company, 1948), 46.

3. Ribalow, 45.

4. William Simons, "The Athlete as Jewish Standard Bearer: Media Images of Hank Greenberg," *Jewish Social Studies* 44, no. 2 (1982), 106.

5. Eric Jacobson, letter to author, 25 November 1992.

6. Aviva Kempner, letter to author, 14 September 1988. My initial Greenberg article has followed an idiosyncratic trajectory. Peter Levine commented in his *Ellis Island to Ebbets Field: Sport and the American Jewish Experience* (New York: Oxford, 1992), 305 that "William Simons...tells this story." See also William Simons, "Hank Greenberg: The Jewish American Sports Hero," in *Sports and the American Jew*, ed. Steven A. Riess (Syracuse: Syracuse University Press, 1998); and William Simons, "The Athlete as Jewish Standard Bearer: Media Images of Hank Greenberg," in *Baseball History from Outside the Lines*, ed. John E. Dreifort, (Lincoln: University of Nebraska Press, 2001).

7. Joseph Campbell with Bill Moyers, *The Power of Myth*, ed. Betty Sue Flowers (New York: Doubleday, 1988), 15.

8. Joseph Campbell, *The Hero with a Thousand Faces* (Princeton: Princeton University Press, 1949), title page.

9. Joyce Wadler, "Public Lives: a Not-So-Old Professor's Take on Baseball," *The New York Times*, 20 October 2000, M1.

10. Marshall Smelser, *The Life That Ruth Built: A Biography* (New York: Quadrangle/ The New York Times Book Company, 1975), 142.

11. Edgar Guest, "Speaking of Greenberg," Detroit *Free Press*, 4 October 1934, 6.

12. Sean P. Means, "Hank Greenberg, Fighting Prejudice with a Baseball Bat, Opens Tower's Film Series," *The Salt Lake Tribune*, 20 August 2000 [cited 25 August 2000]: available from *http://www.sltrib./com/2000/aug/08202000/arts/13960.htm.*

13. Gary Arnold, "Greenberg Film Took Big-League Effort," *The Washington Times*, 26 May 2000 [cited 27 May 2000]: available from *http://www.washtimes.com/entertainment/default-200056222228.htm.*

14. Aviva Kempner, "You Can Go Home Again," [cited 27 April 2000]: available from *http://www.cinimax.com/rellite/greenberg,htm.*

15. Richard Sandomir, "He Batted for the Tigers, Himself and American Jews," *The New York Times*, 9 January 2000, AR38.

16. Marsha Fischer, "Filmmaker Pays Tribute to Hank Greenberg," *South Florida Jewish Tribune*, 8–14 April 1994, 5.

17. Elli Wohlgelernter, "Not Just a Ballplayer, *The Jerusalem Post*, 19 July 1999, 7.

18. Arnold.

19. Fischer, 5.

20. "Director Pays Tribute to Slugger and to Dad," *The Albuquerque Tribune* [cited 21 October 2000]: available from *http://www.abqtrib.com/diversions/101300hank .shtml.*

21. Paul Farhi, "A Tiger Tale," *The Washington Post*, 26 May 2000 [cited 27 May 2000]: available from *http://washington.post.com/wp-dyn/articles/A9506-2000March25 .html*

22. Arnold.

23. Kempner, "You Can Go Home Again."

24. Fischer, 5.

25. Sandomir, AR38.

26. "About the Ciesla Foundation," *The Ciesla Foundation Presents The Life and Times of Hank Greenberg* [cited 27 March 2000]: available from *http://www.hankgreen bergfilm.org/hank-facts.htm.*

27. Means.

28. Loren King, "Reliving the Tales of a Tiger," *The Boston Sunday Globe*, 20 February 2000, M7.

29. *The Life and Times of Hank Greenberg*, written, produced, and directed by Aviva Kempner, 95 minutes, presented by The Ciesla Foundation, distributed by Cowboy Booking International, 1999.

30. *The Life and Times of Hank Greenberg.*

31. William Simons, "Homage to Hank Greenberg," *The Shofar*, August 1992, 3–4.

32. *Sports Century: Hank Greenberg*, Produced by ESPN *Classic*, 45 minutes, 2001.

33. Sandomir, AR38.

34. Farhi.

35. Megan Turner, "Hank's for the Memories," *NY Post. Com* [cited 12 January 2000]: available from *http://www.nypost.com/entertainment/21852.htm.*

36. *The Ciesla Foundation Presents The Life and Times of Hank Greenberg* [cited 27 March 2000]: available from *http://www.hankgreenbergfilm.org/hank-facts.htm.*

37. "Review of *The Life and Times of Hank Greenberg*," *All Things Considered*, National Public Radio, January 12, 2000; and Richard Schickel, "Cinema: *The Life and Times of Hank Greenberg*," *Time*, 5 June 2000, 87.

38. Deron Snyder, "New Film Tells of Bigotry Hank Greenberg Faced," *Baseball Weekly* [cited 30 January 2000]: available from *http://www.usatoday.com/sports/baseball/bbw2/v4/bbw0412.htm.*

39. Meredith Berkman, "Yesterday's Bronx Ethnic All-Star," *NYPost.Com* [cited 27 July 2000]: available from *http://www.newyorkpost.com/postopinion/opedcolumnists/7621.htm*; Lawrence Van Gelder, "He Fell Short of Babe Ruth, but Not for Jews," *The New York Times*,12 January 2000, E5.

40. David Denby, "The Idiot and the Adonis," *The New Yorker*, 24 January 2000, 95.

41. Dick Heller, "Documentary Effort of Love, Baseball," *The Washington Times*, 22 May 2000 [cited 27 May 2000}: available from *http://www.washtimes.com/sports/default-200052222335.htm*; and Stephen Hunter, "'Hank Greenberg': The Inspiring Tale of a True Tiger," *The Washington Post*, 26 May 2000 [cited 27 May 2000]: available from *http://www.washingtonpost.com/wpndyn/articles/A9501-2000May25.html.*

42. *CieslaFdn@aol.com,e-mail* letter to author (undisclosed-recipients), 6 December 2000.

43. Marc Fisher, "Great Casting Makes the Scene at a D.C. Salon," *The Washington Post*, 27 May 2000, BO1 [cited 31 May 2000], available from *http://www.washington post.com/wp-dyn/articles/A1682-2000May26.html*.

44. Alex Wohl, "Conversations: Aviva Kempner," *Detroit Free Press*, May 29, 1988, 7.

45. Fisher.

46. "Greenberg Hailed as Greatest Player Jews Have Contributed to Baseball," Detroit *Jewish Chronicle*, 2 September 1934, 1.

47. Hank Greenberg, *Hank Greenberg: The Story of My Life*, ed. Ira Berkow (New York: *Times* Books, 1989), 233.

48. Greenberg, 234.

49. Greenberg, 239.

50. Lawrence Ritter, *The Glory of Their Times: The Story of the Early Days of Baseball Told by the Men Who Played It*, new enlarged ed. (New York: Morrow, 1984), 330.

51. *The Life and Times of Hank Greenberg.*

"Your" Bears to "Our" Bears: Race, Memory, and Baseball in Newark, New Jersey

Robert Cvornyek

On July 16, 1999, professional baseball returned to Newark, New Jersey after a fifty-year absence. The city's legendary Bears had returned home and the celebration surrounding their arrival sparked historical interest in the team and its storied past. On opening night, sportswriter Jerry Izenberg remarked that after five long decades the mythical "**NO GAME TODAY**" sign was finally removed as baseball made its comeback to a city whose fans once appreciated it with "semi-religious devotion." In particular, the Bears' homecoming stirred the individual and collective memory of those who lived in the city during the 1930s and 1940s when baseball resided at the "core of its [Newark's] very fiber." Embedded in this collective memory was the belief that the Bears represented the city's white community, especially its ethnic working-class neighborhoods. Baseball, like most aspects of Newark's social and cultural history in the Jim Crow era, revealed an acute racial awareness. When newspaper advertisements encouraged support for "your" Bears, whites knew exactly what that meant.[1]

The decision to name Newark's new minor league franchise after the Bears reflected, among other things, the private memory of Rick Cerone, the team's principal owner. Cerone, a former New York Yankee All-Star catcher, lived in Newark and grew up listening to stories about the Bears from his parents. It was not surprising that Cerone regarded the Bears as Newark's most cherished and successful baseball club. When asked by reporters the reason for the name, Cerone responded, "The Bears is the name because of the success that team had in the past."[2] While this was certainly true, the adoption of the name raises significant questions over the role of Newark's "other" team, the all-black Eagles. During the decades of depression and war, Newark had, in fact, hosted two professional teams, one white and the other black. The Eagles of the National Negro League and the Bears of the all-white AAA International League occupied the same city, even the same ballpark, Ruppert Stadium, but each represented a distinct racial group. The separate crowds that turned out to watch the Eagles and the Bears created their own unique intimate space within the otherwise public world of professional sports. Because of the Eagles, the city's African-Americans claimed equal legitimacy to Newark's baseball heritage. Consequently, the return of the Bears generated a controversial debate over the contested history of baseball in Newark.[3]

Two sets of critical questions emerge from Newark's disputed baseball history. The first involves understanding what the team meant to the city's whites during the 1930s and 1940s, especially its second-generation immigrant population. Did the team, for example, play a role in the Americanization process and did that role operate within a distinct racial context? In other words, once inside the ballpark did commonality of color erase any sense that immigrants had once been considered separate races themselves? Finally, did baseball serve to further legitimize racial segregation and thus empower immigrants with a sense of white privilege?

The second set of questions relates to current attempts by the Bears' ownership and Newark's city officials to unite the city behind a team that once symbolized segregation and the maintenance of white privilege. Given the city's troubled racial history and significant population changes during the fifty-year interval between 1949 and 1999, what exactly does the history and memory of the Bears mean to the contemporary city?

The purpose of this paper is to make some tentative responses to these questions through an examination of the Bears' role in constructing and sustaining the city's racial identity. Current scholarship on the Bears fails to account for the team's involvement in the complex and dynamic forces that influenced Newark's racial, ethnic, and class relations during the 1930s and 1940s. This preliminary analysis of the team's impact on race formation, identity, and memory attempts to correct this imbalance in the literature.

To start, the answers to these questions require an awareness of the relationship that exists between memory and contested history. In Newark, dependant upon color, the events that baseball fans remembered as defining experiences that shaped their personal and racial identity were quite different. If people develop a shared identity by isolating and agreeing on specific memories, then the segregated nature of Newark baseball precluded the "common ground" necessary for an agreed upon history. In light of this contested history, Cerone's belief that the contemporary city, now mostly black, would embrace the Bears seems illusory. If one draws on Max Weber's notion of *verstehen*, meaning that the legitimization of symbols must arise naturally from the people, then the team's name was problematic. The name simply held a contradictory meaning for the city's blacks and whites.[4]

In the 1930s and early 1940s, Bears fans enjoyed watching one of the most successful minor league teams in baseball history. In 1931, Jacob Ruppert, owner of the New York Yankees, purchased the team from financially strapped newspaper editor Paul Block for an estimated $600,000. The acquisition included a relatively new stadium built in 1926; it was located on Wilson Avenue in the city's East Ward or Ironbound neighborhood. The ballpark was renamed Ruppert Stadium shortly after the takeover. According to historian Neil Sullivan, Ruppert, who amassed a fortune in his father's beer business and later in real estate, wisely surrounded himself with men who knew the game. In particular, he persuaded George Weiss, vice president and general manager of the Baltimore Orioles, to accept an offer to run the Newark club and build a farm system for the Yankees.[5]

Weiss remained with the Yankee organization for twenty-eight seasons, from 1932 to 1960, serving as architect of the farm system and Yankee general manager. By 1940, the Yankees controlled nine minor league teams and operated at all levels of competition. Newark, the "crown jewel" of the Yankee farm system, consistently developed talent for the parent organization, permitting it to win seven American League pennants between 1936 and 1943. During the team's eighteen-year existence in Newark, the Bears finished first in the International League in 1932, 1933, 1934, 1937, 1938, 1941, and 1942. The Bears also advanced to the league playoffs an additional nine times, missing only the 1947 and 1949 seasons. The team defeated its playoff rivals in 1937, 1938, 1940, and 1945.[6]

Understandably, it was the 1937 ball club that received the most praise and attention. Recently named the Minor League Team of the Century by the readers of the publication *Baseball America*, the 1937 Bears captured one of the team's three Little World Series Championships. According to New Jersey baseball historians James DiClerico and Barry Pavelec, the greatness of this celebrated team rested on three achievements. First, the team finished an astonishing 25½ games in front of the International League's second place team, the Montreal Royals. Second, the Bears captured the minor league championship by defeating the Columbus Red

Birds of the American Association in dramatic style. After losing the first three games, the players stormed back to win the last four to capture the Little World Series title. Finally, they managed to send every starter to the major leagues. Among the regular players who graduated to the big league were Joe Gordon, Babe Dahlgren, George McQuinn, Jim Gleeson, Bob Seeds, Nolen Richardson, Buddy Rosar, Atley Donald, Joe Beggs, Vito Tamulis, and Steve Sundra. The most beloved member of the Newark squad, Charlie "King Kong" Keller, would play 13 seasons, mostly with the Yankees, and help comprise New York's most famous outfield of Joe DiMaggio, Keller, and Tommy Henrich. In later years, other minor league stars, including Yogi Berra, Bobby Brown, Johnny Lindell, George Sternweiss, and Hank Madjeski, advanced to the majors after starting their careers in Newark.[7]

At the time, the Bears opened their 1932 inaugural season, Newark was a white working-class city. The 1940 census revealed that whites comprised nearly ninety percent of the city's population. Most whites lived in self-sustaining neighborhoods composed of one or another ethnic group. First and second-generation immigrants remained isolated in these neighborhoods until the end of World War II. According to historian Kenneth Jackson, Newark's Ironbound section (so named because of the railroad tracks that defined its borders) served as a microcosm of the immigrant city where successive waves of Irish, Scottish, Polish, Lithuanian, Italian, Hungarian, Czech, and Russian immigrants "added their muscle to the many industries of the neighborhood." Dubbed the "City of Opportunity," Newark had the "vaunted reputation of producing almost anything," but most foreign-born immigrants and their children worked in nearby factories and machine shops producing such items as steel, machine parts, clothing, paint, beer, and leather goods.[8]

While most foreign-born immigrants spent their leisure time in the neighborhood, their sons and daughters preferred to venture beyond local boundaries. Newark sportswriter Jerry Izenberg recalled that as a youth he rode a "carbon monoxide belching" bus down Wilson Avenue to Ruppert Stadium where he encountered others from various sections of town. Collectively known as the knot-hole gang, youngsters from around the city formed a common identity based on the symbols, rituals, and language of Bears baseball. Izenberg also recognized the power of baseball in creating a cohesive popular culture among the city's diverse ethnic groups. He remembered that on summer nights, "you could pick a block in the city — any block — and in a world without air-conditioning you could hear the sound of Earl Harper's play-by-play through the open windows, walk the length of that block and not miss a pitch." Similarly, *Trenton Times* reporter

Harvey Yavener wrote that "for those of us who grew up in Newark during the Depression and the War, there was only one sports team...the Newark Bears." For Yavener, "baseball was America's unchallenged sport." It introduced generations of immigrants to a common language, culture, and national heritage. Baseball, for Izenberg and Yavener, was part of an Americanization process that people easily recognized and understood. Historian Steven Reiss concluded that throughout the first-half of the twentieth century, the public came to accept baseball's principal function as the ability to "teach children traditional American values and help newcomers assimilate into the dominant WASP culture." Reiss also reasoned that by expecting fans "to identify with the home team" baseball encouraged a "sense of community by promoting hometown pride and boosterism."[9]

Newark's ethnic groups took special hometown pride in watching members of their own nationality succeed on the diamond. Prior to the 1930s, few professional ballplayers traced their ancestry to southern or eastern Europe. Thereafter, fans witnessed a steady increase in the number of Poles, Slavs, Hungarians, and especially Italians. In 1930, the number of "new immigrants" in the professional ranks jumped from less than seven percent to double-digit figures and remained there throughout the decade. By 1940, minor league clubs, such as the Bears, were producing enough ethnic talent to boost the number of second-generation Eastern and Southern European men to 20 percent. Historian Robert Burke argues that during the Great Depression baseball owners sought control over a larger pool of low cost labor and thus opened the door to ethnic ballplayers. At the same time, the decision to hire white ethnics actually postponed the racial integration of baseball. Given the choice to employ either blacks or white ethnics as cheap labor during the Depression, owners opted for the safest available source. Fearing that fans would not accept black ballplayers taking white jobs, especially in a tight and depressed labor market, owners hired white ethnics.[10]

The degree to which the process of Americanization evolved within a racial context has received considerable attention by historians within the past decade. The scholarship on racial identity has emphasized the development of a sense of whiteness common to all European ethnics in the nineteenth and twentieth centuries. According to historian George Lipsitz, this body of scholarship "helps us understand how people who left Europe as Calabrians or Bohemians became something called 'whites' when they got to America and how that designation made all the difference in the world." In effect, before immigrants became hyphenated-Americans, they became white. This investment in whiteness, segregation, and white supremacy eventually yielded high dividends in enhanced economic opportunity and psychological and material rewards. Blacks became the "other" race against which an accepted definition of whiteness emerged. Whiteness, as a social construct, moved across nationality, religion, and economic skill.[11]

When immigrants from southern and eastern Europe began arriving in Newark in the late nineteenth and early twentieth centuries, many found themselves being defined as non-white or a race apart. Early twentieth century publications on Newark's immigrant Ironbound neighborhood frequently listed the various nationalities as separate races. Authors asked why these races tenaciously clung to their old customs and traditions, and emphasized that the "spirit of America" would inspire "these races to greater hope, greater ambition." As a result, immigrants developed a racialized worldview that placed them above African-Americans, but also below whites. The process of becoming white extended to second and third-generation ethnics until by 1950, according to historian Matthew Jacobson, the race issue ceased to focus on the separate races from Europe and instead "came to refer exclusively to black-white relations and the struggle over Negro civil rights." After 1932, Newark had its own white baseball team, one that connected ethnics to white America based on commonality of color. Newark's second-generation immigrants found that support for their team confirmed their whiteness and fitness for republican citizenship.[12]

With the arrival of the all-black Newark Eagles in 1936, the racial dichotomy was complete. The team represented a growing number of African-Americans, especially those migrating from the southern states, and reflected the common concerns of blacks throughout the city. In 1900, Newark contained 6,694 blacks, slightly less than three percent of the total population. By 1930, the number had jumped to 38,880. In 1940, African-Americans comprised nearly eleven percent of Newark's population. According to a 1931 report on *The Negro in New Jersey*, sponsored by the Interracial Committee of the New Jersey Conference on Social Work, the influx of blacks resulted in a more clearly defined pattern of residential segregation. Most blacks were expected to live in a deteriorating and unhealthy section of town called the "Hill District."[13]

Employment discrimination, sanctioned by employers and safeguarded by organized labor, relegated blacks to the bottom of the economic ladder especially during the crises that impacted the city during depression and war. Given white workers determination to preserve their privilege on the shop floor, blacks were either excluded from the workplace or segregated into unskilled or semiskilled positions. Harold Lett, Executive Director of the Urban League between 1934 and 1945, cited discrimination by the city's unions as a critical reason why blacks lost ground in skilled industrial occupations throughout the 1930s and 1940s. Lacking union membership and thus access to organized labor's apprenticeship programs, blacks were denied the protection and training needed for economic advancement. Newark novelist Curtis Lucas characterized the "The Hill" in 1946 as the place where fellow blacks lived in "broken-down houses" and black women worked as domestics "scrubbing white folks' bathrooms" while white women worked in segregated department stores or in doctors' offices. Black men found employment "working at jobs that white men didn't want."[14]

The Eagles provided an escape for Hill residents from all the above. Moreover, they provided a sense of community pride and accomplishment. The team won the Negro World Series in 1946 and ultimately sent five ballplayers, Larry Doby, Monte Irvin, Willie Wells, Ray Dandridge, and Leon Day, to the Baseball Hall of Fame. Newark's blacks supported and identified with the Eagles just as the city's whites identified with the Bears. Black poet and playwright Amiri Baraka grew up watching the Eagles, and in later life, wrote:

> The Newark Eagles would have your heart there on the field, from what they was doing. From how they looked. But these were professional ballplayers. Legitimate black heroes. And we were intimate with them in a way and they were extensions of all of us, there, in a way that the Yankees and Dodgers [and Bears] and whatnot could never be![15]

Few whites attended the Eagles games, and the team received little or no coverage in the city's white press. Not surprisingly, the two teams never met on the playing field. Although the Eagles frequently requested games, the Bears management flatly refused. The reasons appeared simple enough. Why risk losing a game to a team that you were expected to defeat? Why suffer the repercussions of having a black team defeat one of the nation's best minor league teams. But a contest between the teams would also upset the Bears' fans investment in whiteness. To have both teams play each other, even on segregated ball clubs, implied a level of equality on the field and in the stands that ran counter to the privileged racial status white ethnics had created for themselves.[16]

The existence of two separate baseball teams in Newark in the 1930s and 1940s serves as a reminder of the deep racial divisions that defined the city. Today, the return of the Bears reminds scholars of the changes that have occurred in Newark since 1949. On opening night in 1999, for example, the city's African-American Mayor Sharpe James fully expected to see "whites, blacks, yellows, and Latinos here because that's what the city has to offer." Newark had changed considerably in the fifty-year interval between 1949 and 1999. Most importantly, Newark had become a black working-class city. By 1970, African-Americans became the majority population, and this trend intensified over the next thirty years. By century's end, blacks comprised nearly 60 percent of the city's residents. White ethnics began leaving the city after World War II, and this process accelerated with the ensuing loss of the city's industrial base and retail establishments. Additionally, Newark experienced its worst racial riots in the summer of 1967. These disturbances deepened the racial divide and further encouraged whites to flee to the suburbs.[17]

In a calculated effort to have the entire city support its newest team, Mayor Sharpe James invoked the memory of the Eagles, stating, "Let history say that we started with two separate teams. Now we will have a team that will mirror both the Eagles and the Bears, brought about by black and white, Republican and Democrat, urban and suburban, athlete and nonathlete." Although the Bears retained a special appeal to second and third-generation ethnics, most had already left the city. Mayor James's appeal to the city's black residents insisted that all participate totally in the Bears' reincarnation.[18]

Bears president and owner Rick Cerone followed James's lead and requested that several Eagles players attend the Bears' inaugural ceremonies. Jim Carter, a former pitcher, and Bo Wallace, a former catcher, attended the game and watched from the side as Yankee great Yogi Berra threw the first pitch to fellow Hall of Famer and teammate Phil Rizzuto with Cerone catching behind home plate. Conspicuously absent was Larry Doby, Newark's most famous Eagle. Doby shattered the American League color line with the Cleveland Indians on July 4, 1947, eleven weeks after Jackie Robinson's debut in the National League and later took his rightful place in baseball's Hall of Fame in 1998. Reportedly, Doby was unhappy with the lack of attention and respect given to Newark's "other" team. The token presence of a few Eagles players had been overshadowed by the exalted presence of Berra and Rizzuto and the team's historic connection to the New York Yankees. For Doby, the struggle to tell the full story of Newark's gloried baseball past was unfinished. His history had not been told or celebrated.[19]

Within a year, however, Doby did visit Riverfront Stadium, the home of the Bears. Prior to the 2001 season opener, Cerone arranged to have Doby join with Yogi Berra in rededicating the ballpark as Bears Eagles Riverfront Stadium. The newspapers reported the event as a "symbolic bridging of past divides" and a recognition of Newark's role as New Jersey's baseball capital. For Mayor James, it served political ends as well. He sought to recast the Bears identity as a team capable of uniting a city still haunted by the economic, social, and political legacy of segregation. In effect, his wish to transform "your" Bears of the 1930s and 1940s into "our" current Bears had been fulfilled.[20]

The decision to use the Bears' name was an attempt to connect the past with the present. Cerone did not have to romanticize the team's past or fabricate its success. The Bears had, in fact, achieved legendary status in the 1930s and early 1940s. Cerone's private memory, however, involved a degree of selection and choice. The emphasis on the Bears' success obscured the idea that the city was never united behind the club. As Newark became a more racially divided city in the 1930s, it became increasingly more difficult for city residents to have a shared baseball experience. With the arrival of the all-black Newark Eagles in 1936, it became nearly impossible for an agreed-upon collective memory of Newark baseball to exist.

Cerone's belief that his team could recapture the "magic" of fifty years ago by appealing to the collective memory of Newark's second and third-generation ethnics was mistaken. The success of the former Bears had not completely "rubbed off" on subsequent generations and the return of yesteryear's team was not a powerful enough draw to entice white suburbanites to return to the city for an evening's entertainment. The team's name meant little to the African-Americans who remained in the city and even less to the city's newest Hispanic and Asian immigrants. Only time will tell if the symbolic inclusion of the Eagles and the recognition of the team's legitimate claim in Newark's contested baseball history will generate the additional support needed to pack the 6,000 seats at Bears Eagles Riverfront Stadium.[21]

Today, the history of professional baseball in Newark remains as segregated as the city during the Jim Crow era. There are notable studies on the Eagles, including the works of James Overmyer and Lawrence Hogan and a few popular histories of the Bears, but nothing that analyzes both in the context of the city's urban, labor, political, and social history. Regrettably, this precludes important points of convergence between both teams. Ideally, what is needed is a combined history of both. How did the Bears and Eagles interact and influence each other? Moreover, how did the combined presence of both teams affect the city's racial formation? This paper provides a framework within which to better understand what the Bears meant to the city's white ethnics and the role baseball played in establishing a racial identity among Newark's mostly second-generation European immigrants. As such, it offers an initial step in a much-needed comprehensive account of Newark's baseball history.[22]

Notes

I wish to thank Charles Cummings of the Newark Public Library and Ellen Snyder Grenier of the New Jersey Historical Society for their valuable assistance in preparing this paper. I am also grateful to Louis and Lorraine Cvornyek for sharing their recollections of the Bears and Newark's Ironbound neighborhood.

1. Jerry Izenberg, "A Great Baseball Town Reawakens," *Newark Star-Ledger*, 16 July 1999, 1. For an example of an advertisement for "your" Bears see "Images in Time: Newark Bears Advertisement" located at *http://virtualnewarknj.com/imagepages/sports/bearsad.htm*.

2. Dan Castellano, "A Major Player in the Minors: Ex-Yank Going to Bat for the Newark Bears," *Newark Star Ledger*, 16 May 1996, 58. See also "Remembering Newark's Baseball Past" found at *www.newarkbears.com* for additional information on Cerone's relationship with the Bears.

3. The most comprehensive history of the Newark Eagles remains James Overmyer, *Queen of the Negro Leagues: Effa Manley and the Newark Eagles* (Lanham: Scarecrow Press, 1998). For an overview of black baseball see Robert Peterson, *Only the Ball Was White: A History of the Legendary Black Players and All-Black Professional Teams* (Englewood Cliffs: Prentice Hall, 1970); and Donn Rogosin, *Invisible Men: Life in Baseball's Negro Leagues* (New York: Atheneum, 1983). For an excellent chapter length review of the Negro Leagues see Jules Tygiel, *Past Time: Baseball as History* (New York: Oxford University Press, 2000), 116–143. The most comprehensive book on the Bears, despite its limited focus, remains Ronald A. Mayer, *The 1937 Newark Bears: A Baseball Legend* (New Brunswick: Rutgers University Press, 1994). For a chronological History of the team see Randolph Linthurst, *Newark Bears: The Middle Years* (Trenton: Linthurst, 1979) and *Newark Bears: The Final Years* (Trenton: Linthurst, 1981). Chapter length treatment of the team is found in Neil J. Sullivan, *The Minors: The Struggles and the Triumph of Baseball's Poor Relation from 1876 to the Present* (New York: St. Martin's Press, 1990), 132–148; John Cunningham, *Baseball in New Jersey: The Game of History* (Trenton: New Jersey State Museum, 1995), 44–46; James M. DiClerico and Barry J. Pavelec, *The Jersey Game: The History of Minor League Baseball From Its Birth to the Big Leagues in the Garden State* (New Brunswick: Rutgers University Press, 1991), 83–92; and Bruce Chadwick, *The Wonder Team: The Newark Bears* (New York: Abbeville Press, 1994), 118–123. The newspaper article "Newark's Baseball History Has Been a Colorful One," *Newark Evening News*, 13 January 1950, n.p., copy located in the subject files of the New Jersey Reference Room in the Newark Public Library offers a valuable account of the Bears.

4. Two useful sources on collective memory and contested history are Michael Kammen, *In the Past Lane: Historical Perspectives on American Culture* (New York: Oxford University Press, 1997), 189–213; and David Thelen, "Memory and American History," *Journal of American History* 75 (1989): 1117–1129.

5. Sullivan, *The Minors*, 142–144; and Mayer, *The 1937 Newark Bears*, 19–26.

6. Robert F. Burk, *Much More Than a Game: Players, Owners, and American Baseball Since 1921* (Chapel Hill: University of North Carolina Press,2001), 51–52; and Sullivan, *The Minors*, 143–144.

7. Mayer, *1937 Newark Bears*, passim ; DiClerico and Pavelec, *The Jersey Game*, 85–90; and "'37 Bears Named Top Team of Century," Newark Bears Press Release, 14 April 1999.

8. A comprehensive summary of Newark's census data is found in *A Preliminary Report on Past, Present, and Probable Population for Newark, Jew Jersey* (Newark: Central Planning Board, 1944). On Newark's history see John T. Cunningham, *Newark*

(Newark: Jew Jersey Historical Society: 1964); Barbara Cunningham, ed., *The New Jersey Ethnic Experience* (Union City: Wise Publishers, 1976); Charles F. Cummings, "Knowing Newark: Tour the City's Wards, Beginning in the Busy East," *Newark Star-Ledger*, 3 May 2001, 3; and Charles F. Cummings, "Industry, Commerce Sustain Vibrant Soul in Midst of Change," *Newark Star-Ledger*, 19 September 1996, N3. An examination of the city's neighborhoods is found in Kenneth Jackson and Barbara Jackson, "The Black Experience in Newark: The Growth of the Ghetto, 1870–1970," in William C, Wright ed., *Urban New Jersey Since 1870* (Trenton: New Jersey Historical Commission, 1975), 36–59; and Clement J. Price, "The Beleaguered City as Promised Land: Blacks in Newark, 1917–1947," in William C. Wright, ed., *New Jersey Since 1860: New Findings and Interpretations* (Trenton: New Jersey Historical Commission, 1972), 10–45; and Barbara J. Kukla, *Swing City: Newark Nightlife, 1925–50* (Philadelphia: Temple University Press, 1991), 1–10.

9. Jerry Izenberg, "A New Wind Blows Hope Into Newark," *Newark Star-Ledger*, 1 May 1999, 39; Izenberg, "Great Baseball Town"; Harvey Yavener, "Foreword" in Randolph Linthurst, *Newark Bears: The Middle Years* (West Trenton: Linthurst, 1979), 3; and Steven A. Riess, *Touching Base: Professional Baseball and American Culture in the Progressive Era* (Urbana: University of Illinois Press, 1999), 7.

10. Burke, *Much More Than A Game*, 48–50 and 62–63. See also G. Edward White, *Creating the National Pastime: Baseball Transforms Itself, 1903–1953* (Princeton: Princeton University Press, 1996), 245–274.

11. The best examples of the recent literature are found in David Roediger, *Wages of Whiteness: Race and the Making of the American Working Class* London: Verso, 1991) and "Whiteness and Ethnicity in the "House of White Ethnics" in the United States" in Roediger, *Towards the Abolition of Whiteness: Essays on Race, Politics, and Working Class History* (London: Verso, 1994), 181–198; and George Lipsitz, "The Possessive Investment in Whiteness: Racialized Social Democracy and the White Problem in American Studies," *American Quarterly* 47 (1995): 370. See also Russell A. Kazal, "Revisiting Assimilation: The Rise, Fall, and Reappraisal of a Concept in American Ethnic History," *American Historical Review* 100 (1995): 438 and 465–470; and Jonathan Warren and France Winddance Twine, "White Americans, The New Minority?: Non-Blacks and the Ever-Expanding Boundaries of Whiteness," *Journal of Black Studies* 28 (1997): 200–218.

12. See, for example, the early 20th century pamphlet Joseph A. Roney, *Uplifting Down-Neck*, 16–17, located in the New Jersey Reference Room of the Newark Public Library; and Matthew Frye Jacobson, *Whiteness of a Different Color: European Immigrants and the Alchemy of Race* (Cambridge: Harvard University Press, 1998), 247. On the importance of sports in Newark's Americanization process see Ironbound Community and Industrial Service, *The Coming American in Ironbound* 5 (1926): 4–5.

13. Price, "Beleaguered City as Promised Land," 15 and 25–41; and Jackson and Jackson, "Black Experience in Newark," 39.

14. Recent scholarship on black and white labor during the 1930s and 1940s is found in Gary Gerstle, *American Crucible: Race and Nation in the Twentieth Century* (Princeton: Princeton University Press, 2001), 154–185; Jacqueline Jones, *American Work: Four Centuries of Black and White Labor* (New York: Norton, 1998), 337–355; Price, "Beleaguered City as Promised Land," 31; and Jackson and Jackson, "Black Experience in Newark," 49–50.

15. Amiri Baraka, *The Autobiography of LeRoi Jones* (Chicago: Lawrence Hill Books, 1997), 42.

16. Overmyer, *Queen of the Negro Leagues*, 115–117 and Jonathan Schuppe,

"Remember When: Bears Rename Stadium, Hoping to Rekindle Newark's Glory Days," *Newark Star-Ledger*, 9 May 2001, 23.

17. Diane C. Walsh, "First Pitch, First Wave — Newark Revels in It All," *Newark Star-Ledger*, 17 July 1999, 1; and Jackson and Jackson, "Black Experience in Newark, " 39 and 45–56.

18. "Bears, ECIA Reach Stadium Lease Deal," Newark Bears Press Release, 1 April 1999.

19. Walsh, "First Pitch." On Larry Doby see Overmyer, *Queen of the Negro Leagues*, 236–237. The author wishes to thank Lawrence Hogan for his helpful comments on Doby's refusal to attend the inaugural ceremonies.

20. Schuppe, "Bears Rename Stadium,"23.

21. Castellano, "A Major Player," 58; Diane C. Walsh, "Newark Counting on Its Ballpark, Regardless of Unexpected Costs, *Newark Star-Ledger*, 16 July 1999, 7; and Schuppe, "Bears Rename Stadium," 23.

22. Studies undertaken by James Overmyer and Lawrence Hogan speak directly to the Eagles' impact on racial identity and leads explicitly to a better understanding of the city, especially its economic and political history. Overmyer's biography of Eagles owner Effa Manley carefully examines her role as the Negro league's only female owner, but along the way tells the story of the city's black neighborhoods, the debilitating effects of racial segregation, the economics of black baseball, and the pivotal role the team and its owner played in securing civil rights and social equality for Newark's minorities. See Overmyer, *Queen of the Negro Leagues*, passim; and Lawrence Hogan, James Overmyer, and James DiClerico, "Baseball as Black Comfortability: Negro Professional Baseball in New Jersey in the Era of the Color Line," paper delivered on 11 June 1991 at the Third Annual Cooperstown Symposium on Baseball and American Culture. On the Bears see Mayer, *1937 Newark Bears*, passim; and Linthurst, *Middle Years* and *Final Years*, passim.

The House That Ruth Built, and Pop Opened: Negro League Baseball at Yankee Stadium

Lawrence D. Hogan

"The Negro Leagues are like a light somewhere. Back over your shoulder. As you go away. A warmth still connected to laughter and self-love. The collective Black aura that can only be duplicated with Black conversation or music."[1]
— Amiri Baraka

"And herein lies the tragedy of the age: not that men are poor,— all men know something of poverty; not that men are wicked,— who is good? not that men are ignorant,— what is Truth? Nay, but that men know so little of men."[2]
— W.E.B. DuBois

Yankee Stadium has been for close to eighty years the home to many of the great moments in the history of our national pastime, as well as epic events in boxing, football, and numerous other sports.[2] Stadium moments more sublime than mere sporting events have seen Billy Graham calling sinners to repent; Nelson Mandella admitting to being a Yankee; and two Popes celebrating the Holy Sacrifice of the Mass. Yankee Stadium is the baseball cathedral possessed of the prowess and celebrity of the troubled Baltimore youth who in his athletic manhood presided over the House that Ruth Built.

As sublime a Stadium moment as any came in 1930, involving one of New Jersey's adopted sons whose baseball feats were recently commemorated with induction into the New Jersey Sports Hall of Fame. In hosting that 1930 moment, only seven years after the opening of their great ball yard in the Bronx, the New York Yankees brought into their history a Negro League baseball seed that today needs to take its rightful historic place in our nation's most hallowed baseball canyon.

In late June of 1930, banner advertisements in New York's leading black newspapers, the *Amsterdam News* and the *Age* put out the cry:[3]

> *"Let's Fill the Yankee Stadium!"*
> *2 BIG BALL GAMES*
> *A Double-Header — The Clash of the Season*
> *New York Baltimore*
> *LINCOLN GIANTS vs. BLACK SOX*
> *Saturday, July 5th*
> *FIRST GAME AT 1:30 P.M.*
> *Positively the Biggest Event of the Year*
> *For the First Time the Famous*
> *YANKEE STADIUM*
> *Is Donated to the Colored People of Harlem for the Benefit of the*
> *Brotherhood of Sleeping Car Porters by Courtesy of*
> *COLONEL JACOB RUPPERT*
> *Owner of the New York Yankees*

Merely to have been the first appearance of black professional baseball players at Ruth's house would be significant in itself. But a benefit for the infant Brotherhood of Sleeping Car Porters (BSCP) makes the occasion all the more noteworthy. The union that A. Philip Randolph was then struggling to establish is one of the epic stories in the annals of American labor and African-American history. And the name Randolph keeps company with that of Martin Luther King, W.E.B. DuBois, Frederick Douglass, and Booker T. Washington. The Phil Randolph who in the 1930s, through events such as the Yankee Stadium doubleheader, built a union that gave black workers for the first time a significant place within the ranks of the American labor movement, would test with considerable success the tactics of mass protest in his March On Washington Movement of 1941; eventually become the first black vice president of the American Federation of Labor; and in 1963, through his personal prestige and leadership, give Dr. King the magnificent "I Have a Dream" platform of the Lincoln Memorial in our nation's capital.[4]

The BSCP July 5, 1930, benefit doubleheader in the spotlight of Yankee Stadium was a grand success. Between games, the redoubtable Bojangles

Robinson, running backwards, outraced several YMCA track stars. The band of the 369th infantry regiment, Harlem's famous Hell Fighters, entertained the large crowd. And when the receipts were tallied, and expenses paid, Randolph's Brotherhood treasury was more than $3500 to the good.[5]

While there is no indication of Yankee Stadium being donated to other black social and civil rights causes, there would be a significant Negro baseball presence at the Stadium through the remainder of the 1930s, through the years of World War II, and up to the integration of the majors in the late 1940s. When the Yankees were on the road, teams from the Negro leagues played before large crowds at the Stadium with a regularity that is surprising only to those who do not know their baseball history. In a 1986 interview at the Stadium for the documentary *BEFORE YOU CAN SAY JACKIE ROBINSON*, veteran Amsterdam *News* reporter St. Clair Bourne emphasized the significance of that Negro League presence at Yankee Stadium:

> When these guys came along, and they started playing this kind of ball, and people saw them here (Yankee Stadium), people would come out. Usually it would be a Sunday either after the season or on an empty weekend. And I always felt that had something to do with the gradual moving of Blacks into baseball. Because sooner or later the owners were going to get smart enough to realize that the real part of baseball was green, not black or white. They found out — Rickey was the first to realize it — that if you picked a guy who was exciting, and put him on the team, you were going to get people coming through the gates.[6]

The newspaper accounts and box scores for the July 5, 1930, inaugural opening of the "Colored" chapter in the history of the Stadium takes special note of several players. Bill Holland of the Lincoln Giants became the first black pitcher to ever pitch in Yankee Stadium. It was the first time two black umpires ever officiated a game at the Stadium. Lincoln Giants shortstop Bill Yancey had the distinction of being the first black player to set foot on the turf at Yankee Stadium. Yancey's excitement was such that he ran out on the field early, pretended to catch fly balls in right field like Babe Ruth, and stood alone at home plate pretending to hit home runs into the right field stands like the Babe. Bill Yancey counted playing in Yankee Stadium as one of his biggest thrills.[7]

No player on either team that day was given more attention than a fellow the reporters affectionately referred to as "Pop," the player-manager of the Lincolns. On the Stadium field, Pop would steal a base, be credited with a sacrifice, go 4 for 8 at bat, and handle 24 put outs at first base without an error. Not a bad day's performance for a player nearing the end of a career in Negro professional baseball that began in 1906.[8]

There is a plaque at baseball's most hallowed shrine — the Hall of Fame in Cooperstown — bearing the name of that player:

John Henry Lloyd
"Pop"
NEGRO LEAGUES 1906–1932

A line of the inscription on that plaque reads as follows.

INSTRUMENTAL IN HELPING OPEN YANKEE STADIUM
TO NEGRO BASEBALL IN 1930

Who is this John Lloyd who merited baseball highest honor in 1977? And how do his achievements call for commemoration at Yankee Stadium? Testimony from his contemporaries provides an answer.

There are students of our nation's greatest game who claim that Pop Lloyd could well have been the best shortstop to ever play that position in professional baseball. A St. Louis baseball writer of Lloyd's day went even further in his estimate. When asked who was the best player in baseball history, this white journalist replied: "If you mean organized baseball, my answer would be Babe Ruth; but if you mean all baseball, organized or unorganized, the answer would have to be an Atlantic City, New Jersey colored man named John Henry Lloyd."[9]

An echo of this assessment, perhaps apocryphal, is that back in the early days of radio, pioneer sportscaster Graham McNamee was interviewing the great Ruth himself. McNamee asked the Babe whom he regarded as the greatest player of all time. "You mean major leaguers?" Ruth asked. "No," said the broadcaster, "the greatest player anywhere." "In that case," Ruth is reported to have replied, "I'd pick John Henry Lloyd."[10]

Well might the Bambino have so commented if what Alvin Moses reports is accurate. In a feature article in April, 1933 for *Abbott's Monthly*, the black reporter noted "that if you have been in New York when the Yanks were playing and John Henry Lloyd has an off day you'll always find the big Race man seated in the Ruthian dugout. Lloyd and Babe are great friends and often discuss close plays during the progress of the game."[11]

John Henry Lloyd was in his own way the equal of his steel-driving namesake of legend and song. He was affectionately known as "Pop" to generations of youth in his adopted hometown of Atlantic City, New Jersey who took much inspiration from this giant of the baseball diamond. Pop is remembered fondly by his pupil and great Newark Eagles Negro League pitcher Max Manning as a "gentle giant, strong in character, an honest man, a wonderful person. John Henry Lloyd contributed quite a bit to my knowledge about baseball, and also to my knowledge and learning about being a gentleman, because that's what he truly was. It seemed as if adversity would just fall off his shoulders. He would never dwell on adversity. He would always go to the brighter side of whatever would come up."[12]

Former Atlantic City Mayor Jim Usry, a self-confessed angry young man, and a protégée of Pop's, recalls how the great shortstop taught him to be patient, and to persist in the face of difficulties and discrimination that might well have embittered a man of lesser character. "Pop would say, your time will come. I always remember that."[13]

In 1949, when the rest of America was beginning to erase from its memory any recollection of the time of the Negro leagues, Atlantic City dedicated a stadium to its beloved Pop. When asked on that occasion if he regretted that his playing days were long past before the color line in baseball was erased, John Lloyd spoke these humble sentiments:

> I do not consider that I was born at the wrong time. I felt it was the right time, for I had the chance to prove the ability of our race in this sport, and because many of us did our very best to uphold the traditions of the game and of the world of sport, we have given the Negro a greater opportunity now to be accepted into the majors with other Americans.[14]

John Lloyd had no children of his own. But like his purported friend and admirer, Babe Ruth, he found ample opportunity to express his love for young people. In his retirement years, he became a janitor in the Atlantic City school system. In that humble position, he became a living legend to several generations of schoolchildren. Whitey Gruhler, Atlantic City Press sports editor, described Pop's hold over the children:

> The youngsters cluster about him between sessions. They all call him Pop and love to listen while he spins baseball yarns of the past. Sometimes they refuse to break away from him and Pop has to pick them up bodily and carry them into their classrooms. He is their hero, this big, soft-hearted, soft-spoken congenial man with a tired look in his eyes, but the bubbling spirit of youth in his heart.[15]

The Bacharach Giants figure prominently in the numerous years of managing that Lloyd's Hall of Fame plaque notes. Many of Pop's career highlights came with the Bacharach Giant, a charter member of the Eastern Colored Major League in 1923. In 1926, the Bacharachs brought the Negro League World Series to their hometown of Atlantic City.

The feats and exploits of the Bacharachs made for banner headlines on many an occasion in the newspapers of Pop's era. And as frequently as not it would be the great Pop Lloyd who commanded the attention of newspaper readers. Here we have the Philadelphia *Tribune* of July 12, 1924 announcing, "BACHARACH MANAGER NOW SHARES HONORS WITH SPEAKER, LAMB AND CHAS DRESSEN." The opening paragraph reports on an aging John Lloyd surpassing even the feats of his youth:

> ATLANTIC CITY, NJ, July 4 — In conjunction with the explosion of fire crackers during the Fourth of July celebration, John Henry Lloyd, manager of the Bacharach Giants, exploded theory when he banged out his eleventh straight hit and proved that a veteran player who might be expected to be bowing to old age can tie a world's record that youngsters are striving to equal every day.[16]

Pop Lloyd's Bacharach Giants Negro Leagues baseball world was a place largely hidden from the dominant society by a color line that had whites seeing stereotypes, while blacks celebrated the extraordinary baseball talent of men with colorful names like Cannonball, Smokey Joe, Rube, Dandy, the Devil, and Lloyd himself, El Cuchara. These baseball legends played year round for teams like the Original Cuban Giants of Trenton, New Jersey and St. Augustine, Florida; the feared Lincoln Giants of New York City; Chicago's powerful American Giants of black baseball's founding father, Andrew "Rube" Foster; the Monarchs of Kansas City with their great Satchel; the Newark Eagles of "million dollar infield fame;" and Pop's own Bacharach Giants of Atlantic City, New Jersey.

In 1999, led by the John Henry "Pop" Lloyd Committee, the memory of those wonderful nicknamed baseball men, and their colorfully named teams, was celebrated at a community ball yard in Atlantic City that was commemorating its fiftieth anniversary year. John Henry "Pop" Lloyd Stadium, dedicated to New Jersey's greatest baseball player, was officially opened for play by the political fathers of America's premier resort city in October of 1949. Pop Lloyd Stadium was the first, and is still our nation's most substantial monument to the memory and feats of those who played their baseball in "leagues where only the ball was white."

It would be wonderful, and certainly historically appropriate, if that other Pop Lloyd baseball site — the one in the Bronx that his presence graced on July 5, 1930 — would see fit to honor the memory of the man who could well have been the greatest shortstop ... wait a second, maybe the greatest player ever to have played the game of baseball.

It is long past time for the Yankee Stadium history that was Phil Randolph and his BSCP; the Negro League World Champion Cubans of 1947; the New York Black Yankees of Harlem's legendary Mayor, Bill "Bojangles" Robinson; and perhaps most of all of Pop the Steel Driving Man from Atlantic City to be officially recognized in permanent commemoration at America's greatest sports arena. Of all the major league teams whose history connects directly to the history of Negro professional baseball, none has a richer connection than the Yankees. Nor does any team in baseball treasure its historical past as do the Yankees at the Stadium.

If he were with us today, the Stadium's storied Monument Park would undoubtedly elicit from that great Yankee voice of the past, Mel Allen, his famous trademark phrase, "How about that!" Well to paraphrase Mel, Yankee fans, *how about that absence in that monument park of any commemoration of Pop and his history?*

No arena other than Yankee Stadium is more filled with the ghosts of Satchel's incredible pitching feats; and Josh's prodigious home runs, one of which may be the only fair ball ever hit out of the Stadium. And filled too with the baseball prowess of names such as Manning and Day and O'Neil and Seay and Wells. They and numerous others from the Negro Leagues are not as well know as the two super stars, Josh and Satch. And, of course, even the dark hued superstars cannot compete for fan remembrance and esteem with the Ruths, Gehrigs, DiMaggios, and Mantles of Yankee lore. But, in their own Yankee Stadium baseball moments, those Negro Leaguers playing behind the veil of race were every bit as good as all those other Yankee greats. And they are every bit as deserving of permanent commemoration in the House that Ruth built ... and that Pop opened.

When that Pop Negro Leagues plaque is finally placed in Monument Park at Yankee Stadium, it would not be inappropriate for someone to recall the lyrics from the song about that other great John Henry, the one "dey took to de graveyard, and buried in the san." And in this case every elevated train that comes roarin by the Stadium will echo the refrain,

> Dere lays a steel driving man,
> Lawd, Lawd, dere lays a steel driving man.

Notes

James Overmyer assisted in the research for this article.

1. Amiri Baraka, *The Autobiography of Leroi Jones* (New York: Freundlich, 1984), 37.

2. W.E.B. DuBois, *Souls of Black Folk* (Greenwich: Fawcett, 1961), 164–165.

3. "Let's Fill the Yankee Stadium!" (Broadside Advertisement), New York *Amsterdam News*, 28 June 1930, n.p.; and New York *Age*, 28 June 1930, n.p.

4. For A. Philip Randolph and the Brotherhood of Sleeping Car Porters see, Jervis Anderson, *A. Philip Randolph: A Biographical Portrait*, (Berkeley: University of California Press, 1986), and William H. Harris, *Keeping The Faith: A Philip Randolph, Milton P. Webster and the Brotherhood of Sleeping Car Porters*, (Urbana, IL: University of Illinois Press, 1991).

5. Lucien White, "Roy Lancaster Puts Over Big Benefit," New York *Age*, 19 July 1930, 6..

6. St Claire Bourne interview for *Before You Can Say Jackie Robinson* Documentary, transcript in possession of author.

7. Jim Goldfarb, "Harlem's Team: The New York Lincoln Giants," (Unpublished seminar paper in possession of author)

8. "Lincoln Giants Win 5 of 6...," New York *Age*, 12 July 1930, 6..

9. Robert Peterson, *Only The Ball Was White*, (Oxford University Press: New York, 1992) 79.

10. John Holway, unpublished article in possession of author.

11. Al Monroe, "The Big League," *Abbott's Monthly*, April 1933, 6.

12. Max Manning interview for *Before You Can Say Jackie Robinson* documentary, transcript in possession of author

13. James Usry interview, *ibid.*

14. Peterson, 79.

15. *Ibid.*, 78.

16. "Pop Lloyd Ranks With Chas. Dressen, Speaker...," Philadelphia *Tribune*, 6 July 1924, n.p.

Wendell Smith's Last Crusade: The Desegregation of Spring Training

Brian Carroll

One of Wendell Smith's first encounters with racial prejudice came as a high school senior, playing American Legion baseball, in his hometown of Detroit, Michigan. Smith pitched his team to a 1–0 playoff victory. After the game, Wish Egan, one of the Detroit Tigers' top scouts, signed Smith's catcher, Mike Tresh, who would play Major League Baseball for sixteen seasons. Egan signed the losing pitcher, as well, and told Smith he would sign him, too, if only he could. But Smith was black, and Organized Baseball barred black players. Smith dedicated himself that day to doing "something on behalf of the Negro ballplayers."[1]

True to his word, after college Smith became a crusading black press journalist described by contemporaries as one of the very best of his time.[2] His career began at the *Pittsburgh Courier* in 1937 and continued at the *Chicago American* as its first black sports columnist, the *Chicago Sun-Times*, and finally as the sports anchor at WGN-TV.[3] Yet beyond the fraternity of baseball scholars, few have ever heard of Smith. When the literature refers to him, it mentions Smith as the man who recommended Jackie Robinson to Branch Rickey as the Negro League player best suited to break Major League Baseball's color barrier.[4] Smith's ten-year struggle to bring down baseball's color barrier was overshadowed by Rickey's bold stroke. Moreover, Smith's subsequent campaign of the early 1960s, to ameliorate the plight of black players during spring training, merits closer attention. Note that future Hall-of-Famer Ernie Banks, the Cubs slugging shortstop, was amongst those who recognized the importance of Smith's January 23, 1961, *Chicago American* article exposing the racial injustice endemic to spring training: "I am sure I am speaking for every Negro player in the big leagues when I say we are very grateful to the *Chicago American* for bringing this situation to the attention of the American public."[5] Likewise, former Cleveland Indian Larry Doby, who had broken the American League color line in 1947,[6] saluted the campaign "started by the *Chicago American* to secure equal treatment for Negro big leaguers" while in pre-season training camps in the South.

This paper examines the campaign waged throughout 1961 by Smith and the *Chicago American* to ensure equality for black players during spring training. On the field, 1961 was a glittering year.[7] Off the field, as it was for the country in general, the year proved a turbulent one in the area of race relations.[8] Fourteen seasons after Robinson broke into major league baseball, racial prejudice persisted in the national pastime.[9] Smith's approach was consistent with that of Martin Luther King, Jr., in its tone, dignity, and first-hand experience with the conditions being challenged. Though Smith is due credit for the spring training campaign[10] that credit has for the most part eluded him. This important chapter in the histories of the black press, baseball, the South, and Smith himself, therefore, ought not disappear into obscurity.

For baseball and for the nation, 1961 began with a debate over race relations and Jim Crow policies in the South. A front-page story in the January 23, 1961, edition of the *Chicago American* newspaper punctured the picture of racial tranquility in Major League Baseball. In the article, which was tagged, "Spring Training Woes," Smith revealed to the nation the "growing feeling of resentment" among black players who continued to suffer "embarrassment, humiliation, and even indignities" during the six weeks of spring training in Florida.[11] Each spring star players, including Hank Aaron, Willie Mays, Ernie Banks, and Minnie Minoso, were segregated from their white teammates — forced to sleep, eat, and recreate in separate and largely inferior facilities. White players, in contrast, were domiciled in some of south Florida's finest hotels, such as St. Petersburg's Soreno and Vinoy Park, and the Sarasota Terrace in Sarasota.

By 1961, black players had had enough. And Smith, a moral and social conscience for professional baseball and for Americans, continued his career-long fight against racial discrimination by giving black players a voice. Three years before President Lyndon Johnson signed the Civil Rights Act of 1964 to abolish legal segregation, Smith's campaign encouraged strides by baseball to erase the barriers of segregation during spring training. As of spring training 1961, only the Dodgers had yet desegregated their spring training facilities, doing so by leasing a former naval station in Vero Beach, Florida and building their own living quarters.[12] The Dodgers were the only major league players in Florida who could room together, eat together, and train together without confronting local authorities. As one player told the Baltimore *Afro-American*, the only segregation in Dodgertown existed "by ability, not color."[13] In Florida, home to thirteen of the eighteen major league clubs,[14] Jim Crow laws, customs, and unwritten policies kept blacks and whites apart. Seating at ball games also was segregated.[15]

Despite calls to action by Smith, Sam Lacy, and other black sportswriters, black players, for the most part, did not protest Jim Crow practices in the South, and, without complaint from their black players, neither did the ball clubs. Some of the players said they were content just to be in the major leagues. Monte Irvin, former Giants' great, felt that black players "wanted to play so badly, that (segregation during spring) didn't bother us that much."[16] Additionally, a culture among players discouraged disputes with management for fear of expulsion from baseball.[17] Some Southern players had grown somewhat accustomed to segregation and, therefore, did not challenge it, at least not directly.[18]

Not until 1959 had Henry Aaron complained to Milwaukee Braves management about segregated housing during spring training in Bradenton, Florida. Baseball's all-time home run hitter called the segregation in the state's hotels "the hardest thing to break down" because they stuck together, much as the big league clubs had successfully done prior to Rickey and Robinson.[19] The hotels' owners knew that if one gave in, it would make it very difficult on the others. Aaron's complaints were heard, but at a cost to the entire team. Rather than tolerate segregated housing in Bradenton during the spring of 1959, the Braves, black and white, moved to nearby Palmetto for a "two-bit" motel with inferior food.[20] Smith, Aaron, and Jackie Robinson agreed it would require economic pressure to force change, and they believed the clubs had the influence of the millions of dollars spent in Florida each spring.

In an interview with *The Sporting News* in 1956, Robinson blasted baseball, advocating that major league teams should lean on the Florida communities to "remedy a lot of the prejudices that surround the game as it's played below the Mason-Dixon line."[21] Robinson repeated and elaborated on his charges in his controversial 1963 book, *Baseball Has Done It*, in which he eloquently argued that baseball's dollar would speak with more force than anything else.[22]

In the crucial year of 1961, with Smith and the *Chicago American* leading the charge, the Major League Baseball Players Association demanded that the teams do more to integrate spring training.[23] But granting accolades to those responsible for desegregating training in Florida is complex. It is always difficult to know who to give credit to—and everyone wants it. For example, Bill White, in 1961 a first baseman with the St. Louis Cardinals and later president of the National League,[24] remembers telling a UPI reporter about the St. Petersburg Yacht Club issuing invitations only to white players for its annual "Salute to Baseball" breakfast.[25] The reporter, Joe Reichler, ran a story about segregation during spring training, a story White credits for getting "the ball rolling.... (since) After Reichler's article, there was a lot of pressure in St. Louis to do something about the segregation."

White said he believed his words to UPI were what sparked his club to act. The Cards became the first team after the Dodgers to take dramatic measures, leasing an entire hotel in St. Petersburg and housing all its players there. In Hank Aaron's autobiography, White gives his account of the "Salute to Baseball" breakfast. White, along with black teammates Curt Flood and Bob Gibson, certainly had influence, and undoubtedly contributed to the Cardinals' actions. But White, according to Aaron, had the exchange with Reichler during spring training in March, fully two months after Smith launched the *Chicago American*'s campaign to end the segregation of baseball in the South.

White spoke also to the *Pittsburgh Courier* about the yacht club incident specifically and about segregation in general for an article that appeared on March 18, 1961.[26] He told the *Courier* that the segregation policies were "gnawing at my heart. When will we be made to feel like humans?" But baseball historian Jack Davis later described White as merely "following the lead of Florida black citizens who were engaged in their own struggle for equality."[27]

Documenting the activism of these citizens, most notably local National Association for the Advancement of Colored People members Ralph Wimbish and Robert Swain, was the main purpose of Davis' article, in which it is argued that Wimbish and Swain were the change agents. Because the claim relies wholly for its veracity on Wimbish and Swain, who were interviewed about their efforts by Davis thirty years after the fact, it is difficult to dispute. Clearly grassroots efforts contributed greatly to the pressure the individual clubs felt, especially in St. Petersburg by the New York Yankees. Davis states that the NAACP's Florida headquarters joined Wimbish and Swain, hoping to generate national attention and support.[28]

The relationship between the black press and the NAACP clearly was a close one. Baseball scholar David Wiggins, in his exploration of Smith's ten-year campaign to integrate baseball, states that Wendell Smith proposed in a January 1939 column the formation of an organization like the NAACP.[29] Such an organization, Smith wrote, would allow blacks to attack segregation "until we drop from exhaustion." As Smith explained it, twenty-two years prior to the desegregation of spring training, by uniting in one national association, blacks could put more pressure on Organized Baseball to admit players of color. Ballplayers appeared to recognize the importance, it terms of its content and timing, of Smith's campaign.

The chronology of events underlines Smith's role and that of the *Chicago American* in leading the way, however instrumental the contributions of Wimbish, Swain, and others in the St. Petersburg community. According to *The New York Times*, Wimbish held a press conference on January 31, 1961, to announce that he would no longer secure segregated housing in St. Petersburg for dark-skinned Yankees, most notably black catcher Elston Howard.[30] Remember, however, that Smith and the *Chicago American* kicked off their campaign eight days earlier — on January 23, 1961.[31] It is unknown how interrelated were Smith's campaign and indigenous efforts in St. Petersburg and other Florida cities that hosted spring training. According to Davis, the NAACP worked closely with the *Pittsburgh Courier* and Smith's replacement at that paper, Mal Goode, describing the *Courier* as acting as a "public voice for the NAACP in their activities in Florida."[32] This characterization, too, depends on a long memory, however, in this instance that of former Florida NAACP field secretary Robert Saunders, three decades after the struggle.

According to Smith, in two weeks the *Chicago American* campaign already had garnered national support and had led to a competition among newspapers as to which one should get the credit for the progress made thus far. More research is necessary to verify this claim. In an editorial in that same February 6 edition, the *Chicago American* publisher, Stuart List, hailed the progress made toward desegregation in the two weeks since the paper's campaign began and pledged that his newspaper, "which began this campaign for equal treatment, will continue to watch developments carefully and report them fully."[33]

Several aspects of Smith's first salvo on January 23 are interesting. By using personal pronouns, as in, "his patience is growing short," Smith claimed to speak for all Negro players, something few writers could have credibly done. Second, Smith relied exclusively on unattributed sources, presumably to avoid putting the players in jeopardy with their respective clubs. This method also inferred a high level of cooperation and confidentiality with the players. Third, he referenced first-hand experiences, in particular, his successful alliance with Jackie Robinson in breaking the color barrier, to add weight to his description of the problem and to his very specific plan for taking steps to solve it. Finally, Smith prodded baseball's owners carefully, proposing humble first steps and saying that the black players "realize, of course, that the owners are not responsible for their plight." The players were going about their struggle "in their own quiet way" and not enlisting the aid of the NAACP "or any other such group." It was this conciliatory tone that Banks had praised. Similar to Martin Luther King, Jr.'s, espousal of pacifism, Smith's approach was one of conciliation, give-and-take, and dialogue.

Spring training was more than four weeks away at the time of the initial article, and though the players, according to Smith, wanted to avert a "fiery debate" over civil rights in baseball, they were "tired of being second class citizen(s) in spring training." Afforded respectability during the regular season, all the black players wanted was "the same treatment in the South during spring training that they had earned in the North," asserted Smith. This meant no longer staying in flophouses and eating in second-rate restaurants. The article contained muted but perceptible threats, such as when Smith cautioned that "at the moment he [the black ballplayer] is not belligerent. He is merely seeking help and sympathy, and understanding, and a solution ... (but) his patience is growing short."

Now that black players could eat and sleep in the same hotels with their teammates in cities such as St. Louis, New York, Philadelphia, and Chicago, they turned "southward to correct the evils they encounter there," wrote Smith in the 40-inch article, approximately titled, "Negro Players Want Dixie Rights." One of the more bothersome inequities for black players, according to Smith, was the inability of black players to spend spring with their families. It was customary for white players, who were put up by the teams in comfortable hotels close to the training field, to bring their families and make a vacation out of the six weeks spent in Florida. But the Negro players, facing poor housing conditions and discrimination in Florida communities, naturally were reluctant to bring family members into a hostile environment.[34]

The plan Smith proposed, citing the players as its source, included meeting with club owners to discuss the problem, giving player representatives the authority to negotiate and make decisions, and selecting one former player to explain the black players' position to baseball's top executives. Organizing the article like a legal argument, Smith then described the contributions black players had made since Robinson broke through in 1947, specifically those of Hank Aaron, Willie Mays, Ernie Banks, and Minnie Minoso.[35] Echoing Robinson's 1956 argument in *The Sporting News*,

Smith also cited the money clubs spent in and attracted to the Florida towns in which they trained, revenue no community wanted to lose. California towns, for example, would be glad to host spring training, he wrote. Smith followed up two weeks later with a deeply personal article on February 6 that gave the January 23 piece full credit for no fewer than eight measures being undertaken by major league teams. Smith, for example, cited efforts by Chicago White Sox owner Bill Veeck, a long-time critic of segregation. Confronting the common practice of black players boarding in the private residences of local black families, Veeck was in negotiations with the Sarasota Terrace, domicile to white players during the White Sox' spring camp in Sarasota, Florida, to provide accommodations for six black Chicago players.[36]

According to Smith, Veeck also moved reservations for his team from Miami's McAllister Hotel to the more tolerant Biscayne Terrace hotel for a pair of exhibition games, scheduled to take place later in the pre-season, against Baltimore. Davis, however, claims that Veeck was responding to the Wimbish press conference held on January 31 when he canceled reservations at the McAllister. Nonetheless, chronology suggests that Veeck might have decided to cancel the reservations even before the Wimbish press conference.

Also, according to Smith's February 6 story, the Cubs made the decision to house all of their players together in Mesa, Arizona, at the Maricopa Inn, and not to play exhibition games in cities where black Cubs players would be forced to sleep in separate quarters. Baseball Commissioner Ford Frick had said four days prior to Smith's story that he was "sympathetic" with the problems of the black players. Lee MacPhail, then general manager of the Baltimore Orioles, also reported that he was working to keep his team together at a Miami hotel.[37] Finally, Smith listed a formal statement from New York Yankees president Dan Topping that the team wanted all its players training in St. Petersburg to "live under one roof." Davis claims that Topping's announcement was "in response to Wimbish's demands" made at the January 31 press conference in St. Petersburg.[38] In this instance, it is possible that Davis is correct. The *Fort Lauderdale News*, notes Davis, quoted an anonymous source "close to the Yankee organization" as saying that Wimbish's demands had backed Topping against a wall.

As both Smith and *The New York Times* reported, the spring training domiciles of the Yankees (the Hotel Soreno) and the Cardinals (the Vinoy Park Hotel), both located in St. Petersburg, had no intention of changing their policies, advising the two clubs to "look for other hotels."[39] The Yankees did just that, moving to Fort Lauderdale, ending 36 years spent training in St. Petersburg. Topping, however, claimed the move had nothing to do with segregation.[40]

By April 1961, Smith was with the White Sox in Sarasota, Florida, documenting firsthand, with a flood of almost daily copy, the conditions that Chicago's black players faced. This was a situation far different than Smith had known at the *Pittsburgh Courier,* which had published his copy but once a week. The Sarasota Terrace Hotel refused accommodations both to the black players and to Smith, citing economic reasons for refusing blacks.[41] According to Smith, Veeck was working hard to change the situation, as was the Sarasota Chamber of Commerce. Smith chronicled the tedium that he and the players faced at night. Black players had few recreational options. Public eating places, bowling alleys, and most taxis were off limits in white sections of the city. There were no accommodations for black family members. And blacks needed special permission even to visit the Sarasota Terrace, where their white teammates were housed.[42] Smith also reported the story of the two white hotel owners who were scorned by their neighbors and by Florida civic leaders for their willingness to house the White Sox' black players.[43]

Smith's campaign picked up a huge endorsement in June 1961 when the Major League Players Association formally joined the struggle. The MLBPA's legal representative said the association not only approved of the campaign, but said "the issue raised by *Chicago American*" would be "thoro[ugh]ly discussed" at its annual meeting in August.[44] Just prior to the meeting in Boston, Smith published the thoughts of several top black players on spring training segregation. Minoso, Howard, Aaron, and others went on the record with their grievances. Their anger and impatience were clear.

At the same time, the Cardinals, Yankees, and Orioles announced that they had secured integrated spring training housing, but under different circumstances. The Cardinals benefited from the Yankees' decision to vacate St. Petersburg for Fort Lauderdale. The community did not want to lose another club, so the Cardinals were allowed to billet all their players, black and white, in a single facility.[45] The Braves moved their living quarters from Bradenton to nearby Palmetto to keep their team together. MacPhail's Orioles, meanwhile, finally came to terms with their Miami hotel.

At this time, the White Sox, in mid-season, were still in negotiations with the Sarasota Terrace, but eventually announced, in November, that they were buying the hotel outright "so that all of their players can live under the same roof during their training season."[46] Smith called it an "extreme step" that came as "a direct result of the campaign waged thru [*sic*] last season" by the *Chicago American.* In response to the hotel purchase, the city of Sarasota, according to Smith, agreed to grant the White Sox three baseball fields and clubhouse accommodations. There still were teams with segregated spring training in Florida, including Washington (Pompano Beach), Minnesota (Orlando), Detroit (Lakeland), and Kansas City (West Palm Beach), but Smith reported that he had checked in with each team and that all were "taking measures" to end the segregation.

The completion of spring training integration throughout Florida and Arizona would require two more years,[47] but Smith and the *Chicago American* merit recognition for helping to initiate the debate and subsequently raising it to a national level. Smith helped to legitimize black players' complaints and to de-stigmatize them by providing context and first-hand experience, by avoiding winner-take-all confrontations, and by acknowledging progress when and where he saw it.

Areas for future research include examining the level of cooperation between the press and grass roots efforts in the Florida communities, the reactions by the individual local communities in Florida and their governments, and the degree to which coverage in the *Chicago American* was picked up by other papers, how often it was reprinted, and in what ways it was treated. The stance taken by the *Chicago American* so early in the effort and then sustained is significant enough, but additional research is necessary to find greater evidence of the paper's impact. This study depends heavily on evidence found in the *Chicago American*'s own pages, its writers, and their attributed sources. It is an acknowledged trap historians of journalism fall into to assume the centrality of the media to social change, but, in this case, there is corroborating evidence of a significant contribution, if not a decisive one.

As Smith did during his entire career, he gave black athletes a voice. He also kept individual teams accountable as they worked to change their training conditions. As *Chicago American* writer Milton Gross put it in December 1961, perhaps baseball would have made the changes without the newspaper's pressure and accountability, but the swift changes big league clubs made in 1961 to breach Jim Crow barriers, collectively, were "a great step forward."[48] The *Chicago Sun-Times* later credited Smith with having "led the campaign for equal treatment of black baseball players in housing and meals during spring training and on the road"[49] as would prominent black players.[50] The Major League Baseball Players Association cited the *Chicago American* for raising the issue of conditions black players faced each spring, pledging to join the fight. An examination of the chronology and chain of events also point to Smith as an author and a principal sustainer of the fight for equal rights and fair conditions.

Baseball in 1961, as it had in 1945–47, led, and in some ways paved the way for, America's re-evaluation and, eventual, dismantling of segregation. Upon Smith's death in 1972, the *Chicago Defender*, a leading black newspaper, wrote that Smitty had "a vision of an American society, where ability, skill and character are the sole measures of a man and not the color of his skin. He pursued that idealism ... not with the militancy of the new breed of black spokesman, rather with the calm and patient logic of a wise man whose vision was sharp enough to see the light at the end of the tunnel. He has made his contribution. History will not pass him by."[51]

Notes

1. Undated manuscript, n.d., Wendell Smith Papers, National Baseball Hall of Fame Library, Cooperstown, N.Y., MSB 1. A thorough account of the introduction of Jackie Robinson to Branch Rickey by Smith is documented in what appear to be the beginnings of an autobiography written by Smith. The unpublished notes give Smith's account of the events leading up to and those just after Robinson was signed by Rickey in August 1945.

2. Jim Reisler, *Black Writers/Black Baseball: An Anthology of Articles from Black Sportswriters Who Covered the Negro Leagues* (Jefferson, N.C.: McFarland & Co., 1994), 33.

3. *Ibid.*, 36.

4. See, for example, Red Barber, *1947: When All Hell Broke Loose In Baseball* (Garden City, N.Y.: Doubleday & Co., 1982); Harvey Frommer, *Rickey and Robinson: The Men Who Broke Baseball's Color Barrier* (New York: Macmillan Publishing, 1982); Arthur Mann, *The Jackie Robinson Story* (New York: Grosset and Dunlop, 1950); Robert Peterson, *Only The Ball Was White* (New York: Prentice-Hall, 1970); George Ward and Ken Burns, *Baseball* (New York: Alfred A. Knopf, 1994); and Jackie Robinson (as told to Alfred Duckett), *I Never Had It Made* (New York: G.P. Putnam's & Sons, 1972).

5. Wendell Smith, "Negro Players Gain in Equality Bid," *Chicago American*, 6 February 1961, 16. Note: Smith's coverage in the *Chicago American* and the *Pittsburgh Courier* for the years 1938–161 are archived at the National Baseball Hall of Fame Library, Cooperstown, N.Y., MSB 1. Most of the copies of the articles, however, do not include page numbers, especially for Smith's *Courier* articles.

6. Peggy Beck, "Working in the Shadows of Rickey and Robinson: Bill Veeck, Larry Doby and the Advancement of Black Players in Baseball," *The Cooperstown Symposium on Baseball and American Culture, 1997: Jackie Robinson* , ed. Peter Rutkoff [Jefferson, N.C.: McFarland & Co., 2000]: 109–135), Beck made a valuable contribution to the literature by telling the story of Veeck's signing of Doby, an event that came just four months after Rickey's signing of Robinson. Veeck also signed Satchel Paige and Luke Easter, giving Cleveland more black players than even the Dodgers.

7. In 1961, the pastime's "unbreakable" record—Babe Ruth's 60 home runs in a single season—fell at the hands of the Yankees' right fielder Roger Maris, and in the season's final game. Maris toppled Ruth by winning a wrenching, season-long home run race against his roommate, and the fans' clear favorite, Mickey Mantle, who finished with 54.

8. Also in 1961, the United States broke off relations with Cuba after a crisis over weaponry. In Alabama, white and black liberals who had loosely organized to test and force integration were attacked and beaten by white citizens in Anniston and Birm-

ingham, where riots would make national headlines in May 1963 . Sit-ins swept through as many as seventy Southern cities as part of a protest movement started in part by North Carolina A&T University students at the Woolworth lunch counter in Greensboro, N.C. See Bernard Grun, *The Timetables of History*. 3rd ed. [New York: Simon & Schuster, 1991); and William Chafe, *Civilities and Civil Rights: Greensboro, North Carolina, and the Black Struggle for Equality* [New York: Oxford University Press, 1980).

9. Jules Tygiel, *Baseball's Great Experiment: Jackie Robinson and His Legacy* (New York: Vintage, 1997), 14. The 1887 season represented the "apex of black acceptance" in baseball. Cap Anson, manager and star player of the Chicago White Stockings that season, is blamed for leading the segregation of baseball and for being "one of the prime architects of baseball's Jim Crow policies." Moses Fleetwood Walker was the last black player in Major League Baseball. His release began a 57-year exclusion of blacks.

10. Milton Gross, "Baseball's Negroes Facing Brighter Spring," *Chicago American*, 1 December 1961, 3–23. Gross wrote an obituary, albeit a bit prematurely, for "that quaint southern custom" of segregation, saying that it is being breached ... it is a great step forward."

11. Wendell Smith, "Negro Ball Players Want Rights in South," *Chicago American*, 23 January 1961, A1.

12. Tygiel, *Baseball's Great Experiment*, 316. Called "Dodgertown," the training complex was built in 1948 to fulfill Branch Rickey's dream of operating a "college of baseball." Tygiel describes it as being a "haven of tolerance" (317), but that as soon as a black player stepped off the base, Jim Crow was waiting.

13. Sam Lacy, "Looking 'em Over," Baltimore *Afro-American*, 10 April 1948, 19.

14. Jack Davis, "Baseball's Reluctant Challenge: Desegregating Major League Spring Training Sites, 1961–1964," *Journal of Sport History* 19, no. 2 (Summer 1992): 145. The other five teams trained in Arizona.

15. For more on conditions and daily life in the South during spring training, see Tygiel's *Baseball's Great Experiment*, 303–27.

16. Tygiel, *Baseball's Great Experiment*, 318.

17. *Ibid.*, 318. Chuck Harmon, also in an interview with Tygiel, said, "Anytime you dispute with the management, whether you're white or black, or indifferent, you're gone."

18. Hank Aaron (with Lonnie Wheeler), *I Had a Hammer: The Hank Aaron Story* (New York: HarperCollins, Harper Paperback, 1992 {1991}), 153–4.

19. *Ibid.*, 153.

20. The inferior quarters were, according to Aaron teammate Joe Torre, Palmetto's Twilight Motel, which did not have a restaurant. See Ken Shoulder, "Grand Yankee, Brooklyn-bred Joe Torre Steers the Yankees to a World Championship, Overcoming Personal Troubles and Personal Trauma," *Cigar Aficionado* (February 1997), passim.

21. Jackie Robinson, "Jackie Tells What He Likes and Dislikes — About the South," *The Sporting News*, 6 June 1956, 9.

22. See Jackie Robinson, *Baseball Has Done It* (Philadelphia: Lippincott, 1964). As Tygiel points out in *Baseball's Great Experiment*, Robinson interviewed major league players for the book and "almost every player" complained about the conditions in Florida, particularly the discrimination faced in the local communities (319).

23. This demand by the MLBPA's Robert Cannon, its director, is stunning given Cannon's well-known sympathies with the team owners. Judge Cannon had aspirations of becoming Commissioner of baseball, a pursuit wholly dependent on the owners. Cannon would never become Commissioner, however . See "A History of Baseball Disputes," *USA Today*, 19 March 1990, 8C.

24. When White was named president of the National League in 1989, he became the first black to head a major professional sports league and the highest-ranking black official in the history of pro sports. See Laura Randolph, "Bill White: National League president," *Ebony* 47, no. 10 (August 1992): 52.

25. Aaron, 154.

26. In Davis, "Desegregating major league spring training sites," 144.

27. *Ibid.*, 145.

28. *Ibid.*, 148.

29. David Wiggins, "Wendell Smith, the Pittsburgh *Courier-Journal* and the Campaign to Include Blacks in Organized Baseball: 1933–1945," *Journal of Sport History* 10, no. 2, 11. The NAACP Web site (<http://www.naacp.org/>) states that the organization was founded in 1909 by "group of black and white citizens committed to social justice."

30. Davis, 152.

31. Wendell Smith, "Negro Ball Players Want Rights in South," *Chicago American*, 23 January 1961, A1.

32. Davis, 153.

33. Stuart List, "Progress in Fair Play," 6 February 1961, *Chicago American*, Editorial Page, 8.

34. Davis, 156. Elston Howard is quoted telling the *St. Petersburg Times* that white players could make all their arrangements in advance through an agent. Howard had to wait to see what living conditions he could secure before bringing his family down.

35. Baseball historian Bill James conducted a statistical study in 1987 comparing 54 black rookies with 54 white rookies, expecting to find "nothing in particular," (in Jon Entine, *Taboo: Why Black Athletes Dominate Sports and Why We Are Afraid to Talk About It* [New York: Public Affairs, 2000]: 23). James found that the black players had better playing careers in 44 of the 54 cases, played 48% more games, and clubbed 66% more home runs.

36. Leo W. Banks, "An Oasis for Some Pioneers; Lucille and Chester Willis Put Up Black Ballplayers When Tucson's Hotels Wouldn't," *Sports Illustrated*, 8 May 1989, 116–117.

37. Wendell Smith, "Negro Players Gain in Equality Bid," *Chicago American*, 6 February 1961, 16.

38. Davis, 152.

39. Wendell Smith, "Negro Players Gain in Equality Bid," *Chicago American*, 6 February 1961, 16. The two hotels were owned by the same Kansas City-based company.

40. Davis, 159.

41. Wendell Smith, "What a Negro Ballplayer Faces Today in Training," *Chicago American*, 3 April 1961, 16. The owners were afraid of losing business from white guests if the hotels risked integration.

42. Wendell Smith , "Negro Stars Find Themselves Caged," *Chicago American*, 4 April 1961.

43. Wendell Smith, "Houses Sox Negro Stars," *Chicago American*, 6 April 1961.

44. Wendell Smith, "Player Chief Backs Negro Plan," *Chicago American*, 19 June 1961. Presenting the players' grievances at the meeting were Bill White for the National League and Bill Bruton for the American League. The official, Robert Cannon, told the paper that after discussions with team owners he was confident the problem could be solved to everyone's satisfaction.

45. Wendell Smith, "Players Take Up Color Bar Issue," *Chicago American*, 31 July 1961, 15.

46. Wendell Smith, "American's Campaign Succeeding in Florida," *Chicago American*, 9 November 1961, 33.

47. Paul Meyer, "Columnist Was 'Baseball' Star," Pittsburgh *Post-Gazette*, 29 September 1994, D1. Meyer described Smith as a "leader in getting the big leagues integrated" who "pushed hard for equal housing during spring training, winning that battle in 1963."

48. Milton Gross, "Baseball's Negroes Facing Brighter Spring," *Chicago American*, 1 December 1961, 3–23.

49. Brian Ettkin, "Smith Helped Smash Color Barrier," *Chicago Sun-Times*, 31 July 1994, 9.

50. Banks was the first black to play for the Chicago Cubs, signing in 1953. Doby signed with Cleveland late in the 1947 season. Howard played his first game with the Yankees in 1955. And Cuban-born Minnie Minoso played at least one game in five different decades, beginning with Cleveland in 1949 and finishing with the White Sox in 1980 (From *The Baseball Encyclopedia*, Tenth ed. (New York: Macmillan, 1996).

51. Reisler, 34.

Part 2

MEDIA MYTHOLOGY

Baseball and Supernatural Intervention: Cinematic Reflections on the Crisis of Confidence in Post–World War II America

Ron Briley

During the late 1940s and early 1950s, three baseball fantasy films opened to mixed reviews and mediocre box office. *It Happens Every Spring* (1949), *Angels in the Outfield* (1951), and *Rhubarb* (1951) were initially perceived as lightweight cinema in which supernatural intervention of some type was required to rescue the protagonist from the clutches of evil or corrupt forces. However, a closer reading of these films within the historical context of post–World War II America reveals societal insecurities regarding the promise of American life. Film historian Gary Dickerson finds these films enigmatic, suggesting, "Maybe the answers to many questions that Americans had about future wars, technology, Communism, and bombs simply could not be supplied. Possibly, these films were a response to that predicament."[1] Interpreting this supernatural baseball cinema within the cultural framework of the early Cold War years may shed some light on the development of American ideology and values during this crucial time period. Examined within historical and cultural context, and when compared to other Hollywood features of the period, perhaps these films are neither light fare nor atypical productions. They may reflect fundamental insecurities and doubts regarding the postwar world and attaining the American Dream. In short, they may be read as indicative of a crisis of confidence in post–World War II America.

Many Americans continue to view the early postwar years and 1950s through the rose-colored glasses of television family situation comedies such as *The Adventures of Ozzie and Harriet, Father Knows Best,* and *Leave It to Beaver.* In these television programs, idealistic white suburban families are portrayed with fathers commuting to the office, mothers at home preparing pot roast for dinner, and children whose most complex problems involve a crush on a teacher or asking for an increased allowance.[2] But the reality of the 1950s was far different than these media-constructed families. Nostalgia usually fails to take into account the fear that depression would return with the decline of wartime production. Accordingly, Americans clung to the notion that conformity, the organization man, and following "outer" directed values rather than "inner" direction would allow them to participate in what economist John Kenneth Galbraith termed "the affluent society." To make sense of the period, scholars often use the ideological construct of the postwar liberal consensus.[3] This concept is best exemplified by the twin pillars of anti–Communism and capitalist economic expansion eschewing the inequities of race, gender, and class. Since increasing prosperity will cure all the nation's ills, there is no reason for dissent or protest. Within the confines of this ideology, the American government is as understanding and reasonable as Jim Anderson of *Father Knows Best* and Ward Cleaver in *Leave It to Beaver.*

However, the corporate state, enhanced productivity, and technology did not necessarily usher in a safer and more secure world. Many historians, such as William H. Chafe, perceive the immediate postwar years as better characterized by ambiguity and paradox rather than consensus. Chafe writes that the 1950s appear "as much a time of complexity and contradiction as of blissful complacency."[4] As Michael Harrington documented in *The Other America,* pockets of poverty remained invisible in the tranquil suburbs.[5] The independence of owning one's home in suburbia was limited by community conformity; women were discouraged from pursuing professions but had to work outside the home to support the consumerism which fueled the affluent society. Moreover, the ideology of consensus was challenged by teen rebels, the image of James Dean, the beat culture, and the civil rights movement.

Thus, a more sophisticated examination of the postwar period should take the themes of insecurity and instability into consideration. Spy scandals, the explosion of an atomic bomb by the Soviet Union, and a shooting war in Korea reminded Americans that the world was a very unpredictable place. Frustrated by the failure of the liberal consensus to provide the promised land, many Americans sought scapegoats in the anti–Communist crusades of the postwar period, which limited freedom of expression, silencing political, cultural, and artistic discourse.[6] Some social scientists blamed mothers in the work force for contributing to the problems of juvenile delinquency, for many teens were alienated from the culture of affluence.[7]

These insecurities were reflected in Hollywood feature films of the postwar years. A darkness in the soul of America after the war was evident in the development of *film noir* as a genre. *Film noir* is characterized by such elements as characters who are corrupt and corruptible, often victims of dark forces which they are unable to control or comprehend. The settings are usually an urban environment of moral ambiguity, and the plots "frequently focus on deadly violence or sexual obsession, whose catalogue of characters include down-and-out private eyes, desperate women, and petty criminals." Postwar examples of the *film noir* genre include such Hollywood classics as *The Postman Always Rings Twice* (1946), *The Blue Dahlia* (1946), *Naked City* (1948), and *Kiss Me Deadly* (1955).[8]

Elements of corruption were also evident in sport films of the post war era. Many film scholars view the period between 1947 and 1957 as the golden age of boxing cinema. In features such as *Body and Soul* (1947), *Champion* (1949), *The Set-Up* (1949), and *The Harder They Fall* (1956), promising fighters are betrayed by dishonest gamblers and mangers, who are driven by the evil influence of money. In these films, several of which were composed by writers later subjected to the Hollywood blacklist, greed denies fighters control over their means of production. Accordingly, the sleaze found in the underworld of boxing mirrors the moral ambiguity of the larger society, raising questions regarding American individualism and the possibility of attaining the American Dream.[9]

Even the seemingly more heroic baseball biographical features of the period were burdened by the forces of darkness and instability looming on the American horizon. In films such as *The Stratton Story* (1949), *The Jackie Robinson Story* (1950), *The Winning Team* (1952), *The Pride of St. Louis* (1952), and *Fear Strikes Out* (1957), ballplayers overcome physical disability, racism, alcoholism, lack of education, and mental breakdown in order to participate in the American success epic. But a closer reading of these films reveals a crisis within American masculinity and the patriarchy, for these baseball heroes are insecure, often weepy with feet of clay, and are increasingly dependent upon female assistance or rescue. For example, Grover Cleveland Alexander (portrayed by Ronald Reagan in *The Winning*

Team) is unable to achieve his heroics in the 1926 World Series until his wife Aimee (Doris Day) arrives at the ballpark.[10]

And the self-proclaimed national pastime of baseball was also experiencing difficulty adjusting to the postwar environment The end of the war in 1945 witnessed a new high of nearly eleven million fans attending major league games. This mark was shattered in 1946, when over eighteen million spectators jammed major league parks, perhaps reflecting a "pent up" demand for the sport following the turbulent war years. Attendance continued to climb in 1947 and 1948, reaching a figure of over twenty million customers in the latter year. However, major league attendance took a nosedive in 1950, dropping over 13 percent from 1949. In addition, Congressman Emmanuel Celler's subcommittee on monopoly was investigating allegations of antitrust violations by the sport. Meanwhile, fan support continued to erode. Paid admissions were down over 8 percent from 1951, itself hardly a banner season. A multitude of factors were blamed for baseball's apparent decline in popularity: huge bonuses for signing young players, selective service, the domination of the sport by the New York Yankees, lack of good business promotion skills by some owners, contemporary players who (unlike old-timers) were more interested in salaries and golf rather than competition, the challenge of television, and the fact that children were watching Westerns rather than playing baseball.[11] The changing demographics of American life in the suburbs were initially lost upon much of baseball ownership.

It is within this context of societal and baseball insecurities in the late 1940s and early 1950s that the film productions *It Happens Every Spring*, *Angels in the Outfield*, and *Rhubarb* must be placed. How were Americans and the sport of baseball to extricate themselves from their discontent? In seeking supernatural solutions to the personal problems of their protagonists and the playing field misfortunes of their teams, the producers of this trio of baseball fantasy films found themselves in a situation similar to that confronted by filmmaker Frank Capra. In a series of brilliant films in the 1930s and 1940s, including such works as *Mr. Deeds Goes to Town* (1936), *Mr. Smith Goes to Washington* (1939), and *Meet John Doe* (1941), Capra discovered it increasingly difficult for his populist heroes to overcome the sinister forces threatening the American family and way of life. In the classic holiday film *It's a Wonderful Life* (1947), Capra was unable to extricate his hero George Bailey (James Stewart) from the clutches of Mr. Potter. Bailey and Capra could only find redemption through divine intervention. However, this supernatural solution apparently drained Capra's creative juices, and the director was never again to recapture his earlier commercial and critical acclaim.[12]

A turn to more supernatural answers in postwar America was hardly surprising. Fears of instability in the postwar world, along with a militant crusade against the atheistic principles of Communism, led to a resurgence of religion in the United States. By the end of the 1950s, an astonishing 63.6 percent of the population was affiliated with some religious group, while 60 percent of Americans reported they went to weekly religious services. Within popular culture, films with religious themes, such as *Quo Vadis* (1951), *The Robe* (1953), *The Ten Commandments* (1956), and *Ben Hur* (1959) enjoyed considerable commercial appeal. Norman Vincent Peale celebrated the power of positive thinking; Billy Graham led international religious crusades; Reinhold Niebuhr articulated the theology of neo-orthodoxy; and Martin Luther King, Jr., advocated social activism.[13]

While a muscular Christianity was being activated in the war against Communism and as a support system in times of instability, *It Happens Every Spring* focused its plot upon that other quasi-religious belief system of the 1950s: science and technology. The production was released in 1949 by 20th Century Fox, from a screenplay by Valentine Davies, and directed by veteran filmmaker Lloyd Bacon, best known for such Warner Brothers films as *42nd Street* (1933), *Knute Rockne — All American* (1940), and *Action in the North Atlantic* (1943).[14] The film also featured Ray Milland (who earned an Oscar in 1945 for Billy Wilder's *Lost Weekend*), Jean Peters, Paul Douglas, Ed Begley, Ted de Corsia, and Ray Collins. However, this veteran line up was granted little respect by film critics, who found the picture's supernatural scientific formula plot unrealistic. In a play upon baseball vocabulary favored by many publications, *The New Republic* found *It Happens Every Spring* to have "too many errors even for the bush leagues." Bosley Crowther of *The New York Times* described Bacon's uninspired direction "as monotonous as the script," an opinion supported by John McCarten of *The New Yorker*, who concluded that the baseball film was comprised of simplistic "variations on one joke." On the other hand, *Christian Century* termed the baseball fantasy "delightful comedy fare," and *Newsweek* insisted that *It Happens Every Spring* was an "unorthodox comedy that holds good for any season of the year."[15]

Yet, none of these reviewers made any effort to place the fantasy film within historical and cultural context, which is certainly not surprising considering that the political climate tended to stifle social criticism and commentary. But in ignoring this larger context, film critics failed to recognize that a mediocre Hollywood feature like *It Happens Every Spring* offered insights into the insecurities plaguing Americans during the early years of the Cold War. In a culture where political discourse was viewed as controversial and job threatening, filmmakers increasingly turned to allegory, exemplified by such films as *High Noon* (1952), *On the Waterfront* (1954), and *Invasion of the Body Snatchers* (1956), to provide social and political commentary.[16] While not exactly political allegory, *It Happens Every Spring* does, nonetheless, reflect many of the fears confronting Americans in the postwar period and deserves more serious consideration than contemporary viewers gave the film.

It Happens Every Spring tells the story of chemistry professor Vernon Simpson (Ray Milland), who teaches at a small Midwestern university.[17] By all accounts the professor is an outstanding instructor, except every spring when his mind wanders during lecture as he listens to St. Louis baseball games on a concealed radio (Evidently, the producers failed to secure the authorization of Organized Baseball for the use of team logos. Thus, one is uncertain of whether Simpson is affiliated with the St. Louis Cardinals or Browns.). However, Simpson's major concern is his romance with one of his students, Debbie Greenleaf (Jean Peters), who just happens to be the daughter of the university president (Ray Collins).

But there seems to be no problem with Simpson dating his student. The real issue is whether the professor will be able to financially support Debbie and a family. And Debbie appears much more interested in acquiring a husband than learning the periodic table. In fact, her fixation upon marriage and family fits well with the postwar feminine mystique for middle- and upper-class white women described by Betty Friedan.[18] Simpson, a World War II veteran, displays an insecurity regarding his economic prospects, an apprehension shared by Americans who feared a return to the depression conditions of the 1930s. However, Simpson looks to the World War II alliance between science and industry for his financial salvation. He brings Debbie to his laboratory where the professor has concocted an insect repellent formula for tree bark. He hopes to sell his discovery to a chemical company and pursue a research career in industry.

As they enthusiastically embrace, evidently contemplating their contributions to the postwar baby boom, their loving moment is shattered by a baseball that crashes through the window and smashes Simpson's experiment. A despondent Simpson proclaims he cannot replicate the formula (Evidently, he is a scientist who does not take careful notes.), and he sends Debbie away. Their dreams of a family have been destroyed by an outside force over which they have no control. Americans who had suffered through the dark days of the Great Depression and World War II would have little problem identifying with such a perspective. With the end of what Thomas Engelhard terms America's historical victory culture, due to the advent of the atomic bomb and Cold War, Americans were exposed to a threat of nuclear annihilation over which they exercised little direction.[19]

Following the dismissal of Debbie and what he assumes is the dashing of his hopes for the American Dream, Simpson begins to clean up the debris of the laboratory. When he attempts to throw away the baseball that shattered his domestic bliss, the professor discovers that the ball, which was covered with the insect repellent formula, is impervious to wood. In fact, the ball swerves around chunks of lumber, such as baseball bats (This film, of course, was made before the introduction of metal bats into the collegiate game.). This amazing disclosure provides Simpson with an idea, and he retrieves what is left of his formula.

The next morning he tests his hypothesis by tossing batting practice to two dimwitted but athletic chemistry students, who are unable to hit Simpson's pitches as he doctors the baseball from a cloth soaked in the formula and concealed in his baseball glove. His success with the collegiate ballplayers gives Vernon the inspiration to become a self-made man in the Horatio Alger tradition. He marches off to Professor Greenleaf's home and asks the university president for an emergency leave of absence. The president, along with his wife and daughter, assume that Simpson has made a major scientific breakthrough and is off to share his findings with chemical company representatives.

Instead, Simpson is traveling to St. Louis, seeking a major league tryout. He bursts into the office of St. Louis manager Jimmy Dolan (Ted de Corsia), whose team is languishing in the standings due to a pitching shortage. The young upstart insists that he be given an opportunity to pitch for the St. Louis franchise. As he is being thrown out the office door, Simpson insults the team owner, Mr. Stone (Ed Begley). Demonstrating the superiority of ownership over management, Stone decides to make an example of the impertinent young man, ordering manager Dolan to let Simpson pitch batting practice. To the astonishment of Dolan and Stone, the pitching prospect, aided by the concealed substance in his glove, proves unhittable. Stone immediately proposes a contract, and Simpson makes it clear that his interest in pursuing a baseball career is based on financial concerns. The unheralded pitcher insists that he be promptly paid a thousand dollars for every victory. In the era before free agency, Simpson drives a tough bargain, motivated by his desire to secure enough money to marry Debbie and attain the American Dream.

However, Simpson does not want his fiancée and her family to learn that he is pursuing success in baseball rather than science. So he assumes the alias King Kelly. After his first pitching victory, Simpson/Kelly uses his money to purchase a diamond engagement ring for Debbie, who mistakenly believes that her lover has procured his wealth through criminal activity. The rapidity with which Debbie and her family come to this conclusion is illustrative of the culture's uncertainty regarding financial stability and a reminder of how some Americans had been forced into a life of crime in order to survive during the troubled 1930s.

The club assigns Kelly's catcher Monk Lonigan (Paul Douglas) to room with the rookie phenomenon and keep a close watch on its investment. Although not the most intelligent man in the universe, Lonigan is able to discern Kelly's true identity and informs Debbie, although Kelly/Simpson remains unaware that she is cognizant of his pitching career. As Kelly/ Simpson goes on to win thirty-eight games for St. Louis, including a no-hitter which the film carefully documents. Thus, Kelly earns thirty-eight thousand dollars (a rather hefty baseball salary for the late 1940s) and pitches St. Louis into the World Series against New York (Although one may assume the Yankees, team logos are not used.).

As many critics suggested, Kelly's rise to baseball prominence included numerous implausible plot devices. For example, Kelly's ball dances all over the plate as batters are unable to make contact with the doctored baseball. Therefore, the logical viewer might conclude that Kelly pitched a no-hitter every outing, for until the film's final game, no batter is shown making contact with one of Kelly's offerings. Furthermore, no umpire ever checks the hurler's glove to see if the pitcher is defacing the ball to make the pitches hop. Hall of Famer Gaylord Perry, amongst other pitchers accused of doctoring the ball, would have loved to pitch with the umpiring crews officiating Kelly's games. More astute baseball fans will also have trouble with the fact that in his first relief appearance, with runners on base, Kelly goes into his patented double pump wind up rather than work from the stretch.

However, Kelly gets into trouble as he prepares to start the seventh game of the World Series against New York. He cannot locate his last bottle of formula, for Lonigan assumes that the container is hair tonic. Although he is unable to comb his hair with a wooden brush after applying what he considers to be hair grooming preparation, Lonigan loans the bottle to manager Dolan, who is losing his hair. When an alarmed Kelly attempts to retrieve the formula, the container is accidentally dropped, and Kelly has to pitch the most important game of the season without the aid of his concoction. The result is that the New York club is able to hit Kelly, but the St. Louis offense keeps Kelly in the game, and he enters the ninth inning with a one run lead. With two outs and the bases loaded, Kelly spears a line drive with his bare pitching hand, and St. Louis wins the World Series.

Following the game, a medical examination reveals that the injury to Kelly's hand will end his pitching career. Kelly is barely able to suppress a smile when he hears the news, for the scientist/pitcher realizes that without his secret formula his career is already finished. With the excuse of a broken hand for his retirement, the secret to his success need never be revealed.

Although, Kelly/Simpson did gain considerable money from his baseball season, he remains worried about his long-term financial prospects. He returns to his fiancée, assuming that his unexplained disappearance will make it impossible for him to regain his university position. However, Debbie reveals to her parents and the university community that Kelly is, in actuality, Vernon Simpson. When Simpson arrives at the university, he is met by an enthusiastic crowd who want to congratulate the professor on his World Series triumph.

Also present at the reunion is university president Greenleaf, who informs Vernon that he may not retain his position as a chemistry instructor. Instead, Simpson is asked to head the university's new research facility, which is a donation from the St. Louis team owner Stone, who stipulates that his former pitcher must direct the new center. Simpson now has the financial means and security to marry Debbie and live happily ever after.

There are several disturbing aspects to this postwar success parable. Like many of the characters in the Horatio Alger stories, Vernon Simpson has not achieved the American Dream through the Benjamin Franklin recipe of hard work. Instead, Simpson has to rely upon guile and cheating to navigate the difficult shoals of the post–World War II economy. While this point was lost upon most reviewers, Philip T. Hartung of *Commonweal* found it troubling that the film's happy ending was established through "quite unethical" means, which never seemed to prompt any soul searching on the part of the film's protagonist.[21]

Hartung's observation has considerable merit, and one is left with the question of why few other commentators took issue with the means employed by Simpson to secure a foundation for his anticipated family. Some of this moral ambiguity is perhaps reflective of the nation's insecurities regarding its economic future. It may also be indicative of the paradoxical attitudes concerning the role of scientists and science in the postwar world. The development of the atomic bomb was initially hailed as a great accomplishment; according the conventional wisdom of the time, it ended World War II and prevented the loss of countless American lives in the anticipated bloody invasion of the Japanese islands. However, with the advent of the Cold War and Soviet detonation of a nuclear devise, the atomic bomb's presence was less reassuring to Americans. In *Screams of Reason*, critic David J. Skal suggests, "From its first deployment, the atomic bomb began radiating metaphors about knowledge, sin, and science that gave startling new life to ancient ideas."[22] Skal argues that the promise of nuclear energy was quickly transformed into images of Frankenstein monster who might devour the nation which created it. Popular manifestations of the ambiguity with which the American public perceived science is apparent in the box office success of the science fiction film genre of the 1950s. In films, such as *The Thing* (1951), *Them* (1954), and *The Amazing Colossal Man* (1957), scientific research unleashes forces over which the scientists have no control, and nature, like the Frankenstein monster, seeks a harsh revenge.[23] Perhaps these popular attitudes of moral ambiguity regarding scientists and their work explain why viewers and critics were not more alarmed by Vernon Simpson's lack of ethics. The concept of by any means necessary was not invented by Malcolm X.

A softer note is struck in the 1951 production of *Angels in the Outfield* in which the fantasy component comes from heaven rather than secular science. Nevertheless, reviewers were no more poised to accept the divine intervention of angels than scientific formulas into the realm of baseball. Hollis Alpert of *Saturday Review* described *Angels in the Outfield* as "bogged down in the worst kind of corn, involving nuns, miracles, and a heavenly baseball team." In *The New Yorker*, John McCarten remarked that star Paul Douglas looked uneasy in his role, "as well he might, wading around in this sort of treacle." But other reviewers found the film pleasing light fare. Philip T. Hartung of *Commonweal* thought the film "almost sentimentally sticky at times," but the critic concluded it was "so amusing that it should appeal to all moviegoers even if they don't care for movies about baseball players, nuns, and angels." *Christian Century* was not offended by the film's treatment of religion, describing the picture as "fun, performed with zest and good timing for comedy."[24]

Released by MGM to take advantage of interest in the 1951 World Series, *Angels in the Outfield* was based upon a screenplay by Dorothy Kingsley and George Wells and directed by Clarence Brown, who was nearing the end of a film career which included such outstanding films as *Anna Christie* (1930), *Ah Wilderness* (1935), and *The Yearling* (1946).[25]

The film stars Paul Douglas as the temperamental Guffy McGovern, manager of the inept Pittsburgh Pirates. Focusing the film on the Pirates brought a note of realism to this fantasy feature, for the Pittsburgh franchise was the doormat of the National League in the early 1950s. The film even includes a cameo from Bing Crosby, who was one of the team's owners.[26] The losing ways of the Pirates are hardly helped by McGovern's anger and constant cursing, which is intentionally garbled on the film's soundtrack so as not to offend family audiences. Rather than reflecting the optimism often associated with America in the 1950s, McGovern's animosity and insecurity might be more accurately described as the American nightmare. However, McGovern mends his ways when he is visited by the Archangel Gabriel and the Heavenly Choir Nine, whom Gabriel informs McGovern, have a lifetime batting average of .321. The Archangel observes that McGovern's language and negative attitude have drawn the attention of Heaven, which is not pleased with McGovern. The shaken manager begins to control his cursing and temper, offering compliments and encouragement to the players. McGovern even attempts to expand his cultural horizons, reading Shakespeare's *The Tempest* during the club's road trips. As McGovern transforms, so do the Pirates, as the team commences to win and move up the National League standings. All seems fine until Sister Edwina (Spring Byington) takes orphan Bridget White (Donna Corcoran) to a Pittsburgh home game. The orphan claims to see angels guiding the actions of the Pirate players, although film viewers never actually observe the heavenly representatives, who remain off-screen. Reporter Jennifer Page (Janet Leigh), who has been assigned to provide a female perspective on the game, writes a newspaper piece on Bridget White and her angels. The story brings unwelcome publicity to the orphanage, and Page apologizes for her lack of sensitivity. However, an unanticipated result of this story is to drive the beleaguered participants, Page, White, and McGovern, together into a family situation as they face the scrutiny of more cynical reporters and outsiders.

When McGovern is hit in the head by a foul ball, he inadvertently informs reporters that he speaks with angels. Disgruntled radio announcer Fred Bayles (Keenan Wynn), who has a personal vendetta against McGovern, proclaims that the manger's pronouncement is a disgrace to the game of baseball. The Commissioner of baseball vows to investigate, arriving in Pittsburgh on the eve of the season's last game, which the Pirates must win to achieve their miracle pennant drive. Bayles seems to represent the forces of cynicism, insecurity, and corruption threatening the American family. A Freudian psychologist, and Freud was in vogue during the 1950s, concludes that McGovern is delusional. However, an ecumenical assemblage of theologians, consisting of a rabbi, priest, and minister, step forward in support of the Pittsburgh manager and the possibility of miracles in everyday life, although they have to cut their testimony short for the men of the cloth have tickets to that afternoon's game. Then Bayles questions the young orphan, but McGovern, feeling paternalistic and protective, is unable to control his temper, slugging the inquisitor.

After angel feathers fall on his desk, the Commissioner declares McGovern competent, urging everyone to get out to the ballpark. The Archangel Gabriel chastises McGovern for not maintaining control over his temper. The penalty for striking Bayles is that the manager is on his own; the angels will not intervene in the final game. Left to his own devices, the Pittsburgh skipper decides to name aging veteran Saul Hellman (Bruce Bennett) as his starting pitcher, for McGovern has learned that the athlete will be joining the Heavenly Choir Nine during the off season. Hellman struggles throughout the game, but enters the ninth inning with a one run lead. McGovern tells the veteran that it is his game to finish, and Hellman rewards McGovern's confidence by striking out the final batter. Divine intervention has helped Pittsburgh achieve a miracle pennant.

But beyond the narrow confines of baseball, McGovern has been rehabilitated, and, as part of his redemption, he forms a family with Page (Although Douglas does seem a little old for Leigh.) and White. But the final shot of the film suggests a considerable lack of confidence in the American family's future. In a darkened and deserted stadium, which looms menacingly over the newly constructed family, McGovern embraces White and Page, invoking the names of the baseball deities, Babe Ruth, Lou Gehrig, and Christy Mathewson, who will be needed for guidance and protection during the troubled days ahead. The film's conclusion may certainly be condemned as overly sentimental and corny, but, on the other hand, it hardly evokes an optimistic image for the American family in the postwar era. In addition, the film implies that the heavenly forces have tamed the rugged individualism of McGovern. He has been domesticated and is better prepared to take his place within the organizational society of the 1950s. Yet, McGovern now seems dependent upon divine intervention to safeguard his family.[27]

Again seeking to cash in on World Series interest, Paramount released its fantasy baseball picture *Rhubarb* in the fall of 1951. However, this film about a cat inheriting a major league team failed to capture the box office of *Angels in the Outfield*, and critics were nearly universal in their panning of the picture's production values. Hollis Alpert of the *Saturday Review* found *Rhubarb* "utterly unconvincing," with the quality of the baseball action in the film reaching a new low for Hollywood. *The New York Times*, in sync with most reviews of *Rhubarb*, argued that the film paled in comparison to the satirical novel by H. Allen Smith, upon which the screenplay was based. Nevertheless, *Newsweek* did publish a positive notice, extolling the comic genius of director Arthur Lubin, who was best known for a series of films featuring Francis the talking mule.[28]

Smith's novel *Rhubarb* was published in 1945 and was a wide ranging satire of American life, but the Dorothy Reid and Francis Cockrell screenplay chose to focus upon the baseball aspects of the story.[29] The film begins with the decision of millionaire Thaddeus J. Banner to will his estate and business enterprises, including the abysmal Brooklyn Loons baseball franchise, to his cat Rhubarb.[30] Banner's press agent Eric Yeager (Ray Milland) is tapped by the deceased to serve as Rhubarb's manager and guardian. The will's provisions are a shock to Banner's estranged daughter Myra (Elsie Holmes), who immediately seeks court action to challenge Rhubarb's inheritance. Yeager's private life is also disrupted when his girlfriend Polly Sickles (Jan Sterling), daughter of the Loons manager, begins to sneeze when Rhubarb is in her presence, apparently displaying an allergic reaction to the feline.

On the baseball front, the inept Brooklyn Loons are embarrassed that their new owner is a cat, and the players subject both Rhubarb and Yeager to considerable ridicule. Yet, after inadvertently touching Rhubarb, one of the players contributes a key hit to a Brooklyn rally, and the Loons break a long losing streak. The players then change their tune on Rhubarb, constantly rubbing the feline for good luck, and Brooklyn starts to rise in the standings. The team even alters its name to the Brooklyn Rhubarbs.

When the Rhubarbs reach the World Series, the plot thickens. Myra Banner, whose court action to overturn Rhubarb's inheritance was denied, throws in with gambler Pencil Louie (the Damon Runyon influence is obvious here) to fix the series by kidnapping Rhubarb. The Brooklyn players have grown dependent upon the feline, assuming that they cannot win without their good luck charm. Again the viewer of these baseball fantasy films is presented with a sense of corruption and instability at the heart of the American dream. Just as with Vernon Simpson and Debbie Greenleaf in *It Happens Every Spring,* the achievement of success is precarious and may be snatched away at any moment by outside forces over which the individual has no control. And, of course, the image of baseball and gamblers brings to mind allegations of the Chicago White Sox conspiring with gamblers to "fix" the 1919 World Series with Cincinnati, thus evoking the dark side of America and its national pastime.[31]

These baseball fantasy films prefer to flirt with but not give in to the dark side. Therefore, Rhubarb escapes from his captors and heads for the ballpark. He arrives in time to restore the confidence of his players, and the Brooklyn franchise captures the World Series. However, Rhubarb's interest in escaping and getting to the ball game was more motivated by love for the feline Su-Lin, rather than the sport of baseball.

The film concludes with a brief epilogue in which Eric Yeager and Polly Sickles are strolling through Central Park, accompanied by Rhubarb, Su-Lin, and a litter of kittens. We learn that Polly's sneezing fits are due not to Rhubarb but to the vicuna lining of his cage. The American family has been reunited and preserved from the forces of corruption. Yeager and Sickles have achieved the American Dream. But their success has little to do with the work ethic of the self-made man championed by Benjamin Franklin in *Poor Richard's Almanack*.[32]

In conclusion, the baseball fantasy films of the late 1940s and early 1950s, *It Happens Every Spring*, *Angels in the Outfield*, and *Rhubarb*, provide viewers with optimistic happy Hollywood endings. But in order to attain this outcome, supernatural forces, whether it be a scientist's secret formula (the alchemist's stone), angels, or good luck associated with an animal, are necessary to save the American family from the threat of instability and dissolution. While these films fail to directly confront such issues as the Cold War, nuclear energy, the atomic bomb, changing family structure, and fears of another depression, which were clear and present dangers to the American family, the theme of supernatural intervention does imply strong elements of pessimism and a lack of confidence regarding the American Dream. It should also be noted that these films create a white universe of baseball and suburbia in which Jackie Robinson, the civil rights movement, and an integrated society seem to have no place. Perhaps another unmentioned fear for white America, indirectly captured in these baseball fantasy films, is the threat posed by the civil rights movement to an already precarious economic position.[33] The prosperity of the 1950s was often more apparent in hindsight.

It is also worth observing that supernatural themes in baseball films would once again become popular in the 1980s, a time period of apparent conservatism and economic growth in which, nevertheless, many Americans did not share. In films such as *The Natural* (1984) and *Field of Dreams* (1989), there appears a yearning for a purer, more innocent America, "to the mythic American past evoked by that quintessential conservative Ronald Reagan."[34] While Reagan did portray Grover Cleveland Alexander in the 1951 picture *The Winning Team*, these were not exactly the happiest of personal times for the actor whose career and marriage were languishing.[35] Nostalgia is a powerful but dangerous concept, in which the mythology of baseball may be employed in a manipulative fashion. There is often a tendency to view both the 1950s and 1980s through rose-colored glasses, a perception encouraged by the fantasy baseball films of the two periods. But these films require a closer reading, for buried within these film texts are clues for better understanding the complexities, paradoxes, and ambiguities of American history and culture. *It Happens Every Spring*, *Angels in the Outfield*, and *Rhubarb* may be light fare, but they also provide a glimpse into the darker side of the American Dream, which we should not allow nostalgia to eclipse. Calls for supernatural intervention in America's past cannot be ignored if we are to successfully grapple with the lack of confidence and insecurities which plagued Vernon Simpson and Debbie Greenleaf, Guffy McGovern and Jennifer Page, and Eric Yeager and Polly Sickles. We ignore this historical legacy at our own peril.

Notes

1. Gary Dickerson, *Cinema of Baseball: Images of America, 1929–1989* (Westport, CT: Meckler, 1991), 86. While the musical *Damn Yankees*, based upon Douglas Wallop's novel *The Year the Yankees Lost the Pennant* (1954), was produced in 1955, the film version of the Broadway hit was not released until 1958 and is thus outside the parameters of this study. Although many of the comments made in this paper would apply to *Damn Yankees*.

2. For a more realistic examination of families in the 1950s, see: Stephanie Coontz, *The Way We Never Were: American Families and the Nostalgia Trap* (New York: Basic Books, 1992).

3. For historical interpretations and sociological insights into the Cold War period of the late 1940s and early 1950s, see: John Kenneth Galbraith, *The Affluent Society* (Boston: Houghton Mifflin, 1970); William H. Whyte, Jr., *The Organization Man* (Garden City, NY: Doubleday, 1957); David Riesman, Nathan Glazer, and Reuel Denny, *The Lonely Crowd* (Garden City, NY: Doubleday, 1955); and Godfrey Hodgson, *America in Our Time* (Garden City, NY: Doubleday, 1976).

4. William H. Chafe, *The Unfinished Journey: America Since World War II* (New York: Oxford University Press, 1995), 111–145.

5. Michael Harrington, *The Other America* (New York: Macmillan, 1963), passim.

6. For the impact of McCarthyism, see: David Caute, *The Great Fear: The Anti-Communist Purge Under Truman and Eisenhower* (New York: Simon and Schuster, 1978); Richard Fried, *Nightmare in Red: The McCarthy Years in Perspective* (New York: Oxford University Press, 1990); and Ellen Schrecker, *Many Are the Crimes: McCarthyism in America* (Boston: Little, Brown, and Co., 1998).

7. James Gilbert, *A Cycle of Outrage: America's Reaction to the Juvenile Delinquent in the 1950s* (New York: Oxford University Press, 1986), passim.

8. Alian Silver and Elizabeth Ward, *Film Noir: An Encyclopedic Reference to the American Style* (Woodstock, NY: Overlook Press, 1980),passim; and Michael L. Stephens, *Film Noir: A Comprehensive Illustrated Reference to Movies, Terms, and Persons* (Jefferson, NC : McFarland, 1995), passim.

9. For the golden age of boxing cinema, see: Marc P. Singer, "Fear of the Public Sphere: The Boxing Film in Cold War America (1947–1957)," *Film & History*, 31.1 (2001), 22–27; Grindon Leger, "Body and Soul: The Structure of Meaning in the Boxing Film Genre," *Cinema Journal*, 35 (1996), 54–69; and Donald Mrozek, "The Cult and Ritual of Toughness in Cold War America," in David Wiggins, ed., *Sport in America: From Wicked Amusement to National Obsession* (Champaign, IL: Human Kinetics Press, 1995), 257–268.

10. For the baseball bio-pics of the post war era, see: Dickerson, 58–88; Howard Good, *Diamonds in the Dark: America, Baseball, and the Movies* (Lanham, MD: Scarecrow Press, 1997), 53–80; and Rob Edelman, *Great Baseball Films* (New York: Citadel Press, 1994), 75–85.

11. Bill James, *Bill James Historical Baseball Abstract* (New York: Villard Books,1986), 193, 209; U. S. Congress, *Organized Baseball: Report of the Subcommittee on Study of Monopoly Power of the Committee on the Judiciary*, House Report No. 2002,

82 Cong., 2 Sess. (1952), passim; and Stephen R. Lowe, *Congress and Professional Sports, 1910–1992* (Bowling Green, OH: Bowling Green State University Popular Press, 1995), passim.

12. For Frank Capra and *It's a Wonderful Life*, see: Jeanine Basinger, ed., *The It's a Wonderful Life Book* (New York: Knopf, 1986); James Agee, "*It's a Wonderful Life*," *The Nation*, 164 (February 15, 1947), . 193–194; Richard Griffith, "*It's a Wonderful Life* and Postwar Realism," *New Movies: The National Board of Review Magazine*, 22 (February–March, 1947), 5–8; and Raymond Carney, *American Vision: The Films of Frank Capra* (Cambridge: Cambridge University Press, 1986), 377–435.

13. "Religion," in Richard Layman, ed., *American Decades, 1950–1959* (Detroit: Gale Research Group, 1994), 377–398.

14. For additional information on *Bacon*, see: Douglas Gomery, "Lloyd Bacon," in Laurie Collier Hillstrom, ed., *International Dictionary of Films and Filmmakers: Directors* (Detroit: St. James Press, 1997), 51–52.

15. "Movies," *The New Republic*, 120 (June 27, 1949), 22; Bosley Crowther, "*It Happens Every Spring*," *The New York Times*, June 11, 1949, 11; John McCarten, "Baseball Tricks and Royal *Waves*," *The New Yorker*, 25 *(June 18, 1942)*, 52; "Current Feature Films," Ball," *Newsweek*, 33 (June 13, 1949), 82–85; *Christian Century*, 66 (July 20, 1949), 879; and "On the Ball," *Newsweek*, 33 (June 13, 1949), 82–85.

16. For the impact of what would become known as McCarthyism upon artistic and political expression in Hollywood, see: Peter Roffman and Jim Purdy, *The Hollywood Social Problem Film: Madness, Despair, and Politics from the Depression to the Fifties* (Bloomington: Indiana University Press, 1981), 84–299.

17. For a detailed plot summary of *It Happens Every Spring*, see: Hal Erickson, *Baseball in the Movies: A Comprehensive Reference, 1915–1991* (Jefferson, NC: McFarland, 1992), 168–173. The film is also available on videocassette from Fox Video, Inc., Beverly Hills, California.

18. Betty Friedan, *The Feminine Mystique* (New York: Dell Publishing, 1963), passim.

19. Thomas Engelhard, *The End of Victory Culture: Cold War America and the Disillusioning of a Generation* (New York: Basic Books, 1995), passim.

20. For Horatio Alger, see: Horatio Alger, *Ragged Dick and Mark the Match Boy* (New York: Collier Books, 1962); and Richard Hofstadter, *Social Darwinism in American Thought* (Philadelphia: University of Pennsylvania Press, 1944).

21. Philip T. Hartung, "How Those Boys Do Cut Up!," *Commonweal*, 50 (June 24, 1949), 272.

22. For post war attitudes regarding science, see: Paul Boyer, *By the Bomb's Early Light: American Thought and Culture at the Dawn of the Atomic Age* (New York: Pantheon Books, 1985); David J. Skal, *Screams of Reason: Mad Science and Modern Culture* (New York: Norton, 1998), and Andrew Tudor, *Monsters and Mad Scientists: A Cultural History of the Horror Movie* (Cambridge: Basil Blackwell, 1989).

23. For a good interpretive history of the science fiction genre during the 1950s, see: Patrick Lucanio, *Them Or Us: Archetypal Interpretations of Fifties Alien Invasion Films* (Bloomington: Indiana University Press, 1987).

24. Hollis Alpert, "*SRL* Goes to the Movies," *Saturday Review*, 34 (September 22, 1951), 30; John McCarten, "The Current Cinema," *The New Yorker*, 27 (October 27, 1951), 82; Philip T. Hartung, "*Angels in the Outfield*," *Commonweal*, 55 (October 26, 1951), 64; and "Current Feature Films," *Christian Century*, 68 (October 17, 1951), 1,207.

25. DeWitt Bodeen, "Clarence Brown," in Hillstrom, ed., *Directors*, 118–119.

26. For a detailed summary of *Angels in the Outfield*, see: Erickson, 29–33. The film is also available in videocassette from Warner Home Video, Santa Monica, California.

27. For the post–World War II American family, see: Arlene Skolnick, *Embattled Paradise: The American Family in an Age of Uncertainty* (New York: Basic Books, 1991).

28. Hollis Alpert, "*SRL* Goes to the Movies," *Saturday Review*, 34 (September 22, 1951), 31; *The New York Times*, August 31, 1951, 12; *Christian Century*, 68 (October 24, 1951), 1,239; and "*Rhubarb*," *Newsweek*, 38 (September 3, 1951), 72.

29. For a detailed plot synopsis of *Rhubarb*, see: Erickson, 254–261.

30. While the Brooklyn Dodgers would become one of baseball's power houses in the post-war era, the franchise symbolized on the field baseball frustration and ineptitude during the 1930s and 1940s.

31. Elliot Asinof, *Eight Men Out* (New York: Holt, Rinehart, and Winston, 1963), passim.

32. Ben Franklin, *Poor Richard's Almanacks*, introduction by Van Wyck Brooks (New York: Paddington Press, 1976), passim.

33. For the concept of whiteness in America, see: Grace Elizabeth Hale, *Making Whiteness: The Culture of Segregation in the South, 1890–1940* (New York: Vintage Books, 1999).

34. Stephen Holden, "Today's Hits Yearn for Old Times," *The New York Times* , August 13, 1989, A&L25; Alan Nadel, *Flatlining on the Field of Dreams: Cultural Narratives in the Films of President Reagan's America* (New Brunswick, NJ: Rutgers University Press, 1997), passim; and Edmund Morris, *Dutch: A Memoir of Ronald Reagan* (New York: Random House, 1999), passim.

The Actor as Ballplayer, the Ballplayer as Actor

George Grella

Anyone who has ever watched a baseball game of any kind at any level of competition, and anyone who has ever seen a baseball movie of any level of quality — a broad category which probably includes just about all of the American population out of diapers — no doubt recognizes the profound difference between the two representations of the sport, on the field and on the screen.[1] One of the most obvious sources of that difference lies in the character and meaning of the particular performance within the construct of the two activities, that is, the actions and behavior of the people involved, the actors and the ballplayers, or in other words, to end the elaborate windup and get to the delivery, the actual play of the game. As even the most inexperienced fan and the least perceptive observer will recognize, baseball players on the screen differ considerably from those in what we like to think of as real life. Most actors play baseball as if they were only, well, acting, most look discernibly less talented and skilled than the Little League, sandlot, scholastic, collegiate, minor league, or major league players they impersonate. Most of them, in fact, perform in all areas of the game with a spectacular, sometimes laughable, incompetence. They tend to run the bases as if they were still back in ballet class; they usually swing the bat with the power, grace, and efficiency of ancient ladies beating dusty carpets; in the field, they slap their gloves at the ball like a jungle traveler flailing at mosquitoes; and they throw with a motion resembling the gestures of monarchs greeting their loyal subjects or clerics blessing their congregations.

The concept of the art of acting, of impersonation, of playing a part, however, should surely encompass the task of portraying a baseball player. Actors, as we all understand, play all sorts of roles, some of them far removed from their particular backgrounds, knowledge, experience, even training. It's their profession, it's what they do—as one of my favorite characters in Conrad states, in a somewhat different context, "the trade demands it."[2] Often with extraordinary success, actors therefore play heroes and villains, saints and sinners, cops and crooks, cowboys and Indians, vampires and priests, good guys/girls and bad guys/girls, Hamlet and Claudius, Othello and Iago, Sam Spade and Captain Queeg, Stanley Kowalski and Willy Loman, even people of other sizes, ages, colors, sexes. On the one hand, the art *is* called acting, after all, a kind of beautiful and inspired pretending, in which a man or woman attempts to look, speak, and behave like someone else, who may be entirely different from themselves, and convince onlookers that, if only for a little while, he or she actually is that other person.

On the other hand, the famous magic of cinema, that most miraculous of the arts, can work wonders, creating faraway places of great strangeness or beauty, transporting audiences to outer or inner space, moving backward or forward in time; motion pictures can make monsters, beasts, and aliens; recreate ancient Rome or show us the world of tomorrow; boldly violate the laws of physics and biology; deceive viewers with optical effects, computer wizardry, chemistry, and advanced technology. The arts by their very nature deal in the business of illusion, but the cinema must be the most illusionary of them all: King Kong, you must remember, was only three and a half feet tall. Even those many great actors who practice the famous Stanislavski Method, which dominates most modern film technique over the last half-century, seldom attain a credible performance as athletes. They delve into their roles, immersing themselves fully in their characters, examining personalities, thinking not only about lines and meanings, but also about the famous subtext, all that the character thinks or feels but does not say, the unspoken truths we all sense in others and ourselves. Whatever their other demonstrated abilities and accomplishments, however, even the finest practitioners of the Method cannot in fact investigate fully enough or descend deeply enough into a particular part, or dwell inside the role in a manner that convinces most audiences that they are the athletes they play: somehow, for whatever reasons, they cannot fake that.

A number of examples chosen from some extraordinarily varied films demonstrates the talents and skills of some well known and in many cases distinguished actors, along with their limitations as ballplayers. The pairing of the particular motion pictures, the side-by-side comparison, may reveal both the virtues and the defects in the performances of some famous and even remarkable artists. Although an uncountable number of actors have appeared either in baseball movies, in baseball uniforms, or have played baseball in some form on-screen, a mere selection of citations from only a few motion pictures should provide a reasonably typical demonstration of both acting and playing ball. The moments, scenes, and sequences from several different decades and featuring several generations of actors, will, I hope, serve to represent the hundreds of other films, scenes, sequences, and performers.

In *High Noon* (1952), for example, the retired marshal, played by Gary Cooper, a grizzled veteran who rode the dusty trails of many Westerns over the course of his grand career, makes the fateful decision to return to his home town on his wedding day, despite the pleas of his pacifist Quaker wife (Grace Kelly), and, of course, ends up defending the unworthy pop-ulace of the wretched little burg, achieving a most ambiguous victory over the bad guys and coming to understand the loneliness of a good man in a bad time. As in many other movies, he demonstrates that he can handle a horse and a gun far better than the horsehide and hickory of another activ-ity in his role as Lou Gehrig in *Pride of the Yankees* (1942), one of the most popular and, frankly, one of the most overrated baseball movies of them all. A montage that shows Gehrig honing his skills through college and minor league ball until he makes it to the major leagues provides several examples of an actor desperately attempting to look like a first baseman and quite obviously failing, especially in the fielding, throwing, and run-ning aspects of the game. (Notice too, that in the most famous farewell to baseball of them all, Gehrig's own words and his peculiar moment of bittersweet triumph prove as ambiguous as the Marshall's in *High Noon*).

If Cooper became identified with a number of important American heroes, including, in particular, the cowboy, so Tony Perkins, oddly, became identified with a series of psychologically disturbed characters. A few years before he took on his most famous role, of Norman Bates in *Psy-cho* (1960), quite surprisingly, he played an emotionally unbalanced ballplayer, the very real Jimmy Piersall, in the screen version of the outfielder's memoir, *Fear Strikes Out* (1957); it seems more than passing strange that his portrayal of the troubled Piersall may have inspired the choice of Perkins for the serial killer and amateur taxidermist of Hitch-cock's classic. His appearance in the picture suggests a further, unexplored dimension to the artistic potential of baseball movies as a place where the actor can showcase perhaps other than athletic skills. Interestingly enough, the fictional innkeeper and the real life outfielder apparently share some roughly similar Oedipal problems, the former acting out a pathological devotion to his mother, the latter enduring the bullying domination of an irascible, obsessive father. Despite the important affinities between the two roles, the actor obviously suffers greater inadequacies masquerading as an athlete than as an apparently pleasant, if repressed young man who also happens to be a sexual psychopath. Perkins' fielding and throwing, jerky and graceless, need a great deal of work, even resembling that battery of tics, stutters, and twitches Perkins developed for Norman Bates. Perkins may not swing a bat with much potency, but wields that chef's knife with deadly skill and efficiency (in fact, it became the cinematic serial killer's weapon of choice and truly deserves to be named the Tony Perkins autograph model).

In a later decade, Robert De Niro, one of the most honored and admired actors of our time, played, among a long list of memorable roles (including mental defectives, psychopaths, gangsters, and, yes, athletes) in scores of very different movies, including *Mean Streets* (1973), *The Godfather, Part II* (1974), and *Awakenings* (1990). In one of his earliest successes, *Taxi Driver* (1976), as the title character, De Niro appeared just as crazy, violent, and sexually confused as Norman Bates; he works out fanatically, collecting an arsenal of weapons and strengthening his body for some as yet unclear purpose, but after shooting a pimp and a drug dealer in a cleansing bloodbath, his Travis Bickle ends up as a hero. In *Raging Bull* (1980), he underwent rigorous training to play the middleweight boxing champion Jake LaMotta, and then famously gained 40 pounds to show the fighter at a later time. Although he certainly made a convincing boxer — some commentators even suggested he could be ranked among the top twenty middleweights in the world — as the catcher Bruce Pearson in the much loved *Bang the Drum Slowly* (1973), his performance at the plate, on the bases, and in the field, let alone his stature and his apparent physical frailty, suggests that baseball, as its students understand, remains the most difficult and demanding of all the popular sports (consider Michael Jordan's record in the minor leagues a few years ago). Against the evidence of his and our eyes, his manager (Vincent Gardenia) asserts that his catcher is a big, strong young man who should be able to hit home runs; apparently the director, John Hancock, forgetting that King Kong was only three feet, six inches tall, believed such assertions constituted the celebrated magic of cinema.

A younger actor, one of the more talented of his generation, John Cusack started his career in teen movies like *Sixteen Candles* (1984), then, growing up on the screen in effect, appeared in such movies as *The Sure Thing* (1985) and *Say Anything ...* (1989), matured into somewhat larger and more significant roles, as with his Nelson Rockefeller in *The Cradle Will Rock* (1999). Some students of cinema and sport may remember him as Buck Weaver, third baseman for the 1919 Chicago White Sox in *Eight Men Out* (1988). In that movie, he gets the opportunity to deliver a set speech on the joys of baseball, its everlasting youth and innocence, to some kids, and swings the bat with at least some competence, but at his first fielding opportunity throws the ball as if he had learned the craft on some minor league team, perhaps playing alongside his famous colleagues, Gary Cooper and Tony Perkins.

Many of those same students of the cinema and the sport would probably be surprised to realize that James Earl Jones, of all people, enjoys what may be the longest and oddly, perhaps the most varied baseball career among contemporary stars. Although sometimes overacting with a powerful screen presence that tends to overpower other cast members, he also possesses an undeniable *gravitas*, and he also actually plays ball with some discernible competence; as the years go by, however, and his girth increases, that *gravitas* turns into inertia, and his association with the game evolves into one of vicarious activity and memory. In *The Great White Hope* (1970), as the heavyweight champion Jack Jefferson (obviously based on Jack Johnson), he eludes law enforcement authorities by dressing up in the uniform of a Negro league team and leaving his mother's home with the other players. In *The Bingo Long Traveling All-Stars and Motor Kings* (1976), his size and presence enable him to make an acceptable fictionalized catcher based on Josh Gibson–he squats behind the plate like a veteran of the diamond, throws and hits with an acceptable semblance of actual athletic skill.

Out of uniform but very much in the game, and growing larger and slower, he swings the bat and runs the bases in a pickup game that joins Italian and black miners in *Matewan* (1987), another instance of baseball on film serving as a means of assimilation.[3] As an aged, blind former Negro league star, a sort of Tiresias figure, in *The Sandlot* (1993), he recalls his playing time with Babe Ruth, shows some boys pictures of his glory days in the Negro leagues, and instructs them in the proper conduct of the game. He probably enjoys his most memorable moments, however, in the most successful baseball film of them all, *Field of Dreams* (1989), where he delivers the famous oration, an eloquent set speech, on the beauty and meaning of baseball in American culture, and perhaps most important, in effect, becomes an honorary member of the Chicago White Sox, the same team featured in *Eight Men Out*. Shoeless Joe Jackson invites him to join the heavenly team, a gesture of integration which the movie otherwise entirely ignores. Laughing with delight and a nervous unease about what he will encounter, Jones leaves the baseball diamond to enter the rows of corn and thence, presumably, to sport forever on the Elysian Fields.

While considering the varying levels of ability amongst actors portraying baseball players, an amusing reversal can occasionally occur, with the actor turning out to be a better athlete than a thespian. Robert Redford, a great star and a most underrated actor, demonstrated in *The Natural* (1984) that he could throw the ball and swing the bat with conviction. Although far inferior as an artist to Redford, the best athlete on screen today, however, must be Kevin Costner, who exhibits genuine ability playing tennis in *Revenge* (1990) and golf in *Tin Cup* (1996). More important, he starred in *Field of Dreams*, of course, as well as in the recent *For Love of the Game* (1999); his best performance as a ballplayer, though, must be as Crash Davis in *Bull Durham* (1988), incidentally perhaps also the best contemporary baseball picture, where he most convincingly plays a veteran minor league catcher and swings the bat with a great deal of authority. A comparison of his performance in baseball films with his appearance in his most highly praised work — the long, sentimental, self-indulgent, Oscar-winning *Dances With Wolves* (1990) — suggests the highly unusual conclusion that for once a movie star in almost all his athletic parts proves to be a better ballplayer than an actor.

Reversing the usual direction but underlining the reciprocity between the two endeavors, a genuine baseball player now and then enjoys the chance to appear on screen. In the first film made of his life, *The Jackie Robinson Story* (1950), the pioneering star played himself; handsome, intelligent, and of course, a great baseball player. He also performs at least competently as an actor in an otherwise mediocre propaganda flick masquerading as an inspiring biopic.[4] Mickey Mantle, Roger Maris, and a couple of their teammates on the Yankees played themselves in a flat, dull, and entirely horrible movie called *Safe At Home* (1962), happily unavailable anywhere for anyone, even diehard Yankee fans. One of the few major league baseball players who actually enjoyed a career on-screen, however, was Chuck Connors. A tall, left-handed first baseman, he played two seasons in the National League, for the Dodgers and the Cubs, attaining a lifetime batting average of .238, with two home runs: no wonder that after a stint with the old Hollywood Stars, he turned to acting, at which he made a good living in many films and television shows, including *The Rifleman*, his first series. His height, masculinity, and rawboned physical presence made him a credible cowboy — always important to baseball — and more frequently in his later years, a convincing villain, as in the post-apocalyptic science fiction (and non-baseball) movie, *Soylent Green* (1973), where he gets an obvious hit, shooting a priest in a confessional.

To scrutinize the subject slightly more seriously, gazing retrospectively into the dark backward and abysm of time, the two endeavors, acting and baseball, share a long, complicated, and illustrious history—and even pre-history—which now and then some diligent research unearths for aesthetic and athletic contemplation. As I have discussed in previous essays and papers (themselves indebted to a number of other scholars), stick and ball games begin in ancient ritual practices, probably in prehistoric fertility rites, perhaps in those same vegetation cults that inspire so much anthropological research and literary creation in the twentieth century (see, for example, that key work of Modernism, *The Waste Land*).[5] A great many written records, paintings, carvings, and statues, moreover, establish conclusively the existence of such games in Pharaonic Egypt some 3,000 years ago.[6] The connection between sport and religion also leads, most importantly for this study, to the origins of the drama, an art that itself shares rich and profound associations with sport, demonstrating the remarkable nexus of practices that magnificently inspires the human spirit–faith, art, and sport all apparently originate in the same communal actions conducted for the same reasons. The songs, dances, pageants, plays, and games all grow from the human need to form a community and eventually a society, to gather in groups to worship and celebrate.[7] At some point, constructing a ritual, staging a play, and creating a game become essentially the same activity intended for the same purpose within a similarly sacred space.

More immediately for our purposes, the art of the drama and the sport of baseball display some amusing and inspiring similarities, some superficial, others profound. The very concept of gathering a crowd together in an arena to observe a group of selected performers conducting a ceremony involving singing, dancing, the acting out of parts, and a kind of ball game immediately suggests a resemblance between antiquity and today, between the contests of the past and the games of the present. Certainly the pageantry and entertainment that too often surround and interrupt professional baseball in this country connect in some way to those ancient practices. Various representations of ritual ball games show some of its particular and unusual evolution—drawings, bas-reliefs, and vase paintings portray the playing of ball and stick-and-ball games, which incidentally continue as a sort of cultic practice throughout the history of civilization. The vase paintings of Greek and Roman actors from various eras of antiquity also suggest some of the same movements and gestures, as the grace and elegance of both the paintings and the subjects, I believe, demonstrate a certain affinity with the stances and gestures of the athletes.[8] Certainly, the representations of actors and of athletes suggest a close resemblance between the two.

The concept of presenting a dramatic performance in front of an audience, moreover, appears to influence our general sense of the customary and proper exhibition of athletic contests. We have all heard the familiar, tired refrain from so many practitioners of and commentators on sports, that they work in the business of entertainment, that in effect the athletes differ not at all from the singers, dancers, and actors who also ply that trade, that contemporary athletics in America is simply another version of showbiz. To support that contention, consider the geography, geometry, and architecture of the playing field, which closely resemble those of the traditional theatrical space, demonstrating that the twentieth-century ballpark and the ancient Greek and Roman amphitheater look remarkably alike.[9] The innumerable photographs, diagrams, and architectural sketches of the two ostensibly dissimilar arenas reveal some telling affinities.[10] Although baseball most often seems a version of theater in the round, the fanlike pattern of the seating arrangements, for example, opening up from an exactly delimited point, suggests not only the stage and the audience, but home plate and the outline of the stands that roughly follow the extended, infinite V of the baseball field. Several pictures, maps, and sketches of ancient Greek and Roman theaters, amazingly, even show a clearly marked diamond in the middle of the stage, hinting at the magical configuration that will eventually express the motions and meanings of the game. The original *proskenium*, the door separating the front of the stage from the area behind the scenes, which ultimately becomes what we know as the proscenium arch of the modern stage, in fact looks like nothing so much as home plate, a resemblance that may explain the peculiar shape of that challenging construct, whose evolution from some crude dish to the puzzling pentagon of American baseball otherwise seems entirely mysterious.

Even more important, however, the correlations between the game and theatrical performance generate some profound aesthetic and metaphysical meanings and possibilities. To produce a work of drama on a stage and to construct a game of baseball on a field derive from remarkably similar intentions and create remarkably similar results. Both activities, whatever their particular outcomes, depend upon a shared sense of the transitory. Although most students of the game (including the present writer) assert the timelessness of a rare sport played without temporal boundaries (and minimal spatial ones as well),[11] that timelessness also translates as ephemeral. Once a game has been played in its entirety, nothing of value — beyond a victory and a defeat — has been exchanged, nothing has been created or produced, nothing has been accomplished beyond the sheer performance of the contest, and once over, the game can never be repeated. The transient but utterly unique nature of each game leads to the familiar observation that a spectator can observe in any given game something he has never seen before–an unusual play, a dumb mistake, a crazy incident, and so on — which makes every game simultaneously both different and the same, following the same patterns as every other in the seemingly infinite series of the sport, but also existing solely within itself, a self-created, self-consuming entity, resembling, in fact anything we tend to regard as a work of art. The game finds its being only in its form, while the action within that form provides a constant dynamic — like the Chinese jar in T.S. Eliot's *Four Quartets*, that "… still/moves perpetually in its stillness." ("Burnt Norton," II). Similarly, as any dramatic actor or director would agree, every performance of even the same play by the same cast is different — something changes, a member of the cast discovers some new aspect of a character or some new interpretation of a line, some additional nuance results; certainly most literary scholars and professional critics (I am both) know full well the virtually infinite possibilities of production and performance in any great and enduring play — *Hamlet*, of course, provides the best single example of that potential.

Interestingly, neither the game nor the play can repeat itself, but perhaps must always be a unique event, one in a series of innumerable other examples, but each sufficient to itself, each with its own ontology. Both activities are often recorded on tapes and films, but surely everyone knows that the visual record, a filmed game or a filmed play, provides at best a flimsy, incomplete, and inadequate version of the actual event. Although both art and baseball endure as expressions of the grandeur of the human spirit, a single performance, a single splendid game by its very nature cannot last beyond itself, but lives only for its moments and in memory, a condition that may constitute the complex beauty and tragedy of all performing arts. At the same time, each game may perhaps resemble a reinterpretation of an original text, each providing some new, fresh, usually small addition or possibility within the structure of the grand Platonic ideal. Every game is a new game, every performance a new performance, all create themselves anew with each opening, each curtain rising, each admonition to begin the festivities, the worship, the prayers, or in other words, to play ball. All the players, then, not only the pinch hitters and relief pitchers, serve as understudies, as stand-ins, as available personnel to impersonate another body, the Platonic conception of whatever position they assume, each imitating in his own way the archetypal shortstop or center fielder or first baseman on whatever team they perform for, proceeding through the movements and gestures the game demands.

Since the Greeks instituted contests for the actors of tragedy as early as 449 B.C.,[12] even the element of a conflict, a complex dialectic leading toward a victory and a defeat, within the several kinds of play seems inherently appropriate, the expected outcome of the original concept of staging a performance. The play as religious ceremony, a ritualized activity on the part of priests chosen for that purpose, later in effect sanctifies both drama and game. The play as play, the play as game, the game as play, and all the rich possibilities in the combination quite logically and naturally follow from that central point, the metaphysical home plate for the beautiful and remarkable nexus of the aesthetic and the athletic, of art and sport.

Thus, the royal Egyptian represented on an ancient tomb, participating in a ceremonial game, with a stick and a ball and helpful outfielders lurking in the distance, is a ballplayer. Babe Ruth, representing the thousands of others who have engaged in the American game at every level, is, of course, a ballplayer, but he acted in silent movies as well and was therefore, like Jackie Robinson and Chuck Connors, also another kind of player. And the Greek actor[13] depicted on a vase, with the buskins of comedy that so resemble a catcher's shinguards, regarding his own kind of mask with a bemused expression and in a familiar pose to any fan, as if about to don the tools of ignorance, is also himself a player, even a ballplayer. All those men caught forever through another medium of art in a timeless moment, engage in that entirely human and necessary, enchanted and ephemeral activity: they play a game, they play a play, they play.

Notes

1. For more detailed discussion of baseball in film, see George Grella, "The Baseball Moment in American Film," *Aethlon: A Journal of Sport Literature* 14, no. 2 (1997): 7–16.

2. The French Lieutenant in *Lord Jim* (1900), speaking of courage.

3. For further discussion of this point see "The Baseball Moment in American Film."

4. For fuller discussion of Robinson in that movie, see George Grella, "Black Players on the Field of Dreams: African American Baseball in Film" in *The Cooperstown Symposium on Baseball and American Culture, 2000,* ed. William M. Simons (Jefferson, North Carolina and London: McFarland & Company, 2001), 296–307.

5. See, for example, George Grella, "Solarball: Baseball, America, Time, and the Sun," *The Cooperstown Symposium on Baseball and American Culture, 1999,* ed. Peter Rutkoff (Jefferson, North Carolina: McFarland, 2000), 9–21.

6. See, for example, Robert W. Henderson, *Ball, Bat and Bishop* (New York: Rockport Press: 1947); and Wolfgang Decker, *Sport and Games of Ancient Egypt,* trans. Allen Guttmann (New Haven and London: Yale University Press, 1992).

7. See Johan Huizenga, *Homo Ludens: A Study of the Play Element in Culture* (New York: Beacon Press, 1955) for one of the richest and most influential discussions of the combination of ritual, drama, and game.

8. Some useful sources for photographs and illustrations of ancient representations of both athletes and actors include John Boardman, *Greek Sculpture: The Archaic Period* (New York and Toronto: Oxford University Press, 1978); and John Boardman, *Athenian Black Figure Vases* (New York: Thames and Hudson, 1972).

9. One of many sources for various views of baseball stadia, both real and ideal, in photographs, blueprints, and architectural sketches, is a short monograph by Philip Bess, *City Baseball Magic: Plain Talk and Uncommon Sense About Cities and Baseball Parks* (Madison, Wisconsin: Wm. C. Brown, 1989).

10. Similarly, among the many places to consult for photographs and sketches of ancient amphitheaters are Margarete Bieber, *The History of the Greek and Roman Theater* (Princeton: Princeton University Press, 1939); Peter D. Arnott, *An Introduction to the Greek Theatre* (London: Macmillan, 1959); Arthur Wallace Packard-Cambridge, *The Theatre of Dionysus in Athens* (Oxford: Clarendon Press, 1946); and John J. Winkler and Froma I. Zeitlin, eds., *Nothing to Do With Dionysos?: Athenian Drama in its Social Context* (Princeton: Princeton University Press, 1990).

11. See also George Grella, "Baseball and the American Dream," *The Massachusetts Review* (Summer, 1975), 550–567; and Grella, "Solarball: Baseball, America, Time, and the Sun." .

12. Niall W. Slater, "The Idea of the Actor," *Nothing to Do With Dionysos?*, 385–395.

13. *Nothing to Do With Dionysos?*, Plate 2, following 405.

"The Curious Case of Sidd Finch" and *For Love of the Game*: The Perfect Game as Mythical Literature

Craig This

Introduction

The perfect game — the mere mention of it conjures up memories, images, and, yes, lively debate among baseball fans. As with presidential assassinations, most baseball fans can tell you where they were and what they were doing when they received word that someone had thrown a perfect game. Consequently, these memories are then passed from generation to generation and become part of baseball lore — its legends and its myths.

Most of us, if not all of us, have seen the photograph of New York Yankees catcher Yogi Berra leaping into the arms of pitcher Don Larsen following Larsen's perfect game in the 1956 World series. Others were fortunate enough either to have witnessed it in person or to remember the live broadcast.

My earliest recollection of a perfect game was watching the news footage of Cleveland Indians' centerfielder Rick Manning catching the final out of Len Barker's perfect game in 1981. Seven years later, I listened on radio, driving home to my parents' house, as Cincinnati Reds' pitcher Tom Browning pitched a perfect game against the Los Angeles Dodgers. I also recall a few years ago seeing news footage of New York Yankees pitcher David Cone sinking to his knees after pitching a perfect game against the Montreal Expos. Memories of these perfect games are etched in my mind.

Certain perfect games bring forth lively discussion about the state of baseball. For example, if you had clicked on any Internet chat room focusing on baseball following David Cone's perfect game, you would have read polemics from individuals who questioned the "purity" of Cone's achievement. After all, it came against the lowly Montreal Expos in interleague play.

Controversy also followed the "perfect games" of Harvey Haddix and Ernie Shore. Did they really pitch perfect games? Harvey Haddix went 12 innings, three past the "typical" nine-inning game, but did not record the win. Was it a perfect game? Do nine innings constitute a game? Can a baseball game be completed in more or less than nine innings?

Ernie Shore came on in "relief" of Babe Ruth after Ruth was thrown out of the game for arguing about the called balls that led to the first batter walking. The runner at first was caught stealing, and Ernie Shore, in relief, then retired the next 26 batters. Was this a perfect game?

Bartlett Giamatti, the late Commissioner of baseball, took a purist stance and defined the perfect game as follows:

> If three strikes were the lot of every batter on one side, then twenty-seven batters would have to go up and go down on one side to fulfill the perfect game. But there is a greater perfection—that the maximum of twenty-seven, which is also a minimum, go up and go down for both sides. That ultimate perfect game could endure in time like the foul lines in space—indefinitely.[1]

The perfect game, what it is and what it is not, and the individuals who have thrown perfect games are prime topics for the hot stove leagues during the baseball off-season. This paper, however, examines how perfect games are portrayed in baseball literature, specifically, "The Curious Case of Sidd Finch" by George Plimpton and For Love of the Game by Michael Shaara. My thesis is that both of these works contain the elements of mythical literature, and, as such, these works portray the perfect game as myth.

I will be quite honest, however; these works are stories. To both George Plimpton and Michael Shaara, they are stories, nothing more and nothing less. They are the stories of the people of baseball—its fans, its players, its managers, its owners, its critics, and anyone else who would consider themselves as part of the baseball culture. I am the one who is interpreting these stories as myths, and I am the one who shall make that argument.

The Perfect Game in Baseball

Before delving into the whole notion of what is a myth and how these stories portray myths, I want to go back to the notion of the perfect game — what it is, how rare it is, and its relationship to American culture. Consider how a perfect game relates to mythology.

Mythologist Joseph Campbell writes, "Not everyone has a destiny: only the hero who has plunged to touch it, and has come up again — with a ring."[2] It can be said that not every pitcher has a destiny to throw a perfect game, and only a few who plunge to touch destiny will come up with the ring — in this case, the ring of the perfect game.

In the history of Organized Baseball, eighteen pitchers have thrown perfect games. An interesting mix of pitchers have thrown perfect games. Six of them (only one-third) have been inducted into the Hall of Fame. Statistics do not adequately tell the story of these eighteen. In fact, the statistics of these eighteen tend only to highlight the oddity and rarity of the perfect game.

Four of the pitchers, Len Barker, Don Larsen, Charlie Robertson, and Lee Richmond, had lifetime losing records. Mike Witt's career statistics reveal that he finished only one game over .500. Barker and Robertson had ERAs over 4.00. Nothing overly spectacular about these pitchers, except we are mindful of Campbell; "they plunged" to get the ring of the perfect game.

These eighteen, however, do fit Joseph Campbell's definition of the mythic hero. The mythic hero is one who ventures forth, overcoming personal limitations, encounters and defeats formidable forces, and returns to society. Some heroes are honored; others are unrecognized or disdained, as with many of these eighteen pitchers.

American society and American culture has taught us to believe that no one is perfect. Gus Osinski, Billy Chapel's catcher, at the end of *For Love of the Game*, says, "All my blood life they been telling me … hee hee …they tell me that, quote: 'nobody's perfect. Always remember, nobody's perfect.'"[3] Americans, like Gus, have been taught, have been told that perfection is not achievable, not attainable, save for exceptional instances.

So, where did this notion, this belief, that nobody is perfect come from? Christianity, and many other major religions espouse the "imperfect" nature of humankind. Christianity has at its roots in the notion of original sin and the depravity of human kind. Perfection, it is believed, can only be achieved in the afterlife — heaven. Nevertheless, Christianity, in various forms, asserts that through sanctification, the sinner can grow closer to God even though human perfection on this earth is unattainable.

Conversely, Buddhism, the religious belief of Sidd Finch (the protagonist of "The Curious Case of Sidd Finch"), holds that it is possible to achieve perfection or Nirvana here on earth, but the growth in holiness can be a life-long task. Buddhism teaches that there are four noble truths that need to be understood. The first truth is the truth of suffering. Human existence is unsatisfactory. We suffer physically through sickness, old age, and other maladies; mentally we suffer by proximity to those we dislike or separation from those we love. The second truth is that our suffering is caused by craving, lust, and greed. The third truth is that it is possible to put an end to the craving that brings suffering. The fourth noble truth is that there is an eightfold path to put an end to the suffering — thus, again, a process leading toward enlightenment.[4]

The notion of no one being perfect underlies our culture. Sport, however, provides the opportunity to achieve perfection. Sport acts as religion — a means to achieve perfection, if only vicariously, through the athletes. Through sport, players, as actors on stage, go through a competition, seeking to create the perfect self. Over and over again, day in and day night, they seek to achieve that perfection through their games. Spectators then identify themselves with the players, through transformation achieving that perfection otherwise unavailable.[5]

Baseball, in its perfect game, provides the opportunity to see perfection achieved. It is the only sport that provides this opportunity. Yes, other sports, such as archery, bowling, figure skating, or gymnastics do offer the opportunity to achieve a perfect score. Yet, baseball provides the only opportunity for a face-to-face confrontation, in which the batter and pitcher are constantly making adjustments to "outwit, outlast, outplay" the other. Baseball is not a matter of shooting at a non-moving, non-thinking target nor is it a matter of flawless execution of routine with artistic interpretation that is then judged by someone else. It is a matter of "the battlefield ... symbolic of life, where every creature lives on the death of another."[6] It is a heroic adventure — a journey.

Other sports, such as football, are symbolic battlefields as well, and they do provide the opportunity for teams to have perfect seasons, such as the 1973 Miami Dolphins, who won every game en route to triumph in the Super Bowl. Basketball can witness near flawless seasons, but only baseball offers the one-on-one competition that can literally result in a perfect game.

Some would argue, however, as George F. Will does in *Men At Work* that perfect games are "helped along by repeated instances of luck:"[7]

> In Don Larsen's perfect game for the Yankees against the Dodgers in the 1956 World Series; the Dodgers' Sandy Amoros missed a home run by a foot; Mickey Mantle made a sparkling running catch at his knees

of a sinking line drive off the bat of Gil Hodges; and Jack Robinson ripped a line drive off Andy Carey, the Yankees' third baseman, but the ball bounced straight to shortstop Gil McDougald, who threw out Robinson.[8]

He does qualify this statement by noting that luck has also helped hitters as well. Joe DiMaggio's 56-game streak in 1941 had some "lucky" hits. "Twice," argues Will, "DiMaggio benefited from close calls by official scorers on hits that could have been called errors. Twice he got dinky hits — a catchable fly ball fell untouched, and a full swing produced a slow roller that dribbled into an infield that was pulled back."[9] Luck, then, is obviously present in baseball.

The "luck" provided by Don Larsen's teammates in his 1956 perfect game speaks to yet another argument offered by George Will: pitchers are aided in the throwing of their perfect games by their teammates. "Baseball," argues Will, "is really a one-against-nine game."[10] This "one-against-nine" represents a tension in American society of the constant pull between individualism and community. Baseball is a team game. Yet, each play begins with the confrontation between pitcher and batter, which only tends to underscore the individualism of the game. However, notes Will, there is "no simple batter-against-pitcher confrontation. The batter is working against a pitcher who is thinking and acting with eight other players."[11] These players behind the pitcher, play together, and with each pitch make some change, some movement, some anticipation to aid the team in getting the opposition out.

This reliance upon luck and teammates, concludes Will, tends to make pitchers go to the mound gloomily convinced that they must pitch nearly perfectly to win.[12] Consequently, the focus returns to the pitcher — who despite the presence of teammates — must take it upon himself to pitch "nearly perfect to win" and, in some instances, that leads to a perfect game.

In these stories, we see two versions of a perfect game. The one in "The Curious Case of Sidd Finch" is almost fantastical — a pitcher who is able to throw a 168 mile per hour fastball perfectly down the middle of the plate every time. The other story, *For Love of the Game*, is the story of a pitcher throwing a perfect game in the last game of his career. Both stories appeal to a dream in all of us. Who has not dreamed of being perfect in what he or she does day in and day out, as in the case of Sidd Finch? And, who has not dreamed of being perfect and going out on top, as in the case of Billy Chapel? These personal dreams that coincide with the dreams of others in society become public dreams or myths. While a dream is a personal experience of that deep, dark ground that is the support of our conscious lives, a myth is society's dream.[13] "In the dream the forms are quirked by the peculiar troubles of the dreamer, whereas in myth the problems and solutions shown are directly valid for all mankind."[14]

Sidd Finch is a Buddhist monk, or rather a Buddhist monk in training. He is an orphan. His mother died when Sidd was very young, and his father died while Sidd was in high school. Sidd's father died when his plane crashed into a mountain side in Nepal, and Sidd traveled to Nepal to find his father's remains. He did not, but Sidd was welcomed there into a Buddhist monastery. There, he learns to concentrate and throw snowballs with perfect accuracy.

After some time in the monastery, he leaves and goes to Harvard University. There, he is discovered by baseball talent scouts. He is brought to Florida for spring training by the New York Mets, with the sole purpose of having him make their roster as a starting pitcher. During spring training, he is befriended by a journalist and a young woman. The young woman becomes his love interest.

Sidd Finch is successful as pitcher in spring training. However, when the love affair ends, Sidd loses control of his pitching, and the fantasy seems to end. The love interest, however, is rekindled, and Sidd regains his control. In his first start in a major league game, Sidd throws a perfect game. In his second start, he retires the first twenty-six batters he faces and then before facing the twenty-seventh, he suddenly, and inexplicably, walks off the mound, never to return. The reader, along with Finch's teammates and companions, is left to ponder why.

Billy Chapel, we learn early on, is recently "orphaned" as well. His parents have died, his team has been sold, and the owner who has been like a father to him is no longer around. To compound his troubles, his girlfriend has left him and now he has to pitch in the last game of the season.

Chapel goes out and pitches a perfect game. While he is making this outward journey, a struggle of physical strength and mental toughness, his mind is making an inward journey toward transcendence and enlightenment. This, too, is part of the heroic journey of the myth. The hero must engage in some outward struggle while at the same time undergoing an inner journey.

Myth

Myths abound in baseball. The question, though, is what is myth and how do we define it? "When we come to mythology," writes Leonard Koppett in *The New Thinking Fan's Guide to Baseball*, "the Hall of Fame both embodies and perpetuates it. Its location and origin are a response to pure myth, its purpose is to confer mythological status on its enshrinees, and its own status is shrouded in mythic significance."[15]

Yes, in the Baseball Hall of Fame — the Mount Olympus of Baseball — the gods of baseball reside forever, preserved in immortality. "The bronze plaques, which commemorate the greatest, are only part of the story," writes Civil War historian Bruce Catton. "The noble deeds of the super-players are handed down in stories, year after year, losing nothing in the telling. The legends are in some ways the most enduring part of the game. Baseball has even more of them than the Civil War."[16]

> Baseball celebrates the vicarious triumph. The spectator can identify himself completely with the player, and the epochal feat becomes, somehow, an achievement of his own. Babe Ruth, mocking the Chicago Cubs, pointing to the distant bleachers, took a host of Walter Mittys with him when he jogged around the bases. (There is some dispute about this, to be sure; he was jawing with the Cubs, but purists say he did not actually call his shot. That makes no difference anyway.) It was the same when old Grover Cleveland Alexander, the all-but-washed-up veteran of many baseball wars, came into the seventh inning of a decisive World Series game, found the bases filled with Yankees, and struck out Tony Lazzeri, going on to win game and series; and this was after a wearing night on the tiles. Alexander [had] supposed that his work was over until next spring. Many an aging fan shared in Old Alex's triumph.[17]

The Hall of Fame, its mythical origin, its legends, and its gods reflect mythology. Myth is the collective creation of an entire people, and, in this case, those people are baseball people. Further, the myth of these people expresses in story form the basic worldview and the view of human nature. Baseball people would say that life imitates baseball and that baseball imitates life.

Myth, however, is also what is other — what does not belong to the person who describes it as myth. For the baseball fan, the baseball person, Babe Ruth calling his shot is not myth. It is a story. Grover Alexander's feat is not a legend. It is a story. I am the one defining it and other memorable baseball moments as myths. These stories do not belong to me. To me, these stories are the "other," and so I call them myth.

Myth is also defined by how it looks and the purpose it serves. The structuralist definition of mythology states that in order for a myth to be a myth, it has to have certain structures. Without going into great detail, the structuralists believe that myth must have a certain form, content, function, and context. The myth takes the form of a narrative account of sacred origins. The myth has the content or contains information about decisive, creative events in the beginning of time. The myth serves the function of an exemplar or model in terms of which a static ontology is determined. The myth is delivered in a context, recited with a ritual pattern, making sacred events repeatable by the human participants.[18]

On the other hand, the functionalist definition of myth states that myth serves society with a purpose. The value of the myth lies in its timelessness; that what it teaches society helps explain the past, the present, and the future. Myth, the functionalists believe, can allow us to define the undefined and remove anxiety and fear.[19]

One of the leading proponents of the functionalist school was Joseph Campbell. Yet, in his definition of myth, which is functional, he provides a very definite structure, which he calls the monomyth. Joseph Campbell's monomyth will be used to interpret the two literary works, "The Curious Case of Sidd Finch" and *For Love of the Game.* In doing so, the interpretation will show that these works contain the various elements of the monomyth and thus can be defined as myth.

It can be argued, however, that Joseph Campbell's monomyth is too simplistic and too generic to apply to literature. This argument contends that Campbell's monomyth seems to fit too neatly to any work of literature to which it is applied. Further, his monomyth is more literary criticism than mythological interpretation of literature.[20] Others find his work too focused on individual heroism and American Romanticism. These critics argue that Campbell focuses too much attention on the political individualism and individual salvation found in American Romanticism.[21]

These criticisms are both valid and justified. Campbell's monomyth does neatly interpret almost any work of literature to which it is applied and it does read more as literary criticism than mythological interpretation. Likewise, he does focus on the heroic individualism and does tend to echo the themes of American Romanticism. Consequently, the counterargument can be made that these criticisms validate employing Campbell's monomyth in interpreting these texts and their relationship to baseball and American culture.

Baseball originated about the same time American Romanticism emerged. Thus, in baseball, we find themes of American Romanticism — those themes, which Joseph Campbell championed: the heroic individual, individual redemption, and individual salvation. These themes are likewise found in *For Love of the Game* and "The Curious Case of Sidd Finch." More importantly, since they are literary works, it might best to view them through the lens of literary criticism, albeit in the guise of mythological interpretation. Joseph Campbell's definition of myth can be summarized in the following way:

> The mythological hero, setting forth from his common day hut or
> castle, is lured, carried away, or else voluntarily proceeds, to the

threshold of adventure. There he encounters a shadow presence that guards the passage. The hero may defeat or conciliate this power and go alive into the kingdom of the dark (brother-battle, dragon-battle, offering, charm), or be slain by the opponent and descend into death (dismemberment, crucifixion). Beyond the threshold, then, the hero journeys through a world of unfamiliar yet strangely intimate forces, some of which severely threaten him (tests), some of which give magical aid (helpers). When he arrives at the nadir of the mythological round, he undergoes a supreme ordeal and gains his reward. The triumph may be represented as the hero's sexual union with the goddess-mother of the world (sacred marriage), his recognition by the father-creator (father atonement), his own divinization (apotheosis), or again — if the powers have remained unfriendly to him — his theft of the boon he came to gain (bride-theft, fire-theft); intrinsically, it is an expansion of consciousness and therewith of all (illumination, transfiguration, freedom). The final work is that of return. If the powers have blessed the hero, he now sets forth under their protection (emissary); if not, he flees and is pursued (transformation flight, obstacle flight). At the return threshold the transcendental powers must remain behind; the hero re-emerges from the kingdom of the dread (return, resurrection). The boon that he brings restores the world.[22]

The mythical journey, as described by Joseph Campbell, can be set forth in three words: separation-initiation-return: "A hero ventures forth from the world of common day into a region of supernatural wonder: fabulous forces are there encountered and a decisive victory is won: the hero comes back from this mysterious adventure with the power to bestow boons on his fellow companions."[23]

Separation

In his monomyth, Campbell states the first stage is separation, which is the call to adventure. Campbell notes, however, that before the call to adventure can take place that the hero must cross a threshold. The threshold crossing may be a brother battle, a dragon battle, dismemberment, crucifixion, abduction, night-sea journey, wonder journey, or whale's belly.[24] These thresholds must be crossed, through either conciliation or defeat, before the hero can be called to adventure.

Both Billy Chapel and Sidd Finch, in their respective stories, do engage in threshold crossings before engaging in the separation. Billy Chapel must cross two thresholds — the first comes when Chapel receives word from Dobby Ross that Chapel is being traded.

> Trade, Chapel said.
> Ross, no word necessary, nodded.

Long moment of silence.
Chapel looked at Gus. Gus had turned away.
Chapel said, after a while. "Traded. Who to?"[25]

Later, Billy Chapel must cross another threshold when his "girlfriend," Carol Gray, announces,

"I won't be back. I won't be in this town anymore. And you ... Billy ... you don't need me."
"Don't say that again," Chapel said. Then he said, "There's also a man involved in this. Fella who needs you. Are you thinkin' of ... getting married?"
Carol looked into his eyes. Voice very quiet. She said: "I haven't decided yet. Not yet."
"But there is a guy."
"Yes."[26]

Billy Chapel's two thresholds are a dragon-battle (owners announced he will be traded) and a brother-battle (Carol Gray is leaving him). In the first one, he slays the dragon when he announces to his catcher Gus that he will quit.[27] He can't be traded. The dragon loses its strength.

Carol Gray, on the other hand, has defeated him. He has lost. There is no conciliation. Having crossed the threshold, he immediately leaves the present world and descends into the world of the baseball game: to do battle, to defeat, and to win. It is the hero's call to adventure.

For Sidd Finch, he, too, crosses several thresholds before entering the world of baseball:

[Frank] Cashen looked down at a page of notes. "He's English. An orphan. He was adopted by a famous anthropologist named Philip Sidney-Whyte Finch when he was about six. His father was a widower, an expert on the mountain tribes of Nepal and Tibet. Out there somewhere he was killed in an airplane crash. At the time the kid was in his last year at the Stowe School — one of those English public schools — where he must have done very well because he was accepted into the Harvard Class of 1980. When he got the news about his father, the kid dropped out of school and spent a couple of months in the summer of 1976 in the Himalayas looking for him. No one actually saw the crash; the plane just disappeared. That's quite something, isn't it — this kid wandering through those mountains looking for his father?
... That same fall he came out of the Himalayas and entered Harvard. He dropped the Hayden and Whyte from his name, and changed Sidney, which he changed to Sidd with two d's ... He didn't stick around long enough. He's not even in the freshman directory. He dropped out after just a couple of months there. Really dropped out. He went back to Nepal, Tibet, somewhere out there, and continued his studies, or looked for his father, whatever, wandering from one

monastery to another, for almost eight years. That was where he learned to throw a baseball. Don't ask me how ...

The first scouting report came in from Bob Schaeffer last year. He's one of our people — the manager of the Tidewater Tides, one of our Triple-A farm clubs. So he tells me this. After the game he decided to walk back to the hotel from the ballpark ... the Tides had played badly and Bob apparently wanted to get the game out of his system. About halfway, this kid — tall, gangly, clean-shaven, wearing blue jeans, a backpack, and a big pair of woodsman's boots, starts walking along-side. Very shy but obviously wanting to say something. Clears his throat a lot, Ahem Ahem. What Schaeffer thinks is perhaps the kid wants to ask for an autograph, or maybe chat about the game. But no, this kid says, "Sir, may I be allowed to show you're the art of the pitch?"

...[Schaeffer] says, "Sure, kid, I'd like to see the art of the pitch."

So the kid points out a soda bottle on a fence post. Maybe seventy feet away. The kid skins off his pack, sits down on the ground and unlaces this big hiker's boot he's wearing. He pulls it off so that one foot is bare. For balance, he explains to Schaeffer. Then he reaches into his knapsack and takes out a baseball. He stands up, kicks that bare footway up into the air and he flings the ball. Schaeffer tells me the bottle on the fence post out there, explodes, just explodes[28]

The threshold that Sidd Finch must cross is a wonder journey — a search for his lost father and for himself that takes him from London to the Himalayas to the United States and back to the Himalayas. Then, again, back to the United States, where he encounters the threshold guardian, in the person of Bob Schaeffer. (A threshold guardian in myth is a custodian who acts as a gatekeeper.) He defeats the skepticism of Bob Schaeffer, who sends word to the New York Mets to invite Sidd Finch to spring training. The invitation is the call to adventure — the hero's journey.

Initiation

"Once having traversed the threshold, the hero moves in a dream landscape of curiously fluid, ambiguous forms, where he must survive a succession of trials."[29] This is the initiation. For Billy Chapel, that succession of trials is the 27 batters he will face during the game. For Sidd Finch, the succession of trials are spring training, making the team, and then pitching two baseball games.

The conclusion of the trials usually results, according to Campbell, in one of four triumphs for the hero: (1) sacred marriage; (2) father atonement; (3) divinization; and (4) elixir theft. In both of these works, Billy Chapel and Sidd Finch achieve, what I would argue, to be two of the four: (1) sacred marriage and (2) divinization.[30]

The sacred marriage for both is achieved through illumination and transcendence, which takes place during their hero's journey — pitching the perfect game. Again, the hero's journey is on one level an outward journey, a struggle against the forces in this world or on the baseball diamond;, it is, on another level, an inner journey — a rethinking, a reawakening — that leads to illumination and transcendence over the world.

Robert Ellwood writes that in the monomyth, the hero achieves three revelations. The first revelation is that "we are inwardly of a different nature from the surrounding evil world, in which we are entrapped through no fault of our own." The second is that "salvation must come from a source outside the present evil environment, which cannot overcome its contradictions on its own terms"; and the third is that "salvation is in the form of secret knowledge or gnosis."[31]

This secret knowledge, according to Campbell, is illumination, which is the recognition of one eternity through all things. Everybody has this possibility of rapture in the life of experience."[32] Campbell refers to this as the cosmogonic cycle or universal round. The individual is awakened, goes into a dream, and then deep sleep. The awakening and the transcendence shows that two worlds are actually one — that the world the hero left at the separation is also the world to which the hero returns and realizes the two are one.[33]

The inward journey that Billy Chapel takes is one of soul-searching, of remembrances, thoughts. While the game is going on, he reflects back over his life in baseball, his relationships with teammates and Carol Gray, his parents, and the Old Man (the owner of the team).

> Inning number two: done. Goin Home, Going Home ... walked slowly, happily to the bench, sat, tucked his cap down over his eyes ... they went to bed that first night — no — early in the morning. It was the wrong time. Too soon, too soon. There should have been more ... time to open. She talked to him for hours about the mess of her life, she poured things out she had told no one else [34]

Later in the game,

> ... and the three were down. Chapel had a moment of splendid peace, warmth in the arm. A rare day. A fine day. All my life ... is what I was born to do. He sat ... went back into the darkness ... and saw his father, Pops, catcher's mitt resting on the left knee. Twelve years old: Billy Boy.[35]

Finally, near the end of the game,

> Then, Billy eased back, went to the sinker, got the last man a high hopper to second. Back off the mound ... a good song. Lesson too late

for learning. I am, I said. Fella used to love Neil Diamond, too, was
Old John. Big John, the Poor Man's John, the ancient owner of the
Hawks who'd own the team when Billy was born ...[36]

Sidd Finch also undergoes an inner journey while engaging in an outward struggle. What makes it interesting in this journey is that Sidd Finch
does not pitch just one perfect game, but comes within one out of pitching a second perfect game — move over Johnny Vander Meer! With one out
to go, inexplicably, Sidd Finch placed the baseball neatly beside the pitching rubber, walked off the mound, left the game, and departed the stadium.
Throughout these two outward struggles, Sidd Finch must have undergone
an inner journey, an illumination. The reader is not privy to Sidd Finch's
thoughts as with Billy Chapel, but a conversation near the end of the book
provides some clues.

This narrative comes from the family of the narrator, Robert Temple.[37]

> ... Perfection seems to have problems, my father said ... Perfection
> meant trying to match the gods, and it was important not to do that.
> Arrogance...
> ... He once said that there were a great number of ways to reach
> tharpa or supreme liberation. I said. Sometimes one achieves tharpa
> by not reaching the goal. Sometimes there are more important goals
> than the one that is visible. Not to give oneself the twenty-seventh K
> is a possibility ...
> ... Perhaps he simply did it for love, [my mother] said. Perhaps she's
> the kind of girl, she went on, who would insist on some proof of his
> love — you know, show me that you love me by walking off the pitcher's
> mound.[38]

Since Sidd Finch did leave the game and go with Debbie Sue to the
airport to fly to London, The comments of Robert Temple's mother may
not be all that far-fetched. In fact, Sidd Finch's inner journey may have led
him to the illumination of his relationship with Debbie Sue. The role of
Debbie Sue is that of the goddess in myth. Sidd Finch has met the goddess
and, so too, did Billy Chapel, through Carol Gray. The hero meeting the
goddess is an important element of myth.

"The ultimate adventure, when all the barriers and ogres have been
overcome, is commonly represented as a mystical marriage of the triumphant hero-soul with the Queen Goddess of the world"[39] — in this case,
Debbie Sue and Carol Gray. Joseph Campbell writes,

> The goddess is many things; She is the paragon of all paragons of
> beauty, the reply to all desire, the bliss-bestowing goal of every
> hero's earthly and unearthly quest. She is mother, sister, mistress,
> bride. For she is the incarnation of the promise of perfection; the soul's
> assurance that, at the conclusion of its exile in a world of organized

inadequacies, the bliss that once was known will be known again: the comforting, the nourishing, the good mother — young and beautiful.[40]

Sidd Finch and Billy Chapel both return to this bliss — the comfort, the nourishing, the young, and the beautiful. They both are reunited with the goddess and return home. "So home," wrote A. Bartlett Giamatti, "is the goal — rarely glimpsed, almost never attained — of all the heroes descended from Odysseus. All literary romance derives from the Odyssey and is about rejoining — rejoining a beloved, rejoining parent to child, rejoining a land to its rightful owner or ruler." [41] And, that is what baseball is all about — getting to home, getting back to where you started (home plate).

True, pitchers do not want batters to return home to where they started — they do not want them to round the bases and score. Pitchers want to get people out. The narrative of baseball, however, is the return to where you started, returning back home. As Billy Chapel, thought, going, going home — when the game was over, he could go home. So, the pitchers want to make the journey home and return home as well. The pitcher wants to retire the side, through nine innings, and then go back home, where he came from.

The return to where you started is the universal round. Sidd Finch and Billy Chapel awaken from their slumber when they cross the threshold. They both leave family and relationships behind. During their outward struggles, they make inward journeys that result in illumination and transcendence. These journeys also bring them back to deep sleep and the realization that the world they left is the world to which they return. Billy Chapel, thinking he has left and lost Carol Gray, returns to her at the end of the story. Sidd Finch, likewise, thinking he no longer has someone who loves him, returns to the world to find Debbie Sue and the family he thought he had left.

The Return

The "other" conclusion that both of these stories bring is the divinization of these two men — Sidd Finch and Billy Chapel. Regardless of whether or not they will be enshrined as members of the Baseball Hall of Fame, their pitching perfect games leads to their divinization. Their feats will be recorded as history, as legends that will be passed down from generation to generation.

The divinization also means that these two have achieved immortality and the goal of the indestructible self. Their bodies will age, and they both leave baseball. But their perfect games will be remembered forever. It is, according to Joseph Campbell, the achievement of the infantile fantasy of the indestructible self.[42]

The fantasy of the indestructible self is also the fantasy of the spectator as well. The spectator lives vicariously through the athlete. The spectator uses the athlete to achieve his or her fantasy of immortality. Consequently, the spectator never allows the athlete to grow up. This heroic adventure is sealed in time and in the mind of the spectator, who will always see this particular athlete as "young and strong and special, somewhere in late adolescence ... [and] profoundly innocent."[43] Billy Chapel and Sidd Finch fulfill those fantasies for spectators and teammates. This is the elixir that these heroes bring back to civilization upon return from their adventures.

This is how Billy brought the elixir to his teammates: "the game was over and it was done, it was done, and Chapel closed his eyes to the explosion that came. A moment later he was being carried in the air. Someone pressed a ball into his hand. The ball. To the victor."[44]

Sidd, however, was received more as the hero who is disdained or unrecognized:

> The Mets streamed out of the dugout at the last pitch, but it was not the pell-mell rush that one might have expected, nothing at all like the cap-throwing euphoria typical with the usual no-hitter. Ronn Reynolds did not launch himself into Sidd's arms, as Yogi Berra did into Don Larsen's after his perfect game in the 1956 World Series. The Mets marched out like people who are a little late for a football game, not quite breaking into a trot. After all, most of them had never said more than a word or two to Sidd. He was that "monk guy." He had been carted into their midst just the week before — like an unpacked piece of furniture. They surrounded him, shouting happily at him, but he was escorted off the field more as if they were an armed guard.[45]

Conclusion

In addition to their divinization, Billy Chapel and Sidd Finch reinforce the notion of the American Dream — the success of the individual through his or her own merit. This is the connection between these two works as myth and American culture. This is why they are myths because they speak to American culture, they echo the themes of American culture, and they explain the American perception of people and the world.

American culture, for better or for worse, believes in the self-reliant individual. Not social standing, not divine intervention, not money, not political influence, but pure merit, hard work, the struggle of the individual, will lead to success.

Baseball and the doctrine of the self-reliant individual emerged around the same time. Through the American Romantics — Ralph Waldo Emerson, Henry David Thoreau, Nathaniel Hawthorne, Walt Whitman — the doctrine of self-reliance took hold in American culture.

And, in these two works of literature, we see the same theme echoed: merit will win. "Baseball," writes A. Bartlett Giamatti, "in its conventions makes a tremendous promise — to play the game of America by the rules of the Constitution and the American Dream. Therefore, merit will win, it is promised by baseball."[46]

Notes

1. A. Bartlett Giamatti, *Take Time for Paradise* (New York: Summit Books, 1989), 89.

2. Joseph Campbell, *The Hero with a Thousand Faces*. (Princeton: Princeton University Press, 1973), 228.

3. Michael Shaara, *For Love of the Game* (New York: Ballantine Books, 1991), 147.

4. William H. Gentz, ed., *The Dictionary of Bible and Religion* (Nashville: Abingdon, 1986), 161–165.

5. Giamatti, 38–39.

6. Campbell, 238.

7. George F. Will, *Men At Work* (New York: Macmillan Publishing Company, 1990), 84.

8. *Ibid.*.

9. *Ibid.*, 85.

10. *Ibid.*, 240.

11. *Ibid.*, 240.

12. *Ibid.*, 241.

13. Joseph Campbell, *The Power of Myth with Bill Moyers*. Betty Sue Flowers, ed. (New York: Doubleday, 1988), 40.

14. *Ibid.*, 19.

15. Leonard Koppett, *The New Thinking Fan's Guide to Baseball* (New York: Simon and Schuster, 1991), 325.

16. Bruce Catton, "The American Game" in *A Sense of History: The Best Writings from the Pages of American Heritage* (New York: American Heritage Press, 1985), 567.

17. *Ibid.*, 566.

18. Elizabeth M. Baeten, *The Magic Mirror: Myth's Abiding Power* (Albany: State University of New York, 1996), 25–28.

19. Ibid., 28–35.

20. See Stanley Edgar Hyman, "Myth, Ritual, and Nonsense," *Kenyon Review* 11 (summer 1949), 455–75; Robert A. Segal, *Joseph Campbell: An Introduction* (New York: Garland Press, 1987); and Robert Ellwood, *The Politics of Myth: A Study of C.G. Jung, Mircea Eliade, and Joseph Campbell* (Albany: State University of New York, 1999).

21. See Karen L. King, "Social Factors in Mythic Knowledge: Joseph Campbell and Christian Gnosis," in Daniel C. Noel, ed., *Paths to the Power of Myth: Joseph Campbell*

and the Study of Religion (New York: Crossroad, 1990); Robert A. Segal, "The Romantic Appeal of Joseph Campbell," *Christian Century*, April 4, 1990, 332–35; and Robert Ellwood, *The Politics of Myth: A Study of C.G. Jung, Mircea Eliade, and Joseph Campbell* (Albany: State University of New York, 1999).

22. Campbell, *The Hero* 245–246.

23. *Ibid.*, 30.

24. *Ibid.*, 245.

25. Shaara, 21.

26. *Ibid.*, 40.

27. *Ibid.*, 55.

28. George Plimpton, "The Curious Case of Sidd Finch" (New York: Macmillan Publishing Company, 1987), 16.

29. Campbell, *The Hero*, 97.

30. *Ibid.*, 246.

31. Robert Ellwood, *The Politics of Myth: A Study of C.G. Jung, Mircea Eliade, and Joseph Campbell* (Albany: State University of New York, 1999), 9.

32. Campbell, *The Power of Myth*, 93.

33. Campbell, *The Hero*, 266.

34. Shaara, 85.

35. *Ibid.*, 89.

36. *Ibid.*, 93.

37. Robert Temple, although narrator, plays an important role throughout the story. Robert Temple plays the role of helper to Sidd Finch. The helper, in mythical literature, is a protective figure who assists the hero in his or her journey. The helper's role is that of guide or teacher. Quite interestingly, Robert Temple's nickname in the book is "owl," which is the mythological symbol for wisdom. Also of interest is the fact that a "temple" is where a religious person, such as a monk, might go to pray, to meditate, to seek guidance.

38. Plimpton, 268–271.

39. Campbell, *The Hero*, 109.

40. *Ibid.*, 111.

41. Giamatti, , 92.

42. Campbell, *The Hero,,* 177.

43. Giamatti, 58–59.

44. Shaara, 138–139.

45. Plimpton, 194.

46. Giamatti, 64.

The Symbiosis Between Baseball and Broadcasting

Paul D. Staudohar

The four principal sources of revenue to Major League Baseball are broadcasting, gate receipts, stadium revenues, and licensing. About 40 percent of total receipts derive from broadcasting — television (national, local, and cable) and radio. By far the lion's share of broadcast revenue is from television, and its substantial payoffs have provided a bonanza to owners and players. But squabbling over the distribution of the broadcast pot has plagued the game with work stoppages. And the economic and competitive disadvantages faced by small-market teams, compared to their large-market brethren, are in major part attributable to disparities in broadcast income.

This paper explores the relationships between broadcasting and baseball, from the early days of radio through the television age. It reviews how baseball was the first sport to receive widespread exposure from broadcasting, the influence of national expansion of broadcast markets, and the role of technology. Reasons for the revenue explosion are provided. Of further interest is the economic impact of television on owners and players. Also examined are ways to make the distribution of broadcast revenues among teams more equitable, so as to promote financial health in smaller clubs and better competitive balance on the playing field.

Radio

The medium of radio is important to baseball for a variety of reasons. One is historical. Radio came first, and until the 1950s it was the exclusive way in which fans received broadcast entertainment. Second, radio provided paradigms that evolved into the format for telecasts, e.g., sale of rights to broadcasters, live programming, use of paid announcers, and commercial sponsors. Third, although overshadowed by television, radio continues to provide broadcasts of virtually all games of individual teams plus national events such as the All-Star Game and World Series.

The first broadcasts of baseball occurred during the 1890s, as telegraph services paid to have reports on games sent to saloons and pool rooms.[1] Major League Baseball's first radio broadcast occurred on August 5, 1921, for the game between the Pittsburgh Pirates and Philadelphia Phillies at Forbes Field in Pittsburgh.[2] The World Series in 1921 was broadcast by relay, and in 1922 and 1923 on a play-by-play basis. Helping to stimulate interest was the involvement in the Series of the New York Yankees and their popular star Babe Ruth. Nationwide broadcast of the World Series did not begin until 1926.Although radio broadcasts began in the 1920s, there was no sale of rights for several years. Instead, the owners gave away the rights as a public service. They generally believed that radio coverage would reduce attendance, but acknowledged that they had to put up with some of it because of public demand. In 1929, NBC and CBS each carried the World Series on their networks, on a pro bono basis.

Radio broadcasts of baseball were commercialized in 1934 when Commissioner Kenesaw Mountain Landis reached a deal with the Ford Motor Company for $400,000 to sponsor the World Series for the next four years. The games were presented on all three major networks of that time, NBC, CBS, and the Mutual Broadcasting Company. In 1939, the Gillette Safety Razor Company took over sponsorship of the World Series, which it presented for the next 32 years[4]. Given baseball's popularity, these broadcasts captured the attention of the entire nation.

Because owners remained wary of radio's supposed affect of keeping people away from the ballpark, local broadcasting of games was not common. The main exception was William Wrigley, a chewing gum magnate who owned the Chicago Cubs. In 1925, Wrigley began giving away broadcast rights to any station that wanted to present Cubs' games, and there were multiple broadcasts of games on Chicago stations over the years. Wrigley viewed the broadcasts as free publicity that would promote the interest in his team. Ultimately he was proved to be right.

Although Cub attendance was not reduced by the broadcasts,

Wrigley's example was not generally followed. In fact, in 1932 the major leagues nearly decided to ban broadcasts entirely, and in 1934 the three New York City teams (Yankees, Giants, and Dodgers) agreed to ban radio broadcasting until 1938. The following year, for the first time, all major league teams allowed broadcast of games on radio, albeit often only road games.

By the 1940s and 1950s, radio broadcasts of games of major league as well as minor league teams really took off. From 1945 to 1950, the number of locally operated radio stations doubled; the "Game of the Day" on the Mutual Broadcasting Company network was broadcast on nearly 500 stations in the 1950s.[5] For many years, one of the oddities of local broadcasts was that games were frequently "recreated" by announcers, based on reports via telegraph from Western Union.[6] The most famous example of this occurred at station WHO in Des Moines, Iowa, where announcer Ronald "Dutch" Reagan recreated Chicago Cubs games in the 1930s.

Radio broadcasts were eventually overshadowed by television, but radio retains some allure today, especially for listening while driving and for fans who treasure the imagery that radio provides. A gifted radio announcer, and there are many of these, can hold listeners in thrall with creative commentary.

A relatively new wrinkle is that many teams in the major and minor leagues are presenting games on the Internet. All big-league teams have the option of presenting audio from their games on their own Website or on the site of their flagship stations[7]. This is providing something of a resurgence for audiocasting, because more teams are migrating from free television to regional cable television networks. Fans who do not have cable access may now have the alternative of a free outlet on the Internet to supplement radio broadcasts in home markets. Also teams can now take local radio rights "in-house" rather than selling them on an exclusive basis to a station. These teams can continue to purchase game time on a station, but as more fans with personal computers listen to Webcasts, the costs to the team for broadcasting on radio stations are reduced. Teams also view Webcasts as a marketing tool which allows them to reach fans outside of their home territory.

Television

Baseball was the first sport to be televised. On May 17, 1939, an Ivy League game between Columbia and Princeton, played at Baker Field on the Columbia campus in New York City, was televised on NBC's experimental station. With the famous sports announcer Bill Stern broadcasting, several hundred people watched the game on a small silver screen located at the RCA Building in New York.

On August 26, 1939, the first exposure of Major League Baseball on television occurred, at a double-header at Ebbetts Field in Brooklyn between the Dodgers and the pennant-bound Cincinnati Reds.[8] It is estimated that fewer than 1,000 persons saw the show on nine-inch or less television sets in metropolitan New York. RCA presented the telecast, using two cameras, one behind home plate and the other at ground level near the third base dugout. Reds catcher Ernie Lombardi said that he felt as though someone was "looking over his shoulder" all day.

The Yankees in 1946 paid $75,000 to become the first team to acquire television broadcast rights. The World Series was presented live on television for the first time on NBC in 1949. A major breakthrough occurred in 1951 when a coaxial cable was completed to enable presentation of live broadcasts coast to coast.[9] This allowed the 1951 National League playoffs between the New York Giants and the Brooklyn Dodgers to be nationally televised. Viewers were treated to Bobby Thomson's "Shot Heard Round the World," the most dramatic home run in baseball history, winning the pennant for the Giants in the bottom of the ninth inning of the decisive game.

In 1950, only about 12 percent of American households had television sets. While reception, in black and white, was sometimes of marginal quality, the share of households with television grew rapidly, to 67 percent in 1955 and 87 percent in 1960.[10] Baseball responded to this growth in positive ways, although the lords of the game remained skeptical of the impact of television on attendance at live games, similar to their earlier reservations about radio. By the early 1950s, owners had warmed to radio, perceiving that it actually stimulated demand for live attendance. Television, however, was bad for attendance in their opinion, and it was especially troublesome to the minor leagues because some viewers who could watch major league ball on television lost interest in their local minor league teams.

Prominent baseball executives Branch Rickey and Clark Griffith determined in the early 1950s that the owners should seek to collectively gain control of television broadcasting, limit its exposure, and pool income from the sale of rights.[11] The major leagues established rules prohibiting teams from broadcasting into the territory of another franchise and requiring visiting teams to get permission to broadcast. By 1953, rights to telecast a limited number of games were sold by nearly all teams.

In 1954, the major leagues submitted a plan to the Department of

Justice for a "Game of the Week," to be negotiated by the Commissioner of baseball. The Justice Department, however, advised the leagues that their proposal would violate federal antitrust law. A 1922 Supreme Court decision granted baseball immunity from the antitrust law prohibition on monopolies that restrain competition. But Congress in 1951 had conducted an investigation of this exemption, and owners were also wary of challenges to the legality of the reserve clause, binding players to clubs, which was a clear restraint of the labor market.

The owners went ahead with their plans for a game of the week on television, but the arrangements were made between individual teams and the networks, rather than by the Commissioner on behalf of all teams. Teams whose games appeared more often received greater revenues. Then, in 1961 Congress passed the Sports Broadcasting Act. This law granted an antitrust law exemption to professional team sports, enabling leagues to negotiate national broadcasting rights packages that provided for pooling of income among teams. This law cleared the way for the major leagues to establish tight control of their television rights.

With this control, the symbiosis between baseball and television came into sharper focus. The owners realized that television, used judiciously, would not negatively affect attendance. They viewed it as a revenue source and a way of marketing their team to increase the size of the live gate. Television, for its part, needed sporting events to utilize airtime and attract sponsors. In the early days of live video broadcasting, baseball, then still accepted as the national pastime, was highly valued as a means of legitimizing television programming. This demand translated into hefty financial rewards to team owners. The synergism continues to the present, although the needs may not be as compelling as in the past.

An important reason why the bloom is somewhat off the rose for baseball and television is that the sports calendar has become crowded with events. Once baseball stood alone as *the* professional team sport with national attention. Football was the first to challenge this supremacy, and others followed. Today, all manner of sports and pseudo-sports flood the market with alternatives.

Also, baseball is a sport not altogether suited for television. Football and basketball games, for instance, move laterally across the television screen and utilize a larger ball that is easier to see. The baseball field, on the other hand, is spacious and features a more geometric than linear flow of play. Action away from the ball may be missed on the screen. The smaller baseball moves at high speeds, curves, and can be hit high in the air. Action is less continuous, with numerous "dead spots" that can be boring to viewers. Of course, to true fans, there is nothing as intellectually stimulating as baseball, with its tradition, endless variety, subtlety, and sophistication of play. But, similar to hockey, these nuances do not translate well on television. With its 162 games, baseball has far more availability than pro basketball (84 games), hockey (82 games), or football (16 games), giving the sport a prolonged exposure that can dampen enthusiasm over the season, especially if playoff races are not close.

Television ratings for baseball — regular season, All-Star Game, and post-season — are all at or near historic lows. There are simply too many other things to do. Yet, baseball is hanging on, with fairly robust live attendance. Although the All-Star Game ratings are way down from earlier levels (44 percent in 1982, 22 percent in 1999), they are still far higher than those in other major sports' all-star games.[12] Pro football may be the most popular sport, but baseball continues to possess the hearts of a great many fans.

Broadcast Rights

In contrast to the $100,000 that it cost the Ford Motor Company to sponsor radio transmission of the World Series, its successor, Gillette, had to pony up $400,000 in the late 1930s. By the end of World War II, all teams in the major leagues were selling radio rights for regular season games. Whereas teams received an average of under $1,000 each in 1933 from local broadcasts, by 1950 each franchise averaged over $200,000 annually.[13] The arrangements for the sale of radio rights were similar to those adopted for television. That is, rights to present national telecasts of regular season games, the All-Star Game, and the post-season are sold to networks by the leagues, with equal sharing of revenue by teams. Until 1982, local rights proceeds were exclusively retained by team owners. Some sharing has occurred since then, particularly as a result of arrangements following the 1994–95 player strike.

National Television

National television rights fees on a total annual basis and per team are shown in Table 1. The rights fees have risen steadily over the years, with especially large rises from 1980–93. For instance, the total revenue package of $1.125 billion for the six-year period from 1984–89 ($187.5 million per team on an annual basis) was an increase of nearly four times over the previous period.

TABLE 1.
NATIONAL TELEVISION RIGHTS FEES
(MILLIONS OF DOLLARS)

Year	Amount Per Year	Annual Amount Per Team
1950	1.2	0.1
1960	3.3	0.2
1970	16.6	0.7
1976–79	23.2	0.9
1980–83	47.5	1.8
1984–89	187.5	7.2
1990–93	365.0	14.0
1994–95	190.0	6.8
1996–00	340.0	12.1
2001–06*	559.0	18.6

*The six-year agreement with ESPN began in 2000 and expires at the end of 2005. The bigger six-year agreement with Fox runs from 2001–06.

Source: Data for 1950–79 from Andrew Zimbalist, *Baseball and Billions* (New York: Basic Books, 1992), 49. Data from 1980–1995 from Paul D. Staudohar, *Playing for Dollars* (Ithaca, NY: Cornell University Press, 1996), 21. Data since 1995 determined by the author as presented in various published sources.

The 1990–93 agreement approximately doubled the revenues per team.[14] CBS, trailing the other major networks in overall ratings, sought to enhance its image by paying $1.1 billion over four years. The package included rights to the World Series, League Championship Series, All-Star Game, and 12 regular season games. Shortly after the CBS deal, baseball agreed to its initial national cable contract for games with ESPN. This was a four-year deal, totaling $400 million, providing for rights to 175 games per season.

The 1990–93 agreements were disastrous for the networks, with CBS losing about $500 million and ESPN about $150 million. CBS had rights to less than half the number of annual regular season games that had been shown under the 1984–89 agreements with NBC and ABC, and ratings were low. Besides the low ratings, ESPN's problem was that about half of America's homes did not have access to the cable network. This marked the first time that networks had lost such large amounts on sports programming.

As a result, the 1994–95 national television rights deal was restructured downward, cutting revenues to teams by approximately half. Baseball made an error by agreeing to a joint venture with NBC and ABC called the Baseball Network. Under this arrangement, which was originally set for six years, Major League Baseball received 85 percent of the first $140 million with the networks, and got to keep 80 percent of additional revenue. This arrangement was a mistake because it put baseball in the advertising business, responsible for selling time to sponsors on the Baseball Network, a new role that it was not well suited to perform. The ESPN agreement provided for "up-front" money to baseball, but at $235 million over six years it was less than half the rights fees under the old agreement, and the number of weekly games was reduced from six to three.

The drastic reduction in revenue was felt most acutely by the small-market teams that were more dependent on their equal share of the national television pot. This, in turn, led to a tough stance by the owners at the bargaining table with the players in the 1994–95 negotiations, and was a major factor precipitating the big strike that was so debilitating to the game.[15] Adding to the problem, refunds had to be made to advertisers for the cancellation of the 1994 post-season games. When baseball stubbornly refused to restructure the deal, the networks angrily terminated the agreement after only two of the six years had been completed.

Termination of the television contracts turned out to be a blessing in disguise for baseball, enabling negotiation of replacement contracts totaling $1.7 million with NBC, Fox, and ESPN. This event marked the initial entry of Fox, owned by Rupert Murdoch of News Corporation, into the national baseball telecasts. Apart from the broadcast network, Murdoch's company also controls Fox Sports Net and the FX cable operation. These networks are a major force in local and regional broadcasting.

The new national network television contract is exclusively with Fox. From 2001–06, Fox has rights to the playoffs and World Series, plus 18 Saturday afternoon telecasts each year, during which it can air four different games regionally at the same time. At approximately $419 million per year, the contract provides for about a 45 percent increase from the previous payment for the same package.

In 1999, a dispute arose between ESPN and Major League Baseball. ESPN announced that it was switching three games from its Sunday Night Baseball program to ESPN2, the network's smaller station that reaches fewer viewers. The reason for the switch was that ESPN wanted to show three NFL games in September because of their higher ratings (in 1998 the ratings were 8.1 for the NFL and 1.8 for baseball).[16] In a huff, baseball terminated ESPN's rights contract, effective at the end of the year. This prompted a lawsuit by ESPN to maintain its contract, and baseball filed a countersuit.

After several months of meetings, the parties agreed to a settlement. Under its terms, ESPN went forward with the football telecasts but made up for the lost baseball games by showing extra games on Friday nights on ESPN and ESPN2. More importantly, the parties agreed to extend and enhance their basic rights agreement. A new six-year contract, beginning in 2000, will pay baseball an estimated $851 million. The number of telecasts will increase from 90 to 108 per season, and the deal includes Internet rights and rights to interactive games.[17] Although the television contract is for regular season games only, a separate radio arrangement was reached that includes post-season games, including the World Series, on ESPN radio. The radio rights were acquired for $46 million, or $7.7 million a year.[18]

Local Television.

Unlike national television revenues, which are divided equally among teams, local broadcasting agreements are negotiated separately by the teams. The teams in the most lucrative markets share small amounts of their local revenues with small-market teams, but they get to keep by far the biggest part.

As shown in Table 2, there is a great disparity in local broadcasting revenue. In 1999, all teams received the same amount of $15 million from national broadcasting rights (including radio). But the local broadcast revenues of teams like the Yankees ($58 million) and Cubs ($56 million) is enormously greater than that of the Minnesota Twins ($5 million) and the Montreal Expos ($3 million). The lowly Expos were in even worse shape in 2000, when they failed to renew their local television and English-language radio agreements.[19]

Until 1984, local authorities regulated the rates charged and services provided by telecommunications firms. Pursuant to the National Cable Broadcasting Act of 1984, however, cable television companies could base their charges on what the market would bear. Because some markets do not have competing firms, these companies could be monopolies. The problem that has emerged in these relatively unregulated markets is what is called "cable-ization" or "sports siphoning," resulting in much higher monthly fees to customers.

Suppose, for example, that games are provided to customers in a local market via "free" public television. Teams sell rights to these games and, depending on the size of the market, may reap a tidy reward from the station. A team, however, may be able to significantly increase its revenue by selling the rights for some of its games to a cable provider which charges customers a monthly fee for its service. What is happening is that fewer

TABLE 2.
BROADCASTING REVENUE
(MILLIONS OF DOLLARS)

Team	Local	National	Total
NY Yankees	58	15	73
Chicago Cubs	56	15	71
Atlanta	51	15	66
NY Mets	39	15	54
Los Angeles	33	15	48
Baltimore	25	15	40
Arizona	24	15	39
Anaheim	23	15	38
Chicago White Sox	23	15	38
Boston	21	15	36
Cleveland	21	15	36
Colorado	19	15	34
Philadelphia	18	15	33
Detroit	17	15	32
San Francisco	17	15	32
Seattle	17	15	32
Toronto	17	15	32
Florida	15	15	30
Houston	15	15	30
St. Louis	15	15	30
Texas	15	15	30
Cincinnati	12	15	27
Oakland	12	15	27
Tampa Bay	12	15	27
San Diego	10	15	25
Milwaukee	9	15	24
Pittsburgh	7	15	22
Kansas City	6	15	21
Minnesota	5	15	20
Montreal	3	15	18

Source: Bob Costas, *Fair Ball* (New York: Broadway Books, 2000), 65.

games are being provided on free television and more games on pay cable. Thus games are siphoned from a situation of no charge to customers to a situation where customers have to pay extra for baseball.

The siphoning is illustrated in Table 3. It shows that the average number of broadcast (free television) games per team fell from 65.5 in 1996 to

TABLE 3.
BASEBALL GAMES SHOWN ON
BROADCAST AND CABLE TELEVISION

	Broadcast TV		Cable TV	
YEAR	Total games telecast	Average # of telecasts per team	Total games telecast	Average # of telecasts per team
1994*	1,823	65.1	1,432	51.1
1995*	1,784	63.7	1,232	45.9
1996	1,835	65.5	1,287	50.9
1997	1,668	59.6	1,737	62.0
1998	1,656	55.2	2,059	68.6

	Combined	
YEAR	Total games telecast	Average # of telecasts per team
1994*	3,203	114.4
1995*	3,016	107.7
1996	3,259	116.4
1997	3,405	121.6
1998	3,715	123.8

*Numbers reflect games planned prior to strike-shortened season. Actual numbers were lower

Source: "Cable's Batting Average Keeps Climbing," *Broadcasting and Cable*, Vol. 128, No. 13, March 30, 1998, .24.

55.2 in 1998. This is a decline of 16 percent over three seasons. Meanwhile, the average number of games presented on cable television rose from 50.9 in 1996 to 68.6 in 1998, an increase of nearly 35 percent. Only a few years ago more games were shown on free television than cable. Now the situation has reversed, as significantly more games are shown on cable. On the plus side, however, more games are being televised on the *combined* broadcast and cable outlets, as seen in Table 3.

The impact of this trend is that fans are paying more money to see baseball on local television. Proportionately more games are shown on pay cable, as games move from the free tier to a higher-paid tier. What is more, as noted by Andrew Zimbalist, this escalation does not necessarily stop with basic cable. There is a higher tier of "expanded cable service," where more games are being shown, and beyond that would come the still higher tier of pay-per-view (PPV).[20] PPV has been successful for major boxing events and is used for college football game viewing. It may be that PPV will appear on the baseball menu in the future.

Two other points should be noted briefly. One is the compensatory payments by superstations. The Braves, Cubs, Yankees, and Mets games are televised on stations that can transmit signals nationally. For example, Atlanta Braves' games are broadcast throughout the nation on the cable television network founded by Ted Turner. This aroused the attention of other owners who felt that Turner should pay for this privilege. Therefore, in 1985, at the urging of Commissioner Peter Ueberroth, Turner agreed to pay nearly $30 million to Major League Baseball over five years in exchange for no restriction on the number of games he could telecast.[21] It is only fair that superstations share with baseball owners some of the money they make from advertisers on the broadcasts.

A second point concerns the recent network strategy of trying to squeeze money out of local affiliates. As noted above, the costs to the networks of broadcasting baseball have escalated over the years. Added to this are the big rights fees that networks pay to football, basketball, hockey, and other sports. Traditionally, the major television networks — NBC, CBS, and ABC — have paid their affiliated stations between $150 and $200 million annually.[22] Cable television companies, on the other hand, are paid by their affiliates for the programming they provide.[23] Because of the spiraling costs of programming, especially for buying sports rights, the networks are seeking to phase out payments to affiliates, and hope eventually to reverse the money flow so affiliates are paying them, similar to what happens with the cable providers.

Returns to Owners

Television technology is changing rapidly. High-definition programming is already available, with its images that rival movie theater clarity. The technology is still evolving. The equipment that most people have in their homes limits the reception of high-definition signals. Similar to the transition from audio to video in the 1950s, the early 21st century holds great promise for expanded forms of entertainment with interactive qualities. Who will control the flow of programming to households, through sources such as satellite, fiber optic wire, and coaxial cable remains to be seen. Competition among content providers and distributors will likely create numerous options for consumers. But they will pay a higher price.

One of the interesting challenges for owners in baseball and other sports is how technology will affect the electronic transmission of games to viewers and how to take advantage of the changes. Baseball ownership is gravitating increasingly toward individuals and corporations that can facilitate vertical integration of the sport, such as broadcasters and broadcast sponsors.

The future may foretell rapid rises in domestic revenues to baseball due to technological changes in broadcasting creating an increased demand by viewers. Nonetheless, for several years, prior to the late 1990s, this was not the case (as illustrated in Table 4). Revenues after the 1994–95 strike slowed for a time and then picked up as fan interest revived. Both the networks and baseball are looking for new ventures to increase profitability. League expansion, PPV, and new stadiums with luxury boxes galore are important aspects of this quest. International marketing of the sport is also attractive. In this regard, baseball has lagged behind football, basketball, and hockey. However, Major League Baseball is seeking to increase its international exposure. The 2000 season began with a two-game series in Japan between the Cubs and Mets at the Tokyo Dome, the first ever outside North America. The 2001 season opened with a game in Puerto Rico between the Rangers and the Blue Jays. Baseball has several foreign television rights holders, including NBC Europe; Channel 5 in England; TBS, NHK, and FUJI-TV in Venezuela; Televisa in Mexico; TSN in Canada; and iTV in Korea.[24] With about one-fourth of the players in the major leagues born outside of the United States, the potential for international marketing would seem bright.

Even though baseball's television ratings are down, rights fees have been rising at a reasonably healthy clip. This seems to defy rationality. Why would networks continue to shovel out money to baseball when ratings are low and money might be lost? The answer is that the networks view their sports contracts beyond the simple issue of direct profit or loss. For instance, Fox has paid enormous sums for sports television rights, a money loser in its own right. But ownership of major league sports programming has provided significant increases in the overall prime-time ratings on Fox, and the value of its affiliated stations has increased by far more than the cost of the sports telecasts.[25] Disney, which owns ABC and ESPN, stimulates sales at its theme parks, catalog, broadcasting, film, and team-sports units (Anaheim Angels, Anaheim Mighty Ducks) through sports programming.

The international angle is also part of the symbiosis. At the time,

TABLE 4.
MAJOR LEAGUE BASEBALL'S MEDIA REVENUES
(MILLIONS OF DOLLARS)

Team	1990	1993	1996	1999
NY Yankees	69.4	63.0	69.8	73.0
Chicago Cubs	24.2	36.0	29.3	71.0
Atlanta	20.0	35.0	30.3	66.0
NY Mets	38.3	46.1	30.9	54.0
Los Angeles	29.7	34.0	31.8	48.0
Baltimore	22.5	27.4	30.6	40.0
Arizona				39.0
Anaheim	24.0	26.7	18.3	38.0
Chicago White Sox	24.2	26.2	24.3	38.0
Boston	34.1	38.0	30.9	36.0
Cleveland	20.0	23.7	21.6	36.0
Colorado		5.0	22.8	34.0
Philadelphia	35.0	28.0	21.4	33.0
Detroit	22.3	30.3	24.7	32.0
San Francisco	23.3	27.5	25.5	32.0
Seattle	17.0	21.0	17.2	32.0
Toronto	28.0	31.6	28.4	32.0
Florida		5.0	23.9	30.0
Houston	24.2	26.2	22.3	30.0
St. Louis	27.4	27.0	25.7	30.0
Texas	24.6	27.5	24.3	30.0
Cincinnati	21.8	25.0	21.5	27.0
Oakland	21.2	27.4	25.2	27.0
Tampa Bay				27.0
San Diego	25.1	25.0	16.5	25.0
Milwaukee	19.0	21.5	15.1	24.0
Pittsburgh	20.0	23.5	17.7	22.0
Kansas City	19.0	21.0	16.5	21.0
Minnesota	19.6	22.3	20.4	20.0
Montreal	20.0	24.0	19.4	18.0
Average	25.9	27.7	25.2	35.5

Source: Financial World, July 9, 1991, 42–43; May 10, 1994, .52; June 17, 1997, 47; and Bob Costas, *Fair Ball* (New York; Broadway Books, 2000), 65.

Rupert Murdoch of News Corp. was buying the Los Angeles Dodgers from Peter O'Malley, one of the attractions to Murdoch was his international presence, with broadcasting and sports (soccer, rugby) holdings in Europe and elsewhere in the world. O'Malley was quoted, regarding baseball's missed opportunities internationally, as follows: "We're behind basketball, behind football, behind hockey — we're fourth in that race. That is sad to me. And there's no doubt in my mind that Fox — and Mr. Murdoch — will bring that to the party...He will help internationalize the game more than anyone else on the horizon."[26] Also, the concept of integration among units of a media company like Disney or News Corp. has international application. Murdoch recognized this advantage when he said at New Corp.'s 1996 annual meeting: "We have the long-term rights in most countries to major sporting events, and we will be doing in Asia what we intend to do elsewhere in the world — that is, use sports as a battering ram and a lead offering in all our pay-television operations."[27]

When Peter O'Malley sold the Dodgers for $311 million in 1998, they were the last family-owned team whose revenues were the owner's sole support. The trend, as illustrated by News Corp. and Disney, is for media companies to enter baseball as owners. Tribune Company, which owns the *Chicago Tribune*, WGN-AM radio and WGN-TV television superstation, bought out Times-Mirror Corporation, which owns the *Los Angeles Times, Newsday*, and other media properties. Ted Turner sold his broadcasting and cable stations (TBS, TNT, CNN) to Time Warner and continues to be an executive for that business as well as the Atlanta Braves and Atlanta Hawks. Fox owns local broadcast rights to nearly all major league teams. These are illustrations of vertical integration in baseball, with media companies owning teams, broadcast sources, and sports-programming rights.

Benefits to Players

In an attempt to undercut the newly-formed American Baseball Guild, a union of players in 1946, the owners offered a pension plan to be funded by contributions from players and owners.[28] The owners decided unilaterally to fund the pension program from the sale of national television and radio rights. The players were kept in the dark about details of the program for the time being.

Upon the death in 1949 of a ten-year veteran ballplayer, Ernie Bonhaur, there was no available money in the pension fund to provide for his widow. Consequently, Commissioner Happy Chandler hurriedly obtained funds by selling the television and radio rights to the World Series and All-Star Game to Gillette for the next six years, at $1 million per year.[29]

When the pension plan was revised in 1956, the players were consulted. They were given a choice of a flat $1 million annual contribution or a 60 percent share of All-Star Game receipts and all radio and television profits from the game, plus radio and television receipts from the World Series.[30] Wisely, Ralph Kiner, a player representative, thought that television's promising future justified taking the percentage rather than the flat fee. This would prove to be a boon to player pensions.

In 1972, the players went on strike over the extent and nature of pension funding, causing the cancellation of 86 games at the start of the season. As a result, funding levels were raised and a cost-of-living increase was provided for retirement benefits. This successful strike, the first in the modern sports era, was conducted with Marvin Miller at the helm of the union.

The Major League Baseball Players Association (formed in 1952) hired Miller as its first full-time executive director in 1966. A former official of the Steelworkers Union, Miller brought the players together in an adversarial relationship with the owners, erasing the paternalism of the past. By 1975, in a grievance arbitration involving pitchers Andy Messersmith and Dave McNally, baseball players won the rights to become free agents (currently after six years major league experience.) Combined with the opportunity of salary arbitration for players with 2.7 to 6 years of major league experience, free agency has become the engine for the huge increases in player salaries over the years.[31]

If free agency and salary arbitration are the engine for player salary increases, television provides the fuel. There is a strong correlation between player salaries and television revenues, both national and local. It is no coincidence that the Yankees, the team with the richest revenues from sale of local broadcast rights, is also perennially the team with the biggest payroll. As noted in Table 1, revenues to baseball from national television were reduced by about half as a result of the rights sale for the 1994 and 1995 seasons. Not surprisingly, average player salaries were essentially flat during the period from 1994–96 (not considering salary reductions as a result of the strike).[32] The large increase in television revenue from the 2001–06 rights sale practically guarantees that average player salaries will rise at a rapid pace in future years.

Given the growing gap in local television revenues between the highest and lowest revenue teams, a question arises as to whether this disparity translates into success on the playing field. There has always been a positive correlation between high salaries and winning teams. If a club is successful on the playing field, salaries increase because players are compensated on the basis of past performance. Teams like the Yankees can afford to pay players more, to replace players who are injured, and to attract free agents from other clubs. The correlation is not perfect, however, as for many years small-market teams like the Oakland Athletics, Cincinnati Reds, and Minnesota Twins won the World Series. The Yankees did not even make the playoffs from 1983–93.

But beginning in 1995, big-market teams have dominated the playoff positions. That year, Atlanta, with the fourth-highest payroll, won the World Series over Cleveland with the seventh highest. In 1996, the three teams with the three highest payrolls — the Yankees, Baltimore Orioles, and Atlanta Braves — were joined by the team with the fifth-highest payroll, St. Louis, as the final four teams in the playoffs. In 1997, Florida (fifth highest) beat Cleveland (third highest) in the World Series. In 1998, the Yankees (second-highest) swept San Diego (tenth-highest); and in 1999 it was the highest-paying team, the Yankees, sweeping the third-highest-paying team, the Braves.[33] In 1999, all eight teams that made the playoffs were among the top ten payrolls in baseball. The highest-payroll Yankees ($112 million) won again in 2000.

Of the sources of revenue to baseball, only licensing is relatively constant. Local broadcast revenue, gate receipts, and stadium revenues can be highly variable. Some so-called small-market teams like Texas and Colorado have relatively high gate receipts and stadium revenues from recently built ballparks. Thus, while the size of the media market is a crucial factor to team revenue and success, it is not the whole story.

Bellamy and Walker have done some interesting modeling to show how cities of about the same size can have significantly different revenue streams from television and attendance, with relatively high revenues in Baltimore and St. Louis, and low revenues in Milwaukee and Pittsburgh.[34] They offer a "pinned-in" model to explain a large part of Pittsburgh's financial difficulties, in that several major league teams surround this city geographically, such as Cleveland, Cincinnati, New York, Philadelphia, Baltimore, and Toronto. In contrast, under what Bellamy and Walker call the "hinterlands model," St. Louis has little major league competition to the immediate west and south, giving it a large potential broadcast market. Also, unlike the Pirates, the Cardinals realized early the advantages of using radio and later television to expand its broadcast market and lock in generations of fans.

Although other variables weigh heavily, the local broadcast revenue factor is crucial to financial success as well as success on the field. There is some sharing of these revenues at present, but it is relatively minor. It will have to be beefed up so that rich clubs share far more of their local broadcast revenue with geographically disadvantaged clubs. Bob Costas recommends the radical change of giving half of each team's local broadcast money to its opponents, or placing this half into a national pool that would then be divided equally among all 30 clubs.[35] Naturally, well placed owners, like the Yankees' George Steinbrenner, the Braves' Turner, or the Dodgers' Murdoch oppose significant revenue sharing. They contend that it is a free enterprise capitalistic economy. Let competition determine survival. These owners paid proportionately more to buy their clubs, so the higher returns should be theirs to keep.

On the other side are the poorer teams who feel that they are not really competitive on the playing field, because they can not afford to pay the high salaries that attract outstanding players. It seems unfortunate that a team like Montreal was unable to retain such excellent players as Randy Johnson and Pedro Martinez. Even though Montreal has done surprisingly well in maintaining a good record on the field with a very low payroll, the club has little chance of retaining superstars or advancing to the post-season.

A practical argument endorsing greater revenue sharing is that teams are organized under the umbrella of a league. Leagues are joint ventures with monopoly control (territorial rights) in the defined geographic area of team operation. Unless the large-market teams play games exclusively among themselves, the small-market teams are part of the show. It has been suggested that some of the worst off of the small-market teams, such as Minnesota and Montreal, should have their franchises cancelled by the leagues. This might improve economic competition, but it would be highly unfair to local fans in those cities. Assuming the leagues remain in their present form, the only way for the economically disadvantaged teams to compete effectively is to share more of the local broadcast revenue from the high-income clubs. This would appear almost certain to occur in years to come.

Notes

1. Andrew Zimbalist, *Baseball and Billions: A Probing Look Inside the Big Business of Our National Pastime* (New York: Basic Books, 1992), 148

2. *Ibid.*

3. Doug Battema, "Baseball Meets the National Pastime: Baseball And Radio," in *The Cooperstown Symposium on Baseball and American Culture, 1999*, ed. by Peter M Rutkoff (Jefferson, NC: McFarland & Company Publishers, 2000), 148 and 168.

4. Benjamin G. Rader, *In Its Own Image: How Television Has Transformed Sports* (New York: The Free Press, 1984), 25.

5. *Ibid.*, 26.

6. *Ibid.*, 27.

7. *Broadcasting & Cable*, Vol. 127, No. 28, July 7, 1997, 48.

8. Information about this game was obtained by the author from the archives at the National Baseball Hall of Fame and Museum in Cooperstown, New York.

9. Bobby Thomson with Lee Heiman and Bill Gutman, *The Giants Win the Pennant! The Giants Win the Pennant!* (New York: Zebra Books, Kensington Publishing Corp., 1991), 232.

10. Andrew Zimbalist, *Baseball and Billions*, 149.

11. James Edward Miller, *The Baseball Business: Pursuing Pennants and Profits in Baltimore* (Chapel Hill, NC: University of North Carolina Press, 1990), 6.

12. Nathan Hegedus, "Baseball Banks on All-Star Game Ratings," *The Wall Street Journal*, July 10, 2000, B12.

13. Benjamin G. Rader, *In Its Own Image*, op. cit., 26.

14. Portions of the data on the two rights contracts from 1990–95 are based on Paul D. Staudohar, *Playing for Dollars: Labor Relations and the Sports Business* (Ithaca, NY: Cornell University Press, 1996), 20–21.

15. Paul D. Staudohar, "The Baseball Strike of 1994–95," *Monthly Labor Review*, Vol. 120, No. 3, March 1997, 24.

16. "ESPN Countersued Over Schedule Switch," *San Francisco Examiner*, May 23,1999, C5.

17. Larry Stewart, "Baseball, ESPN See Air of Ways," *Los Angeles Times*, December 7, 1999, B1.

18. *Ibid.*

19. John Walters, "Broadcast Blues," *Sports Illustrated*, April 4, 2000, 20.

20. Andrew Zimbalist, *Baseball and Billions*, 156.

21. Paul D. Staudohar, *Playing for Dollars*, 21.

22. Joe Flint, "How the Top Networks Are Turning the Tables on Their Affiliates," *Wall Street Journal*, June 15, 2000, A1.

23. *Ibid.*, 8.

24. Chuck Johnson, "America's Pastime Crisscrosses the Globe," *USA Today*, March 7, 2000, 16 C.

25. John F. Geer, Jr., "Fox's Law," *Financial World*, June 17, 1997, 52.

26. Connie Bruck, "The Big Hitter," *New Yorker*, December 8, 1997, 82.

27. Cited in *Ibid.*, 86.

28. David Q. Voigt, "Serfs versus Magnates: A Century of Labor Strife Major League Baseball," in *The Business of Professional Sports*, ed. by Paul D. Staudohar and James A. Mangan (Urbana, IL: University of Illinois Press, 1991). 113.

29. Kenneth M. Jennings, *Balls and Strikes: The Money Game in Professional Baseball* (Westport, Conn.: Praeger Publishers, 1990), 13.

30. *Ibid.*, 14.

31. See Paul D. Staudohar, "Baseball's Changing Salary Structure," *Compensation and Working Conditions*, Vol. 2, No. 3, Fall, 1997, 2–9.

32. *Ibid.*, 5.

33. Bob Costas, *Fair Ball: A Fan's Case for Baseball*, (New York: Broadway Books, 2000), 56.

34. Robert Bellamy and James R. Walker, "Baseball and Television: The Case of the Cubs," paper presented at the annual NINE Spring Training Conference on Baseball History and Social Policy Issues, March 18, 2000, in Tucson, Arizona, 7–10. (mimeographed).

35. Bob Costas, *Fair Ball*, 66–67.

The Pitch:
Baseball and Advertising
in the Late Nineteenth and
Early Twentieth Centuries

Roberta Newman

In the mid-nineteenth century, two powerful forces arrived on the American scene, one, strictly a business, the other, seemingly only a game. Each had a major impact on American culture, and each was, and continues to be, intimately connected to the other. The game, our game, baseball, as the Madison Square Garden cable network regularly assures us, is "more than just a game." The business, advertising, is one of the central institutions in contemporary American culture. Indeed, it would be difficult to argue that advertising does not permeate virtually every aspect of American culture, that it does not dominate American cultural production.[1] Advertising, like baseball, taking the excepted evolutionary stance that our national pastime developed from rounders, may have existed in embryonic form in England prior to taking root in America. But it took a nation of hustlers, a nation of hucksters, a nation of snake-oil salesmen, to turn it into a major industry.

From the outset, professional baseball has had a close relationship with advertising. Rather than souring with time, this relationship, almost a love affair, has grown ever stronger. Where would professional baseball be without the beautiful new retro-ballparks named for giant corporate entities, Bank One, Pacific Bell, Enron, and the Coors and Miller brewing companies, for example? Certainly, the new ballparks have relied heavily on the largesse of the municipalities for which they were built, but it can be argued that these stadiums might never have been completed were it not for corporate sponsorship. At first glance, stadium sponsorship agreements seem to be one-sided. Baseball would appear to need large corporate sponsors more than the sponsors need baseball. After all, even without baseball, telecommunications giants, major breweries, banking institutions, and the like, would, have football, basketball, hockey, and stock car racing as available avenues for sponsorship agreements. But baseball has something to offer that these other professional sports do not. For unlike other popular spectator sports, baseball carries with it its iconic image as the national pastime and, by extension, its role as an icon for America.

Sponsorship, per se, differs from other forms of advertising. Rather than giving consumers explicit reasons for purchasing a given product, sponsorship pitches products by association, implicitly.[2] What professional baseball has to offer its sponsors is the association with its perceived wholesomeness, its down-right, all–American essence. That professional baseball may not, in fact, be all that wholesome is unimportant. That it is perceived as wholesome is what matters. It is an example of the theory suggested by social scientist, W. I. Thomas, referred to as the definition of the situation, which states that if you treat something as real, it is real in its consequences.[3] Thus, if consumers and sponsors alike treat professional baseball as wholesome and all–American, then it is wholesome and all–American in its consequences. Any number of recent television commercials bear this out. An apt example might be the Mastercard ad in which a group of suitably gap-toothed, adorable children attend their first major league ballgame, a "priceless" American experience, if ever there was one. Because both the advertiser and the viewer treat this scenario as typical Americana, it is, in effect, typical Americana. The implication is that, because Mastercard makes participation in this priceless slice of wholesome American life possible, Mastercard, itself, must also be wholesome and all–American. Perhaps, because of the strong association of baseball and baseball imagery, and, by extension, products advertised using baseball and baseball imagery, with a symbolic America, the marriage between baseball and advertising, implicit and explicit alike, was already entering middle age before the NFL, the NHL, the NBA, and NASCAR (the all–American bastard child of Prohibition), were even glints in the eyes of their organizers, or their sponsors.

The relationship between baseball and advertising actually predates the advent of the Madison Avenue agency as we know it. Modern American advertising, which counts humbug peddler PT Barnum among its early acolytes, actually has its roots in Philadelphia, where the first advertising agency, Volney Palmer, was established, in 1843, just two years before Alexander Cartwright codified the rules of baseball in New York. But Volney Palmer was but a distant cousin to contemporary advertising giants with their extensive copy and art departments. Volney Palmer's sole undertaking was to peddle space in print publications to advertisers. Preparation of advertising copy, however, was the job of the advertiser, not of the agency.[4] In 1880, the first professional ad man, John E. Powers, was hired by John Wanamaker, also of Philadelphia, to write ad copy for his department store,[5] just eleven years after the first acknowledged professional baseball team, the Cincinnati Red Stockings, was established in 1869. Powers, who was fired and rehired by Wanamaker almost as many times as Billy Martin was fired and rehired by George Steinbrenner, was apparently born in central New York state in the late 1830s,[6] the very time and place of baseball's mythic, if not its real, conception. Although these are just a series of coincidences, their concurrence may stem from the fact that social and economic conditions were right for both the development of advertising and the spread of baseball.

In the second half of the nineteenth century, the growth of industrialism, leading to an increase in urbanization, also contributed to an increase in the number of people with more disposable income and more leisure time than they might have had in the past.[7] In the period immediately following the Civil War, a surplus of consumer goods, on which the new urban working and middle classes might spend some of that disposable income, also flooded the market.[8] These factors led, on one hand, to an increase in recreational activities, among them both participatory and spectator sports, and, on the other, to the spectacular rise of American consumerism. Thus, the mechanism making the marriage of baseball and advertising all but inevitable seems to have been in place at the inception of both industries.

Perhaps the earliest and most enduring link connecting professional baseball and advertising is ballpark signage. Traditional ballpark advertising signs — large, clear messages painted or posted on perimeter boards and scoreboards — have, it seems, always been a part of the American baseball experience. Archival photographs of long demolished nineteenth- and very early twentieth-century ballparks indicate that the practice of on-sight advertising has been around since the earliest days of baseball's life as a spectator sport. Indeed, it is difficult to find an archival photograph of the interior of a professional ballpark that does not have advertising signage. The rationale behind on-sight advertising appears to be quite clear. In the days when mass media was limited to print, and advertising in print media was often prohibitively expensive, the opportunities presented by ballpark signage were invaluable. The obvious advantage of advertising at an event which attracts large crowds is that marketers have a captive audience. As people became active consumers of professional baseball, they also became passive consumers of advertising. Fans, like the batters they came to watch, were faced with a barrage of pitches from a variety of pitchers.

On-sight advertising in ballparks was an ideal way to familiarize attendees with the name of a given product, and name recognition was, for the most part, what this type of advertising had to offer. Although ballpark signs were necessarily large, there were limitations inherent in the form. A product's name and perhaps a single slogan, suggestive of the product's virtues, were all that there was room for on a given sign, if the ad was to communicate clearly.[9] Ads with abundant text touting the specific qualities of a given product were not really an option. For example, Lever Brothers, the makers of Lifebuoy Soap, could not really tell fans in attendance at Philadelphia's Baker Bowl much about Body Odor or how their product worked to eradicate this socially fatal disease, a condition essentially created by advertising agencies in the early 1920s.[10] But it could associate itself with the power to cure the condition with the legend "Health Soap Stops B.O." What Lever Brothers could do, by placing a giant sign on Baker Bowl's right field wall, reading "The Phillies Use Lifebuoy," was to induce fans to associate the Phillies, and, by extension, baseball, with their product. That this strategy worked in this particular instance is evidenced by a graffito amendment to the billboard added some years after it was posted at the stadium, reading "But they still stink."[11] In this regard, on-sight advertising worked a lot like sponsorship. Rather than aiming to pitch specifics, name recognition was its goal, as it still is today.

America's ballparks would not, in all probability, have been effective venues for on-sight advertising, were it not for the advent of star players to bring in fans. To contradict W.P. Kinsella's mysterious, fictional voice, heard in an Iowa cornfield, it was probably not enough to build ballparks. There had to be some additional attraction. It is no coincidence, therefore, that baseball's first star pitcher was also its first star pitch man. Indeed, Alfred Goodwill Spalding was a man of firsts. He was the first player to pitch a shut-out, the first pitcher to win 200 games, and arguably the first to tie his own name, the name of his sporting goods company, inexorably to baseball.[12] Spalding was a genius of marketing and promotion. Already associated with the baseball as a player in the early 1870s, Spalding's real impact on the sport, the one that has endured for over a century, came from his promotion of baseball in order to sell sporting goods. According to Spalding Worldwide's official Web site:

> When youngsters get together for a ball game on a sandlot field, its often the child who brings the ball that gets to be the pitcher. That's the way it has been for generations. That wasn't usually the case, however, at the Major League level... except where Albert Goodwill Spalding was concerned. Then again, AG Spalding wasn't your ordinary pitcher.[13]

Spalding opened his first sporting goods emporium in 1876, his first season as a pitch man and his final season as a pitcher. At the same time, his eponymous company began to manufacture baseballs. Spalding paid the National League, which he was, not so coincidentally, involved in establishing, a dollar for every dozen balls it used, thus making his product the official ball of the National League.[14] This familiar marketing strategy, a form of sponsorship now known as licensing, whereby an institution, be it commercial or otherwise, sells the rights to use its name, has brought us everything from the "official" mustard, peanut butter, and snack cracker of Major League Baseball to the "official" allergy medicine and real estate agency of the game.[15] While the patent medicine industry, which lays claim to many advertising firsts, may have employed this form of sponsorship to sell some of its magic potions before Spalding entered the market, licensing in sports can be traced back to Spalding and his Official National League Balls.

The same year Spalding began marketing Official National League Balls, he also published the first of his official baseball guides. While the ostensible purpose of the *Spalding Guides* was to provide information pertaining to the game, their real purpose was advertising, the promotion of the Spalding brand, both implicitly, by associating the name with the game, and explicitly, in advertisements for Spalding products. Eventually, *Spalding Guides* would become a medium for other advertisers, as well. However, Spalding reserved advertising space on the covers exclusively for his company's products. Long before newspaper advertising became the norm, Spalding recognized the marketing potential of print media. That Spalding was able to exploit the print media was made possible by several nineteenth-century innovations. In 1841, a process by means of which cheap paper could be manufactured was developed in France. In addition, later in the century, the invention of both lino-type, by means of which type could be set rapidly and relatively inexpensively, and the half-tone process, which, by converting solid areas of color to a pattern of dots, allowed for the printing not just of stark black and white, but of various tones of gray, made print advertising more affordable and more visually interesting.[16] The very fact that until a generation ago, New York's children played street games, many of them based, however loosely, on baseball, with "Spaldeens" is evidence of Spalding's genius for promotion, for his ability to use the new advertising media available to him to the fullest.

The marketing techniques introduced by Spalding with his *Guide* were frequently copied. Most notable was the *Reach Guide*, which began publication in 1883, six years after the Spalding's first *Guide* was issued in 1877. Like the *Spalding Guide*, the *Reach Guide* was the product of a sporting goods company, A.J. Reach, owned by Reach, a former catcher, who became the first ballplayer to receive a regular salary in the 1860s, and a partner, Ben Shibe, later part-owner of the Philadelphia Athletics.[17] The *Reach Guide*, also a potent venue for advertising, was positioned as the official year book of the American League in 1906. At first glance, Reach appears to have taken a page from Spalding's marketing book, but closer investigation shows that, in fact, Reach sold his company to Spalding in 1889, but retained the Reach name on certain products, most notably, his *Guide*. In addition, Reach retained some control over the products that bore his name. For example, he patented lively cork centered balls, perhaps developed by Shibe, under the Reach name in 1909. The Reach balls, which replaced those with a hard rubber core, were then licensed as the official balls of the American League.[18]

The *Spalding* and *Reach Guide*(s) were not the only dedicated baseball publications to serve as venues for advertisers of sporting goods and other products. In addition to scorecards and programs, which, like the ballparks in which they were sold, were always adorned with advertisements, various newspapers and publishing houses issued unofficial baseball guides and yearbooks. *How to Play Baseball, by League Stars*, complete with schedules and records, published by the *Brooklyn Daily Eagle* in 1921, is just one example. Along with the requisite ads for sporting goods, this guide contained ads for any number of local Brooklyn banks, private detective agencies, and several phonograph dealers. Most interesting, perhaps, were the half-page advertisements for Sylvan Electric Bath, supposedly a harmless, drugless, invigoration treatment for rheumatism, gout, lumbago, and other treatments, as well as a full page ad for another publication, the first yearbook, undoubtedly with its own ads, of the League of Nations, *What the League of Nations has Accomplished in One Year*, by Dr. Charles H, Levermore of Adelphi College, which, perhaps not so coincidentally, also advertised in the *Brooklyn Eagle* baseball guide.[19]

With Spalding's official National League balls and his *Spalding Guides*, the man with the genius for pitching also relied on another marketing technique which has become the meat of the relationship between baseball and advertising over the passing years, the celebrity product endorsement. Aside from the occasional celebrity endorsements attesting to the miraculous curative powers of one or another patent medicines, the practice of celebrity product endorsements was uncommon prior to the twentieth century. Spalding may very well have been one of the first, if not the first, celebrity to pitch something other than a patent potion aimed at the alleviation of human suffering. Certainly, images of specific baseball players appeared on trade cards in the nineteenth century, and these were, indeed, used to sell products. However, baseball trade cards were frequently produced without the consent of the ballplayers pictured thereon. In contrast, by deliberately tying his name, as a pitcher, to his original product, the baseball, as well as to other sporting goods and to his *Guide*, Spalding deliberately engaged in a practice that has become the norm.

Why was Spalding's endorsement so effective? Stanley Resor of J. Walter Thompson, one of the architects of the boom in celebrity endorsements in the 1920s, noted that we wish to imitate people who we assume to possess taste and knowledge superior to our own. Thus, by using a product associated with a celebrity, we show the world that we, too, possess superior taste and knowledge.[20] In the case of a celebrity ballplayer, we wish to associate ourselves with more than just his good taste in choosing to play baseball and his knowledge of the sport, we wish to share in his glory, to own a piece of his superior, almost supernatural, physical skills.[21] In effect, when Spalding put his name on baseballs and baseball guides, he invested his products with almost magical powers and properties. In this way, his products, the balls in particular, became like relics, objects handled by or closely associated with saints, the possession of which, brings the owner, user, or viewer closer to the divine.[22] The magic with which the Spalding balls were invested became even more potent when the product became the official ball handled by all National Leaguers. Consumers of the Spalding balls shared not only in his glory, but in the collective divinity of the National League.

Spalding's attempts to market his company and its products did not end with guides and official baseballs. He knew that the best way to sell more stuff was to create a demand for it. And, the best way to create a demand for his stuff was to spread the gospel of baseball, not only around the country, but around the world. As Spalding wrote in what was touted as "Base ball's first official bible," *Base Ball, America's National Game*:

> An event of considerable importance in its influence upon the American national game was the world's tour of Professional National League Base Ball Players in the winter of 1888–89. Base Ball had been advancing in popularity with such rapid strides in our own land during the preceding years, that I felt the time had come when this great

pastime should be introduced wherever upon the globe conditions
were favorable to our peculiar form of outdoor sport. [23]

Clearly, the introduction of our peculiar form of outdoor sport to the
world would be accompanied by the introduction of Spalding's equipment
to be used wherever upon the globe conditions were favorable. Spalding's
tour, perhaps the first example of sponsorship in baseball, was largely a failure, but not every attempt at advertising is successful, not even for an
advertising genius like Spalding. Witness another of Spalding's failures. In
1882, he concocted and sold the idea that each fielding position should
have its own color-coded uniform, which his company, quite naturally,
would produce.[24] Fortunately, this experiment in advertising went the way
of the dead ball. But despite these minor set backs, Spalding succeeded in
making his name, the name of his company, a household name.

With the exception of sporting goods advertising, like Spalding's,
nineteenth-century print ads, for the most part, pitched patent medicines,
intended to treat female complaints, and were aimed, almost entirely, at
women.[25] Indeed, women, who made most of the household purchases,
were the primary demographic of most early advertising.[26] The original
lyrics to *Take Me Out to the Ball Game* not withstanding, women were not
the ideal demographic to be pitched to by advertisers using baseball
imagery. Of course, there were exceptions to the rule that women were the
primary purchasers of consumer goods, even in the patent medicine business. In 1886, John Stith Pemberton, one of so many self-proclaimed doctors, mixed up a batch of syrup containing two powerful stimulants,
extracts of cola nut and coca leaf, from which cocaine also derives. He also
added wine. Thus was born Pemberton's French Wine Cola, one of hundreds of patent medicines containing coca, which was marketed as a brain
and nerve tonic. Shortly thereafter, Georgia, the home of Pemberton's
tonic, became a dry state, forcing him to replace the alcohol with caffeine.
By 1887, the name of Pemberton's concoction, now a temperance drink, was
changed to Coca Cola, thereby emphasizing its most potent ingredients.
In 1893, Asa Briggs Chandler, an Atlanta pharmacist, made advertising
history when he registered the first trademark in United States history, the
name Coca Cola written in the now familiar script.[27]

Although by 1905, only spent coca leaves, largely devoid of their active
ingredient, were used in brewing Coca Cola, it continued to be marketed
as an elixir capable of curing headaches and providing imbibers with a
quick lift. One particularly successful ad campaign, touting the near miraculous qualities of Coke, featured a large arrow encircling text and drawings, and often included the slogan, "Whenever you see an arrow, think

of Coca Cola." The ads, which ran in newspapers, included a series of testimonials by prominent baseball players, among them Frank Chance, Miller
Huggins, and Eddie Collins, to name but a few. Of particular note is an
arrow ad from 1905, in which Napoleon Lajoie and Rube Waddell attested
to the near miraculous restorative powers of Coca Cola. Waddell's testimonial may be particularly telling: "More than once a bottle of your Coca
Cola has pulled me through a tight game. There is nothing better for pitchers in hot weather. I find Coca Cola stimulating to both body and mind,
and is the only beverage of the kind that does not leave an after effect."[28]
Whether Coca Cola, most notably before its reformulation in 1904, helped
or hindered the pitcher's famous ability to be distracted by shiny objects
and the sirens of fire engines while on the mound, is a question which may
never be answered.

Interestingly, patent medicine testimonials, such as those represented
in the Coke arrow ads, have their roots in American evangelical culture.
In the earliest days of advertising, even before Spalding put his name on a
baseball, snake-oil salesmen (itinerant preachers of a sort) were responsible for pitching magical elixirs that could alleviate all suffering, at the same
time they pitched God, thereby mixing salvation from discomfort with
salvation from sin.[29] Therefore, the product, as well as the pitch man with
whom it was associated, took on mythic proportions. This was particularly
true when the endorser was a celebrity. In fact, the very term celebrity
comes from the Latin, *celebratus,* the condition of being honored, from
which also comes the term, celebrant or priest.[30] That the celebrity endorsement was far from common, made the testimonials all the more potent.

In 1906, the patent medicine industry was dealt a near fatal blow by
the passage of the Pure Food and Drug Act.[31] Gone were the ads making
claims for miraculous cures. But baseball players continued to endorse
Coca Cola as a refreshing soft drink, rather than as a magical potion. This
was attested to on trade cards as well as in the arrow ads, which continued to run in newspapers as late as the second decade of the twentieth century. Decades before Madison Avenue told television viewers that drinking
Gatorade would help them "Be Like Mike," American consumers, whenever they saw an arrow, were instructed to think of Coca Cola, and by
extension baseball's greats, America's greats.

Along with baseball and the advertising businesses, another nascent
American industry made its first mark on American culture in the mid-
nineteenth century. Tobacco, as a cash crop, was central to the settlement
and development of colonial America. However, the mass-marketing of
tobacco did not begin until the nineteenth century. Familiar to most Americans is the earliest form of tobacco advertising, the cigar store Indian,

which, in the mid-nineteenth century, became a fixture outside tobac-conist's shops. Though not as common, a number of tobacconists chose an alternative figure to advertise their wares, the cigar store baseball player. The connection between tobacco and Indians by tobacconists clearly plays on tobacco's roots as an indigenous, American product. So, too, perhaps, does the connection between tobacco and baseball.

While tobacconists sold cigars, loose tobacco for pipes, and, in the late 1850s, following the Crimean War, when they were introduced to British officers by the Turks, the makings of cigarettes, the marriage of tobacco advertising and baseball, at this point a protracted engagement, was not consummated until later. During the Civil War, John Green marketed a brand of golden Bright Leaf tobacco, the variety used predominately in cig-arettes, as "genuine Durham Smoking Tobacco." After Green's death in 1869, W.T. Blackwell bought the company and began to advertise the tobacco by the name of its already familiar trademark, the Bull.[32]

So was born Bull Durham tobacco, perhaps the most widely copied brand in tobacco advertising history. In 1902, when more Americans were smoking Bull Durham tobacco than any other brand, the Durham Bulls of North Carolina State Professional Baseball League were founded. Although the league folded after just 48 games, the Durham Bulls were to reappear in a number of incarnations, and still exist today as the AAA affiliate of the Tampa Bay Devil Rays.[33] Naming a team after a region's most impor-tant product appears to have been a particularly effective form of adver-tising. Durham, North Carolina was the home of the American Tobacco Company, which, in 1902, had monopolistic control over the tobacco industry in the United States, Blackwell having merged his company with that of ATC founder James Buchanan "Buck" Duke in 1890.[34] Naming a team the Durham Bulls was essentially different from simply naming a team after a local industry, the Milwaukee Brewers, for example. They were not, after all, the Durham Bright Leaves or even the Durham Ciga-rettes, but rather, the Bulls. This was an early example of "branding," con-necting the product with a brand, and by extension, linking the name of the brand with baseball.[35]

Show a pack of Bull Durhams, now factory rolled, to anyone today, and they will at once conjure up an image of Kevin Costner in a baseball uniform. This association persists despite the best anti-tobacco efforts. Indeed, the beleaguered Tampa Bay organization appears to be in no hurry to discourage this connection. This is particularly interesting, since the Devil Rays are in the process of attempting to drop the Devil from their name, given its negative connotations. In fact, a mural, featuring Bull Durham's enduring bovine trademark as well as the legend, "hit bull, win suit," a prop constructed for the 1988 film, the name of which might be construed as one giant product placement, was installed in the Durham Bulls Athletic Park, opened in 1995. In many ways, this has been, inadvertently, one of the most successful ad campaigns in history. Legend even has it that the Bull Pen is so named because, in the area where Durham pitchers warmed up, there was a giant billboard advertising Duke's product, also embellished the trademark bull. In fact, the Durham Bull graced the wall in a number of bullpens across the country. Whether the origin of the bullpen is true or simply another apocryphal story, it serves as another form of implicit advertising.

Bull Durham loose smoking tobacco may have become synonymous with baseball in the early twentieth century, but the American Tobacco Company staked its real claim in the factory rolled cigarette trade, linking its many brands with baseball, as early as the mid–1880s. Increased industrialization and urbanization effected the growth of the cigarette industry as it did that of its companion industries, advertising and baseball. The cigarette business, and the cigarette advertising business, like baseball was born in New York City, not in North Carolina. In 1884, Buck Duke left Durham, temporarily, and set up shop in a loft on Rivington Street, on the Lower East Side. With a newly invented cigarette rolling machine, the brainchild of Virginian James Bonsack, Duke's company produced a number of brands, among them Mecca and Sweet Caporal, and advertised them heavily.[36]

Although Duke advertised on billboards and in newspapers, by far his most successful advertising strategy was the introduction of trade cards, embellished with pictures of athletes, actresses, and pictures of exotic locales. Most popular and most significant were the trade cards illustrated with pictures of baseball players, the first baseball cards. Trade cards were an ingenious form of premium advertising, a marketing strategy originally introduced in the late nineteenth century. At the outset, consumers were induced to collect wrappers or labels from soap, which they could redeem for valuable gifts, the actual cost of which were generally covered by the shipping and handling charges consumers were required to remit.[37] Trade cards were simpler and more direct. There was nothing to save, nothing to send for. Like little billboards that fit in your pocket,[38] baseball trade cards, also called pack stiffeners, for the ability to do just that, were issued in numbered sets in order to provide added incentive for repeat purchasing.[39] In fact, in the early days of cigarette advertising, individual brands were not marketed based on taste, as they are today. Instead, different brands were sold based on the cards inside the pack.[40]

Unlike product endorsements, baseball trade cards did not depend on the cooperation of the players pictured thereon. The famously rare Honus Wagner card, pulled from production in 1909, shortly after being introduced, supposedly because Wagner objected to promoting the use of tobacco, was intended to be included in packs of American Tobacco's Sweet Caporals. That Wagner was so violently opposed to tobacco marketing may be nothing more than a legend. According to Frank Ceresi, curator of the MCI Sports Gallery, citing Keith Olbermann, Wagner's objection may have stemmed from the fact that he was not paid for the use of his image, as he would have been if trade cards were treated as product endorsements. The famed shortstop was, in fact, pictured in advertisements for other tobacco products, although these predate the trade card.[41]

The American Tobacco Company also used trade silks and flannels, little pieces of cloth printed with images, to sell cigarettes. These items were aimed at women, who presumably collected the bits of fabric with an eye to making quilts from them. While baseball images were not common on silks and flannels, nevertheless, a small proportion bore the pictures of popular players.[42]

Trade card collecting was something of a craze among adults, like the recent crazes for collecting Beanie Babies and bobble head dolls. However, it is impossible to ignore the fact that the demographic Duke intended to reach with baseball trade cards included boys as well as men. The introduction of RJReynold's phallic cartoon character, Joe Camel, in the late twentieth century, as a device to sell tobacco to children, was nothing new. RJR was simply following in a long tradition of cigarette advertising. Eventually, other industries would follow the lead of big tobacco. Trade cards bearing the images of baseball players were also included with such items, also attractive to children, as candy, chewing gum, and that famous nineteenth-century patent medicine, the ever stimulating Coca Cola. In fact, one of the ball players to be pictured on Coca Cola trade cards was none other than Honus Wagner.[43]

After the breakup of the American Tobacco trust, the packaging of baseball themed trade cards and other premiums along with tobacco products, known as "cigarette sandwiches" to the trade, entered its heyday.[44] Because, all of a sudden, there was competition in the tobacco business, baseball trade cards and premiums flourished.

But by the end of World War I, with the advent of cheap newsprint, the popularity of cigarette sandwiches declined.[45] Trade baseball cards, though still available with some brands, were no longer the norm. Certainly, the craze for baseball cards has not disappeared with the decline of the tobacco trade card. Indeed, the production of baseball cards in their own right, not as ad premiums, is still going strong. Lately, there seems to be a resurgence of trade card advertising. A trip to the supermarket revealed that Skippy peanut butter, certain Nabisco crackers and cookies, and selected Post cereals all feature trade card promotions. Unlike the Nabisco and Skippy cards, which feature young fan favorite Derek Jeter, the Post promotion is aimed at adults. Post's cards depict vintage Hall of Famers and are included in boxes of cereals, among them Raisin Bran, pitched to the aging baby boomer demographic.

Following World War I, tobacco advertising was no longer the bailiwick of trade cards. This is not to say that tobacco advertising ceased to look to the diamond for imagery. Even before the popularity of tobacco trade cards declined, tobacco manufacturers sought other ways to rely on their perceived connection to baseball in order to sell their products. For example, in 1910, in the midst of its dismantling in wake of anti-trust legislation, the American Tobacco Company introduced lower priced, massproduced Home Run cigarettes, marketed to working class baseball fans as having "Quality, Not Style." Unlike the more expensive brands, which cost ten or fifteen cents a pack, Home Runs were sold for five cents for packs of twenty.[46] Much like the current radio ad campaign, connecting the image of a couple of self-proclaimed, "hard-working union plumbers" with their requisite thick, blue-collar, New York accents, to hard-working ballplayers, the manufacturers of Home Run cigarettes played on perceived anti-elitist sentiments of the average sports fan to sell their product.

Styles of advertising, like styles, in general, are subject to change. While tobacco trade cards waned in popularity, newspaper advertising waxed. Perhaps the most important style of print advertising, including newspaper advertising in the first decades of the twentieth century is known as Reason Why advertising. George Washington Hill, who succeeded Buck Duke as President of American Tobacco, was a great proponent of Reason Why advertising. Rather than luring consumers with flashy graphics, Reason Why advertising concentrated on attracting buyers to a product with dense copy, intended to convince them that they had a specific need for a particular product.[47] A favorite of early advertising agencies, Reason Why's strategy was ideal for the increasingly more affordable print media.

Before the advent of the first powerful agencies later in the decade, Hill wrote Reason Why copy himself. One of the products he focused his personal creative efforts on was Tuxedo Pipe Tobacco.[48] Hill's American Tobacco Company, like Coca Cola, counted celebrity athlete endorsements, most notably that of Ty Cobb, among the tools of its trade. Indeed, in the early days of celebrity athlete endorsements, Ty Cobb seems to have been a ubiquitous figure. Given his reputation for unpleasant behavior, it is highly unlikely that his testimonial would appear in any early twenty-first century print ad. After all, how often are the faces of Albert Belle or John Rocker pictured pitching products in major non-sports related publications?

Eventually, Hill was forced to give the American Tobacco account to one of the newly powerful and effective advertising agencies. His choice, a natural one given his predilection for Reason Why advertising, was Chicago's Lord and Thomas agency, under the auspices of Albert Lasker. Of all the early advertising executives, Lasker relied most heavily on Reason Why to sell products throughout his career, even when other admen had abandoned the style. In fact, it was Lasker's contention that an ad agency did not really need an art department, if it had good copywriters.[49] Lasker, the man who is considered to be one of the fathers of modern advertising, was for a time, the largest minority owner of the Chicago Cubs and had considerable impact upon the professional game of baseball both inside and outside the advertising arena.[50]

Lasker, the author of a number of landmark ad campaigns, was, among other things, the first to "market" a president. As Warren Harding's director of public relations, he married politics and advertising. Harding was an avid golfer. Lasker was concerned that the candidate would be perceived by the public as an elitist. Golf was, after all, the sport of the elite. But Harding was also part owner of a minor league baseball team, the Marion club in the Ohio State League. Baseball, unlike golf, was the national pastime, the people's game. In order to pitch Harding as a man of the people, Lasker emphasized the candidate's connection with baseball, all the while playing down Harding's love of golf. For public relations purposes, Lasker even attempted to arrange an exhibition game between Harding's minor leaguers and Lasker's Cubs. Apparently, however, the game never took place.[51]

That Lasker's strategy regarding Harding's image was apparently so effective that it seems to have been revived by George W. Bush's handlers during the 2000 Presidential election. After all, the fact that the Bush family augmented their wealth in the oil business, certainly an industry that is perceived as elitist, was not stressed during his campaign. Bush's connection to baseball, however, seemed to be mentioned whenever possible. Perhaps this helped burnish Bush's image as a man of the people, as it did Harding's eighty years earlier.

Albert Lasker was also responsible for the eponymous Lasker plan, proposing that the professional baseball needed oversight by a commissioner.[52] In fact, it was he who proposed that trustbuster Kenesaw Mountain Landis be the first named to that position.[53] It is certainly ironic, in this regard, that the same man who was genuinely horrified by the 1919 Black Sox scandal, was partially responsible for giving the nation the leader responsible for the Teapot Dome scandal.

As an advertising man, Lasker handled various accounts that were either directly or indirectly related to baseball. Prior to landing American Tobacco, Anheuser Busch and Pabst breweries were among Lord and Thomas's biggest clients. Although, when Lasker first joined Lord and Thomas in 1898, the agency also counted the William Wrigley Company as its client, Lasker never personally handled the account.[54] In 1925, when he sold his share of the Cubs to Wrigley, his close friend with whom he could not work effectively, Lasker, ever the ad man, suggested that the chewing gum magnate change the name of his ballpark from Cubs Park to Wrigley Field.[55] Lasker convinced Wrigley that calling the park Wrigley Field would do his "chewing gum business a lot of good," increasing name recognition, thereby selling more gum.[56]

Certainly, ballparks had been named for owners and industrial giants prior to this. After all, Shibe Park was named for sporting goods manufacturer Ben Shibe. However, Shibe's company bore the name of his partner, A.J. Reach. Thus, the rationale for naming the park after Shibe was not, primarily, to sell sporting goods and *Reach Guides*. Lasker, in contrast, was directly responsible for naming the first ballpark not for its team, its city, its neighborhood, or for the personal aggrandizement of its owner, but for its owner's corporate identity. Thus we can see Lasker's ghost in shiny new Enron Field, Coors Field, PacBell Park, Miller Park, and a host of other ballparks bearing corporate monikers. A practice routinely criticized by baseball media as well as fans for taking some of the romance and tradition out of the national pastime, of debasing the great cathedrals of the American church of baseball, of commercializing the sport, the naming of ballparks as a means of branding is very much in the American professional baseball tradition, dating back, if not to the very origins of the professional sport, then to the early decades of the twentieth century. And, somehow, it seems only right that this tradition, alive and well today, should have begun with the naming of one of the last of the great old ballparks still standing, Wrigley Field.

Accusations abound that America's game is being corrupted by commercialism. But professional baseball is and has always been a business. That the professional sport has ever been pure, free from the specter of advertising, is as much a myth as is baseball's invention in Cooperstown by Abner Doubleday in 1839. Even baseball's adopted anthem, *Take Me Out to the Ball Game*, invokes a branded snack food when its narrator sings, "Buy me some peanuts and Cracker Jack." Professional baseball, that most

American of spectator sports, has always been intimately connected with advertising, that most American of businesses, that most American of cultural products. Indeed, these two powerful American cultural institutions will continue to be linked for the foreseeable future.

Notes

1. James B. Twitchell, *AdCultUSA: The Triumph of Advertising in American Culture* (New York: Columbia University Press, 1996), 1.

2. Steve Sleight, *Sponsorship: What It Is and How to Use It*, (Maidenhead, U.K: McGraw Hill UK, 1989), 75.

3. Robert E. L. Faris, *Chicago Sociology, 1920–1932* (Chicago: The University of Chicago Press, 1970), 15.

4. Stephen Fox, *The Mirror Makers* (Urbana: University of Illinois Press, 1997), 4.

5. *Ibid.*, 25.

6. *Ibid.*, 27.

7. Steven A. Riess, *Touching Base: Professional Baseball and American Culture in the Progressive Era* (Urbana: University of Illinois Press, 1999), 12.

8. Twitchell, 72.

9. Sleight, 75.

10. Donald J. Mrozek, "From National Health to Personal Fulfillment, 1890–1940," in *Fitness in American Culture: Images of Health, Sport and the Body, 1830–1940*, ed. Kathryn Grover (Amherst, MA: University of Massachusetts Press, 1989), 32.

11. Sam Carchidi, "A Marker to Aid in Remembering the Baker Bowl," *Philadelphia Inquirer*, 5 August 2000, E1.

12. Sam Coombs and Bob West, Preface, in Alfred Goodwill Spalding, *Base Ball: America's National Game, 1839–1915*, (San Francisco: Halo Books, 1991), x.

13. "Classic Name Revolutionizes Sporting Goods Industry," in *Spalding Sports Worldwide* [cited 14 April 2001], available from <http://www.spalding.com/history.html>.

14. Geoffrey C. Ward and Ken Burns, *Baseball: An Illustrated History* (New York: Alfred A. Knopf, 1994), 27.

15. Sleight, 4.

16. Fox, 34.

17. Jonathan Fraser Light, *The Cultural Encyclopedia of Baseball*, (Jefferson, N.C.: McFarland, 1997), 606.

18. "Al Reach," in *The Online Baseball Library* [cited 1 June 2001], available from <http://cbs.sportsline.com/u/baseball/bol/ballplayers/R/Reach_Al.html>.

19. *How to Play Baseball, by League Stars* (Brooklyn: Brooklyn *Daily Eagle*, 1922), microfilm.

20. Fox, 89.

21. Twitchell, 132.

22. Michael Costen, "The Pilgrimage to Santiago de Compostela in Medieval Europe," in *Pilgrimage in Popular Culture*, ed. Ian Reader and Tony Walter (London: Macmillan, 1993), 138.

23. Alfred Goodwill Spalding, *Base Ball: America's National Game*, 155.

24. Ward and Burns, 28.

25. Fox, 16

26. *Ibid.*, 284.

27. "History," in *Soda Fountain* [cited 1 June 2001], available from <http://www.sodafountain.com/softdrink/cocacola.htm>.

28. Lawrence S. Ritter, *The Glory of Their Times* (New York: William Morrow), 88, unnumbered figure.

29. T.J. Jackson Lears, "American Advertising and the Reconstruction of the Body, 1880–1930," in *Fitness in American Culture*, 21.

30. Twitchell, 131.

31. Fox, 65.

32. American Tobacco Company, *Sold American: The First Fifty Years* (Durham, N.C.: American Tobacco Company), 18.

33. "Team History/ Milestones," in *Durham Bull's Page* [cited 26 April, 2001], available from <http://www.dbulls.com/teamhistory.html>.

34. American Tobacco Company, 22.

35. Twitchell, 54.

36. American Tobacco Company, 21.

37. E.S. Turner, *The Shocking History of Advertising* (New York: E.P. Dutton, 1953), 123.

38. Twitchell, 78.

39. American Tobacco Company, 20.

40. Twitchell, 79.

41. Frank Ceresi, "The Wagner Card," in *Baseball Almanac* [cited 28 June, 2001], available from <http://www.baseball-almanac.com/autont005.shtml>.

42. American Tobacco Company, 25.

43. "History," in *Soda Fountain*.

44. American Tobacco Company, 23.

45. Twitchell, 80.

46. American Tobacco Company, 36.

47. Fox, 50.

48. American Tobacco Company, 51.

49. John Gunther, *Taken at the Flood: The Story of Albert D. Lasker* (New York: Harper, 1960), 96.

50. *Ibid.*, 117.

51. Riess, 69.

52. Gunther, 121.

53. *Ibid.*, 122.

54. *Ibid.*, 42

55. *Ibid.*, 123.

56. *Ibid.*, 119.

Baseball Fiction for Youth

Pamela Barron and Gail Dickinson

Choosing books for children based on interest is considered one of the best ways to encourage reading.[1] Jim Trelease, author of *The Read-Aloud Handbook*, discusses the concept of the "home run" book.[2] Trelease and other authors maintain that if children find that one book, "the home run" that exactly matches their interests, it will touch a chord deep inside them and spark a lifelong love of reading. Baseball provides the subject matter for a number of home run books.

Baseball used to be the sport of choice for children, but competition from soccer, football, swimming, and other sports has changed that. Baseball stories are no longer the only sport featured in children's literature. Have the nature and content of baseball books changed over time? This paper explores books with the subject heading of "baseball—fiction," published since 1950.

What Is Children's Literature?

There are many definitions of children's literature. For the purposes of this paper, children's literature is defined as those books published specifically for children. Children and young adults have been informally defined by two divisions of the American Library Association. The Association for Library Services to Children of the American Library Association defines children as "birth up to and including age fourteen."[3] The Young Adult Library Services Association defines teens as ages "twelve through age eighteen."[4]

For this paper, the authors looked at books written for both children and teens. For most children, the first book they are introduced to is a picture book. In a picture book, both the text and the illustrations tell the story. Picture books are shorter in length as well, generally 32 pages long. A picture book is a unique genre, because one must learn to "read" the illustrations. Many of the clues of characterization are given in the illustrations, not the text. For instance, we know that children notice elements in the illustrations of picture books that elude adults. Even though the text and illustrations may be done by two different individuals, they end up as a unified whole, a seamless blend of the two.

When looking at fiction written for children and teens, the same literary criteria is used as in the evaluation of adult titles. The only difference concerns the age appropriateness of the writing. For example, is the characterization appropriate for a 7-year-old child? Would the child talk this way, and act this way? If told in the first person, as many of these books are, is the voice accurate for that age character?

Authors of children's fiction are not necessarily expected to be experts in the subject area; however, they should be accurate. When writing about baseball, or using baseball as the setting for a story, basic rules of the game should be followed, and correct terminology must be used. References to real people and events should be historically accurate. Historical fiction for youth, just like historical fiction for adults, should be held accountable. In a novel of historical fiction in which Babe Ruth is a character, the author is allowed to make up conversations, but the author will violate conventions of the genre if the author has Ruth doing things he never did, visiting places he did not visit, or playing games in which he did not play. Authors cannot rewrite history for the fictional stories they are creating. Fictional characters may be placed anywhere, in any time, but real characters must be set where they were in real life.

Awards

The Newbery and Caldecott Awards are the two most prestigious awards given in the field of children's literature. They are awarded by the American Library Association. The award winners are announced each January, and are selected from the field of children's literature published during the previous year. The Newbery is given for the most distinguished work of children's writing, and the Caldecott Award is given for the most distinguished illustration of a children's book.[5] Several volumes are also selected as Honor Books (or runners-up) for each award.

Amongst the 2001 awards, one of the Newbery Honor Books was *Joey Pigza Loses Control*, by Jack Gantos.[6] Joey has Attention Deficit Disorder. His parents are divorced, and Joey is sent to spend the summer with his father, whom he does not remember. The father, an alcoholic, convinces Joey to stop taking his medication. By having Joey participate on the Little League team he coaches, the father helps his son gain control over life.

Casey at the Bat, illustrated by Christopher Bing, was a 2001 Caldecott Honor Book.[7] It is an illustrated version of the original poem published in 1888 by Ernest L. Thayer. Bing's version looks like a scrapbook, with old newspaper clippings, artifacts, tickets, period baseball cards, and other memorabilia. Bing notes that he was inspired by Wallace Tripp's earlier illustration of Thayer's poem.[8]

The fact that both of these awards recognized baseball books is evidence that baseball is still a viable subject area for children's fiction.

Reading for Children

Like any skill, reading is developed with practice, and the way students learn to read affects their reading throughout their entire life.[9] Reading as a free voluntary activity has long been associated with academic achievement. Recent research suggests that children and youth view reading as a positive activity. Reading is a foundation skill, and all other skills in life depend on it to some extent. Children who choose reading over other leisure activities tend to read faster, have a higher level of reading comprehension, and retain more information from their reading.[10]

On the other hand, children who do not willingly choose reading as a leisure activity are usually slower readers, who never have the chance to develop the speed or skills that will increase their reading ability. One proven way to encourage reading is to encourage the child to choose reading material written on a topic in which the child has a natural interest. In *Hooked on Books*, Fader bought paperback books for teens with no previous interest in reading. Allowing the teens free access to books and the freedom to choose their reading turned these students onto reading.[11]

The use of appealing baseball books is a way to hook reluctant readers. However, with fewer children playing baseball as they grow up, we do not know if baseball books will still catch children's interest. This paper is a discussion of issues and interests in children's baseball fiction.

Methodology

A review of the literature revealed only one in-depth study of children's baseball fiction. Debra Dagavarian did a content analysis of stories published in magazines for children from 1880–1950.[12] Stories were chosen with the following characteristics:

• Playing baseball was an element of the plot.
• Baseball figured in either the interaction of the characters with each other, or the characters interacted with the structure, process, or physical imperatives of the games.

Dagavarian found five general themes. Interpersonal support, individual responsibility, sacrifice, modesty, and fair play were seen as American values strengthened by the playing and retelling of baseball. Dagavarian commented,

> The structure of the game is such that democratic principles are inherent, and a collective orientation is required. The pace of the game, the configuration of players on the field, the structure of the process and the function of the coach — all of these unique aspects of baseball serve to initiate the youngster into certain culturally-sanctioned normative patterns and value orientations.[13]

Compilation of Bibliography

Using the Library of Congress search terms of Baseball-Fiction and Baseball-Juvenile Literature, library databases were searched to determine baseball holdings. Other bibliographic tools were used as well to begin compiling an annotated listing of baseball books for youth, from 1950 to the present. As the list grew, certain types of books were excluded. Baseball books featuring anthropomorphic animals as the main characters were amongst those eliminated. Basically, the criteria used for this research was the same as Dagavarian's research above, that baseball and the playing of baseball was an element of plot.

Books from the list were found in nearby libraries and a sampling selected for further study. A content analysis instrument based on current research in the field of children's literature was developed. Themes and issues for further research emerged from this framework.

Findings

Several findings emerged from the analytical framework. These are listed below, with books listed under each discussion point to illustrate and highlight the text.

Baseball as Elements of Plot. In the earlier baseball fiction, having knowledge of baseball was essential to understanding the plot. In these books, the plot was generally protagonist against self. The main character's ability to play baseball was threatened, and the resolution of that conflict was baseball-centered. In other words, these earlier books were about playing the game of baseball. An example of such an earlier book is Joe Archibald's *Southpaw Speed.*[14] The main character has great skill as a pitcher, but his ego overshadows his ability. An injury forces him out of the major leagues, and then to the minor leagues, where he learns humility and the true meaning of heart. In *The Great Pete Penney*, Priscilla Penney, otherwise known as Pete, strives to develop her curve ball, playing as the only girl on a Little League team. [15]

The level of baseball knowledge required to read and understand the plot is quite high in these earlier books. In Archibald's book, the following passage illustrates this:

> Tozar, the Jay hitter, let a fastball go by, and the count was even. He got a small piece of the next pitch, and ahead of the batter, Billy threw his idea of a slider again. Thomas lined it into right for a single, and the Jay pilot went to his bench.[16]

A passage from the Tolle book reveals a similar approach:

> I warmed up with seven pitches over the plate to Vince and I felt ready to go. My fastball was zinging like it never did before, and I fanned the first batter. The second batter fouled two and was thrown three balls before he popped out to third. I lost some of my confidence then, and the next batter got a walk. With two away and one on first, the next batter hit a double, sending the walk to third, ready to score.[17]

Contrast this plot and level of assumed baseball knowledge with *Painting the Black*, by Carl Deuker. [18] During his senior year in high school, Ryan Ward's friendship with a new kid in school helps him recover his love of baseball after an injury ended his career as star Little League player. However, Ryan is faced with the moral dilemma of turning in the new star athlete of the team for a sexual harassment incident at school, or winning the state championship. Like the Archibald book, the plot conflict is protagonist against self; however, baseball is used as a backdrop to the conflict, rather than the focus of the conflict.

Also, rather than assuming a high degree of baseball knowledge, the author explains baseball terminology. The book opens with an explanation of the title:

> Lots of guys can stand on the pitcher's mound and throw a baseball hard. But they aren't pitchers. A pitcher does more than throw: he knows what he's doing out there. He changes speeds; he works the corners, inside and outside, tying batters up or making them reach out awkwardly. And once he owns the corners, once the umpire is calling all those pitches strikes, then he really goes to work. He moves his pitches out or in another inch, so that instead of going over the plate, the ball passes over the edge of the plate. Painting the black, they call it.[19]

Gender

Title IX, part of the Education Amendments of 1972, was an attempt to equalize opportunities for girls in sports. It could be assumed that previous to Title IX, or at least around the same time, the appearance of girls in baseball stories would be limited by the opportunities girls had in real life to play baseball. Since literature tends to reflect the issues and trends of society, it could also be assumed that as the opportunities for girls to participate in sports grew, the sports literature would reflect that increased opportunity. A look at the baseball fiction for youth provides contradictory evidence for that assumption.

In 1972, as the issues surrounding girls in Little League Baseball began to make national news headlines, Isabella Taves' *Not Bad for a Girl*[20] was published. In this book, Sharon is described as an attractive and charming girl of twelve. However, her tryout and subsequent selection to her brother's Little League team drew jeers and insults from the crowds. After her coach is fired and Sharon herself is removed from the team, she is interviewed by the national press. Nonetheless, Sharon was not restored to the team, and her exile from baseball continued.

In the 1990s, girls on Little League teams were not unusual. However, books from this decade reveal little change. The *Boonsville Bombers* by Alison Herzig, published in 1993, still has a sister attempting to make it on her brother's baseball team, where she will be the only girl.[21]

Role of Adults

The role of adults in most children's and young adult books is minor. Children and young adults are the audience for these books, so adults are usually flat characters, stereotyped, and not essential to the plot. In some books, adults are even the cause of the conflict, and the adults are rarely helpful in solving problems. In the baseball fiction reviewed for this paper, coaches and teachers, although still minor characters, are portrayed more positively than parents in most instances. Young adults prefer to read stories featuring characters their own age, in a believable life situation. A typical teenager's life centers around friends and school, sports, and extra-curricular activities, and this is reflected in the literature.

One would expect the coach to have a major role in a sports' book; that, however, was often not the case. Although the coach was the most significant adult character in most of these books, the resolution of the conflict was still the responsibility of the young adult. In the children's books, the coach was more involved with the children's lives outside of the team practices and games than the coaches for the young adult teams. Since these books are in the category of contemporary realism, this wider level of concern by adults for children is expected, more so than in the young adult books.

In the majority of both the children's and young adult's titles, parents were rarely directly involved in the plot of the books. A few parents were encouragers, who came to the games and showed empathy for wins and losses. Most parents were portrayed as neutral and stereotypical, with moms baking cookies for the teams and washing uniforms. Some parents were active discouragers of the baseball aspirations of their children. In these instances, another relative, such as an uncle, as in *Choosing Up Sides*, by John Ritter,[22] or an aunt, as in *The Great Pete Penney*, by Jean Bashor Tolle[23] became the enabler, taking the child's side and standing up to the parents.

Alfred Slote used the father-son conflict as a basic plot line in *My Father, The Coach*.[24] Ezell Corkins was excited to finally have a Little League team to join. His father, a parking lot attendant at the local bank, views the team as his opportunity to humiliate his boss, the vice-president of the bank, who coaches last year's championship team. Ezell's father's lack of knowledge about the game of baseball becomes quickly and publicly evident. Ezell, torn between loyalty to his friends and the embarrassment of having his father use the team to create power situations, comes to an understanding of his father's motivation and learns to support him.

Race and Ethnicity

All children need to be able to see themselves and their culture reflected in the books that they and their peers are reading. Issues of race and ethnicity are carefully considered in the study of literature for children and youth to ensure accurate and realistic portrayals of all children. The presence of minorities in contemporary literature text and illustrations should reflect our diverse society. This is an area of concern for the baseball fiction reviewed for this paper. The characters in these baseball books were overwhelmingly portrayed in the characterizations and the illustrations as white. In most of these books, there was no evidence of differences of race, ethnicity, and culture.

Most African-American characters were based on famous historical players, such as Satchel Paige or Jackie Robinson. Several books by Walter Dean Myers, who portrayed the struggles of a multicultural baseball team with players dealing with issues of adoption, step-parenting, and homelessness, provided an exception to the standard presentation.[25] Tales with contemporary, realistic Hispanic characters appeared in only one of the short accounts in Gary Soto's *Baseball in April and Other Stories*.[26] Nonetheless, Dean Hughes' series books, *The Scrappers* and *Angel Park All-Stars*, had some characters with Hispanic names.[27] Asian-American or Native American characters were not present.

There were two books with Jewish characters. In *About the B'nai Bagels* by E.L. Konigsburg,[28] Mark is preparing for his Bar Mitzvah, and dealing with his mother and aunt as new inexperienced coaches for his Little League team. In Miriam Rinn's *The Saturday Secret*,[29] Jason's new stepfather imposes strict restrictions on the family, including banning the playing of baseball on Saturday afternoon.

There were some books set in other countries. An example of this is David Klass' *The Atami Dragons*,[30] in which an American boy travels to Japan with his family, where he plays Japanese baseball. These books offer only one view of each of these cultures, rather than the rich diverse cultures found in both the United States and other countries.

Other themes

Americanization. Earlier in this paper, it was noted that Dagavarian equated American values with baseball. Some books used baseball as a metaphor for the process of Americanization. In Bette Bao Lord's *In the Year of the Boar and Jackie Robinson*,[31] Shirley Wong became more Americanized as she learned the game of baseball. The book's climax had Shirley introducing Jackie Robinson to the class as she realized that although she could never be President, her children would have that opportunity if they chose.

Matt Christopher's *Look Who's Playing First Base*[32] and *Shortstop from Tokyo*[33] depicted new immigrants adapting to American customs and baseball. Although this theme of Americanization was common in books published in the 1970s and early 1980s, the connection between baseball and Americanization was not prevalent as a plot line in more recent books.

Historical Fiction. Many of the books with African-American characters were historical fiction, based on the old Negro baseball leagues. Robert Newton Peck's *Extra Innings*[34] and Walter Dean Myer's *The Journal of Biddy Owens*[35] were two of the most recent additions to this genre. In David Adler's *The Babe and I*, Ruth[36] gave aspiring "Newsies" a chance to watch a Yankee's game. Bill Gutman's time travel fantasy series had a young boy traveling back in time with the magic of a baseball card.[37]

These authors were reaching back to a time in which baseball captured the heart and soul of America, without the distractions of competing sports and other leisure activities. They were tapping into previously unexplored territory of the golden times of baseball, such as the Negro baseball leagues and women's professional teams. New mechanisms of reaching that time included time travel and fantasy.

Calls for Further Research

It is interesting to note that the baseball players referred to in the books were players from another era, usually Babe Ruth or Jackie Robinson. Contemporary baseball players were rarely mentioned. It is unknown whether this is because of the historical reverence authors have for the game, admiration for past players, or because of current scandals of some of today's players. Children need role models that they can see every day, and Babe Ruth, Jackie Robinson, Lou Gehrig, and Mickey Mantle are only shadowy historical figures for today's children and youth.

Gender presented several areas of concern. Overwhelmingly, girls are still struggling to find a place to play, especially when they reach their teens. Perhaps this is because soccer, tennis, and other sports can maintain the interest of girls into their teens and beyond. Conversely, baseball gives way to softball after a girl's Little League years. This dead end to girls playing baseball is partly responsible for the portrayal of girls as still struggling to make the boys' baseball teams.

The role of mothers as coaches carries this further. Even if mothers were directly involved in the teams, they were the coaches of their sons' teams, not of their daughters' squads. While some mothers encouraged their daughters, they facilitated their sons' participation.

Beginning in the mid–1980s, there was a shift away from issues of race and culture as central to the book's plot. Today's characters are more self-absorbed, dealing with their own personal issues. The interplay and team spirit of the past are not present, except in areas of direct conflict. Characters are increasingly white, suburban, and middle class.

There is little research on the attitude of youth towards baseball as the sport of choice. We do not know if there is a specific lack of interest by certain geographic, cultural, or racial groups. However, if the available titles of baseball fiction are indicative of reality, then it would indicate that baseball is a white, middle-class, male sport. As baseball books become less inclusive, less representative of our increasingly diverse society, and require less knowledge about the game, it becomes less likely that the baseball-hungry child will find the "home run" book in baseball fiction.

Notes

1. Stephen Krashen, *The Power of Reading, Insights from the Research* (Englewood, Co: Libraries Unlimited, 1993), passim.

2. Jim Trelease, *The Read-Aloud Handbook* 2nd rev. ed. (New York: Penguin, 1989), passim.

3. For more information on the Association for Library Service to Children, look at the ASLC website at *www.ala.org/alsc*.

4. For more information on the Young Adult Library Services Association, check the YALSA website at *www.ala.org/yalsa*.

5. A complete Newbery and Caldecott Awards listings is available at the website of the Association of Library Service to Children at *www.ala.org/alcs*.

6. Jack Gantos, *Joey Pigza Loses Control* (New York: Farrar, Straus, Giroux, 2000), passim.

7. Ernest Lawrence Thayer and Christopher Bing, *Casey at the Bat: A Ballad of the Republic Sung in the Year 1888* (Brooklyn, NY: Handprint Books, 2000), passim.

8. Ernest Lawrence Thayer and Walter Tripp, *Casey at the Bat* (New York: Coward, McCann & Geoghegan, 1978). Although Bing gives credit for inspiration to the Tripp version, a side-by-side examination reveals interesting similarities and differences. Even though the illustrations show generally the same scenes for each passage, the perspectives are more often then not reversed. A scene in the Tripp book may show the players on the field looking up at the fans, but the Bing illustration for the same scene will show the fans looking down at the players.

9. Bruno Bettelheim, *On Learning to Read* (New York, Knopf, 1981), passim.

10. Krashen, passim.

11. Daniel Fader, *Hooked on Books: Program and Proo.* (New York, Putnam, 1968), passim.

12. Debra Dagavarian, *Saying It Ain't So, American Values as Revealed in Children's Baseball Stories, 1880–1950* (New York: Peter Lang, 1987), passim.

13. Dagavarian, 118.

14. Joe Archibald, *Southpaw Speed* (Philadelphia : McRae Smith, 1965), passim.

15. Jean Bashor Tolle, *The Great Pete Penney* (New York: Atheneum, 1979), passim.

16. Archibald, 93

17. Tolle,. 27

18. Carl Deuker, *Painting the Black* (New York: Camelot, 1997), passim.

19. Deuker, 3.

20. Isabelle Taves, *Not Bad for a Girl* (New York: M. Evans, 1972), passim.

21. Alison Cragin Herzig, *The Boonsville Bombers* (New York: Puffin, 1991), passim.

22. John Ritter, *Choosing Up Sides* (New York: Puffin, 2000), passim.

23. Tolle, passim.

24. Alfred Slote, *My Father, The Coach* (Philadelphia:Lippincott,197), passim.

25. Walter Dean Myers is one of the most prominent African-American authors writing books for youth. Myers has won several awards for his writing, including a Newbery Honor.

26. Gary Soto, *Baseball in April and Other Stories* (San Diego: Harcourt, Brace, Jovanovich, 1990), passim.

27. *The Scrappers* series was published in the early 1990's by Bullseye Press, and Hughes began the *Angel Park All-Stars* series in the later 1990's, published by Aladdin, a division of Atheneum..

28. E.L. Konigsburg, *About the B'nai Bagels* (New York: Atheneum, 1969), passim.

29. Miriam Rinn, *The Saturday Secret* (Los Angeles: Alef Design Group, 1999), passim.

30. David Klass, *The Atami Dragons* (New York: Scribners, 1984), passim.

31. Bette Bao Lord, *In the Year of the Boar and Jackie Robinson* (New York: Scholastic, 1984), passim.

32. Matt Christopher, *Look Who's Playing First Base* (Boston: Little, Brown, 1971), passim.

33. Matt Christopher, *Shortstop from Tokyo* (Boston: Little, Brown, 1970), passim.

34. Robert Newton Peck, *Extra Innings* (New York: Harper Collins, 2001), passim.

35. Walter Dean Myers, *The Journal of Biddy Owens* (New York: Scholastic, 2001), passim.

36. David Adler, *The Babe and* I (New York: Avon Camelot, 1999), passim.

37. Bill Gutman's series focus on famous historical baseball players, including Babe Ruth, Honus Wagner, and Jackie Robinson. This continuing series was begun in the late 1990's, and is published by Avon Camelot.

For the Record and Lives That Mattered: American Baseball Autobiographies

Thomas L. Altherr

Ever since 1782, when that consummate patriot Benjamin Franklin agreed to the publication of his autobiography (which he had written eleven years earlier), Americans have had a special penchant for that form of writing. Imbued with a millennial sense of purpose, at least since the American Revolution, if not earlier, Americans have had a special compulsion to tell the stories of their lives. Whether fashioning exemplary parables, confessing failures, embellishing otherwise lackluster life narratives, or simply stating the facts and opinions for the record, Americans have churned out millions of pages (and miles of audio and videotape) of autobiography. Scholars study the form as a specific literary type and English departments often offer courses and hold workshops on writing one's own autobiography. In our age, few Americans keep a diary or a journal, and fame is fleeting. Still, we have an abundance of autobiographical materials. The historian Martin Duberman once claimed that all history boils down to biography, but he might have just as well said autobiography.

Certainly, Americans were not the first humans to write or tell autobiographies — after all many civilizations, classical and otherwise, had their own forms. Yet Americans have appropriated the type as if it were uniquely suitable for the American experience. Celebrating rampant individualism throughout the late eighteenth and nineteenth centuries, autobiographies became the easy vehicle for self-made men to recount their ascent from poverty to affluence. Others, blending in romanticism, penned narratives in which they unburdened their souls and memories of emotional troubles and triumphs, the all-purpose confessional and therapeutic disclosure. Many autobiographers have taken the opportunity to write a revisionist interpretation of themselves, to gussy up their image for posterity, to "set the record straight" while often cobbling a new set of misty myths and self-aggrandizements. Some escaped slaves and escaped captives from imprisonment by indigenous peoples found their stories movingly retold for humanitarian or racist reasons. Whether starting with the present or near past and working backwards, or following the birth-to-the-present pattern, American autobiographers possess purpose, as though the meaning of the lives chronicled would vanish unless committed to paper.[1]

It should be no surprise then that people connected with the national pastime have themselves left a plethora of autobiographies. Players, ex-players, managers, coaches, umpires, executives, baseball wives, and fans have all chimed in this historical chorus. Among the thousands of baseball autobiographies (many of them co-written or "as-told-to" versions) have been the life stories of Hall-of-Famers and not-so-Hall-of-Famers, longtimers and flashes-in-the-pan, can't-misses and did-misses, fringe characters and those at the center of baseball power. Some are short (and geared often for a juvenile market) and some are fragments, and others are longer (and some long-winded) expositions. Several baseball people have had more than one autobiography. Perhaps only Richard Nixon wrote more books about his life than did Mickey Mantle! Some baseball autobiographies are autobiographies in a looser sense of the word, serving as frameworks for extended editorials and personal gripe sessions about the sport. Nonetheless, many baseball autobiographies are superficial (mere chronicles of I played here, I played there, I hit such-and-such an average, I won so many games, etc). and fail to explore the deeper meanings of the game. Fortunately, that is not the case with all baseball autobiographies. Quite a few merit extended examination.

Given space limitations, this paper will concentrate on six such autobiographies: Pat Jordan's *A False Spring*, Kirby Higbe's *The High Hard One*, Al Schacht's *Clowning Through Baseball*, Tug McGraw's *Screwball*, Hank Aaron's *I Had a Hammer*, and Charlie Metro's forthcoming *Safe by a Mile: A Heart Full of Baseball*.[2] *A False Spring* is a heart-wrenching, but brutally honest telling of Jordan's rapid drop from unlimited potential as a "bonus baby" with the Milwaukee Braves in 1959 through his descent to the low minor leagues to his exit from baseball in 1962. *The High Hard One* is a forthright account of Higbe's hard-bitten major league career (most notably with Brooklyn), his harrowing combat experiences in Europe during World War II, his minor league fadeout years , and his subsequent sixty-day stint in jail, which led to a job with the criminal justice system. *Clowning through Baseball* records Schacht's mediocre major league pitching and coaching career and his long stint as one of the game's premier funnymen. *Screwball*, as the title suggests, details Tug McGraw's career of throwing his signature pitch (the screwball), achieving something approaching stardom with the Mets; it also looks at the eccentricities of McGraw's personality. *I Had a Hammer* chronicles superstar Hank Aaron's rise to fame with the Braves, his chase of the career home run record, and his front-office experiences, all against the backdrop of racial tensions and the civil rights movement. *Safe by a Mile* offers a unique sixty-plus year perspective on the game, following Charlie Metro's baseball career on every level of the sport, from a tryout camp with the Browns in 1937 to a baseball sculpture project, "Hitters' Hands," in retirement; it delivers assessments on the developments within the game over those decades. Several other autobiographies, including Curt Flood's *The Way It Is* and Hank Greenberg's *Hank Greenberg: The Story of My Life*, certainly merit inclusion, but for this paper six will suffice[3]

Jordan's narrative is arguably the best baseball autobiography ever published. From its dripping-with-irony title onwards, *A False Spring* sparkles with metaphor and a candor usually absent from baseball books. Departing from the long tradition of American success stories embodied in autobiographies from Benjamin Franklin to Donald Trump, Jordan takes the reader on a painful journey through his descent from fame and promise.

Early in the account, Pat established his reasons for writing the book:

> Yet it [his baseball career] never seemed to end properly, neatly, all those bits and pieces finally forming some harmonious design. It just stopped, unfinished in my memory, fragmented, so many pieces missing. Over the years I have begun sorting and resorting those bits and pieces — delicately, at first — finding every now and then a new one to further flesh out that design, finally discovering the pieces had always been there and that what had been missing was in me. This book, then, is an attempt not to relive that experience but to resee it, once and for all, as it truly was, somehow frozen in time, unfragmented, waiting only for me to develop the perception needed to see it whole. [4]

Writing a decade after his exit from the Braves' organization, during a time of national disillusionment, with the debacles of Vietnam and Watergate still fresh, Jordan chose the autobiographical format as an exercise in self-realization, a therapeutic approach. "Baseball was such an experience in my life," he declared, "that … I have still not shaken it, will probably never shake it. …It's as if I decided at some point in my life, or possibly *it* was decided, that of all the things in my life only that one experience would most accurately define me." [Jordan's italics] Moreover, he contended, objectivity is not the sole goal of this examination: "It hardly matters whether this is a fact or a private delusion. It matters only that I devoted so great a chunk of my life to baseball that I believe it's true. I believe that that experience affected the design of my life to a degree nothing else ever will."[5]

The very process of memory is an important element in Jordan's self-narrative. His depictions, for instance, of his first professional season, with the McCook Braves in the Nebraska State League, brim with sharp detail. A sense of time and place is vivid in his evocative descriptions of the town, its people, his teammates, his colorful manger, Bill Steinecke, and the Midwestern customs so foreign to a young man from Connecticut.[6] Similarly his beautifully drawn pictures of his initial reaction to the Braves' spring training facilities, at Waycross, Georgia and Bradenton, Florida are themselves worth the price of the book.[7] And yet, when he summed up his performance of that year in McCook, the clarity of his memories blurs:

> I finished that first season with a 3–3 record and a 3.54 earned run average. I gave up 41 hits in 56 innings. I walked 55 batters and struck out 56. I obtained these statistics from a back copy of *The Sporting News*. I'd forgotten them. I'd forgotten so much about those games, which, at the time, were so important to me. Small fragments, like the hailstones in Holdrege [Nebraska], they have melted in the warm waters of my memory.

But other experiences maintained a stronger hold on Jordan's personal archives:

> There are some fragments, however, that have not melted but have surfaced, hard and cold and sharp, from my subconscious. They seldom concern those games ("my only reality"), but deal instead with all that "dead time" I passed in McCook. These float about, knocking against one another in a disturbing way, until the two at length fit together to form a large piece and, repeating that process, a still larger one, until they have taken on a shape I can now recognize.[8]

Even then, the process can be tricky. Years later, while writing the book, Jordan mused, "And as I go about my ordinary day, I'll wonder, now, what people are passing, unseen, through my life, only to be remembered years later with a warmth I never felt at their moment of passing."[9]

A False Spring is especially poignant when it treats the discrepancies between expectations, particularly those of his older brother George (who worked out frequently with Pat when Jordan was an up-and-coming phenom in Little League and high school) and the ensuing realities. Jordan wrote thus of George's misperceptions:

> What I had been is still clear to my brother. It is a picture whose lines have been redrawn so often, retracing identical successes year after year, that it has become etched in his memory. He never saw those lines erased during my years in the minor leagues and then somehow redrawn, without his knowledge, until what they defined when I was released by the Braves in 1962 was something unrecognizable to him.[10]

During Pat's abbreviated career, George refused to give up his conception of Pat as a strikeout pitcher. After one game in which Jordan pitched very well, but struck out only two batters, George upbraided him for not striking out more.[11] There are many valuable insights and hard won lessons in Jordan's account, but one of them may be the persistence of the past, the death grip it has on a person's abilities to respond to a changing present and future.

Kirby Higbe's autobiography, *The High Hard One*, took almost the opposite approach to that of Jordan's. Although Higbe salted his narrative with plenty of down home Southernisms, the tale is relatively unadorned and straightforward. As if the title itself was indicative, Kirby tossed the readers the high hard one: this is how it was, hard, tough, plain and simple. Of his childhood baseball abilities, Kirby wrote matter-of-factly, "I developed my strong right arm early in life by getting in rock fights and by making bets I could throw rocks farther than anybody thought any boy ever could. I didn't know then that later in life my right arm would be my sole means of support." [12]

Born in 1915, Higbe came of age during the tough times of the Great Depression. Jobs and money were scarce for his family in South Carolina, so young Kirby took what was available: "I was a real puny kid, so I started cutting trees and logs all over the countryside, both to build myself up and to make some money. In those days, all the people in the country needed wood both for their cookstoves and to heat with. I would walk out in the country, sometimes a good many miles, and cut wood all day for 25 cents and a good country meal. They really put out some good country food. Cutting wood with a 12-pound ax gives you a good appetite."[13] His raw physical talents helped him survive: "After grammar school I went one year to Wardlaw Junior High School, where I got more practice for my baseball career. There was a pretty good-sized field behind the school, about 300 feet from home plate to the center-field fence. Money was so scarce the only way I could eat was bet 10 or 15 cents I could throw the ball over the center-field fence from home plate. That is the way I ate lunch the whole year at Wardlaw."[14]

For all of his perceptive comments on baseball and his career, Higbe remained imprisoned by his racial perspectives. The South that Higbe grew up in was one of hardened racial segregation. Around Columbia, African-Americans and whites kept a wary distance, but according to Higbe, there was little of the racial violence that occurred in Northern cities. Thus, he wrote later, "We didn't have anything personal against Jackie Robinson or any other Negro. As Southerners who had played ball up North for several years, we heard a lot of talk about how we abused and mistreated Negroes down South, and we knew we never had. We never had any race riots or trouble with Negroes in my neck of the woods down South, but I had seen and heard of plenty of trouble in Detroit, New York, and St. Louis."[15] When he and other white youths crossed over into the black residential district, they themselves became targets of rock-throwing retaliation. Higbe recalled the incidents thus:

> I was on the radio one time with Bill Stern in New York, and he asked me how I ever got such a strong arm. I told him throwing rocks at Negroes, and he cut me off the mike right away. I don't think he understood.
>
> We were Southern boys, brought up to believe in the separation of the races, but we didn't hate Negroes. The rock fights were more of a game on both sides. It was a challenge on both sides. They threw as many rocks as we did, sometimes more, being on their home field, so to speak, and not having to scramble up that clay bank.[16]

In this autobiography, Higbe soft-pedaled the degree of real racism in his South and in baseball. He described the many reminders of the Confederacy's cause in his hometown and took pains to distinguish such as a proud heritage, not destructive racism. In 1947, when Jackie Robinson broke the racial barrier in the major leagues, Higbe was one of several Dodgers who protested Jackie's arrival. Branch Rickey granted his wish not to play with Robinson by trading Kirby to the Pirates. Twenty years later, while writing these memoirs, Higbe still remained a bit obtuse about the impact Robinson had on the game. Although by that time he generally had praise for Jackie's playing abilities, Higbe asserted that it was probably the expanded chances for education that changed baseball more than did the cracking of the color barrier.[17]

Indeed, his regret over never graduating from high school was a constant refrain throughout the autobiography. He made his choice early on to make a living throwing a ball. After losing a Little World Series championship game, Higbe gained a new approach to life: "Losing that ball game was the end of my boyhood. In the morning and from then on I began thinking about baseball as the main business of my life. You can't see ahead. You go a pitch at a time, an inning at a time, one game at a time."[18] When he hung up his spikes in 1953, the pain was palpable: "Baseball had been my life for twenty-five years. I hated to quit. God, I hated to quit. I loved the game so much, and there wasn't anything else I knew." [19] A page later, he offered more details: "Driving home that night, I thought about my years in baseball, how I had given it everything I had for twenty-five years. When you love the game and the fans, you have to quit when you can't give what the game demands and the fans want. When I got home I told my wife, 'That was it. It's over.' I couldn't comb my hair for a week."[20]

Yet looking back over his career, Kirby lamented not having the credentials to get a decent position after baseball ended. He counseled college-age players to focus on getting an education. "I have wished a thousand times I had not quit school without at least a high-school education. I have talked to a good many boys who are prospects for professional ball, and I tell them all to finish college before they sign for professional ball," he remarked. He urged them then to give "four hard years" to baseball, and then if they didn't make it by then, go on to another career choice. "An education is something you don't have to carry on your back," he stated, "They can't take it away from you. I am speaking from experience. I learned the hard way. Baseball was all I knew."[21] That declaration summed up the baseball life of Kirby Higbe.

Much more light-hearted was Al Schacht's account, *Clowning through Baseball.* In breezy fashion, Schacht recounted his efforts to land a mound job with John McGraw's New York Giants, his bouncing around the minors and majors, finally landing with Bucky Harris' Washington Senators during their glory days in the mid–1920s. All through his campaign in the minors, however, he discovered hints of his true calling as a clown. In 1913, for example, after riding a horse into the stadium at the start of a game, he commanded the uproarious applause of the Newark crowd; it was incidental that he survived, on the mound, for less than three innings. "But on that day," Schacht writes, "I discovered it was easier to make people laugh than it was to retire those batters."[22] Combining the sort of brazen fool image that Ring Lardner used to great effect in his 1920s baseball stories with a heavy dose of the sort of self-deprecation that Bob Uecker made his stock and trade later in the century, Al elucidated the possibilities for humor within the game. Describing his encounters with umpires, he wrote:

> "They took great delight in fining me or chasing me out of ball games. One ump even took a decided interest in me and my well-being. He used to give me the proverbial thumb at the slightest provocation,

with the following explanation: "I know you're a bug on hot water, so I'm kicking you out while there's still some in the shower. I don't want you taking risks by showering in cold water.'"[23]

After his American League debut, in which he faced the Tigers' Harry Heilmann in a close game with disastrous results, Al philosophized, "And a few moments later, when I was under the shower bath, I realized that a fellow can lose a ball game quite easily on only one pitch."[24] Luckily for him, a career in baseball comedy waited down the road.

In 1937, Schacht "assumed the fancy title of 'Clown Prince of Baseball,' and became the Vagabond Zany — a one-man circus — a traveling fool."[25] On the circuit constantly, Schacht honed his *schtick* in many a minor league park — an account of a performance at Pennington Gap, Virginia, in which he had to go up an eight-thousand foot cable to a mine head to rouse the miners to come to the park that evening, is superb.[26] Eventually, Schacht solidified his hold as the major leagues' designated humorist, either alone or with another Senators' veteran, Nick Altrock. Throughout the last part of the book, Schacht moaned and groaned about his persistent problems with chauffeurs and paid tribute to other eccentric characters in baseball, such as Moe Berg, Smead Jolley, and Art Shires. More informational than penetrating, Schacht's book leaves a reader hungering for a little less foolery. All told, however, *Clowning through Baseball* is an enjoyable read and a fascinating, if somewhat restrained, look at the intersection of humor and sport.

Early in his autobiography, *Screwball*, Tug McGraw stated, "It's hard to describe yourself the way other people do…. They see you as a nut, flake, freak, screwball. I think I'm basically an honest person."[27] That comment fairly well crystallizes the tone of his book. He played off his screwball image and yet tries to escape it. For example, Tug became identified with his battle cry, "You gotta believe!" during the 1973 season when the Mets fought back to win the pennant and go to the World Series. But, as he explains it, the slogan came about almost accidentally. While the Mets were mired in last place earlier in the season, McGraw had a conversation with an insurance salesman named Joe Badamo, who convinced Tug of the power of positive thinking.[28] Tug integrated the salesman's credo into his mental approach to the game. Then, as the Mets fought their way into the pennant race, McGraw, after winning a game, entered the clubhouse, shouting "like a madman," "You gotta believe." He confessed, "I suppose I meant you gotta believe that sooner or later you're bound to win one." But the phrase caught on and helped energize the surging Mets.[29]

Like Pat Jordan, McGraw had a brother who had a direct influence on him, but whereas George Jordan was nowhere near the athlete Pat was,

Tug's brother Hank was larger and more athletically talented. "I had an older brother who was a super athlete," Tug recalled, "he was everything to me growing up, but I didn't envy him, I loved him. Maybe there was a little bit of envy. I wanted to be as good as he was, but not because he was getting all the attention. Just because he was my brother."[30] McGraw wrote, "Hank was my number one hero in those days. He had forty pounds and five or six inches on me, and he got into sports right away ...Hank and I already had built our time around sports because we got a boot out of it. We were very close."[31]

Hank signed with the Mets for a $15,000 bonus. Later during an exhibition game in Williamsport, Pennsylvania, Tug and Hank faced each other. The showdown was a draw of sorts. Hank popped out in his first time up, but slammed a double the next at bat.[32] All this spurred Tug on in his own athletic endeavors: "Because I was a shrimp, I also had an inferiority complex, and I became very competitive in sports because of it."[33] When a college coach once said, "[L]ook, McGraw, you're not going to play pro baseball anyway," Tug's drive and cockiness proved that coach dead wrong.[34]

McGraw's life and times included a lot of playfulness. A confirmed prankster, Tug kept the clubhouse loose with imitations and other stunts. He revealed that an ankle injury was due to some reckless tobogganing with fellow Met Ron Swoboda on Long Island.[35] But sometimes his humor was self-deprecatory. For example, note this account of his first slide into home plate as a boy:

> Once I tried to imitate the TV stars by sliding home. I hit a ball between the outfielders and starting racing around the bases. We didn't have fences or anything like that, and you had to run out a home run. As I rounded third base, I remembered the guys on TV sliding across the plate, so I decided to slide, too. But I didn't know *where* to slide because I'd never done it before. So I hit the dirt halfway between third and home, a long ways from nowhere, and then had to crawl the rest of the way to the plate with a home run and a red face.[36]

For all his merrymaking, however, McGraw displayed a more introspective side. For Tug, pitching itself could be an existential scenario: "Who am I? Where am I? Why am I? That's often what comes out of the blur when you're trying to narrow everything down to you and the hitter."[37] A stretch in the United States Marines during the Vietnam War caused some of this change, as did the shooting of students at Kent State in 1970. Thinking about his military service, McGraw wrote, "Sometimes during a ball game now I'll remember some grinding thing that happened to me in the Marines. And I realize that those six months in service left me with a lot of scars and bruises. Emotional ones, like when my folks split up or when I couldn't get people to understand something I was trying to do. They also left me tougher in some ways." "But I'm no psychologist," he demurred, "so I'm not going to try to 'sum it all up.'"[38] Towards the end of the book, McGraw reprinted a long diary entry ruminating on his belief in God, his own confusions with current events, his anguish over Vietnam and Kent State, ending with this pronouncement: "I think the reason I love baseball so much is because when I come into a game in the bottom of the ninth, bases loaded, no one out and a one-run lead … it takes people off my mind."[39]

When many white fans read Hank Aaron's autobiography, *I Had a Hammer*, they are surprised to encounter such a passionate account of his life. During his playing days, Aaron did not have the flashy image of a Willie Mays or fiery temperament of a Frank Robinson or a Roberto Clemente. For all his steadiness and greatness, Hank impressed many who saw him play as sort of a sleepy, laidback player. Indeed, whites accepted that image because as Aaron noted, it "wasn't regarded as bigotry for a white person to make lighthearted reference to a black person's laziness or ignorance — it was just being a good ol' boy."[40] Of course, the stereotype was inaccurate, as Aaron waged his battles and showed his pride in his own ways. Still, the average reader is unprepared for the candor and even anger that pervades his narrative. Aaron, and his co-writer Lonnie Wheeler, anticipated this. In the first chapter, Hank explained why he was recounting his story:

> The way I see it, it's a great thing to be the man who hit the most home runs, but it's a greater thing to be the man who did the most with the home runs he hit. So long as there's a chance that maybe I can hammer out a little justice now and then, or a little opportunity here and there, I intend to do as I always have — keep swinging. I'm taking my cuts as you read this. I'm telling my story, and when everything's said and done, maybe it'll mean more than a bunch of home runs. I can only hope and keep hammering.[41]

In the last chapter, Aaron amplified his point: "Baseball needs me because it needs somebody to stir the pot, and I need it because it's my life."[42] "Maybe the day will come when I can sit back and be content with the changes that have taken place in America," he pondered, "or, at least, in my part of it, which is baseball. Maybe in a few years, baseball won't need somebody like me anymore. But until that day comes, I intend to stay in the batter's box — I don't let the big guys push me out of there anymore — and keep hammering away."[43]

For most baseball historians and many fans, the contours of Hank

Aaron's career are well-known. *I Had a Hammer* faithfully outlined them. Coming up with the Braves in 1954, Hank put together a string of All-Star seasons, including leading Milwaukee to the World Series in 1957 and 1958. As Aaron snuck up on Babe Ruth's career home run record in the early 1970s, the baseball public either cheered or derided his achievements. When Aaron finally broke the record in 1974, it was greeted with a good deal of relief by Hank himself and many well-wishers. Only then did fans become aware of how much torment Hank had undergone, how many pieces of hate mail and death threats had shown up at his doorstep. Having run that gauntlet and survived, Aaron faded as a focal point for racial divisions within the game. His post–715 home run career seemed anti-climactic, especially his designated hitter stint with the Milwaukee Brewers prior to his retirement in 1976. But Aaron's book went further, providing an extended civics lesson about the struggles of the Civil Rights Movement. Perhaps only Robert Creamer's *Baseball in '41* took as many pains to relate what was happening outside the ballpark to the happenings on the field.[44]

The most pervasive theme of Aaron's narrative, of course, is the omnipresent presence of racism and segregation, which haunted his career. As might be expected, Hank experienced many instances where he had to eat in restaurants or sleep in hotels apart from his white teammates. Like Jackie Robinson and other pioneer black ballplayers, Aaron heard his share of racist taunts, which, of course, increased during his pursuit of Ruth's record. But an earlier episode, narrated in the book, exemplifies the bigotry encountered by Aaron.. After playing in Baltimore, Aaron and his team, the Indianapolis Clowns, moved on to Washington, but had to wait out a storm. Aaron recorded the episode in all its bitter irony:

> We had breakfast while we were waiting for the rain to stop, and I can still envision sitting with the Clowns in a restaurant behind Griffith Stadium and hearing them break all the plates in the kitchen after we were finished eating. What a horrible sound. Even as a kid, the irony hit me: Here we were in the capital in the land of freedom and equality, and they had to destroy the plates that had touched the forks that had been in the mouths of black men. If dogs had eaten off those plates, they'd have washed them.[45]

Repeatedly, Aaron documented the patterns of racist stereotyping, exclusion, neglect, and abuse that he and so many other African-American players had to endure. *I Had a Hammer* is all the more powerful because Aaron and Lonnie Wheeler refused to settle for the typical and superficial as-told-to autobiographies. The book ranks with the great moral testimonies of all time.

Last, Charlie Metro's autobiography, *Safe by a Mile*, shows yet other dimensions of the genre. Hardly a household name like superstar Aaron, nor the glorious failure of a Pat Jordan, nor the hard-bitten Depression-era player of the Kirby Higbe mold, nor a slap-happy Al Schacht clown, nor a wacko Tug McGraw goofball, Metro occupied a rather unique territory in baseball. Involved in the game directly and constantly from 1937 to his retirement in 1984 and indirectly with his "Hitters' Hands" project since then, Charlie had the opportunity to witness the game from many different angles, to accumulate a wealth of baseball anecdotes and tales, and to achieve a long-grounded perspective on the past, present, and future of the sport. Indeed, his life, from his fortuitous tryout camp at Johnstown, Pennsylvania during his senior year in high school to his yeoman scouting service in the 1970s and 1980s, represents a "Pilgrim's Progress" of sorts, a quasi-allegorical journey through the hustlings of the minor leagues, a treasured stint of three years in the majors, several years of trials in the minors, leading back up to the top — as a manager with the Cubs and Royals, a coach and scout with the White Sox, a scout with the Reds, director of players with the Kansas City franchise, seven years of scouting with Tommy Lasorda's Dodgers, and a year of coaching with Billy Martin's Oakland club in 1982. Perhaps only Jimmy Reese and Dave Garcia were in uniform longer. In some important ways, Metro became baseball's Everyman, or as he might put it less graciously, horse manure, always around and always underfoot.

And yet through all these wanderings, Charlie constantly kept a sense of humor and captured the crazy happenings of the game in the numerous anecdotes that punctuate the narrative. Two will suffice here to illustrate the flavor:

> But there were always other mysteries and uncontrollables. One day in the early 1950s, we were whomping Hudlin's Jackson team something like fifteen to two. I was playing right field. Near the end of the game, I looked into the dugout and saw the batboy and the rest of the guys packing up the bats and other equipment. I couldn't believe it. They were violating one of the sacred rules of baseball: never pack up the equipment until the game is over! I was out there yelling, "Unload the bags" and everything else, but nobody knew why I was going crazy. The blacks were in the bleachers down the right field line out there, and they were giving me all kinds of heck. They had a lot of fun with me, and I was answering them back. "We're going to get you, Charlie," they said, "We're going to get you. We're going to beat you." One black guy had a rabbit's foot, and he kept teasing me with it. Can you guess what happened? You're right. In the bottom of the ninth Jackson put together a rally, and we helped them out with some bonehead defensive mistakes. Their hits fell just beyond our fielders. Our second baseman thought there were two outs and put the ball in his pocket instead of relaying it to first for what would have been a game-ending

double play. When the commotion settled, the final score was sixteen to fifteen, Jackson. If you go down to that Jackson ballpark today, you'll probably find them still hitting! We never did get them out. Every time I saw Willis Hudlin after that, he would point his finger at me and laugh. And I'd say, "Willis, we're both old guys now. Look out." That day, however, I was so mad at everybody that I walked home in my uniform. I wouldn't even ride the bus. I walked all the way back to the hotel in Jackson...[46]

My Montgomery team was playing in Savannah one steamy evening in 1951, when the mosquitoes were pretty thick and angry. They were like dive-bombers, so many of them occasionally the groundskeepers had to smoke the field. We were losing, down by five runs, and I was standing in the coach's box wondering how I'd gotten us into this mess. It was the top of the ninth and we were down to our last out. Dick Greco, our big right fielder and quite a home run hitter, was the batter. He drew a walk, but that didn't seem promising, because Dick wasn't much of a runner. Well, at that time my steal sign was skin on skin. As I was coaching over there at third, a mosquito nailed me and instinctively I slapped at it. Dick Greco's eyes must have gone full wide, because the next thing I know, he took off for second base on the next pitch. Even more surprisingly he made it! Now I was getting quite irritated. Even the greenest rookie knew that you didn't steal a base with your club down by five runs in the top of the ninth. While I was fuming, another mosquito attacked me and again I swatted my arm. Again the next thing I realized was that big Dick Greco was rumbling into third base with another steal. I muttered to him, "Wait till I get you in the clubhouse after the game," as he lay there after his slide with a slap-happy grin on his face. I turned back to watch the pitcher work to our batter, but somehow I slapped my arm again at another mosquito. Greco, probably as bewildered as the opposing team at this point, nevertheless took off for home and slid in safely! As if that wasn't astonishing enough, our next few batters connected and put up four more runs on the board to tie it up. Then in the tenth, we pushed across another one and won the game. The newspaper the next day proclaimed me an absolute genius for such daring base coaching. I didn't have the heart to tell them that it was just the dang mosquitoes.[47]

Many additional stories expand on this humorous side of the game, which serve as counterpoints to the inexorable chronology of countless hours of hard work, waiting and moving on, releases and hirings, many miles of rail travel, constant air flights across North America and the Caribbean in search of talent, spring trainings, long seasons, and playoffs that marked Metro's steady sojourn in the sport.

Finally, then, baseball autobiographies share some common ground with much good literature. The process of memory, especially in *A False Spring*, brings forth a shock of recognition, self-recognition, for sure, but at the same time elicits some shared experience with the reader. By asserting that my life, or at least my baseball career mattered, baseball autobiographies offer an affirmation of both the individual and communal aspects of the game. Baseball, our venerable national pastime that may, in its folk antecedents, pre-date the American Revolution, has produced autobiographies that serve up multiple perspectives on the game's history, texturing the past in ways that statistics and passing anecdotes can not.[48] For, essentially, the game is long with us, accumulating in our consciousness, even as it sloughs off or reinvents details. For some baseball may indeed be life, as the T-shirt proclaims, but, more likely, it is life, the raw stuff of these autobiographies, which is the matrix in which baseball resonates.

Notes

1. For some convenient summaries and studies of American autobiography, see Barbara B. Oberg and Harry S. Stout, eds., *Benjamin Franklin, Jonathan Edwards, and the Representation of American Culture* (New York: Oxford University Press, 1993); G. Thomas Couser, *American Autobiography: The Prophetic Mode* (Amherst, Massachusetts: University of Massachusetts Press, 1979); Albert E. Stone, ed., *The American Autobiography: A Collection of Critical Essays* (Englewood Cliffs, New Jersey: Prentice-Hall, 1981); Thomas Cooley, *Educated Lives: The Rise of Modern Autobiography in America* (Columbus, Ohio: Ohio State University Press, 1976); Joseph Fichtelberg, *The Complex Image: Faith and Method in American Autobiography* (Philadelphia: University of Pennsylvania Press, 1989); and D.H. Lawrence's delightful take on Franklin and his *Autobiography* in *Studies in Classic American Literature* (New York: Viking Press, 1961 [1923]), chapter II.

2. Pat Jordan, *A False Spring* (New York: Dodd, Mead Company, 1975); Kirby Higbe (with Martin Quigley), *The High Hard One* (Lincoln, Nebraska: University of Nebraska Press, 1998 [1967]); Al Schacht (with Murray Goodman), *Clowning through Baseball* (New York: A.S. Barnes and Company, 1941); Tug McGraw and Joseph Durso, *Screwball* (Boston: Houghton Mifflin Company, 1974); Hank Aaron (with Lonnie Wheeler), *I Had a Hammer: The Hank Aaron Story* (New York: HarperCollins, Harper paperback, 1992 [1991]); and Charlie Metro (with Tom Altherr), *Safe by a Mile: A Heart Full of Baseball* (Lincoln, Nebraska: University of Nebraska Press, forthcoming, January, 2002).

3. Curt Flood (with Richard Carter), *The way It Was* (New York: Trident Press, 1980); and Ira Berkow, ed., *Hank Greenberg: The Story of My Life* (New York: Times Books, 1989).

4. Jordan, 11.

5. *Ibid.*

6. *Ibid.*, 54–126.

7. *Ibid.*, 127–148 and 194–237.

8. *Ibid.*, 124.

9. *Ibid.*, 166.

10. *Ibid.*, 8.

11. *Ibid.*, 228.

12. Higbe, 3.

13. *Ibid.*, 9.

14. *Ibid.*, 12.

15. *Ibid.*, 104.
16. *Ibid.*, 11.
17. *Ibid.*, 100–109.
18. *Ibid.*, 19.
19. *Ibid.*, 153.
20. *Ibid.*, 154.
21. *Ibid.*, 147.
22. Schacht, 28.
23. *Ibid.*, 29–30.
24. *Ibid.*, 75–76.
25. *Ibid.*, 119.
26. *Ibid.*, 131–136.
27. McGraw, 20.
28. *Ibid.*, 23.
29. *Ibid.*, 25 and 35.
30. *Ibid.*, 19.
31. *Ibid.*, 19 and 63.
32. *Ibid.*, 97–98.
33. *Ibid.*, 56.
34. *Ibid.*, 77.
35. *Ibid.*, 122–123.
36. *Ibid.*, 60.
37. *Ibid.*, 17.
38. *Ibid.*, 108.
39. *Ibid.*, 155–157.
40. Aaron, 117.
41. *Ibid.*, 6.
42. *Ibid.*, 456.
43. *Ibid.*, 457.
44. Robert Creamer, *Baseball in '41* (New York: Viking Press, 1991), passim.
45. Aaron, 47.
46. Metro, chapter 5.
47. *Ibid.*, chapter 5.
48. For evidence of pre–1839 baseball and baseball-type games, see Thomas L. Altherr, "'A Place Level Enough to Play Ball': Baseball and Baseball-type Games in the Colonial Era, Revolutionary War and Early American Republic," *NINE* 8, no. 2 (Spring 2000), 15–50.

Baseball Haiku: Basho, the Babe, and the Great Japanese-American Trade

Edward J. Rielly

The introduction of baseball into Japan from the United States and haiku into the United States from Japan was one of the great cultural trades between these two countries, even if the adoption of haiku by Americans must be viewed as akin to a transaction involving a "player to be named later." This paper outlines some of the important people and events involved in the rise of baseball in Japan and haiku in the United States, and in the wedding of haiku and baseball in recent years.

Baseball has long been considered America's national pastime. Since the 1870s, when baseball was first introduced into Japan by Americans, it has steadily gained importance in Japan as well. The two Americans most responsible for the popularity of Japanese baseball are Babe Ruth and General Douglas MacArthur, but many other individuals also played important roles. Credit for introducing baseball to Japan is usually given to two American missionary teachers in the 1870s: Horace Wilson, who taught history and English in Tokyo at Kaisei Gakko (the future University of Tokyo), where he instructed his students in the rudiments of the game; and Albert Bates, who apparently organized the first formal baseball game while teaching at Kaitaku University in Tokyo in 1873. Horoshi Hiraoka, a Red Sox fan while studying in Boston, formed Japan's first team, the Shimbashi Athletic Club Athletics, in 1878. In the same year, F. William Strange, an English lecturer at Tokyo University, provided Japan with the rules of baseball in his book *Outdoor Games*.[1]

Baseball quickly caught on with the Japanese, who found the game, especially individual competition between pitcher and hitter, similar to the martial arts, and viewed the sport as a way to build character through hard work and discipline. Baseball, also called *yakyu* (field ball), became a sport of the upper classes played by high school and university students.[2] A visit by the University of Wisconsin's baseball team in 1878 inaugurated numerous future sojourns, in both directions, by amateur teams.[3] The first tour of Japan by American professionals occurred in 1908, sponsored by A. J. Reach & Company, a sporting-goods firm. The "Reach All-Americans," as they were called, although the team actually consisted of minor leaguers and fringe major league players, won all seventeen of their contests.[4]

Japanese baseball progressed so quickly that by 1911 Albert Spalding, the great pitcher, club president, and sporting goods magnate, devoted a chapter to it in his book *Base Ball: America's National Game*. Spalding refers to the sport as "the most popular form of outdoor pastime" for students at Japan's leading universities and discusses various trips by Japanese and American college teams to each other's country.[5] Spalding quotes E. S. Wright reporting in the *Philadelphia Evening Telegraph* that the Japanese play the game of baseball "with the rowdy part kept out."[6] Almost eighty years later, in his book *You Gotta Have Wa*, Robert Whiting would explore in much greater depth the Japanese approach to playing:

> The concept and practice of group harmony, or *wa*, is what most dramatically differentiates Japanese baseball from the American game. It is the connecting thread running through all Japanese life and sports. While "Let It All Hang Out" and "Do Your Own Thing" are mottoes of contemporary American society, the Japanese have their own credo in the well-worn proverb, "The Nail That Sticks Up Shall Be Hammered Down."[7]

The 1908 visit by Reach All-Americans was followed by the joint world tour undertaken by the New York Giants and Chicago White Sox after the 1913 season. John McGraw's Giants lost to the Sox twice in Japan, and a joint Giants-Sox squad defeated the Keio University team.[8]

Herb Hunter, who played in only thirty-nine games in the majors from 1916 to 1921, proved more successful arranging tours of American players to Japan.[9] He took the so-called "Herb Hunter All-Americans," a mixture of minor and major league players, to Japan in 1920 and 1922. The latter, which included more top players (e.g., Herb Pennock, Waite Hoyt, Casey Stengel), had the distinction of being the first group of American professionals to lose to a Japanese team.[10]

A women's team, the Philadelphia Bobbies, journeyed to Japan in 1925. Although to the Japanese, the players appeared even younger than their ages of thirteen to twenty-three, the Bobbies held their own against their male opponents, winning some and losing some.[11]

Hunter arranged for still another American team to visit in 1931. This squad featured some of the game's biggest stars, including Mickey Cochrane, Lou Gehrig, and Frankie Frisch, and had no trouble handing their Japanese opponents seventeen consecutive drubbings.[12] The following year, the Negro League Philadelphia Royal Giants returned, having first played there in 1927.[13] Also in 1932, Hunter came back with three instructors to help the Japanese elevate their level of play: National League batting champion Lefty O'Doul, pitcher Ted Lyons, and a backup catcher named Moe Berg.[14]

Berg played fifteen seasons in the majors, ending in 1939. Not much of a hitter, he compiled a batting average of just .243 for his career, most of which he spent with Chicago, Washington, and Boston in the American League. A Princeton graduate and outstanding scholar who majored in modern languages, Berg supposedly knew a dozen languages and, as the saying went, could not hit in any of them. It supposedly was Berg who led scout Mike Gonzalez to coin the famous assessment "Good field, no hit." However, Berg endeared himself to his guests by learning enough Japanese on his trip to Japan to converse somewhat in it and to do some basic writing with *katakana*,[15] the Japanese syllabary used especially for loan words.[16] Berg later went to work for the Office of Strategic Services (forerunner to the Central Intelligence Agency) as an espionage agent during World War II.

Then came the 1934 trip to Japan by another team of all-stars, this one including Babe Ruth, as well as the non-all-star Moe Berg. By 1934, relations between Japan and the United States had soured due to Japan's invasion of China and the United States' attempts to restrict development of Japan's naval fleet. Foreigners generally were neither popular nor trusted, as the Japanese assumed that they were spies.[17] However, the Japanese loved Babe Ruth, who despite being almost at the end of his career, batted .408 with thirteen home runs in seventeen games. The closest that the Americans came to losing was a 1–0 decision over an eighteen-year-old pitcher, Eiji Sawamura. Sawamura struck out Charlie Gehringer, Ruth, Lou Gehrig, and Jimmie Foxx in a row.[18] He later died in World War II, his name remaining alive in the Japanese equivalent of the Cy Young Award named after him.[19]

Matsutaro Shoriki, owner of the newspaper the *Yomiuri Shimbun*, sponsored the 1934 trip. He arranged to have five games played at Tokyo's

Shingu Stadium, originally a shrine to the Emperor. Members of an ultra nationalist group, the War God Society, were outraged that a foreign sport was played in a place they considered sacred. In February 1935, a member of the group stabbed Shoriki, who survived the attack, and, inspired by the outpouring of enthusiasm for Ruth, organized the first professional Japanese team, the Dai Nippon Tokyo Yakyu Kurabu (the Great Japan Tokyo Baseball Club). When the team toured the United States later in 1935, Shoriki changed its name to something easier for foreigners to pronounce, the Tokyo Giants.[20] By 1936, the first professional league in Japan was established. The memory of Babe Ruth remained very much alive. A plaque at Osaka's baseball stadium commemorated his visit, and the annual day devoted to encouraging boys' baseball was called Babe Ruth Day.[21]

World War II strained but did not destroy veneration for Babe Ruth in Japan, even if Ruth did destroy most of his Japanese souvenirs after the attack on Pearl Harbor,[22] and Japanese soldiers sometimes tried to antagonize American troops by yelling "To Hell with Babe Ruth!"[23] Ruth remained so respected in Japan that the United States government gave some thought to having him broadcast messages to the country prior to the nuclear attack on Hiroshima.[24] When Commissioner A.B "Happy" Chandler declared April 27, 1947, Babe Ruth Day in American ballparks, the Japanese joined in to honor the beloved player they called "Beibu Rusu." Instead of speeches, they gave a thousand yen to each player who hit a home run that day.[25]

Moe Berg did not play much during that 1934 tour, but he did a lot of sightseeing with his movie camera. He ducked out of one game in Tokyo, dressed in Japanese clothing, hid his camera under his kimono, and, ostensibly visiting a patient at the seven-story Saint Luke's Hospital, managed to reach the top floor. From there, he ascended the bell tower by way of a narrow staircase. With a panoramic view of Tokyo stretching about him, he proceeded to film the city, including shipyards and a variety of important industrial and military sites. During the war, Berg passed his film along to the Office of Strategic Services. Various accounts of this story have Lieutenant Colonel Jimmy Doolittle using the film in planning his 1942 attack on Tokyo, although Nicholas Dawidoff, in *The Catcher Was a Spy: The Mysterious Life of Moe Berg*, convincingly argues that American intelligence had far better information than that contained in an amateur's eight-year-old film. Dawidoff asserts that the Berg film was not relevant to planning for the Doolittle raid.[26]

World War II brought baseball largely to an end in Japan. With many of the top players gone to war, the 1943 season, for the professional league, was reduced to 84 games from the 105 of the previous season. The 1944 season was abbreviated to just 35 games, and 1945 competition was dropped entirely. During the war, anti–American sentiment led to abandonment of many English terms routinely used in Japanese baseball, with Japanese approximations taking their place.[27]

It surely would have taken much longer for baseball to make a strong comeback in Japan had General Douglas MacArthur not been in charge of the occupying force. MacArthur, Supreme Commander for the Allied Powers (SCAP), wanted to bring Japan back into the family of nations as soon as possible, and he sought to transform Japan into a democratic nation modeled after the United States. One of MacArthur's decisions to help refashion Japan in America's image was to encourage the rebirth of baseball, America's national pastime. MacArthur decided to retain as many useful traditions as possible, including the position, albeit revised significantly, of the Emperor.

Yet there was more behind MacArthur's decision than political calculation. MacArthur had a long love affair with baseball going back to his youth. At West Texas Military Academy in San Antonio, this son of another famous general, Arthur MacArthur, Jr., played baseball for the academy team in the 1890s. He was a good fielding shortstop also known for his skill as a bunter but was not much of a hitter. During his senior year in 1897, the team went undefeated.[28]

At West Point, MacArthur's love for baseball threatened his academic status despite his talents as student, and he gave up the game for his senior year. That must have been quite a personal sacrifice for MacArthur, who, despite modest baseball skill, was known as "Dauntless Doug" for his perseverance and ability somehow to get on base, often by drawing a walk or laying down a successful bunt. He was even chosen team captain and scored the decisive run in his team's 4–3 triumph on May 18, 1901, at Annapolis, in the first ever Army–Navy baseball game.[29] Playing left field for the cadets, MacArthur was taunted from the stands in reference to his father's role as Governor General of the Philippines:

> Are you the Governor General
> Or a hobo?
> Who is the boss of this show?
> Is it you or Emilio Aguinaldo?[30]

Aguinaldo had declared himself president of the Filipino Revolutionary Government and was waging a guerrilla war to gain independence from the United States. MacArthur described his deciding run against Navy after reaching base on a walk:

I was no Ty Cobb, but in those days I could run. I went down on the first pitch and, sure enough, the catcher threw wild, allowing me to go on to third. The throw from the outfield went over the third baseman's head, and I trotted home with what proved to be the winning run in a 4–3 contest. They are fine sportsmen, those Navy files, and when the game was over they treated me as though I really were the governor general. I was far from a brilliant ballplayer, even by the limited standards of college baseball, but that game will always stand out as one of my happiest memories.[31]

Years later, as Superintendent of West Point, MacArthur was not averse to stepping into the batter's box to give a hitting tip to a cadet named Earl Blaik, later a famous football coach at West Point.[32] During his early years as Superintendent, he removed the ban on playing sports on Sundays.[33] In the aftermath of World War II, when driving between his residence at the American Embassy in Tokyo and headquarters, he enjoyed watching sandlot games from his car.[34] That love for the game remained with him. Near the end of his life, living at the Waldorf in New York, MacArthur watched baseball on television and enjoyed discussing the sport with visitors. He invariably knew the players' batting averages before the statistics appeared on the screen.[35]

MacArthur's directives to resurrect baseball and clean out the stadiums, which had been used for such purposes as ammunition dumps, brought the sport back quickly.[36] Eight professional teams played a schedule of 105 games in 1946. By 1950, there were two leagues, the Central and Pacific, with a total of fifteen teams. The Mainichi Orions of the Pacific League won the first Japan Series. The number of teams later would stabilize at six per league, and Americans in limited numbers would join the Japanese teams. Occasionally an American, such as Cecil Fielder, has used his Japanese experience as a springboard to a comeback or even stardom in the United States. Edwin O. Reischauer, who was born in Japan and served as Ambassador to the country under President John F. Kennedy, noted in his book *The United States and Japan*, first published in 1950, that baseball for decades had been the national pastime as much in Japan as in the United States.[37]

In recent years, Japanese teams have become more competitive in contests with American squads and, in the Olympics, a serious medal contender. Japan won the Gold medal in 1984, and while the United States and Cuba have gathered the Gold since then, Japan has added several more medals. Perhaps nothing testifies as much to the success of the sport that Douglas MacArthur brought back into prominence as the increasing number of Japanese players joining United States teams. Pitcher Mashi Murakami performed effectively for the San Francisco Giants in the mid–1960s, but after his departure there was a lengthy hiatus of Japanese players in this country until Hideo Nomo joined the Dodgers in 1995. His success was immediate, as he led the National League in strikeouts and earned Rookie of the Year honors. The following year he threw a no-hitter, and, after more modest success during subsequent seasons, Nomo bounced back in 2001, with the Boston Red Sox, to pitch another no-hitter. At one point in the 2001 season, eight Japanese players were active in the majors, most notably two Seattle Mariners. Relief pitcher Kazuhiro Sasaki, named American League Rookie of the Year in 2000 while recording thirty-seven saves, set a new record in 2001 for most saves in April with thirteen. Outfielder Ichiro Suzuki, demonstrating all-around ability at bat, in the field, and on the bases, helped Seattle open the 2001 season as the hottest team in the majors by hitting safely in twenty-three consecutive games. In 2001, Suzuki, the American League MVP, had a .350 batting average, 242 hits, and stole 56 bases.[38]

Although the United States is now receiving this new type of recompense for its conveyance of baseball to Japan, the country has profited for many years in other ways: financial benefits from selling sporting goods to Japan, the diplomatic power of a shared sport, and the opportunity for both Japanese and Americans to learn more about each other through baseball tours. Still another benefit of increased interaction between Japan and the United States has been the subsequent enrichment of American poetry, notably though haiku.

Poetry has been closely associated with baseball since the days of Walt Whitman in the nineteenth century. Perhaps the ultimate poet of America, Whitman was a sports reporter for Brooklyn newspapers and followed baseball all his life. In the poem "Song of Myself," in *Leaves of Grass* (1855), he included "a good game of base-ball" among the positive, manly sports. After he suffered a stroke in the 1870s and could no longer attend games, he continued to enjoy discussing baseball and lamenting the growing use of the deceitful curveball, which he considered a dishonorable tactic.[39]

Baseball remained the poet's game through the work of such great American poets as Robert Frost (who, a year before reading a poem at President Kennedy's 1961 inauguration, wrote an essay on baseball for *Sports Illustrated*, noting, "I never feel more at home in America than at a ball game be it in park or sandlot"[40] and an all-star team of poets, such as William Carlos Williams, Richard Hugo, Carl Sandburg, David Bottoms, Donald Hall, and Marianne Moore.[41] As the twentieth century drew to an end, baseball had found its way also into American poets' haiku, probably the most revered of all poetic genres in Japan, and increasingly popular in the United States over the past half century.

The history of haiku in the United States is substantial but considerably younger than the history of baseball in Japan. Haiku may be thought of, in a phrase already used in this paper, as the player to be named later in this cultural interchange between the two nations.

In Japan, though, haiku has a long and honored history.[42] Its origins are to be found in the *renga*, a linked-verse form popular in Japan as early as the thirteenth century. The *renga* traditionally consisted of alternating stanzas of five-seven-five and seven-seven *onji* (sound symbols), with the complete poem often consisting of thirty-six, fifty, one hundred, or even one thousand stanzas. Usually two or more poets would compose the *renga*, alternating stanzas, and employing more of an associative link from stanza to stanza than a continuing narrative. *Renga* were routinely referred to as *haikai-no-renga*, with the opening stanza of the poem called the *hokku*. By the seventeenth century, poets were beginning to treat the *hokku* as a separate poem that would come to be called a haiku.

The first great master of haiku was Matsuo Basho (1644–94), as revered in Japan as Shakespeare is in England or the United States. Basho accumulated many students and disciples, ensuring that his contributions in haiku and other genres would endure. Other great practitioners of haiku included Yosa Buson (1716–84), Kobayashi Issa (1762–1826), and Masaoka Shiki (1867–1902). Haiku continued to prosper throughout the twentieth century and remains enormously popular in Japan today.

Large numbers of people compose haiku in contemporary Japan. Many belong to the hundreds of haiku clubs throughout the country, which in turn publish club magazines. Newspapers include haiku sections, and there are national mass-circulation haiku magazines. It is a poetic genre for the masses rather than for an elite, much as baseball is a sport for the masses in both Japan and the United States.

The haiku, heavily influenced by Zen Buddhism, is deceptively challenging. In this country, due to ignorance of the form's long history and philosophical underpinnings, it was once viewed as primarily a child's type of nature poem and so taught in elementary schools. The haiku is short, often but not always in seventeen Japanese *onji*, and combines surface simplicity with a profound depth. The haiku seeks to relay in vivid images the poet's experience of oneness with the natural world. Through a careful choice of words, the poet relays that experience to the reader so that both poet and reader have something approximating the same experience of reality. Because of this unity of existence, a haiku often includes images of both nature and humanity without editorial comment, just as the tree, mountain, wild geese, or ocean waves make no comment beyond their being.

A traditional (although not universal) aspect of haiku is the season word (*kigo*), and somewhere within the haiku is often a shift so that two images or parts of the total experience reinforce, contrast, or in some other way convey a relationship. The haiku poet usually seeks photographic realism but focuses on the small detail to convey the whole rather than a broad and generalized panoramic view.

A once common but receding fallacy regarding haiku in English is that they must be written in seventeen syllables, a "rule" born from misunderstanding the nature of Japanese *onji* (which have a one-to-one relationship between symbol and sound) and equating them with English syllables (which often include more than one sound). Thus a seventeen-syllable haiku in English is apt to be longer and wordier than a seventeen-*onji* haiku. In recent decades, both Japan and the United States have seen considerable experimentation with the form and subject matter of haiku.

United States poets such as Ezra Pound, Amy Lowell, Wallace Stevens, and William Carlos Williams composed haiku and haiku-like poems in the early decades of the twentieth century,[43] but World War II, as with baseball in Japan, figured prominently in the history of haiku in the United States.

Harold G. Henderson and R. H. Blyth were the two most important figures in the transformation of English-language haiku from something occasionally practiced by a few elite poets into a medium through which large numbers of people sought to share their experiences. Henderson, who had published English translations of Japanese haiku in *The Bamboo Broom* in 1934, served on the staff of the United States occupation forces in Tokyo after the conclusion of the war. Returning to the United States, Henderson taught at Columbia University and, among several books on Japanese language and culture, published *An Introduction to Haiku* in 1958. The book includes an analysis of the characteristics of haiku and discussions of Japanese haiku poets from the genre's origins through the nineteenth century. Henderson's book became something of a haiku bible for American poets.[44]

R. H. Blyth, an Englishman, spent part of the war in a Japanese internment camp. After the war, he continued his study of the Japanese arts, Zen Buddhism, and haiku. He became a tutor to the Crown Prince of Japan and published a series of books, most importantly four volumes on haiku from 1949 to 1952. The four volumes became popular in the United States and also contributed greatly to an American understanding of haiku.[45] Blyth, along with his contributions to the advancement of English-language haiku, played another role in the converging story lines of this paper. Blyth apparently served as a mediator between General MacArthur and the

Japanese Imperial Court in the aftermath of World War II.[46] According to Harold G. Henderson, Blyth "was in great degree responsible for the Emperor's giving up his divinity... ."[47]

From the 1950s on, the advance of haiku in the United States was like a snowball rolling down a mountain. Famous writers (Gary Snyder, Allen Ginsberg, Jack Kerouac, Richard Wright, United Nations Secretary General Dag Hammarskjöld) and large numbers of talented but less well known poets turned to haiku.[48] *Haiku* magazine began in the United States in 1963 with *American Haiku*, published in Platteville, Wisconsin. Many other haiku magazines would follow. The Haiku Society of America was born in 1968, with Harold Henderson one of its founders.[49] By the end of the twentieth century, the snowball had become an avalanche of individual poets, magazines, publishers, and haiku organizations, far too great even to begin cataloging in this paper.

Finally, the two great cultural worlds of baseball and haiku came together. Along with individual haiku about baseball in various magazines, baseball has become the primary subject of some haiku publications. Mike Schacht, editor of *Fan Magazine*, produced a special issue of baseball haiku in 1998. Jim Kacian, who operates Red Moon Press, edited, with longtime haiku editor and poet Cor van den Heuvel, a book of baseball haiku entitled *Past Time* in 1999.[51] In the same year, Kacian published a book of baseball haiku by van den Heuvel called *Play Ball*.[52]

Past Time includes one haiku each by thirty-one poets, each poet listed by favorite major league team and preferred position. In my own haiku, for example, I found myself in the outfield, my team the White Sox, along with:

> the boy not chosen
> steps over home plate,
> picks up his books[53]

Baseball is an especially appropriate subject for haiku in the United States, where the sport developed its present form (although antecedents such as rounders and cricket were brought to this country by the English).[54] Haiku usually seek some union of nature and humanity, and baseball grew out of a pastoral setting. The game still retains something of that natural setting, even in modern stadiums, but more so in minor league parks (the term "ballpark" itself recalls the game's origins) where the diamond is outdoors, the fans close to the field, the grass real, the dirt rises in small puffs as the runner slides into base, and trees and hills loom beyond the fences. So, among the major team sports, it is baseball that most clearly touches the natural world that is a vital dimension of haiku.

Haiku poets talk much about the "haiku moment"—that brief experience, intuitively recognized as significant, that the poet seeks to re-create through a few vividly descriptive (rather than explanatory) words.[55] For one seeking haiku moments, what sport, especially among the team sports, is more appropriate than baseball? The pace of baseball permits fans to view the game in distinct moments rather than as a blur of action or a complex fusion of bodies whose individual motions are almost impossible to decipher. Fans watch the individual fielder or batter, the baseball rising toward left field, the pitcher starting his windup, the graceful shortstop flying through the air to encircle a liner in his glove, the fleet runner stealing a base. Even when more than one player is involved, as in a double play, the viewer easily follows the movement from player to player, the experience so readily divisible into its component moments that the parts may even be immortalized (Tinker to Evers to Chance). These are moments that invite reflection and haiku.

The haiku poet attempts to invite vividly felt moments into the here and now. There is no past separate from the present. Similarly, people continue to hold in memory moments of their own baseball days: at recess in the playground of a country school, dreaming of making the big leagues, sharing sunny days in a minor league ballpark with one's parents (later with one's children or grandchildren).

When a haiku poet writes "choosing sides at recess/in the dirt-packed playground —/the bat slips from my hand," or "spring melt.../a baseball rises/beneath the forsythia," or "knuckleball twists/in the afternoon sun —/my stiff neck," or "April shower —/obituary leads me/to an old baseball card," a trade of sorts is being concluded, although neither portion of the equation ever truly concludes.[56] Baseball to Japan, haiku to the United States, now both in harmony. Harmony is an important element of haiku. It also is a long-lived effect of baseball, uniting past and present, young and old, country and country.

Notes

1. For this early history of Japanese baseball, see Robert Whiting, *You Gotta Have Wa* (1989; New York: Vintage Books, 1990), 27–28.

2. Whiting, 28–29.

3. Joel Zoss and John Bowman, *Diamonds in the Rough: The Untold History of Baseball* (Chicago: Contemporary Books, 1996), 409.

4. Whiting 39.

5. Albert G. Spalding, *Base Ball: America's National Game 1839–1915* (1911; San Francisco: Halo Books, 1991), 255.

6. Spalding, 259.

7. Whiting, 70.

8. Whiting, 39–40.

9. Hunter played with New York and Chicago in the NL in 1916; Chicago, 1917, and Boston, 1920, in the AL; and St. Louis in the NL in 1921. His lifetime batting average was just .163. For players' statistics, I have used John Thorn et al., eds., *Total Baseball*, 6th ed. (New York: Total Sports, 1999).

10. Whiting, 40.

11. Gai Ingham Berlage, *Women in Baseball: The Forgotten History* (Westport, Conn.: Praeger, 1994), 40–42.

12. Whiting, 40–41.

13. For a thorough list of visits by U.S. professional baseball teams to Japan, see Daniel E. Johnson, *Japanese Baseball: A Statistical Handbook* (Jefferson, N.C.: McFarland, 1999), 335–36.

14. Nicholas Dawidoff, *The Catcher Was a Spy: The Mysterious Life of Moe Berg* (New York: Pantheon, 1994), 78.

15. Dawidoff, 78–80.

16. *Hiragana* is used for native words, sometimes with Chinese characters. For a succinct differentiation between *katakana* and *hiragana*, see Victoria Fromkin and Robert Rodman, *An Introduction to Language*, 6th ed. (New York: Harcourt, 1998), 501.

17. Dawidoff, 87–88.

18. Robert W. Creamer, *Babe: The Legend Comes to Life* (New York: Simon and Schuster, 1974), 378–79; Marshall Smelser, *The Life That Ruth Built* (New York: Quadrangle/New York Times Book Company, 1975), 480–82.

19. Among those who comment on Sawamura's death are Yoichi Nagata and John B. Holway, "Baseball in Japan," *Total Baseball*, 6th ed., 527; and Harrington E. Cressey, Jr., "Baseball in the Armed Services," in the same edition of *Total Baseball*, 2518.

20. Smelser, 485; and Whiting, 43–44.

21. Smelser, 482.

22. Smelser, 481–82.

23. Smelser, 527; and Whiting, 46.

24. Whiting, 46.

25. Smelser, 535–36.

26. Berg, 133–36, 385–86. Among those who perpetuate the theory of Berg's having aided the raid on Japan is Whiting, 43. Doolittle himself does not mention Berg in his memoir: see James Doolittle, *I Could Never Be So Lucky Again* (New York: Bantam, 1992).

27. Whiting, 46.

28. William Manchester, *American Caesar: Douglas MacArthur 1880–1964* (Boston: Little, Brown, 1978), 44–45. The father won the Congressional Medal of Honor for a successful assault on Missionary Ridge during the Civil War, was a veteran Indian fighter, participated in the Spanish-American War, and served as a Military General of the Philippines; he was relieved for insubordination by President William Howard Taft, thus foreshadowing his son's later difficulties with President Truman during the Korean War.

29. Manchester, 56.

30. Douglas MacArthur, *Reminiscences* (New York: McGraw-Hill, 1964), 26.

31. MacArthur, 27.

32. Manchester, 123.

33. Manchester, 124.

34. Manchester, 478.

35. Manchester, 701.

36. Crissey, 2518–19.

37. Edwin O. Reischauer, *The United States and Japan*, 3rd ed. (Cambridge, Mass.: Harvard University Press, 1965), 15.

38. The other Japanese players in addition to Suzuki, Sasaki, and Nomo were Angels pitcher Shigetoshi Hasegawa, Mets outfielder Tsuyoshi Shinjo, Royals pitcher Makoto Suzuki, Expos pitcher Masato Yoshii, and Red Sox pitcher Tomo Okha.

39. See the chapter "Whitman and Baseball," in Ed Folsom's *Walt Whitman's Native Representations* (New York: Cambridge University Press, 1994), 27–54, for a comprehensive discussion of Whitman's attitude toward baseball.

40. Zoss and Bowman, 273–74. Also see Frost's poem "Birches," which some forty years earlier imagined a boy "too far from town to learn baseball" and consequently finding other pursuits like bending birch branches.

41. For discussions of baseball poetry, see Donald Hall's essay "The Poet's Game" in his collection *Fathers Playing Catch with Sons: Essays on Sport (Mostly Baseball)* (San Francisco: North Point, 1985), 57–63; both the introduction and poems of *Hummers, Knucklers, and Slow Curves: Contemporary Baseball Poems*, ed. Don Johnson (Urbana: Univ. of Illinois Press, 1991); and the selection "Poetry" in Edward J. Rielly's *Baseball: An Encyclopedia of Popular Culture* (Santa Barbara, Cal.: ABC-CLIO, 2000), 232–34.

42. I am indebted to William J. Higginson, with Penny Harter, *The Haiku Handbook* (New York: McGraw-Hill, 1985), 7–76 and 87–114, for the overview of the history and form of haiku that follows.

43. See, for example, Ezra Pound, "In a Station of the Metro"; Amy Lowell, Amy Lowell, "Autumn Haze"; Wallace Stevens, "Thirteen Ways of Looking at a Blackbird"; and William Carlos Williams, "The Red Wheelbarrow."

44. Higginson, 57. See Harold G. Henderson, *An Introduction to Haiku: An Anthology of Poems and Poets from Basho to Shiki* (Garden City, N.Y.: Doubleday Anchor, 1958).

45. David Cobb, "One Hundred Blyths," *Rediscovering Basho: A 300th Anniversary Celebration*, ed. Stephen Henry Gill and C. Andrew Gerstle (Folkestone, England: Global Oriental, 1999), 82–91. See Blyth's four-volume work, *Haiku* (1949–52; San Francisco: Heian International, 1981–82).

46. Cobb, 84.

47. Cobb, 87.

48. See Gary Snyder, *Earth House Hold: Technical Notes and Queries to Fellow Dharma Revolutionaries* (New York: New Directions, 1969); Jack Kerouac, *The Dharma Bums* (1958; New York: Penguin, 1986); Richard Wright, *Haiku: This Other World* (New York: Arcade, 1998); and Dag Hammarskjöld, *Markings*, trans. Leif Sjöberg and W. H. Auden (New York: Alfred A. Knopf, 1964).

49. By 2001, the Haiku Society of America had grown to include over 800 members throughout the United States, Canada, and sixteen other nations.

50. *Fan Magazine*, edited by Mike Schacht, included prose (both fiction and nonfiction), poetry, and art.

51. Jim Kacian and Cor van den Heuvel, eds., *Past Time: Baseball Haiku* (Winchester, Va.: Red Moon Press, 1999).

52. Cor van den Heuvel, *Play Ball: Baseball Haiku* (Winchester, Va.: Red Moon, 1999).

53. Permission to reprint this haiku, which previously appeared in Jim Kacian and Cor van den Heuvel, *Past Time: Baseball Haiku* (Winchester, Va.: Red Moon Press, 1999), n.p. is granted by copyright holder Edward J. Rielly, author of both the haiku and of this paper.

54. For discussions of these British sports, see Edward J. Rielly, *Baseball: An Encyclopedia of Popular Culture*, 262–63 and 69–70.

55. A discussion of these and other aspects of *haiku* occurs in Edward J. Rielly, "Writing (and Understanding) Haiku," *Writers' Journal* 11, no. 6 (1990): 18, 35, 37.

56. Permission to reprint these four haiku is granted by copyright holder Edward J. Rielly, author of both the haiku and of this paper. "spring melt" first appeared in *Modern Haiku* 32.2 (Summer 2001), 4; "April shower" first appeared in *bottle rockets* 2.2 (Spring/Summer 2001), n.p.; and "choosing sides at recess" and "knuckleball twists" are previously unpublished.

Part 3

MYTH AND MYSTERY

Baseball and Freemasonry in American Culture

Charles DeMotte

The life of Alexander Joy Cartwright, the man known as the "father of modern baseball," provides us with a link between baseball and Freemasonry. Born on April 17, 1820, in New York City, Cartwright was an enthusiast of the informal and ill-defined game that passed by the name of rounders, town ball, cat ball, and base. In 1845, he, along with others, put forth twenty rules, which provided uniform standards for the game. With the discovery of gold in California, Cartwright set off for the West Coast with a dozen friends on March 1, 1849, to make their fortune. Along the way, they played baseball with groups of Native Americans and frontiersmen. Arriving in San Francisco in July, Cartwright soon tired of the gold rush. He also became ill. Persuaded to go to Hawaii, Cartwright reached there at the end of August. He so loved the islands that he decided to settle down and resided there for the remaining forty-three years of his life. Shortly after his arrival, Cartwright petitioned to join a Freemasonic lodge, Le Progress de l'Oceanie. This was the start of a distinguished Masonic career during which Cartwright advanced through the various offices, becoming master of the lodge for two terms in 1855 and 1856.[1]

Whether Cartwright ever saw a connection between the game of baseball, which he helped to create, and the ritualized patterns of Freemasonry, which he later embraced, is impossible to say. Contemporary observers of American culture would no doubt have been aware of the dissemination of the ballpark and the lodge into virtually every community across the country during the course of the late nineteenth century.

Over the last third of the century, millions of men were initiated into various Masonic orders and lodges. Based on estimated figures, nearly one million men were members of York or (American) Rite Masonry in 1903; about 750,000 men had, at the same time, gone through the different degrees of Blue Lodge Masonry, with another 330,000 members of Royal Arch lodges. This does not include the many thousands of others who belonged to the Knights Templars, or other lodges whose organization and rituals were derived from Masonry such as the Odd Fellows, the Knights of Pythias, the Patrons of Husbandry (Grange), the Ancient Order of United Workmen, the Improved Order of Red Man, and the Knights of the Maccabees. Add to this other masculine fraternal orders, including the Knights of Labor, the Sons of Temperance, and the veterans of the Civil War, who formed groups with ritualized practices within the body of the Grand Army of the Republic (GAR) and the United Confederate Veterans. Thus we can clearly see that a large percentage of Victorian American manhood was employed in some sort of lodge work.[2]

Baseball also experienced dramatic growth over the latter decades of the nineteenth century. By 1858, there were no less than fifty baseball clubs in New York. During the 1860s, the game moved out of the metropolitan New York area and became embedded in the social life of fraternal clubs and other organizations. In the post Civil War period, baseball ceased to be an isolated club sport and developed as a nexus of teams and leagues scattered across the Northeast and the Midwest. According to historian Warren Goldstein, baseball was grounded in a singular localism that was both literal and figurative.[3]

The years between the Civil War and the First World War witnessed the first phase of baseball's growth as a national sport. Factories, churches, social clubs, fraternal orders, and lodges all fielded baseball teams in a plethora of leagues and associations. One of the giants of American social realism, James T. Farrell, noted that one of the baseball teams he and his friends competed against, in Washington Park on Chicago's Southside, represented a Masonic lodge, consisting mostly of Jewish merchants and salesmen.[4] It was during these formative years that baseball emerged in American life both literally and figuratively as the national pastime.

How baseball and freemasonry in their own separate spheres influenced the character of American society is the subject of this presentation. The thesis offered holds that both baseball and Freemasonry share common subjective qualities that imposed a ritualized order on a transient and volatile nation. It is interesting to note that these two aspects of American culture developed from obscure beginnings. While we have it on good authority that baseball was the offspring of British parents, namely rounders and cricket, the more distant relatives are in question. We are told that ancient Egyptian temples contained drawings of people playing some kind of ball game and that in the British Museum there is a leather ball from the Nile region dating back more than 4,000 years.[5] How many variations of baseball like games there have been remains a mystery and will continue to be so. What seems apparent, however, is that games centered on hitting a ball with a stick are something of a cultural universal.

The origins of Freemasonry are likewise obscure. The Grand Lodge of London was officially opened as the Scottish rite in 1717, but few would accept that late date as its commencement point. The famous historian of Freemasonry, Albert Mackey, presents a number of possible theories as to its starting point, some legendary, others mythical, and a few historical, while C.W. Leadbeater, in his book *The Hidden Life in Freemasonry*, unabashedly holds that Masonry is of Egyptian origins. One plausible theory is that Masonry developed as the legacy of an ancient mystery school of uncertain beginnings that remained an underground secret society during much of the Christian era up through the seventeenth century, and for good reason. Whatever its origins, those who know it from the inside out can attest to the richness of its history, legends, and symbolism.

While both Freemasonry and baseball are, at their root, of foreign extraction, they found fertile soil in the United States to grow and prosper. What made each initially popular in this country was the sense that they contributed to the moral fiber of the nation. The issue of character is an important one and emerges again and again in Masonic literature and in the stories and accounts of writers on baseball in its formative years. The growth of Masonry in the years following the American Revolution owed much to its emphasis on moral training, the importance of individual merit, and social virtue, all ideals essential to the growth of a republican society. Open to all segments of the adult masculine community, Masonry proved to be a leveler among the classes, which conveniently reinforced the democratic ethos of the new American nation. Governor DeWitt Clinton of New York even went so far as to claim that Freemasonry was "co-extensive with the enlightened part of the human race." [6]

Observers of baseball also saw the game as a vehicle for health and moral virtue. One newspaper in the 1850s, quoted by baseball historian Benjamin Rader, observed that a baseball player must exercise sobriety, temperance, patience, fortitude, self-denial, obedience, and other like virtues. [7] This was a view shared by Cartwright and the other organizers of the game; they imposed strict rules on players to prevent improper behavior. One of the game's staunchest advocates, journalist Henry Chadwick, saw baseball as significant in raising the consciousness of Americans.

Morality was also intertwined with the process of socialization. Playing baseball was considered to be part of the training in American values for waves of immigrants who poured into the country, particularly after the 1880s. It was perhaps for this reason that Albert Spalding and others sought to re-invent the history of the game and claim that it was a purely American phenomenon.

Baseball and Freemasonry were also instrumental in promoting the cult of manliness. Victorian society was on one level divided into spheres of influence based upon gender. Middle-class females were expected to manage, if not rule, the home or the private sphere of life. Males dominated the public realm. Public space encompassed not only places of employment, but also the myriad of clubs, societies, fraternal orders, and forms of popular amusement. Baseball and Masonry were both reflections of this masculine world. Mark Carnes in his study of secret societies in Victorian America presents an erroneous case, I believe, in arguing that Masonry, and other groups of that ilk, provided a psychological refuge for the expression of male identity. The appeal of Masonry and the various levels of shared meaning that it offers is far more complex. Nevertheless, in presenting the template for an idealized political and social order, Blue Lodge Masonry epitomized a set of hierarchical relationships that were thought to be within the masculine domain.

With respect to baseball, the game offered men the opportunity to express the physical and aggressive side of their nature. The emphasis, as put forth in Cartwright's original set of rules, makes clear that the intent of baseball was to provide exercise for gentlemen.[8] The ideal baseball player, certainly in the view of Cartwright and the early founders of the game, was a man of refinement and of independent means whose adherence to the rules of the game followed on from a broader acceptance of social norms. Though a form of exercise and entertainment, baseball was also intended to be serious business. The purpose of the game was to foster the development and perfection of skill, and was not viewed primarily as pastime for boyish frivolity. As seen by many traditionalists, the gradual commercialization of baseball within a few decades of its creation, resulting from the pressures of money, power, and greed, was as a dilution of its intent and purpose.

In another juxtaposition of the notion of private and public, it might be said that whereas baseball occupies more the realm of public space, Freemasonry is more akin to the private realm of being. The list of those who were active in Masonic lodges, starting with George Washington, comprise a virtual *Who's Who* of American history, yet only a few of them were ever known to be Masons. In contrast, the vast majority of men who have played in the major leagues were known as ballplayers even after their playing days were over. True, a few, like Jim Bunning, went on to have another public career of some standing, but in most cases retired players either found careers in some other part of the game or drifted into relative obscurity. Ty Cobb will be remembered as perhaps the greatest player to ever step on to a big league diamond but never as a Mason, which he also was.

The inception of baseball and the popularity of lodge work took place within a developing nation. The nineteenth century marked a period of great turbulence in American life. Tides of immigration brought to the United States an influx of displaced persons from all over Europe who flocked into large metropolitan areas and turned villages into towns and cities. It was not until the 1890s that the frontier finally closed and the concept of America as a coherent geographical unit took form. The Industrial Revolution, which hit its stride in the decades following the Civil War, imposed new routines of urbanization and patterns of time-discipline on the mass of skilled and unskilled workers alike. The redefinition of time and space dictated by the clock and the machine tied men and women to a set of repetitive tasks within confined spaces. The monotony and often shear brutality of the industrial system fostered much violence and rebellion, which as part and parcel of America's turbulent labor history has been well documented.

Baseball and the rhythmic patterns of lodge work spoke to a basic need for ritualized play and ceremonial order that had been marginalized by industrial life. Play, wrote the cultural historian Johan Huizinga, explicitly serves to represent a cosmic event and thus bring it into manifestation.[9] What he means by this statement is that play, or sport, dramatizes certain archetypal patterns that speak to some fundamental quality of the human soul. This dramatization often takes the form of a myth. One such myth is the journey home. In the story of the prodigal son, it is the adventurous and rebellious offspring who leaves home to gain experience in the world, only to return again chastened and wiser. Eastern religions teach, at another level, that men and women go through endless rounds of birth and death on the wheel of life prior to gaining enlightenment (the true home). In the Masonic ceremony of initiation, the candidate is taken on three symbolic journeys before he is brought to the altar at the center of the lodge, a symbol of home depicting the light of one's true self, the soul.

Likewise in baseball, the goal is to leave home so as to return home. A. Bartlett Giametti, in an unpublished manuscript entitled *Baseball and American Character*, argues that the search for home is a metaphor linking baseball to the American experience. The journey is not an easy one.

On the way home, there are many casualties. Most batters fail even to reach base. Those runners who reach base safely through a hit, a walk, or a fielder's error are often stranded there. Only a comparative few, in most circumstances, ever complete the cycle and return home. As in any mystery school, such as what Masonry was always intended to be, the arduous road to initiation is characterized by many difficult tests and trials. Many are called, but only those prepared to subject themselves to certain disciplines are chosen. It is these select few who eventually reach the home base of greater self-realization.

Once completed, we are told, the journey must always start again until there is an end to all journeying.[10] Drama, whether acted out in a lodge or on the playing field, relies upon a deliberate repetition of actions, which serves to raise profane activity to the level of the poetic. In baseball, as in lodge work, timing and the repetitive performance of every action, down to the smallest detail, underscores the entire performance. Movement about a lodge is predicated upon precise angles and squares so that the ritual work, to use a phrase from Huizinga, "is seriousness at its highest and holiest."[11] The craft of baseball, in much the same manner as the craft of Masonry, is characterized by the unceasing repetition of coordinated actions that when mastered takes on the beauty of simplicity. The complexities of pitching a ball thrown in various ways at different speeds to a precise target, the fluidity and balance required to perfect a double play, and the split second timing and hand-eye coordination that enables a batter to connect with a pitch are all the result of painstaking repetition and attention to detail. The elaborate process of learning and perfecting one's skills begins in earnest with the Entered Apprentices of the lower minor leagues and intensifies significantly for those who become the Master Masons of Major League Baseball.

All ritual work is confined to an enclosed space. The ritual act does not occur in an undefined sphere but in consecrated space defined by a center and a periphery. According to Huizinga:

> A closed space is marked out for it (play), either materially or ideally, hedged off from the everyday surroundings. Inside this space play proceeds, inside it rules obtain. Now, the marking out of some sacred spot is also the primary characteristic of every sacred act. This requirement of isolation for ritual, including magic and law, is much more than merely spatial and temporal. Nearly all rites of consecration and initiation entail a certain artificial seclusion for the performers and those to be initiated.[12]

In a metaphoric sense, an enclosed space brings order out of chaos. Inside a lodge certain protocols are observed which define discourse and procedural order among officers and lodge members. Baseball, in a similar vein, creates within a given space an area where the rituals of play unfold. In that immortal film *Field of Dreams*, based on W.P. Kinsella's novel *Shoeless Joe*, a space is created out of an Iowa cornfield where the spirits of baseball's legendary greats emerge to engage in the craft of their game and the dreams of their younger years.

The confinement of space not only defines the field of ritual activity but also differentiates participants from non-participants. The foul lines in baseball delineate the sphere where play is fair and where it is out-of-bounds. It is the role of the umpire, the guardian of the rules, to oversee this space and determine, for instance, when a ball is in play. By the same token, there is an outer boundary, often sealed by a fence or a grandstand, beyond which neither outsiders nor other non-participants can enter. The enclosed space allows play to unfold freely without interference and thus solemnizes the ritual.

Freemasonry, in a like manner, is a performance within a closed space. There is both an outer door and an inner door, the latter marking the entrance point to a lodge. The process of opening a lodge involves creating a secure space free from the intrusion of "cowans and eavesdroppers" and then proving the columns so as to make sure that those in attendance are Masons. In Masonry, the officer responsible for securing this space is the *Tyler* who guards the inner door and seals an active lodge. It is within the seclusion of a *tyled* lodge where the labors of the day can commence and the mysteries unfold.

Within this *tyled* and enclosed space, the inner performance of ritualized activity occurs as well as the dramatic unfolding of visible events. There is also *tyling*, of a sort, within baseball. The game takes place on different levels. There is the outer form of the game, which to the average fan is a contest of who can score the most runs, or conversely, who can prevent the fewest runs from scoring. The beauty of the game is contained in the routine and apparently simple actions of executing the various plays skillfully and competently. On the other hand, the inner game is that which is known only to the practitioners and emerges out of an overall game plan. How will a pitcher work a given hitter? To what extent are environmental factors such as wind, humidity, and sunlight influential in how the fielders position themselves? What forms of subtle communication will be employed to give one side a slight advantage over the other?

Baseball, like Freemasonry, has its secrets. The signs flashed by the catcher to the pitcher, directions given from the bench to the coaches, which are then transmitted again to the hitters and base runners, and the informal communication between a pitcher and his fielders all function as a secret code of instructions comprising the inner game. The use of signs, particularly at the professional level, is often the key to success. We now know, for instance, that a contributing factor to the "Miracle at Coogan's Bluff" in 1951 was that the New York Giants were able to secretly steal signs, which proved to be particularly effective in their come-from-behind victory over the Brooklyn Dodgers to win the National League pennant. Apparently, the team stationed an electrician in the clubhouse where, using a spyglass he was able to read the signs of the opposing catcher. He then tapped out a coded message, using a buzzer, by which the intended pitch was passed along to the dugout where it was then relayed to the batter. The fact that this elaborate network of sign stealing did not come to light for fifty years bears witness to its effectiveness.[13]

Secrecy and silence are virtues that speak to the very essence of Free-masonry. They are designed to guard the lodge on two counts: first as to security against the intrusion of non–Masons and, second, to the veiling of certain occult secrets that are part of the degree work. The Entered Apprentice begins his Masonic labors by learning the duty of secrecy and silence. At each level of the Masonic work, new secrets are imparted. Some of these secrets relate to the recognition of a brother of that degree, while others pertain to the more arcane workings of energies and forces. These principles of secrecy and silence can be traced back to the ancient myster-ies and systems of worship found in the Hellenistic world dating back to the fourth century B.C. When asked what was the most difficult aspect of the inner work of these mystery schools, Aristotle is said to have responded, "To be secret and silent."[14]

Both a lodge and a baseball field conform to certain structural prin-ciples predicated upon number and geometry. All ritual is based on num-ber. Not surprisingly, religious practices derived from a close study of scripture follow certain numerical patterns. A few numbers appear to have a universal quality. The number three, for instance, is seen as an archetypal number, and in many traditions takes on a sacred quality. The Christian trinity (Father, Son, Holy Spirit) characterizes the godhead in which three principles make up one entity. There are three stages of consecration in the Catholic Mass and three readings from the scriptures. Interestingly, the Christian Bible contains over five hundred and fifty references to the num-ber three, making it in one sense a source book on numerology. Similarly, the Hindu tradition is structured on the trinity, commencing with the three great deities: Shiva–the destroyer, Vishnu–the sustainer, and Brahma–the creator, and the triadic groups of lesser deities, for instance, Agni, Soma, and Gandharva. Trinities of deities can also be found among the Greeks, the Egyptians, the Babylonians, and the Sumerians, among others.

The number four also figures prominently in baseball and lodge work. Four is a number ascribed to material form and is often thought of in terms of space. We tend to think of space in flat, linear terms. There are four directions, four corners of the earth, and the four qualities of physical matter (earth, air, fire, and water). Add height and depth and the earth resembles a cube. The number four not only governs space but time as well. A day is divided into four parts: sunrise, midday, sunset, and midnight. A month is similarly represented by the four phases of the moon; a year has four seasons and is defined by the cardinal points marked by two solstices and two equinoxes. Likewise, a century is often divided into four quarters. As a representation of time, the number four conveniently conforms to a natural growth cycle. Something is born, develops to maturity, ripens, and then undergoes a process of decline.[15]

Baseball, like Masonry, in the words of A. Bartlett Giamatti, involves "squares containing circles containing rectangles; precision in counterpoint with passion; order compressing energy." In both cases, it could be said that there is a fundamental geometric order based upon the numbers three and four. Masonry is built upon a pavement measured to a perfect square. Baseball is centered upon a diamond square with occupants at each of the four corners. In Masonry, there is also an invisible rectangular diamond linking the three principle officers (the worshipful master, the senior warden, the junior warden, and the chair of the unseen master). Each lodge member in Masonry is seen as a stone in the temple. Newly initiated brothers sit in the northeast corner of the lodge where the corner stone of a building is usually placed, and are viewed as rough ashlars, or stones that needs to be worked into a smooth or perfect stone of equal proportion to fit into the temples' plan with right exactitude. A properly constructed lodge also conforms to the exact ratio of 2:3. This proportion determines not only the dimensions of the lodge building, but also the width and depth of the altar table.

Threes, and multiples thereof, abound in the symbolism of Masonry. At the center of a lodge are the three great lights (square, compass, and book of wisdom), which are supported by three lesser lights representing the three principle officers, who in turn, symbolize three aspects of divinity. A Mason figuratively uses three working tools in his Masonic labors: the chisel, the gavel, and the twenty-four inch gauge. In a lodge, there are nine main officers plus the *Tyler*, who guard the temple. There are three degrees in a Blue Lodge, namely Entered Apprentice, Fellow Craft, and Master Mason. Within Scottish Rite Masonry, there are a total of thirty-three degrees.

The repetition of the number three is readily apparent in baseball (three strikes, three outs, etc.), as well as multiples of three (nine innings, nine players per side, a distance of 60'6" between pitchers mound and home plate, and a possibility of six pitches maximum that can be thrown to a hitter at any one time at bat). According to the original rules, the game would end when one team scored twenty-one runs, or 3:7.

In a ballpark, the distance between bases is well known to be ninety feet, making a total of three-hundred and sixty feet, equal to the equivalent number of degrees in a circle. The circle of the mound is in juxtaposition to the circle around home plate whose radius is thirteen feet containing three squares, including the batter's boxes, which are six by four feet, conforming to the 2:3 ratio. The third square contains three sides and is forty-three inches across. A hitter waiting for a pitch will swing a bat not greater than 2¾" in diameter at a baseball exactly nine inches in circumference. Home plate in baseball represents the point of intersection where lines extend out at an angle of ninety degrees, theoretically forever.[16]

Movement within a lodge stands in counterpoint to that on the ball field. In traversing a lodge, a brother passes from the east to the west by way of the south and from the west to the east again by way of the north in clockwise fashion. By contrast, in baseball the movement of runners circling the bases revolves in a counterclockwise order. In both cases, there is a protocol of movement and direction of energy. Masons who are not officers communicate questions and comments through the wardens of their column, which is then passed on to the master of the lodge.

In baseball, there is a similar economy of movement. An infield hit is fielded and relayed to the appropriate base. Similarly, a base hit to the outfield will result in a direct throw or a series of relays aimed at catching an advancing base runner. The web of connections fostered in lodge and on the playing field lends itself, in the words of poet Donald Hall, to "create an elegant, trivial, enchanted grid on which our suffering, shapeless, sinful day leans for the momentary grace of order."[17]

In Masonry, there is a symbolic association between the four directions and the seasons. Light, symbolically, emerges in the east representing creation or new beginnings; it then moves by way of the south, marking the midway point in the summer of the year, and sets in the west at the autumn equinox, before being plunged into the darkness of winter in the north. Hall observes that baseball also marks the four seasons. It dies into the October ground only to be reborn again in the spring. Like the birds, it migrates north in April and by mid-summer it has reached its peak of activity, in contrast to the dormant period of winter when baseball is relived in the hot stove league or played in the nether fields of the Caribbean.[18]

The fortunes of Freemasonry and baseball in twentieth-century American Culture have taken both co-terminus and divergent turns. Masonry's Golden Age lasted into the twentieth century. It was during this time that Masonry attracted men of prominence across the country, whereby lodge membership was often the key to political and social standing. Like other fraternal movements, the demise of Freemasonry began in the 1930s when the Depression years resulted in a loss of income due to the impoverished condition of many of its members. Over the last half century, membership in Masonic orders has continued to fall and lodges have closed or consolidated as the number of Masonic funerals regularly outweighs the number of initiations. Changes in lifestyle patterns, gender roles, and demographics have all contributed to this decline. Recent efforts, small as they are, to open the lodge doors to women and to bring about a reformation in Masonry through reviving its spiritual heritage may prove to be the salvation of this noble and ancient lineage.

Baseball, on the other hand, has gone through cycles of decline and resurrection and on the whole has fared well. This is not to say that the recent history of organized baseball is without conflict and turbulence, witness its own social and economic transformation of the past half century. It is no longer the game of inner-city neighborhoods, like Brooklyn, or the private fiefdoms of the Lords of the Realm. The abolition of baseball's reserve clause, coupled with free agency, television, strikes, labor troubles, and above all, an explosion of money has enabled the sport to undergo its own capitalist revolution and to become part of the seemingly unlimited entertainment industry. While Major League Baseball has prospered by becoming more of a corporate entity, it has suffered increasing competition from other sports, most notably soccer, especially at the grassroots level. Baseball today is no longer America's game; it is one of America's games.

Whatever becomes of the Masonic idea, or ultimately baseball, there can be little doubt that these two movements have contributed to the richness of American culture, both objectively and subjectively. At its deepest level, both baseball and Freemasonry are rooted in archetypal myths and patterns. At another level, baseball and Freemasonry reflect a certain moral and social order. The catechized definition of Masonry as "a system of morality, veiled in allegory and illustrated by symbols" speaks to its subjective qualities. "The one constant theme through all the years has been baseball," notes Terrance Mann in *Field of Dreams*. "...It reminds us of all that was good and could be good again." We are told that peak experiences and nostalgia provide the basis for religious beliefs, and that these two powerful elements tie people to baseball.[19]

While Cartwright was the first person whose name can be associated with both baseball and Freemasonry, there have been many others. There has been no exact count of the number of Masons who have been ballplayers. There have been, minimally, 411 baseball people, including owners, managers, writers and other media figures, umpires, and ballplayers, who were Masons.[20] In reality, the figure may be markedly higher. What significance this has is far from clear. We know little beyond the fact that a sizeable number of baseball people were Masons of varying duration. Like Cartwright, many may have come to Masonry in later life after their playing days were over. Others may have joined due to family connections or for social recognition. Whatever the connections, it would seem reasonable to suppose that whenever Mickey Cochrane, Bobby Doerr, Carl Hubbell, Cy Young, Tris Speaker, Honus Wagner, and a host of other players "met on the level, acted on the plumb, and parted on the square" whether in lodge or on the ball field, they were involved in an engaging and meaningful experience.

Notes

1. Jerry R. Erikson, "Alexander Joy Cartwright," *Royal Arch Mason Magazine*, Fall (1962), 1–7; and "Alexander Joy Cartwright, Jr., and Masonic Brothers at Bat," *The Pony Express*, October (1966), 3–8.

2. Mark C. Carnes, *Secret Ritual and Manhood in Victorian America*, (New Haven: Yale University Press, 1989), 5–9; and Dale E. Boudreu, "Sources of the Fraternal Spirit," *Gnosis* 44, (1997), 37–38

3. Warren Goldstein, *Playing for Keeps: A History of Early Baseball* (Ithaca: Cornell University Press, 1989), 101.

4. James T. Farrell, *My Baseball Diary* (Carbondale: Southern Illinois University Press, 1998), 81

5. James A. Vlasich, *A Legend for the Legendary: The Origin of the Baseball Hall of Fame* (Bowling Green, OH: Bowling Green State University Popular Press, 1990), 5.

6. Steven G. Bullock, *Revolutionary Brotherhood: Freemasonry and the Transformation of the American Social Order, 1730–1840*, (Chapel Hill: University of North Carolina Press, 1996), 138–139, 153

7. Benjamin G. Rader, *Baseball: A History of America's Game*, (Urbana: University of Illinois Press, 1992), 10

8. Thomas Gilbert, *Elysian Fields: The Birth of Baseball*, (New York: Franklin Watts, 1995), 28

9. Johan Huizinga, *Homo Ludens: A Study of the Play Element in Culture* (Boston: The Beacon Press, 1950), 17.

10. Stephan Lehman, "Baseball Is About Going Home," *Elysian Fields Quarterly* 13, no. 3 (1994), 1.

11. Huizinga, 18.

12. *Ibid.*, 19–20.

13. Joshua Harris Prager, "Giants' 1951 Comeback, the Sport's Greatest, Wasn't All It Seemed," *The Wall Street Journal*, 31 January 2001, 1.

14. Albert G. Mackey, *An Encyclopedia of Freemasonry and Its Kindred Sciences* (Chicago, The Masonic History Company, 1927), 2:675.

15. A. Bartlett Giamatti, *Take Time for Paradise: Americans and Their Games* (New York: London, Summit books, 1989), 85.

16. *Ibid.*

17. Donald Hall, *Fathers Playing Catch with Sons* (New York: Laurel Books, 1985), 51.

18. *Ibid.*, 47–48.

19. Russell Hollander, "The Religion of Baseball: Psychological Perspectives," *Nine: A Journal of Baseball History and Social Perspectives* 3 (1994), 11–12.

20. Erikson, 8–11.

Claude Hendrix: Scapegoat or the Ninth Man Out?

George M. Platt

Myths and legends provide fuel for hot stove leagues and pass traditions from one generation to the next. As building blocks of culture, they usually deserve protection from people with a predilection to separate fact from fiction. Now and then, however, in the spirit of fair play, some myths need to be scrutinized. Such is the case with Claude Hendrix, one of the finest players in the days when baseball was young. Although the recipient of only modest attention since after he left the diamond, Hendrix, according to a number of posthumous assessments, merits inclusions amongst baseball's outcasts. Yet, the question lingers: was Hendrix's fall from grace the fruit of history or of mythology?

From 1911 to 1920, pitching for Pittsburgh and Chicago of the National League and Chicago of the Federal League, Hendrix won 143 and lost 117 with an ERA of 2.65. During his best pitching years, he won 24 and 29 games respectively, and his career statistics include 1,092 strikeouts, a no-hit game, 27 shutouts, 17 saves, a .241 batting average, and a .962 fielding average. He led the National League in winning percentage in 1912 and 1918. A good hitting pitcher, Hendrix also had 13 home runs. His first full year in the majors, 1912, may have been his best. With a record of 24 and 9, he trailed only Grover Cleveland Alexander in strikeouts—176 to 195. He also hit .322, which places him in a very elite group of pitchers who won 20 games and hit over .300 in the same year.[1]

In 1920, Hendrix was part of an incident that triggered the grand jury investigation leading to the famous Black Sox scandal and placed a cloud

276

over his place in baseball history, a cloud that slowly mushroomed into a storm of highly questionable conclusions about his career. It began shortly after his death when the publisher of *The Sporting News* stated, erroneously, in a 1947 biography of baseball Commissioner Kenesaw Mountain Landis, that Hendrix had been "dropped from league baseball."[2] The assumption that some form of official action had been taken gained momentum with the claim in David Voigt's three-volume history of baseball that Hendrix had been "axed" by Landis. Subsequent use of phrases such as "barred for life," "suspended from baseball for life," and was "dropped from Organized Baseball" further spread this falsehood.[3] Other writers concluded that there was some sort of unofficial ban to keep Hendrix out of the game, and they employed terms like "he never played in organized baseball again," "unable to sign with any other club," "persona non grata in baseball after 1920," "no other major league team signed him," "found the doors of baseball closed to him," "unofficially blacklisted," and "the Cubs suspiciously released Hendrix without explanation or public disclosure."[4]

Only a few chroniclers of the 1920–21 baseball years hesitated to indict Hendrix. Warren Brown, author of the Cubs' book for the Putnam baseball series, made no mention of Hendrix's connection to the events of 1920. In *Eight Men Out*, the classic account of the Black Sox, Eliot Asinof simply states that Hendrix was the scheduled pitcher in the game that sparked the grand jury investigation, making no inference that he was dropped from baseball. Hendrix does not appear in the movie adaptation of the Asinof book.[5]

Was Hendrix "axed" or "blacklisted," officially or unofficially, making him in essence the *ninth man out*, or has he been wrongfully treated by many historians and baseball writers in recent years? The full story will probably never be known, but this account attempts, in the parlance of baseball, to "clean the plate."

The Early Years

Claude Raymond Hendrix was born in 1888 in Johnson County, Kansas, a rolling prairie of farms and small towns (which today is part of the Kansas City metropolitan area, home to a half million people). His father, Price (P.K.), grew up on a farm, worked for farmers and merchants, and was in business for himself when, in 1902, he became the first Democrat elected county sheriff. He was reelected in 1904, running on a platform of cutting expenses, arresting "horse and harness thieves," and opposing the "whiskey convicts," who were supporting his opponent. Price did not seek reelection in 1906, and he settled in Stilwell, purchasing a large home, a business block, and a farm outside of town. The local businessmen organized a bank, and Price served as cashier.[6]

Claude, a right-hander, attended school in Olathe and pitched for local teams, crediting his father with the development of his baseball skills. In 1906, when his parents were in the process of moving from Olathe to Stilwell, which had no high school, Claude enrolled as a junior in the commercial course in the preparatory program at St. Mary's College, where he received a grade of "C" for the year and a commendation for "excellent deportment."[7] Under Coach Ernest Quigley, St. Mary's had one of the finest college baseball program in Kansas, and in 1907 Claude was the number two pitcher for a team that won 17, lost 2, and tied 1. St. Mary's was victorious over Nebraska, Missouri, the Fort Riley team, Fairmount College, and the second squad for St. Paul's American Association team. The student newspaper lauded Claude's pitching but also noted that he hit home runs each of his first five times at bat, "and whenever a man was in a hole from that time on …(he) was marched to the bat, and he always made connection with the ball…."[8]

In February 1908, Claude, by then a lanky six-footer with a square jaw, transferred to Fairmount Academy, the preparatory program at Fairmount College (which is now Wichita State University). At Fairmount, he joined one of the Wheatshockers' best teams of that era.[9] The team had two outstanding pitchers, Hendrix and Percy Bates, who also went on to play as a professional. *The Sunflower*, the campus newspaper, noted that Claude's "name is not unknown in the baseball world." *The Wichita Eagle* commented that "he is young but is reputed to be the fastest college pitcher in Kansas," and "he works the spitball to perfection."[10]

The Shockers went 7 and 4 that season, defeating the "B" team of the Jobbers, Wichita's entry in the Western Association, by a score of 12–4, although the Jobbers apparently inserted some of their regulars in the late innings in an attempt to avoid defeat. The Shockers played the Jobbers' regulars in a match just before their season opened and lost 16–0. They won one of three at Arkansas, with Hendrix the pitcher in both defeats. An eastern Kansas trip that would have included a game with St. Mary's was canceled because of bad weather.

Hendrix was active in campus social life, placed fourth in a boxing tournament, was the best shot-putter at Fairmount, and never turned down a chance to go fishing. But baseball was clearly his main interest, and he did not return to college. In the summer of 1908, he pitched for the Greenbacks of Lincoln, Nebraska in the Class A Western League. He also began the 1909 season with the Greenbacks. Control problems plagued him, however, and he was sent to Peoria, Illinois, of the Three-I League, and then given an unconditional release.

Claude had to drop down a notch and signed with Salina in the Central Kansas League, which was managed by Ernest Quigley, his former college coach at St. Mary's. (Quigley later became a well-known umpire in the National League, working six World Series, including the 1919 Black Sox infamy. Quigley concluded his career as athletic director, from 1944 to 1950, at the University of Kansas.) In his first game with Salina, Hendrix threw a one-hitter, but his control problems continued, and he walked ten. Claude soon became the mainstay of the pitching staff, however, and when the season ended, he and another player were invited to join Omaha, Nebraska, in the Western League. They delayed reporting, however, to play in a nearby tournament because they could "make more money," a move which the reporter for the Salina newspaper did not seem to consider unusual.[11] Hendrix pitched only a few innings in Omaha before the season ended.

Farther west, the frontier city of Cheyenne, Wyoming, was promoting baseball, probably in an attempt to get a Western League franchise. In 1910, Cheyenne secured a young baseball wizard from Kansas City named Ira Bidwell to organize and manage a semi-professional team. Bidwell recruited Claude to join an eleven-man roster of three pitchers and eight others, mainly from the Kansas City area. Several went on to play in the major leagues. They launched their campaign in early April and played through Oklahoma, Missouri, and Kansas before arriving in Cheyenne to open the season in late May with games against teams from Wyoming, Nebraska, Kansas, Colorado, and New Mexico. Although Claude often pitched three or four times a week, he still was able to add trout to his fishing repertoire.

The Cheyenne Indians dominated the field, and following a late September series with the Trinidad Miners, the *Cheyenne State Leader* proclaimed "Indians Win Championship of the West."[12] The team then went on a "barnstorming" tour in Colorado, New Mexico, and Texas, an aspect of baseball that Claude perhaps always liked most. Since the Indians did not play in a league, it is difficult to identify a specific number of games for the season. Claude clearly pitched in more than 40 games, winning about 38 of them. On June 25, he pitched a no-hit game against the Union Pacific team of Omaha. When not pitching, he often played left field. A number of major league representatives watched the team, and 1911 found Claude Hendrix starting the season with a minor league team affiliated with the Pittsburgh Pirates.

The Major Leagues

By June, Hendrix was ready for the majors and posted a 4–6 record with the Pirates. The following year he quickly established himself as a star, leading the National League in wins (24), losing only 9 games, and registering the best fielding percentage amongst pitchers. During spring training in 1913, he was a holdout. In 1914, he jumped to the Chicago team in the newly established Federal League, managed by fellow Kansan Joe Tinker. Hendrix was the Federal League's top pitcher, winning 29 games and placing first or second in almost every pitching category. His move to the Feds not only disappointed his mentor Honus Wagner and the Pittsburgh fans, but earned him the wrath of Pirate's owner, Barney Dreyfuss, who felt Hendrix was ungrateful and "money-mad."[13]

For Claude, however, the move to Chicago brought him within a day's train journey of his childhood sweetheart and the financial security to get married. On January 23, 1914, after receiving a telegram from the Chifeds, Claude and Mabel Nelson, daughter of Mr. and Mrs. S.A. Nelson of Spring Hill, "motored to Paola and were quietly married." (Mabel's father was a successful farmer and also engaged in the feed and livestock business.) The newlyweds then returned to the Nelson home, where both sets of parents gathered. After Claude and Mabel "were forgiven" by their elders, they promptly departed so Claude could sign a three-year contract, with Chicago, for $6,000 a season plus a $5,000 signing bonus.[14] Spring Hill, just south of Kansas City and a few miles from Stilwell, was to be their home for the next decade.

On opening day in 1914, the Chifeds, later known as the Whales, played the Packers in Kansas City. Eight thousand fans were on hand, including a large delegation from Stilwell and Spring Hill, to see "banker" Claude Hendrix pitch — he was also the assistant cashier in his father's bank. Chicago won 3–2, as Hendrix put the Packers down in order in four of the nine innings. A few days later, the Chifeds held their home opener with the Packers as the visitors. Hendrix again pitched, allowing only six hits, as he won 9–1 before 25,000 fans in a new stadium at the corner of Clark and Addison, a stadium later named Wrigley Field (which is now the second oldest ballpark in the major leagues). The Chifeds outdrew both the White Sox and the Cubs that year.

Chicago returned to Kansas City in early June, and Hendrix pitched 13 innings before winning 5–2. *The Kansas City Times* reported that "Claude had his saliva dip doing seven kinds of tango steps."[15] Tinker's team finished second in 1914, but the following year they won the pennant. Hendrix slipped to 15–16, but pitched a no-hit game against Pittsburgh on

May 15. He was also seen driving a new Case five-seater, which the Spring Hill newspaper called a "real beauty."

The Federal League was the product of businessmen who wanted to participate in the lucrative, but closed, business of baseball and of players who felt that they worked for unfair wages.[16] When the upstart league was "bought out" in late 1915 by the American and National Leagues, Charles Weeghman, the owner of the Whales, was allowed to purchase the Chicago National League team, and Hendrix became a Cub. In 1916, the Cubs moved to Weeghman Park at Clark and Addison, and Claude again pitched the opening game as the Cubs beat Cincinnati 7–6. He slipped to 8 and 16 but with a respectable ERA of 2.68. It was a bad year for the pitching staff as the Cubs set a record by losing ten games with a 1–0 score. In 1917, the Cubs remained in fifth place, but Hendrix improved to 10 and 12 with an ERA of 2.60.

In 1917, Hendrix registered for the draft in Kansas. He drew a high number and was not called, making him eligible to play in the war-shortened 1918 season, during which he still won 19 or 20 games, depending on the source one accepts.[17] Despite the loss of Grover Cleveland Alexander to the military, the Cubs other starting pitchers — southpaws Jim "Hippo" Vaughn and George "Lefty Tyler" and right-handers "Shufflin" Phil Douglas and Hendrix — helped Chicago win the pennant by more than 10 games.

In the World Series against Boston, Cubs' manager Fred Mitchell elected to start only his two southpaws in an effort to keep Babe Ruth's bat silent. At that time, the Babe played left field only against right-handers. The strategy worked, but Boston still won the series, 4 games to 2. Hendrix and fellow "righty" pitcher Phil Douglas saw only limited action. Hendrix pitched the final inning in game six, surrendering no hits and no runs. Claude's big moment came in the eighth inning of game four with Ruth pitching for the Red Sox. Bill Killefer walked, and Claude came in to bat for the pitcher. He promptly drove a single to left field. A ground-out scored Killefer, ending Ruth's Series record at 29 2/3 scoreless innings. Ruth still got the victory as the Red Sox scored in the bottom of the eighth. It appears ironic that Hendrix, who had the best winning percentage in the National League but was kept out of a starting role in the Series because of the awesome Babe, helped put the limit on what Ruth would later call his most important record.

With one hit in his only time at bat and a scoreless inning on the mound to his credit, Hendrix still remains one of the few World Series players with perfect lifetime batting and earned run averages. After the Series, Claude worked in a Wisconsin shipyard until the Armistice, and both he and Vaughn were holdouts the following spring. In 1921, Hendrix's arm was showing signs of age, and he slipped to 10 and 14, but Claude still had a respectable ERA of 2.62.

The Autumn of 1920

For both baseball and Hendrix, 1920 was a pivotal year. The season began with widespread rumors about control of the 1919 World Series and baseball in general by organized gambling. Claude's career appeared to be nearing the end. On August 31, he was 9 and 12 with an ERA of 3.58, well above any of his nine previous years, and scheduled to start against last-place Philadelphia. Cubs president William L. Veeck received phone calls and telegrams stating that Detroit gamblers were betting heavily on the Phillies, and just before the game Hendrix was replaced by Grover Cleveland Alexander. The Cubs lost anyway, 3–0, and Hendrix denied any knowledge of an attempt to "fix" the game. The phone calls and telegrams made no mention of Hendrix, a fact often ignored in baseball history. Charles C. Alexander in *Our Game* records that the tips identified Hendrix as having been bribed to throw the game.[18]

Veeck hired private detectives, but the story soon broke in the press. A September 4, 1920, front page headline in *The Kansas City Times* proclaimed, "K.C. Bookmakers Drop $101,000 in 'Philly Run.'" A grand jury was convened to investigate, and its charge included examination of gambling in baseball. The focus of the grand jury, and of the national press, quickly shifted to the 1919 World Series where the favored White Sox had lost to the Cincinnati Reds.[19]

The Cubs were no longer in contention, and Claude traveled with the team on its final eastern road trip, but did not pitch. On September 22, 1920, he was sent back to Chicago, with three other players, to be available to the grand jury, but was not called to testify. On September 29, Hendrix pitched in an exhibition game against the Peru (Indiana) Greys, which the Cubs won 7–0.[20]

By this time, a serious struggle had developed, with the National League and three American League teams on one side, and Ban Johnson, president of the American League, and the remaining AL teams on the other. At issue was a revised governance plan that would have significantly reduced Johnson's domination of baseball. Feelings were bitter between the two groups, particularly between Johnson and Charles Comiskey, owner of the Chicago White Sox. One of Johnson's strong advocates, sportswriter Otto Floto of *The Kansas City Post*, responded in his column on September 11. Under the heading, "First It Was the World's [sic] Series Scandal and Now It's the Cub 'Thing,'" he commented:

> And yet we have implicit faith in Ban Johnson. We realize he is the man of the hour in a crisis of this sort. If any of the players have *[sic]* been guilty of dealing with gamblers and he can be shown the proof to that effect it is needless to say that player's career is ended for all time in the national sport. However, Johnson cannot act on the strength of mere idle gossip. He must be shown tangible evidence.[21]

On October 1, 1920, Veeck told the grand jury that there was no evidence that any member of the Cubs was involved with gamblers. In fact, he concluded, the gamblers apparently had tried to make a "sucker" of the Cubs to get them to make a last minute shift and start their best pitcher for the August 31 game.[22]

On October 29, 1920, the grand jury indicted thirteen individuals — the eight White Sox players and five others. On the same day, Johnson stepped forward with "new evidence." He had received a letter from Otto Floto in which Floto stated that a Kansas City gambler named H. A. "Frock" Thompson had received a telegram before the August 31 game, telling him to "Bet $5,000 on the opposition." Floto could not remember for sure, but he thought the telegram was signed by Claude Hendrix. Floto also tied Gene Packard, who had been a popular pitcher with the Kansas City Packers of the Federal League, to baseball gambling.[23] Hendrix, who was on his way to southern Kansas and Oklahoma to pitch in exhibition games, spoke to reporters in Kansas City:

> The report that I wired this fellow Thompson is a lie. I don't know Thompson. Someone is going to get into trouble for tacking my name to such a wild tale. The more they investigate this affair the better satisfied I'll be, because I know they will find there is not one word of truth in it. I know my name has been connected with the stories about that game of August 29 [sic]. These stories surprised and embittered me. I have been honest in my baseball and private life and it is tough to be falsely accused of such a dirty deal. Any time they want to question me, I'll be ready. They'll find my record clean.[24]

Thompson agreed, "There is absolutely nothing to the yarn. I am not even acquainted with Claude Hendrix and wouldn't know the gentleman if I met him on the street."[25] Unfortunately, *The New York Times* in its October 21, 1920, story about the incident identified the Kansas City gambler as "Frog" Thompson, a name that perhaps seemed more typical of a gambler when a half-century later it became popular to assume that Hendrix was guilty.[26]

Hendrix was not called by the grand jury, which submitted its final report on November 6, 1920. Following a meeting of the minor leagues in Kansas City, the American and National League teams gathered in Chicago and reached a settlement. Newspapers across the country carried front page stories on November 13, announcing that Judge Kenesaw Mountain Landis had been named "czar" of baseball. Commissioner Landis later banned the eight Black Sox players for life.

Claude dropped out of the news until early February 1921 when the Cubs gave him his unconditional release. In reporting the release, the *Chicago Daily Tribune* said that the "general belief is that Claude will not be back in organized ball." The story also specified that "President Veeck stated yesterday that Hendrix wasn't released because of any evidence against him, but was let out with the general idea of disposing of veteran material and building up a young team." Buck Herzog and Fred Merkle, it was noted, had been released for the same reason several weeks previously.[27] A few days later, a *Tribune* story by I.E. Sanborn reviewed the players forced out of baseball by the gambling scandal. In addition to the eight from the White Sox, he mentioned Hal Chase plus Heinie Zimmerman of the Giants, Joe Gedeon of the Browns, and Lee Magee of the Cubs. He did not include Hendrix in his list.[28] It is unfortunate that *The New York Times* did not mention Veeck's comments in its brief notice about the release on February 8. Later writers may have used the *Times* as their single source of information. In reporting Claude's release, *The Kansas City Star* included Veeck's disclaimer.[29] Floto's *Post* did not:

> Claude Hendrix, veteran spitball pitcher of the Chicago Cubs, was unconditionally released Monday, according to announcement made by President W. L. Veeck. Hendrix had been named last fall in reports of alleged collusion with gamblers and reports had been current for some time that he would not be retained by the Cubs.[30]

Hendrix spoke with Kansas City reporters the same day, and the *Times* stated:

> Claude Hendrix has pitched his last game of ball for a major league club. Even a big salary offer and a long term contract would not lure the Kansas boy back to baseball's big show for he made it known yesterday that he was through, following the announcement of his unconditional release by the Chicago club.
> "I told my friends at the close of last season that I was through with major baseball," said Hendrix, "and I still stick by my decision. Mr. Veeck of the Cubs always has treated me as a gentleman and I most certainly appreciate his kindness in giving me my unconditional release. Now I am free but I don't expect to take advantage of it and offer my services to any big league club. I have a good position here as a salesman for the Oakland Motor Car Company and next summer I

expect to spend my spare time pitching for semi-professional teams in Missouri, Kansas, and Oklahoma."[31]

Otto Floto, whose journalist style would be typical of "tabloids" or "talk radio" today, termed the eight Black Sox players "members of the Pillow Lifter's union," castigating them for "making an attempt to back pedal and refute the confessions they made to the grand jury" and predicting "they will not get very far, neither will the 'remember-the-wife-and-kiddies' outfit who hope to escape the just punishment they so richly deserve." He then concluded:

> There are a lot of other players still to be mentioned. Two of them in particular who came from the Federal league, where all the crookedness seems to have been hatched, will be questioned by Judge Landis and when they get through will wish they had never been summoned....[32]

As he had announced, Claude worked in Kansas City and pitched independent ball while he and Mabel made their home both there and in Spring Hill, where they were active in community affairs. The Spring Hill Christmas dance they hosted with their friends, Dr. and Mrs. Gast, was a popular event. But tragedy beckoned; Mabel became ill in 1923. An operation proved futile, and, within a few months, Mabel died a painful death.

The following spring Claude's father retired from banking, just as the agricultural depression hit rural Kansas, and moved to Wellsville, a small community about twenty-five miles west of Spring Hill. The elder Hendrix engaged in insurance and real estate, and he and Claude purchased the Liberty Theatre, showing films like *Rin-Tin-Tin* and *The Hunchback of Notre Dame*.[33] Without Mabel, however, Kansas was no longer home for Claude, and in the summers of 1924 and 1925 he played ball with some old Pennsylvania friends in the Lehigh Valley, a hotbed of semi-pro baseball. He first signed with the Emaus [now Emmaus] Moravians, producing immediate cries of "outlaw" from neighboring towns. Hendrix was kept on the bench while team management sent a night-letter to baseball Commissioner Landis, who responded with a telegram on June 20, 1924: "PITCHER HENDRIX HAS AN UNCONDITIONAL RELEASE. HE IS A FREE AGENT."[34]

The Moravians finished their season on August 10, and Claude joined the Allentown Dukes, owned by the well-known baseball magnate Ernest "Duke" Landgraf. The Dukes had defeated the Yankees in an exhibition game the previous year. The "Big Kansan" became the ace of a staff that included former major leaguers "Jing" Johnson, Bill Pertica, and Weldon Wyckoff. Claude finished the season with 8 wins and a tie. Over the next few years, he pitched for Allentown and Camden. And, during the winters, he played in Mexico. In 1928, Claude had trouble getting his arm ready for the season, and even the "emery and bottle cap" balls, common in semi-pro games, did not help. Allentown lost to the Phillies in an exhibition game although Claude pitched three scoreless innings, a feat that must have given him some satisfaction as he thought back to 1920. For both Claude and Allentown, however, the season disintegrated, and in what apparently was his last appearance, he started a game against the Cleveland Indians on July 9 and was "yanked" in the fourth after giving up six runs.[35] These two exhibition games provide important documentation, as Judge Landis would not have allowed major league teams to play exhibitions against a semi-pro team that used a player banned from the majors.

The Verdict

Did Claude Hendrix plan to throw the game to the Phillies on August 31? That question probably will never be answered. The only evidence to support such a charge is the letter from Otto Floto, alleging that Hendrix placed a bet against his own team. The grand jury ignored the letter. It can be suggested that he had a history of bouncing from team to team, looking for a bigger pay check. But so did Joe Tinker. Actually, Claude initiated only one move in his major league career. The opinion of Hendrix's former coach, Ernest Quigley, might have been relevant. Unfortunately, Quigley (who was famed for ignoring his whistle when officiating on the basketball courts of America, instead pointing a finger at the guilty party, and shouting, "YOU can't do that!") apparently left no record of his assessment. Quigley did not umpire the Cubs-Phillies game of August 31, but he was behind the plate a few days earlier when the Pirates shelled Claude. He would have known whether Claude's arm was finished or not.

Was Hendrix embittered because he, like Douglas, did not start a game in the 1918 Series?[36] Or was Claude in some form of financial trouble? There is no evidence to support either assumption. Claude liked playing baseball, but he also liked hunting and fishing. Moreover, he owned grain and livestock land in Kansas, and in 1920 his father, P. K. Hendrix, a perceptive businessman, was president of a bank in Bonner Springs, Kansas. It is possible that P. K. served as Claude's financial advisor and counseled him to "hold out."

Was Hendrix officially banned from baseball? The answer to that question is clearly "no." Was he "unofficially" banned by some form of agreement among the owners and Commissioner Landis? There is no evidence to support such a conclusion.

Another concern is that he did not attempt to clear his name as did, for example, Buck Weaver. Weaver, the outstanding third baseman for the White Sox, admitted that he knew about the plan to "fix" the 1919 World Series, but played to win in every game. Landis repeatedly turned a cold shoulder on Weaver's efforts to be reinstated. Hendrix, however, had retired from Major League Baseball. He was 33 years old and had pitched 2,372 major league innings, plus at least 400 innings with Cheyenne in 1910. Not many pitchers lasted that long. Of the 1,090 individuals who pitched in the majors from 1901 thru 1919, only 49 had more career innings than Claude. He had 1,092 career strikeouts; only 32 others in that group had more. He had 27 shutouts, a substantial figure. His 2.65 ERA and .241 batting average still place him amongst the top fifty pitchers of all-time in those categories.[37]

For Claude, the war-shortened 1918 season and the 1920 campaign both ended by Labor Day, and a comparison reveals the extent to which his career was declining. In 1918, he started 32 games, completed 21, pitched 233 innings, and led the National League in winning percentage. In 1920, he started 23 games, completed only 12, pitched 203 innings, and won only 9 games. On June 10, 1920, Hendrix failed to retire a single batter in the third inning, causing *Philadelphia Inquirer* writer Jim Nasium to gloat, "Claude Hendrix essayed to pitch the Cubs to victory over our Phils and Cravath's clouters tore the quivering hide off his palpating form in the very first period... ."[38] A month later, Claude lasted only seven innings against Boston, and Ed Cunningham wrote, "[The Braves] captured the series by falling on Cloudy Claude Hendrix like a flock of eight-cornered confetti."[39] Although still used occasionally as a pinch hitter, his batting average fell from .264 to .181, and he hit no home runs in 1920.

Actually, there was no reason for Hendrix to think that his reputation needed to be defended. It was not until after his death that it became popular to write that he had been banned, either officially or unofficially, from baseball.

Aftermath

In 1926, Claude decided to make Allentown home, and his parents soon retired there. He purchased the AA Café, and it became a downtown watering hole famous for chili con carne and frequented by newspapermen, sports fans, and area residents. At his death, he left it to his best friends, bartender Michael "Chief" Szalay and waitress Margie Miller, who operated it for another decade after his death. In the Lehigh Valley, he is still remembered as a leading sports hero of the past century.[40]

Claude and Mabel had no children, and he had no brothers or sisters. He died on March 22, 1944, of pulmonary tuberculosis, after having been ill for a year. Hendrix's obituary tells us that he coached the Limeport team in the East Penn League, gave advice to youngsters in the game, and enjoyed hunting and fishing.[41] He left no close relatives to defend his name.

Notes

1. *The Baseball Encyclopedia: The Complete and Definitive Record of Major League Baseball,* 9th ed. (New York: Macmillan Publishing Company, 1993), 1010 and 1929. Some published records give Hendrix 144 wins and 116 loses, including 20 wins in 1918; see, for example, John Thorn et. al., *Total Baseball: The Official Encyclopedia of Major League Baseball,* 6th ed. (New York: Total Sports, 1999), 1585.

2. J.G. Taylor Spink, *Judge Landis and Twenty-Five Years of Baseball* (New York: Thomas Y. Crowell Company, 1947), 62.

3. David Quentin Voigt, *American Baseball: Volume II, From the Commissioners to Continental Expansion* (Norman: University of Oklahoma Press, 1970), 144; Joseph M. Overfield, "Tragedies and Shortened Careers" in *Total Baseball,* ed. John Thorn and Pete Palmer (New York: Warner Books, 1991), 438; Doug Myers, *Essential Cubs* (Chicago: Contemporary Books, 1999), 350; and Rich Westcott and Allen Lewis, *No-Hitters: The 225 Games, 1893–1999* (Jefferson, NC: McFarland & Company, 2000), 82.

4. Harold Seymour, *Baseball: The Golden Age* (New York: Oxford University Press, 1971), 298; Edie Gold and Art Ahrens, *The Golden Era Cubs, 1876–1940* (Chicago: Bonus Books, 1985), 84; Bill James, *The Bill James Historical Baseball Abstract* (New York: Villard Books, 1986), 136; Harvey Frommer, *Shoeless Joe and Ragtime Baseball* (Dallas: Taylor Publishing Company, 1992), 131; Daniel E. Ginsburg, *The Fix Is In: A History of Baseball Gambling and Game Fixing Scandals* (Jefferson, NC: McFarland & Company, 1995), 231; David Pietrusza, Matthew Silverman, and Michael Gershman, ed., *Baseball: The Biographical Encyclopedia* (New York: Total Sports Publishing, 2000), 487; and Robert F. Burk, *Never Just a Game: Players, Owners, and American Baseball to 1920* (Chapel Hill: The University of North Carolina Press, 1994), 231. Ginsburg (133) and Pietrusza (487) also have Hendrix attending Fremont College rather than Fairmount College.

5. Warren Brown, *The Chicago Cubs* (New York: G. P. Putnam's Sons, 1946), passim; and Eliot Asinof, *Eight Men Out: The Black Sox and the 1919 World Series* (New York: Holt, Rinehart and Winston, 1963), 149–150. Troy Soos uses the 1918 Cubs for his popular mystery, *Murder at Wrigley Field* (New York: Kensington Publishing Company, 1996) but does not include Hendrix although Claude appears to be one of the players pictured on the dust jacket.

6. Ed Blair, *History of Johnson County Kansas* (Lawrence, KS: Standard Publishing Company, 1915), 428–430; and "Why Hendrix Should Be Elected," *Olathe Register,* 4 November 1904, 1. Blair, who was well acquainted with the Hendrix and Nelson families, lists Claude's birth year as 1888. Most baseball records list it as 1889, and his obituary in the Allentown newspapers stated he was born in 1891.

7. In the late 1800s, many colleges had preparatory programs aimed particularly at rural students or those looking for a church-related high school curriculum. In early years, these students participated on college teams, but by 1907 conferences began to prohibit this practice. Baseball in Kansas was still an exception, partly because the

weather made completion of schedules difficult. At Fairmount, four of the ten team members were Academy students.

8. *Dial*, July 1907, 355. Although there were three weekly newspapers in the area at that time, plus the monthly student newspaper, the record for each game is not complete. Hendrix can be credited with at least three of the victories for that year.

9. There is nothing in the record to suggest a reason for this move. Quite possibly Charles Comiskey, owner of the Chicago White Sox, was responsible for sending Claude to St. Mary's College and then to Fairmount Academy. Comiskey too had attended St. Mary's College, and in 1916, on the way home from spring training, the White Sox played an exhibition game against St. Mary's College. Frank Isbell, one of the co-owners of the Wichita Jobbers, also played for the White Sox where he is remembered for having played every position. "Izzy" spent much of the preseason and periods late in the season in Wichita and other minor league towns, acting somewhat as the unofficial director of the farm system for Comiskey.

10. *Sunflower*, 7 March 1908, 1; and *Wichita Eagle*, 26 May 1908, 7.

11. *Salina (Kansas) Evening Journal*, 2 September 1909, 5. From 1908 to 1911, Hendrix may have pitched for teams other than those listed here. His record is difficult to trace because there were two young men named Hendrix (not related) playing in Oklahoma, Kansas, and Nebraska during this period. Newspaper accounts usually included only last names, and the sports writers frequently confused the two individuals.

12. "Indians Win Championship Of The West," *Cheyenne State Leader*, 27 September 1910, 8.

13. Dennis DeValeria and Jeanne Burke DeValeria, *Honus Wagner: A Bibliography* (New York: Henry Holt & Company, 1995), 260; and "Stars of the Federal League," *Baseball Magazine*, March 1916, 106.

14. *Spring Hill (Kansas) New Era*, 30 January 1914, 1.

15. "Downed In 13 Innings," *Kansas City Times*, 4 June 1914, 8.

16. For a review of the events leading up to the organization of the Federal League and of its short life, see Robert F. Burke, *Never Just A Game: Players, Owners, And American Baseball to 1920* (Chapel Hill: University of North Carolina Press, 1994), 178–209. For a history of the Federal League, see Marc Okkonen, *The Federal League of 1914–1915: Baseball's Third Major League* (Cleveland: The Society for American Baseball Research, 1989).

17. *Olathe (Kansas) Register*, 2 August 1917, 1.

18. Charles C. Alexander, *Our Game: An American Baseball History* (New York: Henry Holt and Company, 1991), 123.

19. For a short history of the Black Sox affair, see Alexander, 118–129. For the best account of the scandal, see Eliot Asinof, *Eight Men Out: The Black Sox and the 1919 World Series* (New York: Holt, Rinehart and Winston, 1963).

20. See *Chicago Daily Tribune*, 1–30 September 1920.

21. Otto Floto, "It's Enough to Shake Anyone's Faith in Honesty of Baseball," *Kansas City Post*, 11 September 1920, 5.

22. "Gamblers 'Chose' Pitcher?" *Kansas City Times*, 2 October 1920, 14.

23. "Now Hendrix is Involved," *Kansas City Times*, 30 October 1920, 16; and "To Probe Charges Against Hendrix," *Kansas City Post*, 30 October 1920, 5.

24. "A Denial From Hendrix," *Kansas City Times*, 30 October 1920, 16.

25. *Ibid.*

26. "Frog" is used by Seymour, 301 and Ginsburg, 134.

27. James Cruisinberry, "Claude Hendrix Handed Release By Boss Of Cubs," *Chicago Daily Tribune*, 8 February 1921, 14.

28. I.E. Sanborn, "Gambler Grip on B.B. Puts Crimp In Majors' Rolls," *Chicago Daily Tribune*, 13 February 1921, Part 2, 2.

29. "Cubs Release Hendrix," *Kansas City Star*, 7 February 1921, 9.

30. "Claude Hendryx [sic] Dropped by Cubs," *Kansas City Post*, 7 February 1921, 6.

31. "Through As A Big Leaguer," *Kansas City Times*, 8 February 1921, 8.

32. Otto Floto, "Rubber Mouthpiece Used by Ted Lewis in Ring Is No Worse Than Employment of Gloves and Pads by Ball Players; Stars of Yesteryear Performed Without Artificial Protection," *Kansas City Post*, 17 February 1921, 8. The two former Federal League players are clearly Claude Hendrix and Eugene Packard, a pitcher for the Kansas City Packers.

33. Hendrix's business activities in Wellsville and in semipro baseball in the area are reported in the *Wellsville (Kansas) Globe*, January 1925 through June 1927.

34. "Hendrix Free Agent, Wires Judge Landis," *Allentown Morning Call*, 21 June 1924, 17.

35. *Allentown Morning Call*, 9 July 1928, 15.

36. See Tom Clark, *One Last Round for the Shuffler* (New York: Truck Books & Pomerica Press, 1979). John Lardner reviewed Douglas's banishment by Judge Landis and concluded that probably the only problem Douglas had was being an alcoholic. "The Crime of Shufflin' Phil Douglas, *New Yorker*, 12 May 1946, 136.

37. Data comparing the 1901 through 1919 pitchers are from David S. Neft, Richard M. Cohen, and Michael L. Neft, *The Sports Encyclopedia: Baseball*, 20th ed. (New York: St. Martin's Griffin, 2000), 110–121.

38. Jim Nasium, "Nearly N-Hit Game for Causey," *Philadelphia Inquirer*, 11 June 1920, 8.

39. Ed Cunningham, "Tribals Capture Final Game from Cubs, 4 to 1," *Boston Herald*, 31 July 1920, 6.

40. Evan Burian, *Sports Legends of the Lehigh Valley* (Emmaus, PA: Evan Burian, 1998), 96.

41. "Claude Hendrix, Ex-Big Leaguer, Dies Here," *Allentown Morning Call*, 23 March 1944, 5.

Baseball, Transcendence, and the Return to Life

Phil Oliver

I believe in the Church of Baseball. I tried all the major religions and most of the minor ones. I've worshipped Buddha, Allah, Brahma, Vishnu, Siva, trees, mushrooms, and Isadora Duncan. I know things. For instance: there are 108 beads in a Catholic rosary, and there are 108 stitches in a baseball. When I learned that, I gave Jesus a chance. — Annie Savoy, Bull Durham[1]

If baseball is Annie Savoy's religion, transcendence is the affective object of her totemic fascination with its equipment and artifacts. Speaking too loosely, we might say that transcendence is to religion as the outfield fences are to (arguably too many) big league hitters and fans: the sine qua non, the aim and fulfillment, even the raison d'etre.

This analogy strains to accommodate the fact that many conventional religionists are not passionately fired by a quest for transcendence at all but are content to enact the habitual motions of religious practice peculiar to their own particular denominations and devotions for their own sake, whether from dutifulness or inertia or simple dearth of imagination. Many profess (but betray no visible passion for) the belief that literal transcendence in the form of everlasting incorporeal "life" awaits the faithful, at least those of the right stripe. Others readily confess an active yearning for transcendence but disavow supernaturalism, religion, or both. Still others just enjoy their transcendent moments, but do not specially mark or otherwise objectify their occasions.

Admittedly, our analogy is flawed. The holy grail of exalted personal experience does not often appear so delightfully, inescapably palpable as

Fenway's Green Monster or Wrigley's ivy. Not everyone prefers, or will confess to preferring, the spiritual equivalent of a big fly to the game's (and to life's) more intricate, subtle, and spread out serendipities. The analogy fails, ultimately, because life bursts the arbitrary bounds it would impose. This is a good thing. Spirit must always answer its own call. If we all heard the same voice in the cornfield, the exceptionality, wonder, and ultimate mystery of *this* exceptional form of experience — in each instance "mine," for some*one*— would be lost. It would become a mere candidate for explanation and easy dismissal. If we value life, we must presume instead to respect the sources that sustain it, especially those sources beyond our own present sight and hearing.

"Transcendence" is a rich but imprecise notion, and an evasive target that calls up a wide range of overlapping associations. It may provoke thoughts of religion, spirituality, serenity, reverie, fantasy, enlightenment, ineffability, meditation, mysticism, metaphysics, the meaning of life, the denial of death, art, aestheticism, psychopharmacology, neuropathology, parapsychology, or even epistemology, to skim only a portion of a list that scrolls on and on. But Andrew Delbanco, bemoaning the spiritual vacuity of an age so caught up in the borrowed prestige of brand identity, writes that "the idea of transcendence has detached itself from any current symbology" save that of mass market advertising ("the golden arches and the Nike swoosh").[2] It may be useful, then, to ponder Peter Ackroyd's novel reconfiguration: "trans-end-dance: the ability to move beyond the end, otherwise called the dance of death."[3] On my reckoning, though, it makes better sense to speak of the celebratory dance of *life*, and of the *return* to life that transcendence can sponsor when it assumes personal form.

I will say more in a moment about why I find Ackroyd's twist helpful, not just for our understanding of transcendence in general but especially in its specific relation to baseball. We should underscore immediately, though, that if transcendence *is* a dance of death, it is nonetheless a dance vitalized by life and, for some, a dance entirely devoted to life's vitalization. For the psychologist, philosopher, and seminal pragmatist William James (1842–1910), the urge to flourish and find personal fulfillment in terms compatible with the view of life as a phenomenon of nature — not a pageant directed by divine intervention or a quest for supernatural immortality — is an oft-neglected catalyst of religion and engine of transcendence. (But just in case that sounds too simple, it must be admitted that reports of Godly incursion can also be accounted as natural phenomena, for a Jamesian; but we can leave that accounting for another day). James was a great friend and defender of supernaturalism but an even greater friend of life and its innumerable possibilities regarded as products of nature. The "return to life" of my title is borrowed from James, an intellectual who never lowered his guard against the evisceration of life by thought.

Life's greatest possibilities culminate in those passionate personal enthusiasms and "delights" of uninhibited subjectivity that can spring from the spontaneity of perception and voluntary attachment that is our natural birthright. Baseball happens to be one of my own spontaneous delights. In my recently published book *William James's "Springs of Delight": The Return to Life*, baseball figures as a leading exemplar of a phenomenon I call "personal transcendence." I will say a bit about how sharply this contrasts with the conventional conception of transcendence as a state of withdrawal, gradual or sudden, from our respective personalities.

But first, let us pull back for a moment from the precipice of potential confusion I may have introduced with that long litany of associations and connotations that are conjured by talk of transcendence. This paper takes a distinct mythic angle, concerned neither with issues of historical veracity or allegorical fancy but rather of what might better be called personal probity. My field of play centers on the varieties of rich inner experience that can be available to the mythic imagination, but that we can rarely find words to match.

In my own work, "myth" has not been an explicit theme. Spirituality, religion, and the philosophical ideas of William James have been. But the late mythologist Joseph Campbell, popularizer of the encomium to "following your bliss," was assuredly (if unintentionally) in James's ballpark and mine. Campbell's critics have impugned him as derivative and superficial, but I think he understood well enough that real bliss is profoundly personal and sui generis.

Richard Ford's magnificent 1995 novel *Independence Day*,[4] with Cooperstown (and Ralph Waldo Emerson) providing a perfect backdrop for the mythically resonant theme of youth's initiation into the world of self-reliant maturity, and of benumbed maturity's self-recovery and return to life, is another contemporary blending of spirit, personal predilection, and philosophy. I am most interested in exploring human subjectivity and the endless ways in which individual human beings find or create significance in life by cultivating specific personal enthusiasms. It will not surprise many in Cooperstown to hear baseball mentioned in this vein. I suppose we are all here because we love to talk about baseball. I am no exception. Yet, and perhaps paradoxically, those of us who are most enthusiastic about baseball know that talk about baseball is ultimately incapable of bearing its own weight. Or maybe the better way to say it is that talk is unbearably light and superficial compared to the depths of personal feeling and association of which it is the merest residue. This is not a comment on baseball per se, but on talk and language and subjectivity.

Please do not misunderstand me here. I am not counseling silence. Those of us who enjoy talking baseball ought to keep on talking. I am suggesting, however, that personal enthusiasms run deep: they run to a place beyond talk and the objectifying intellect. I wish to endorse the view of those who have denied that "language goes all the way down," in full recognition that this point is best pressed non-verbally. But I still trust language to go just far enough down so that talk about the *limits* of talk need not itself descend to babbling and futility.

The mythic imagination largely has to do with how we attach ourselves to cultural meanings, entities, and *stories* bigger and older than ourselves. Baseball serves nicely to illustrate many anthropological generalizations about us.[5] But it also testifies, for some, to ranges of personal significance that cannot be generalized. Myth is a cultural phenomenon, but it can also take strikingly, and to important degrees incommunicably, personal form. Not only are members of different cultures of different mind, but fellow enthusiasts within the same subculture can be mutually opaque in an enthusiasm shared on the surface but possibly not much further. I have friends who share my love of the national pastime but who cannot bring themselves to share my philosophizing approach to the game. For them — and good *for* them — it is just a game. But for those of us who care about baseball's place in the larger scheme, for whatever diversity of reasons, it can be enlightening to realize that the game is also a canvas reflecting the beam and shadow of our inner lives. Woody Allen's character in *Manhattan* drew himself up from despair with a list of things that made his life worth living, a list including Willie Mays as well as some other items I personally find much more difficult to fathom. Doubtless, each of us could very quickly generate such mutually confounding lists — however deeply we may commingle in our shared admiration of Willie (or Mickey, or the Duke).

On June 27, 1998, *The New York Times* ran a feature on the proceedings of the Tenth Cooperstown Symposium. *The Times* reporter found room, between repositioning Carl Yastrzemski to catcher and scoffing at academic (but not, somehow, journalistic) pomposity, to quote our colleague George Grella:

> While the game displays a significant physical beauty and radiates a spiritual transcendence, it also expresses the parallel paradoxical quality of sadness.... If baseball celebrates youth, it also reminds us of mortality; if a game can last forever, it is also an ephemeral endeavor; it usually inspires lyric poetry, but also lends itself to the elegiac

mode.... [I]t instructs us in two crucial American concepts, the loneliness of space and the sadness of time.... It creates an immense green
field, a gorgeous vista invoking the pastoral, the agricultural, even the
peaceable kingdom, but it hints that the lush green garden may also
be a vale of tears. Baseball is the saddest game.[6]

My approach is not to settle for the sadness but to acknowledge its source
and its portion of the truth and then to get past it — to "return to life."
Death is not finally the meaning of life, nor is the sadness that attends
our contemplation of its finality; though of course life in its precious,
finite fullness cannot possibly be grasped in the obtuse defiance of death.
Our games and our play must end, but their impending end is not their
greatest salience. The play *is* the thing. Henry Samuel Levinson, commenting on James's student, colleague, and occasional antagonist George
Santayana, identifies our great challenge: "how to display suffering's mean-
ness and then transcend it by celebrating 'passing joys and victories in the
world.'"[7]

I do not share the belief of many that religion is reducible to an ultimately futile or ineffectual effort to disarm, deny, or otherwise deal
untruthfully with the cold realities of our mortality. It is not necessarily
just about death, any more than it is necessarily just about God. Transcendence may seem to be about God, or it may be sacredly secular and
humanistic. Secular, humanistic, *and* sacred? Those who find "secular
humanism" intrinsically profane will not grasp, as James did, the possibility of this triple yoking. Dewey also affirmed this possibility, as do many
liberals, Unitarian Universalists, and other "progressive" minorities in our
time. Habit and convention, not empirical perspicacity, decree that public-
spirited and earth-centered secularists must disavow a spiritual life. Transcendence may be cosmic or quotidian, reserved or refined, proselytizing
or private. It may suggest supernaturalism, but it need not; indeed, one of
my aims here is to strengthen the claims that, *for a Jamesian*, transcendence
need not imply the supernatural and that strictly speaking, and in the spirit
of James, it need not involve the transcendence *of nature*.

Transcendence may be strictly transient, momentary, and isolated, *an*
experience discontinuous in each instance of its occurrence with the larger
rhythms, patterns, and meanings of the lives it graces. Alternatively, it can
compose the largest meaning in one's life, the pattern of a lifetime. Transcendence may be a fruition, an experience of conclusion — "consummatory," in John Dewey's language — or it may be less punctuated and more
enduring. Dewey himself wrote a great deal about consummatory transcendence, but the latter sort, transcendence of a more stolid and stoical
kind, suggests the consistent pattern and meaning of Dewey's long life's

work. His gravestone paean to "the continuous human community in which we are a link," modestly marked on the campus of the University of Vermont, summarizes that pattern and meaning with simple but powerful eloquence.

Transcendence might strike like a bolt from the blue or be more like the almost imperceptibly accretive sands on a beach. It may be an event in life, small or staggering. It may be a dispositional attitude toward life that raises one's sea-level of happiness and the quality of experience in general, attuning the sensibilities to notice and appreciate a transcendent dimension of events that more somber natures miss. Or it may be the pessimist's prayer of salvation, his escape from an immanent existence he finds all too oppressively real.

Transcendence can be triggered, on the one hand, by a tiny incident, a random sensation, or an excavated memory; or, on the other hand, it can be produced by large and baffling public events. An example of the latter might be the apparently sudden collapse of the Soviet bloc in the concluding years of the last century, especially for those whose entire comprehension of human possibility had been conditioned from birth to accept its permanence. The resulting psychic dislocation and scramble for personal meaning must have occasioned much transcendence, East *and* West.

Transcendence may be unexpected and surprising, or it may be the object of methodical cultivation. My delight in the game of baseball, for instance, or in a particular game, sometimes catches me by surprise but on other occasions has to be tracked down like a shot lined deep into the gap. The national pastime is public, and frequently baffling, but — with a respectful bow to documentary artist Ken Burns ("The game is a repository of age-old American verities ... and yet at the same time a mirror of the present moment ..."[8]) — it may be a stretch to call it "large" without qualification. It is a game, after all, even if many of us resist demoting it as *only* that; there are times, we are sure, when life is best played at, too. And F. Scott Fitzgerald was just wrong when he called it "a boy's game, with no more possibilities in it than a boy could master, a game" without "novelty or danger, change, or adventure." Closer to the mark is the observation that it "has been a touchstone to worlds elsewhere."[9] But for me the transcendent dimension of this game is not "elsewhere," it is (as in *Field of Dreams*) in my own backyard.

Here would be a good place for me to say just a little about "personal transcendence" and how it contrasts with more conventional assumptions about spiritual life. It is the personal turn that opens the door to treating baseball (and much else) as more than a game, at least in the terms of my own approach. Philosophers, theologians, novelists, and others have written of transcendent experiences involving exalted self-surrender, when individual personality and identity are submerged or annexed by some mysterious larger force, power, or entity, and consciousness is pervaded by impersonal awareness, a sense of heightened reality, expanded perception, or unification with "the infinite." The object of so much psychic commotion has been designated "God" and countless cognate terms for divinity by some, but others have proposed different candidates for transcendent attachment. I am partial to a non-supernatural candidate that, I believe, James also especially favored, while yet remembering that he was temperamentally disposed to "favor" as many transcendent objects and ideals — metaphysical, natural, supernatural, or occult — as could be surmised to animate the inner life of even a single soul in the vastness of time and space.

I must, then, issue a caution always to bear in mind the distinction between James's own personal enthusiasms and his pluralistic hospitality to those of others. Tolerance or sympathy being itself one of his ideals, he often enthused over views — more pointedly, over *others'* enthusiasm for views — which in fact he detested personally. He sympathized with almost everyone's spontaneous personal enthusiasms, their ways of meeting and "reacting on" life, without sharing them. And, while he had his own clearly defined philosophical beliefs, he tried to refrain from using philosophy to discredit the experience of other persons. Many a commentator has failed to notice and apply this distinction and has run aground by miscasting James's broad sympathies as personal endorsements.

But James *was* notably drawn to an expansive vision of life rooted in a Darwinian account of our biologically humble (but wondrous) origins and married to pragmatic, pluralistic humanism. He gave voice to that vision in various and sometimes subtle ways, always championing the integrity of personal and even marginal perspectives but never losing the tether of what he called "the really vital question for us all," a question he poses most pointedly in *Pragmatism*: "What is this world going to be? What is life eventually to make of itself?"[10]

James was fond of invoking the image of a chain as life's most apt metaphor, and meant by his and our "vital question" an urgent reminder that our personal commitments and concerns should never be allowed to sever sustaining connections to our communities and our legacy. They should anchor us in the present but also point us to posterity and the future. Such connections begin at home and school, and *preschool*: James was one of the first professional observers of mental life to emphasize the crucial window of receptivity that opens widest while the world is still fresh. All of us who have been privileged to nurture young lives and who have paid attention can corroborate this observation.

For those who compose what the English call the chattering classes (educators, authors, lecturers, maybe even the odd symposium participant), forging those kinds of life connections is also the business of the workplace. But parents and teachers remain our paradigmatic nurturers and, ex hypothesi, those who stand to exert the greatest eventual influence on what life will "make of itself." It may just be possible to take that roll so seriously and perform it so joyously that it becomes a vehicle of transcendence. Don Mattingly said of his active place in the Yankee pantheon, as an outstanding former pinstripe icon who now instructs rookies in spring training, "it feels good to pass stuff on."[11] I don't suppose Mattingly would wish to assert anything like a transcendent connection to George Steinbrenner, but his simple statement mirrors a feeling others have attested in speaking of their own alternative enthusiasms. And something of the same feeling is eloquently and deliberately conveyed, with overtly-spiritual reverberations in The Game, a new baseball book by Robert Benson.[12]

My thesis is that James was an advocate for a type of personal transcendence owing at least as much to subjectivity as to pure experience. The importance and ubiquity of the concept of subjectivity in James's philosophy is directly related to its preeminence in experience and life. "Pure experience" may exhibit salient generic elements that can be abstracted from personal particularity, and that philosophers may find it useful in some contexts of analysis to emphasize; but life experience, as such, is intrinsically and significantly personal. Impersonal experience is not something we live, except in the derivative, discursive form of life that comes later. This is not to say that transcendence must turn its back on analysis and discourse, which in fact provide some persons their highest happiness. But it does imply that such persons should not generalize from their own case about this. If you find your way to a kind of transcendence through words, they still must be words that speak directly to you, not in an argot the rest of us can be presumed to know about. It is not enough to be "present," in some Zen-like fashion of transparent and selfless purity, to our most compellingly significant experiences; we must bring ourselves, our persons, our peculiarities and idiosyncrasies, our histories, and our anticipated futures — in a word, our subjectivity — with us, in our most transcendently stirring moments.

"To the question about the meaning of life everybody answers with the story of his own life," said Hungarian novelist Gyorgy Konrad.[13] James would have heartily approved: this is how we should answer, and the existentialists were not the first to say so. But unlike many existentialists, pragmatist, like James and Dewey, also believe that the primacy of our personal stories need not preempt an inclusive social vision.

The *future* orientation of Jamesian transcendence, in particular, distinguishes it from alternatives and sits least comfortably alongside those more familiar Eastern and quasi–Eastern versions of transcendence that suppress subjectivity and will, renounce the self and its desires, and extol timeless passivity as the highest level of psychic ambition. Kitaro Nishida's Japanese Buddhist version of pure experience, for instance, takes James in a Zen direction that I think false to his own intentions, toward the fusion of self and universe, dissolving into a timeless meditation on nothingness or The Void (as Sidd Finch and Sadaharu Oh, with their "zen way of baseball," might have it). For James, self and universe are never really one — never mind *nothing!* He defends the experience of those who believe in this oneness, but he does not corroborate it. Nor does James concur in the sentiment that "there is nothing that is not a manifestation of God,"[14] though he sympathizes with the affirming sensibility uttering it. Indeed, he sympathizes with whatever secures anyone's happiness and threatens no one else's.

"Happiness is a mystery like religion, and should never be rationalized,"[15] said James's younger contemporary G.K. Chesterton. Happiness may in fact be a mystery and a gift, but for James it was also a pursuit. That is where religion comes in. James defined religion as "the feelings, acts, and experiences of individuals in their solitude, so far as they apprehend themselves to stand in relation to whatever they may consider the divine."[16] He claimed to reject the notion that defining religion so broadly automatically includes any fanatical fascination, systematic obsession, or prolonged piety that anyone may happen to profess for anything at all; presumably, then, he would have applied strictest scrutiny to the late Flip Wilson's "Church of What's Happenin' Now," Garrison Keillor's "Sacred Shrine of the Republican Revelation," *or* Annie Savoy's "Church of Baseball," for instance, before accepting their own self-descriptions as religious. In fact, James thought religion a dignified thing, not to be trivialized or whittled by sensibilities small and silly. We can well imagine his reaction to this statement from the leader of a new religious movement based in Franklin, Tennessee, a faith-based organization dedicated to the convergence of diet and divinity: "God is powerful, rich, famous. He has got on designer clothes." One of her co-religionists proclaims: "The Lord has delivered me from Little Debbie Cakes."[17] James did not trivialize religion, but even less did he favor the suppression of anyone's spontaneous enthusiasms and ideals — even when their special creeds and theories strike some of us as "absurd."

And it must also be said, if in this time of the Taliban in Afghanistan (with their ugly destruction of ancient religious art) and so many other visible outrages committed in religion's name any reminder is still necessary, that religious feeling as such is not an intrinsic good. James was a friend of religion when its fruits were nourishing and sweet, not when it desecrated and embittered the human spirit.

The record seems fairly clear that James remained neutral, publicly, about the extent or the supernatural status of his own personal faith. James's frank responses to a questionnaire on religion in 1904 provide real insight: *Do you believe in personal immortality?* "Never keenly; but more strongly as I grow older." *Do you pray?* "I cannot possibly pray—I feel foolish and artificial." *What do you mean by 'spirituality'?* "Susceptibility to ideals, but with a certain freedom to indulge in imagination about them. A certain amount of 'other worldly' fancy. Otherwise you have mere morality, or 'taste.'" *What do you mean by a 'religious experience'?* "Any moment of life that brings the reality of spiritual things more 'home' to one."[18]

There is a substantial body of precedent supporting liberal inclusivity in the designation of the religious. For instance, many socialist intellectuals earlier in this century — atheists not excluded — considered themselves intensely religious. "Whatever a man will labour for earnestly and in some measure unselfishly is religion,"[19] said writer and mystic D. H. Lawrence. Others have been known to exhibit an astonishing quasi-religious enthusiasm for what non-enthusiasts stubbornly persist in calling mere games, diversions, recreations, or pastimes. We have already alluded to the "Church of Baseball" and its many high-minded penitents who have waxed spiritual and poetic about the national pastime. Some of my fellow enthusiasts are prone to saying, with Tom Boswell, that "time begins on opening day." I do understand the sentiment, though for some of us that is when it *stops* in the salutary sense of transcendence.

But on further reflection, I prefer to think of these personal perceptions of the dawn, and of important beginnings, as neither really starting or stopping our calendars and clocks so much as just putting them in a drawer for the duration of each episode of deep delight, however resonant or fleeting. And, as hinted in this essay's opening remarks, Peter Ackroyd's reconfiguration of this perplexing concept as *trans-end-dance* ("the ability to move beyond the end, otherwise called the dance of death") reminds us that the human spirit enjoys at least the possibility of graceful motion beyond the arrested, contemplative, sometimes stultified, or even terrified mood which can engulf our awareness of mortal boundaries. This is movement towards life, not eternal rest. Satchel Paige said that maybe he would "pitch forever," and in the sense of a naturalized concept of eternity —

stretching time to fit perception that is expansive but unperturbed about the morrow — maybe he did.

James's student, the pragmatist Morris Raphael Cohen, once published an essay entitled *Baseball as a National Religion* in which he reported actually bringing the idea to James's attention. Unfortunately, baseball seems not to have been one of James's own deepest delights. "He listened sympathetically and was amused, but he did not take me seriously enough. All great men have their limitations."[20] But if James could not quite grasp the seriousness of Cohen's proposal, neither would he have brushed off or taken lightly the spirit of the younger man's enthusiasm for the game (or Hall of Fame umpire Bill Klem, whose bronze plaque in Cooperstown records The Old Arbitrator's testimonial that "baseball is more than a game to me, it's a religion") as an idle or misspent passion. James wrote,

> Wherever a process of life communicates an eagerness to him who lives it, there the life becomes genuinely significant. Sometimes the eagerness is more knit up with the motor activities, sometimes with the perceptions, sometimes with the imagination, sometimes with reflective thought. But wherever it is found, there is the zest, the tingle, the excitement of reality; and there is "importance" in the only real and positive sense in which importance ever anywhere can be.[21]

James would also have implicitly understood Paul Simon's plaintive rhetorical lyric "Where have you gone, Joe DiMaggio?" We have a powerful need for inspirational icons we can revere and yet still, somehow, "relate" to. (DiMaggio himself did not understand, insisting that "I just did a Mr. Coffee commercial ... I haven't gone anywhere."[22])

But DiMaggio, the hero and icon (as distinct from the aging ex-athlete/celebrity), *had* "gone away" by the time Simon was crooning his lament: he had come to embody a special status in our culture, a kind of transcendent remoteness from the generational clashes and street protests of the 1960s. He had gone away to a "place" of timeless presence in the untouchable halls of pop culture, mythology, and collective memory — to the place of baseball's past and the "don't look back" safety of a consecrated pedestal. His ascendancy, as it were, may begin to explain the sense of sacrilege that greeted a recent biography's criticisms of the Yankee Clipper.

Beyond the simple "team concept" and its instrumental focus on victory, baseball actively rewards another kind of dwelling in the past and encourages the eager anticipation of future occasions of dwelling there again, at the park and in the imagination. Those creatively spliced video reels in which a swatting Ruth melds with an Aaron, Mantle, Maris, Mays, or McGwire demonstrate at some level how this mere game can encourage its devotees to slip the bonds of time, in transient green reveries. The late Renaissance scholar and baseball Commissioner Bart Giamatti wrote with passion of the inner fields of play where we mortals may visit fields of the mythic consciousness.[23]

Inner fields of play is a wonderfully pregnant notion, alive with the possibility of life's recurrent novelties. It is capable of suggesting a more pliant religious sensibility than most of us may be accustomed to, a flexibility of spirit that does not load the deck either for or against supernaturalism but that is alert and receptive to life's beneficent moments as they come. If only time were so fluid in our world as in Ray Kinsella's — and in a way it is, thanks in no small part to places like Cooperstown and to the preservationist historical spirit — Giamatti's lyricism might have clinched Cohen's case for James. Personal enthusiasms of all kinds can fire spiritual passions and tether their devotees to life in unique and delightful ways. They sponsor our return to life when ardor flags. For some of us, the phenomenon can be no better attested than by just a bit of reflection on the nature of our respective forms of delight in Giamatti's "great and glorious game." I must close with the Jamesian admonition that punctuates my title.

James, like the most thoughtful philosophers and poets, wavered between the earnest wish to affirm and extend our humanistic inheritance of understanding and sympathy through language ("philosophy is essentially talkative and explicit"[24]) and an acute awareness of the intrinsic limitations of language that foreshadows the pragmatic elevation of deeds over creeds, actions over words, and engaged spontaneity over cool detachment. "The philosophy which is so important in each of us is not a technical matter; it is our more or less dumb sense of what life honestly and deeply means,"[25] a sense better enacted and enjoyed than enunciated. This creative tension was not resolved by James, who never stopped talking about the insufficiencies of talk:

> I am tiring myself and you, I know, by vainly seeking to describe by concepts and words what ... exceeds either conceptualization or verbalization. As long as one continues talking, intellectualism remains in undisturbed possession of the field. The return to life can't come about by talking. It is an act; to make you return to life, I must set an example for your imitation, I must deafen you to talk, or to the importance of talk.... Or I must point, point to the mere that of life, and you by inner sympathy must fill out the what for yourselves.[26]

In the spirit of William James, then, we can surely do no better than point ourselves towards that field of dreams outside, and from there to realms beyond and within. There is nothing else we need to say, except: play ball!

Notes

1. *Bull Durham*, written and directed by Ron Shelton, Orion Pictures, 1988.

2. Andrew Delbanco, *The Real American Dream: A Meditation on Hope* (Cambridge: Harvard University Press, 1999), 5.

3. Peter Ackroyd, *The Plato Papers: A Prophecy* (New York: Doubleday/Nan A. Talese), 33.

4. Richard Ford, *Independence Day* (New York: Random House, 1995) passim.

5. Bradd Shore, *Culture in Mind: Cognition, Culture, and the Problem of Meaning* (New York: Oxford University Press, 1996), chapter 3.

6. Edward A. Gargan, "Field for Philosophizing and Other Dreams; Scholars Look Into Baseball and See the American Essence," *New York Times*, 27 June 1998, B11.

7. Henry Samuel Levinson, *Santayana, Pragmatism, and the Spiritual Life* (Chapel Hill: University of North Carolina Press, 1992), 12.

8. Ken Burns and Geoffrey C. Ward, *Baseball: An Illustrated History* (New York: Knopf, 1994), xviii.

9. Quoted in *A Companion to American Thought,* ed. Richard Wightman Fox and James T. Kloppenberg (Cambridge: Blackwell, 1995), 57.

10. *Pragmatism. The Works of William James,* ed. Frederick H. Burkhardt, Fredson Bowers, and Ignas Skrupskelis (Cambridge: Harvard University Press, 1975), 62. This multivolume series is the authoritative source for James's texts and hereafter is referred to by specific volume title, with "Works" and year of publication noted parenthetically.

11. Buster Olney, "It Seems Like Old Times With Mattingly," *New York Times*, 2 March 2000, D2.

12. Robert Benson, *The Game: One Game, Nine Innings, A Love Affair With Baseball* (New York: Tarcher/Putnam, 2001), passim.

13. Wim Kayzer, 'A Glorious Accident': Understanding Our Place in the Cosmic Puzzle* (New York: W. H. Freeman, 1997), xi.

14. Kitaro Nishida, *An Inquiry into the Good*, tr. Masao Abe and Christopher Ives (New Haven.: Yale University Press, 1990), 158.

15. G.K. Chesterton, *Heretics* (Amazon Press e-book edition based on New York: John Lane Company, 1905), 62.

16. William James, *The Varieties of Religious Experience* (Works, 1985), 34.

17. Rebecca Mead, "Slim for Him," *The New Yorker*, 15 January 2001, 48f.

18. *William James: Writings 1902–1910* (New York: Library of America, 1987), 1183–85.

19. D.H. Lawrence to Rev. Robert Reid, 3 December 1907, *The Selected Letters of D.H. Lawrence*, ed. James T. Bolton (New York: Cambridge University Press, 1997), 7.

20. Morris R. Cohen, *Faith of A Liberal* (New York: Henry Holt, 1946), 57. Originally published in *The Dial* 67, 26 July 1919.

21. William James, *Talks to Teachers on Psychology and to Students on Some of Life's Ideals* (Works, 1983), 134–35.

22. Paul Simon, "The Silent Superstar," *The New York Times,* 9 March 1999, A23.

23. See A. Bartlett Giamatti, *Take Time for Paradise: Americans and Their Games* (New York: Summit, 1989); and Kenneth S. Robson, ed., *A Great and Glorious Game: Baseball Writings of A. Bartlett Giamatti* (Chapel Hill: Algonquin Books, 1998).

24. William James, *Some Problems of Philosophy* (Works, 1979), 63.

25. William James, *Pragmatism* (Works, 1975), 9.

26. William James, *A Pluralistic Universe* (Works, 1977), 131.

Part 4

MYTHS IN PROGRESS

From Scientific Baseball to Sabermetrics: Professional Baseball as a Reflection of Engineering and Management in Society

Richard J. Puerzer

Throughout its history, professional baseball has been a mirror of many aspects of American society. This relationship extends to the evolution of attitudes and practices of management in baseball, both on the field and in the front office, and in society as a whole. From the advent of scientific baseball in the late 1800s to the use of sabermetrics and strict pitching regimens today, baseball has reflected the application of engineering and management practices for the improvement of both on-the-field and business performance.

The management of a baseball team is far more complicated than the plan attributed to Casey Stengel of "keeping the guys who hate you away from the guys who are undecided." When formally examined, team management in baseball is a multi-disciplinary task, requiring knowledge of statistics and mathematics, as well as an understanding of the diverse areas of ergonomics, organizational behavior, and management theory. These topics are all prominent areas of study in the field of engineering, specifically in the discipline of industrial engineering. In fact, links to the field of industrial engineering can be seen throughout the history of professional baseball. One reason that this relationship is so strong is that baseball, like industry, is ever evolving. In discussing baseball in the late 1800s, Bill James states what he believes is a fundamental misunderstanding about the way baseball is and always has been played. He states that the way baseball is played is not defined largely by the rules. Instead it is defined by the conditions under which the game is played, specifically the ballparks but also the players, the ethics, the strategies, the equipment, and the expectations of the public.[1] Continuous changes in the game of baseball have and will continue to necessitate the constant evolution of baseball management to lead this change. Likewise, developments in industrial engineering have been and continue to be a bellwether of business and industry trends acceptable within and relied upon by society. Thus, industrial engineering serves as a change leader in industry.

This paper will analyze the development of methods and trends in industrial engineering that have also been applied to baseball throughout its history. This analysis will demonstrate the inextricable bond between the evolution of management in baseball and in industrial engineering. Likewise, it suggests that perhaps a closer formal working relationship, such as the hiring of industrial engineers in the baseball management field, would be advantageous to the business of baseball.

A Brief History of Industrial Engineering

Before looking at its relationship with baseball, industrial engineering as a discipline must be discussed, as it is a little known and often-misunderstood field of engineering. Industrial engineering can be generally described as the study of methods for the improvement of the great variety and multitude of systems used in the working world. These described improvements can be characterized as improvements in the following: productivity and cost-effectiveness in accomplishing a task; the safety, comfort, and satisfaction of workers; and the optimization of related systems achieving work.[2] In more general terms, industrial engineers strive to make things better, faster, and cheaper.

There are four major areas of study in industrial engineering: operations research, ergonomics, manufacturing, and management. All four areas are covered to some degree in an undergraduate program in industrial engineering. Operations research is the term for the many mathematical tools used in industrial engineering, including statistical analysis, linear programming, and simulation modeling. Ergonomics is the study of improvements in the design of the work environment for human beings.

The manufacturing area studies the improvement of methods for the manufacture of goods. Lastly, the field of management studies how businesses operate and how they can be managed to run effectively and successfully. These four fields are not studied independently, but instead are integrated so as to provide industrial engineers with a system-wide view of the problems they address in their work.

Industrial engineering developed in the late nineteenth century in response to the massive increase in large-scale manufacturing to meet the needs of society. As industry rapidly expanded, corporate leaders recognized the need to increase productivity and efficiency in their businesses. Frederick W. Taylor is generally considered to be the father of industrial engineering.[3] He began work in time studies (the study of the standard time required to accomplish a job following the exact methods by which that job was to be accomplished). His work on time study analysis began in 1881 while working for a Philadelphia-based steel company. Taylor went on to develop a system of management know as "Scientific Management." Scientific management describes the use of such tools as time study, standardization of tools and tasks, and bonuses for performance in industry to improve the efficiency of business.[4] Although scientific management and its tools had a turbulent history, it is indisputable that the application of many of its tenets was indispensable in industry as a starting point for business improvements. Later in this paper, the immediate and long-term impact of scientific management on baseball will be examined.

Two other important early industrial engineers were the husband and wife team of Frank and Lillian Gilbreth. The Gilbreths were the founders of modern motion technique, which is defined as the study of the body motions used in performing an operation, to improve the operation by eliminating unnecessary motions, simplifying necessary motions, and establishing the most favorable motion sequence for maximum efficiency.[5] Frank Gilbreth originally introduced these ideas in the early 1900s. At that time, he suggested the filming of work operations and slow-motion analysis of the tasks. These methods are described in the autobiographical work, *Cheaper by the Dozen*, which describes the filming of Gilbreth and his twelve children having their tonsils removed in order to study the motions involved by the surgeon in the operation.[6] Obviously baseball has found this tool to be invaluable as pitchers and hitters watch and analyze video of their motions for flaws and improvement. Lillian Gilbreth was one of the first scientists to study industrial psychology, or the study of the attitudes of people to work and the interaction between management and labor. Baseball history is ripe with examples of applications of industrial psychology, such as the evolving style of field managers and the corporate culture of teams.

Industrial engineering continued to evolve throughout the 1900s with the many improvements in industry and technology. World War II saw the need for massive improvements in the scheduling and optimization of the movement of people and supplies and the use of scarce resources. Research and application of a great many mathematical tools, generally described as operations research methods, addressed many of these needs. Later, the widespread use of statistical analysis in industry was caused in large part by the great success that statistical process control enjoyed in post–World War II Japan. With the advent and quick acceleration of the utility of computers, math tools, such as linear programming and simulation analysis, became widely used. Although baseball has been slow to embrace the computerization and analysis of its many statistics, the impact of accepted analysis on the game is indisputable.

Today, industrial engineers are employed by a wide spectrum of companies in the manufacturing and service industries. Their roles in these companies range from traditional engineering work, such as time studies and statistical process control, to state of the art research in mathematical modeling and design work in ergonomics. Also, as their careers progress, industrial engineers tend to be the most qualified engineers to move into management positions within companies.

Scientific Management and Scientific Baseball

The first link between industrial engineering and baseball dates back to the early days of professional baseball with the application of scientific management to the game. The term scientific baseball dates back until at least the 1870s, and reached great prominence in the 1890s with the increased American faith in scientism, or the passion to apply science to all fields of human endeavor.[7] Scientific baseball, synonymous with the term "small ball" used today, describes using offensive strategy such as place hitting, the hit-and-run, and stealing bases to score a few runs. Having achieved a lead, the pitching and defense are to limit the number of runs allowed and thus enable the team to prevail.[8] At the time of its development, scientific baseball was seen as the opposite of "the manly game" of slugging and aggressive play to pound one's team to victory. Scientific baseball had supporters in some of the elder statesmen of the time, including Henry Chadwick and Harry Wright. Likewise, high-profile players, such as Willie Keeler, were seen as flag-bearers of the scientific game. The best teams of the 1890s, the Boston Beaneaters and the Baltimore Orioles, were purveyors of the scientific game. The Beaneaters are credited by many for the development of the hit-and-run play.[9] Ned Hanlon, whom Bill James calls the great-grandfather of most modern major league managers, managed the Orioles in the late 1890s when they were renown for their core of Keeler, Wilbert Robinson, Hughie Jennings, and John McGraw.[10] Hanlon's philosophy as manager of the Orioles was to have a systematic plan, which sounds much like a business plan, of keeping the opponent guessing and studying the opponents so as to take advantage of their weaknesses.[11] Scientific baseball would remain the dominant philosophy in the on-field management of baseball teams until the 1920s when the predominance of home runs would force it out of widespread use for two generations. Its departure left many, including Ty Cobb and Ring Lardner, to lament the passing of what they considered real baseball.

The term "scientific baseball" mirrored that of "scientific management," then the cutting edge of management theory. Frederick Taylor, the "Father of Scientific Management," used a baseball team as a metaphor in the description of a well working company that he presented before Congress in 1911.[12] Although the prevalence of scientific management disappeared in industry by the 1920s, it was and is still widely applied in baseball. In fact, some facets of scientific management have only recently been employed. For example, one tenant of scientific management is to use the best worker at hand to accomplish a specific task. Platooning, or the use of left-handed hitters against right-handed pitchers and vice-versa, was used as a strategy as early as the 1870s by Cap Anson's Chicago White Stockings and also later by Ned Hanlon's Orioles. It fell into disfavor in the 1930s and 1940s before a successful revival in the 1950s by Casey Stengel and the New York Yankees.[13] Platooning is, of course, widely used today.

The use of relief pitchers is another instance of the specialization of workers to achieve a specific task. Although relief pitchers have always been employed in baseball, they were, prior to the 1950s, often seen as, in Branch Rickey's words, "a necessary evil." Sometimes they were used as pinch runners. Jim Konstanty won the National League MVP for the 1950 Philadelphia Phillies as a reliever. And Joe Black, Hoyt Wilhelm, and Roy Face followed with stellar seasons in the relief pitching role.[14] Relief pitching has continued to adapt and flourish, with the further specialization of relief pitchers as long-relievers, middle-relievers, and closers. Relief pitchers are now developed in the minor leagues. Statistically, saves and holds are specific measures of the performance of relief pitchers. Often, the middle reliever and closer are seen as a specialty team within the team, such as the 1990 Cincinnati Reds' nasty boys of Rob Dibble, Randy Myers, and

Norm Charlton or the 1996 Yankees' tandem of Mariano Rivera and John Wetteland. Today, a team's bullpen is seen as a crucial component of a winning team.

Operations Research and Sabermetrics

A reliance on numerical analysis is another attribute shared by baseball and industrial engineering that has existed and evolved throughout their history. Professional baseball has always had an inextricable relationship with numbers and statistics. Due to the discrete nature of the events of the sport, baseball provides for a multitude of opportunities for the collection and evaluation of numbers. With every pitch, data can be collected and analyzed for trends, meaning, and significance. Sabermetrics is a term derived by combining the acronym for the Society for American Baseball Research (SABR) with the term for measurement. It is defined as the mathematical and statistical analysis of baseball records.[15] Although the descriptive term "sabermetrics" has been around for less than thirty years, the analysis of baseball statistics preceded the organization of professional baseball. The sophistication of the statistical analyses employed in baseball, like those used in business and society, have evolved sporadically over time.

The initial popularity of baseball may have been due to the ease with which statistics were used to describe the game, especially through the box score. As a sportswriter in New York in 1858, Henry Chadwick, an Englishman born in 1824, developed the box score.[16] Chadwick was extremely influential in the early years of professional baseball as he developed tabular standings, the batting average, and most of the statistics and tables used to describe baseball. Branch Rickey has referred to the box score as "the mortar of which baseball is held together." Chadwick was given the moniker "Father Baseball" in his lifetime for the development of the box score and his influence on the game.[17]

Statistics were embraced by society during the early years of professional baseball, again as society sought to become "more scientific" in its look at life. For example, in the early 1900s, the federal Census began collecting demographic information for tracking purposes and became a much more scientific study than a simple count of the population. Likewise, the new social science fields of psychology, sociology, and economics increased the utilization of statistics.[18] Acting much like an industrial engineer, Chadwick's statistical view of baseball was used not only to report the game, but also to improve the game. He was present on the rules committees in the early years of the game and had a lasting impact on all aspects of the game. He sought to perfect the game by making it "more conducive to, and demanding of, skilled play — and consequently more exciting to watch."[19]

The development of statistical analysis in baseball began with Chadwick and his use of such measures as the batting average (although his was initially calculated as hits over games). Chadwick even used a primitive measure of slugging percentage, which he termed "total bases average." This measure is a weighted average, where the elements making up the numerator, the number for each type of hit, are recognized as having different value; singles are unweighted, doubles weighted by a factor of two, triples by a factor of three, and home runs by a factor of four. Thorn and Palmer recognize this weighted average as the cornerstone of today's statistical innovation in baseball. However, they also point out that baseball has been very conservative in its acceptance of new measures, as the National League did not make slugging percentage an official statistic until 1923, and the American League waited until 1946.[20]

In many ways, professional baseball has been slow to recognize the potential impact of statistical and analytical tools. It was not until 1954 that more sophisticated analysis of baseball through mathematics and statistics was pursued. This was at about the same time that American industry was turning towards statistical and optimization tools for the improvement of efficiency and cost effectiveness. In a 1954 issue of *Life* magazine, Branch Rickey, then chairman of the board of the Pittsburgh Pirates, authored an article in which he described use of some new measures of baseball performance.[21] Although not named as an author, Allan Roth, a statistician, played a large part in the development and reportage of the new measures.[22] Among other equally prescient ideas presented in the article, Rickey and Roth rightly devalued batting average and proposed in its place On Base Percentage as a better measure of a batter's performance. This article would serve as the starting point for baseball's new statistics, those that sought to recognize a player's contribution to the scoring of runs.

Baseball and the field of operations research came together in 1959 and again in 1963 as the journal *Operations Research*, published by the Operations Research Society of America, featured papers written by George Lindsay on statistics and strategy in baseball.[23] These papers made considerable headway in the analysis of the use of statistics for the evaluation of baseball strategy. However, perhaps due to the journal in which they were published and the mathematical language used, this work made no impact whatsoever on organized baseball.[24]

The first book entirely devoted to the application of statistical analysis of baseball was *Percentage Baseball* by Earnshaw Cook, published in 1964.[25] Cook, who had previously published several books on the engineering of steel and alloy making, looked at the application of probability theory in baseball strategy. Although the book did garner some media attention at the time, it did not have any impact on organized baseball, again perhaps due to the strictly academic nature of the language. The book did have an impact on Philip Roth's *The Great American Novel*, in which it is credited for the nontraditional baseball strategy employed in the plot of the novel. Specifically, Cook's analysis of the strategy of the sacrifice bunt shows it to be a scoring inhibitor instead of a run producer. One of Roth's characters uses this and other nontraditional strategies in the management of a baseball team.

In the twenty-first century, organized baseball seems to finally be embracing much of what has been learned through the mathematical analysis of baseball. With the advent of the personal computer in the 1980s, the collection, storage, and crunching of the huge quantities of numbers which baseball analyses necessitates have become much easier. With this ability, researchers outside of professional baseball have made a significant impact on the analysis of the game. These include members of The Society for American Baseball Research, founded in 1971, an organization dedicated to the study of baseball history and statistics; John Thorn and Pete Palmer, whose book *The Hidden Game of Baseball*, published in 1984, took an historical perspective on the evolution of statistics and went one step further with the introduction of linear regression analysis as a method of player performance measurement; and Bill James, who began to self-publish his work on the mathematical analysis of baseball in 1977.

In many respects, Bill James has been to sabermetrics what Taylor or the Gilbreths were to industrial engineering.[26] James took the smattering of statistical research that had been done through the history of the game and, with single-mindedness and graceful writing, turned the analysis of baseball statistics into an accepted science. However, the impact of his work has been mitigated by the glacial speed of change in on-field strategy by the baseball establishment. Much like the slow acceptance of the quality movement in the United States, baseball has been shortsighted in assessing the impact of the new science. But, as many baseball observers, such as journalist Rob Neyer, have commented, a new generation of baseball people, especially general managers, who have grown up on the work of Bill James and others, will utilize the new information.[27]

The typical view of organized baseball's attitude towards the numerical analysis of the game is expressed in Roger Kahn's novel *The Seventh*

Game, the prolific baseball writer's only work of fiction. The team on which the story's protagonist plays is owned by a man "with degrees in engineering and business" who has an affinity for using computer programs to calculate statistics for the analysis of strategies for his team.[28] This owner, who is essentially educated as (and playing the role of) an industrial engineer in his effort to improve his team, is seen as an annoyance and a harm to the game. Although statistics have been used in the analysis of baseball strategy and performance essentially since the birth of the game, they are often seen as an impediment to enjoyment of the game. Although some bemoan the fact that statistics take the magic out of baseball, no one can argue that they are essential to the game's history as well as its analysis and strategy. As baseball innovator Branch Rickey was quoted as saying, "Luck is a residue of design."[29] It is virtually impossible to thoughtfully design successful baseball strategy without the use of numerical tools.

Ergonomics and Baseball Training

A third aspect of baseball related to industrial engineering is the study of the ergonomic requirements placed upon the players. Most industrial engineers have some training in ergonomics, also known as human factors engineering. The objectives of the study of human factors engineering are to enhance the effectiveness and efficiency with which human beings accomplish work while improving the safety and reducing the fatigue and stress associated with that work.[30] The study of human factors engineering analyzes work primarily from three perspectives: anthropometrical (the study of the dimensions of the human body); physiological (the study of the demands of physical exertion on the human body); and psychological (the study of the mental affects of work on the body). From these perspectives, the industrial engineer strives to improve the efficiency, safety, and comfort of work through tool, methods, environmental design, and worker training. A baseball player's work necessitates him to excel at the diverse activities required of the game while avoiding the multitude of possible injuries that these activities may cause. Although the work performed by a baseball player is quite unique, it is subject to improvement through the application of techniques akin to those of industrial engineering.

Human factors engineering developed as a segment of industrial engineering in the late 1800s and early 1900s with the increase in the use in technology in society. Frank and Lillian Gilbreth did much of the early work in the field, especially in the study of skilled performance and fatigue with, among other groups, surgeons. However, it was not until the end of World War II, with the massive surge in the use of technology throughout all aspects of labor and society, that human factors became an important field, examining both the physical and psychological impact of work.[31] Since then, a multitude of advances in the design of products for safety and comfort have been made, such as the use of seat belts and airbags in cars. Likewise in the history of baseball, most of the tools for improving the safety and comfort of players have only recently been implemented. For example, batting helmets were not widely used until 1952 when the Pittsburgh Pirates, under general manager Branch Rickey, used special plastic helmets in both the field and at bat.[32] Also, the now ubiquitous batting gloves have only recently come into use. Human factors engineering has evolved through research, which has resulted in standards and legislation regarding the safety and comfort of workers and society in general. Today, as evidenced by the auto industry, which emphasizes the safety and comfort of new vehicles as much, if not more, than the vehicles' performance, human factors engineering has a strong presence throughout society.

A salient example of the application of human factors engineering on a grand scale in baseball was the Kansas City Royals Baseball Academy. The academy, founded in 1970 by Royals' owner Ewing Kaufman, had three goals: first, to increase the supply of talent in the Royals organization; second, to develop the players as people by paying for their college classes taken while in the academy; and third, to test and analyze the skills and performance of baseball players. The academy invited a great number of scientists, psychologists, and inventors whose theories were tested.[33] Kaufman's vision of worker development and task improvement is not unlike that of W. Edwards Deming,[34] the quality guru who helped Japanese industry gain worldwide prominence for the quality of their manufactured goods, specifically electronics and automobiles. Syd Thrift, who was the founding director of the academy, describes the academy as a laboratory and mentions several "discoveries" made through the work at the academy, including stretching programs for every player, the timed, measured baserunning lead, and methods to improve players' reflexes and fielding range. The work at the academy was not limited to on-field performance. Academy research also examined such areas as the psychological and physiological effects of substance abuse on players.

The academy was not long lived, however, lasting only three years. At an expense of four million dollars and after the evaluation of thousands of athletes, only 14 players signed professional contracts and only one player, Frank White, went on to the major leagues.[35] Thrift and Kaufman blamed divisiveness within the Royals organization for the downfall of the academy. Many in the Royals organization thought that resources would be better used in the traditional methods for developing talent, scouting and the minor leagues.[36] Although the experiment of the baseball academy was seen as a failure by many, its discoveries have had a lasting impact on many of the game's training and playing practices. Similarly in industry, industrial engineers often face resistance and failure in their work, although the improvements they work toward do prevail in the long run.

A great many applications of human factors engineering in baseball are centered on the pitcher. For example, the pitch count is a physiological measure applied to the pitcher that tracks the number of pitches each pitcher has thrown in a game. The pitch count is kept in order to keep track of the effort he has expended and toll taken on his arm during a game. Pitch counts have not been kept with great accuracy until recently, perhaps because pitchers are now seen as a more valuable commodity than ever before. The reduction in the average pitch count of most pitchers in recent years is evidence of the newfound concern for the pitcher's well being. For example, Sandy Koufax averaged 155 pitches per game in a season in the early 1960s, which was not an unusual amount for the time. By 1991, the average number of pitches thrown by a starter in a game was down to 82.[37] This reduction in the number of pitches thrown by individual starters is an indication of both the great increase in the use of relief pitchers and the attempt to control and reduce the work done by starting pitchers. The fragility of young pitchers in the recent history of baseball has led many baseball people to worry about their overuse. Another measure, pitcher abuse points, which is based in part on pitch count is used to measure the use and potential abuse of pitchers.[38]

The concern with player well being, both physically and mentally, has increased over the history of professional baseball much as the concern for the worker in industry has increased since the industrial revolution. With additional advances in research in human factors engineering on work and society in general, more change will inevitably come in the baseball community as well.

Industrial Management and Baseball Management

Management in baseball, both on the field and as a business, has gone through a remarkable number of changes through its history. Again, as Bill James states, the way baseball is played depends not on its rules but on the conditions under which the game is played and therefore the way in which it is managed.

Christopher Risker has written that one reason that Americans have been fascinated with baseball can be revealed by examining the similar concerns of management theory, organizational theory, and baseball, which he refers to as the interplay of preparation, spontaneity, and the tension between engineering and genius.[39] Describing management in the early years of professional baseball, Risker describes John McGraw as a purveyor of the scientific management school of thought, popular in industry at the time of McGraw's managerial years. McGraw, for example, took responsibility for all of the decisions made by his players and asserted absolute authority over his players both on and off of the field. Of course, McGraw's style of management had its deficiencies. One large deficiency was the lack of input from the players. McGraw's contemporary and rival, Connie Mack, managed his players quite differently. As Bill James stated, Mack's philosophy of management was "you get good people, you treat them well, and you'll win."[40] Mack's approach very much foretold the view of the human relations school of management, which followed scientific management as the next popular management style in business.

Baseball management style changed with the times in much the same way that management style changed in society. The authoritarian style of McGraw fell aside as players, and workers, were given more rights, either through unionization or simply through changes in society. One manifestation of change in the management of a baseball team that also mirrored industry trends is the increased delegation of authority through an organization. For example, by the 1960s and 1970s, the number of coaches greatly increased as they became an increasingly important component of a team's management unit.[41] Teams began to have specialized management personnel, such as batting, pitching, and bench coaches (in addition to the first and third base coaches traditionally found on the team). With the use of these additional coaches, on-field management essentially constituted a management team. This team approach was exemplified by the experiment in rotating coaches, known as the "college of coaches," used in place of a manager by the Chicago Cubs in the early 1960s. The college was originally made up of eight coaches with equal responsibility (although later one man was named as head coach to lead the group). The novel "college of coaches" included Buck O'Neil, the first black to coach in the major leagues.[42] Although this method was not continued after 1965, the increase in the number of coaches and the delegation of authority to these coaches changed team management. Reflecting upon recent World Series games, it is obvious that the strategies the Yankees employed were conceived by not only manager Joe Torre, but also coaches Don Zimmer and Mel Stottlemyre, with whom Torre appeared to discuss every strategy.

Since the time of Mack and McGraw, the conditions under which baseball is played have changed dramatically and so too have the management styles. Today, baseball managers must be able to reconcile the team concept with the multinational, highly paid, megastar players making up that team. McGraw's method of management would find little success in today's environment. However, Mack's management style is essentially the same as that followed by the New York Yankees' Joe Torre, the most successful manager of recent years.[43]

Training as an Industrial Engineer

The close evolution between baseball and industrial engineering has been documented throughout this paper, especially with respect to important changes in the way business and baseball have been improved. It is clear that baseball is an application of many of the important concepts in industrial engineering based on improvement, whether it be improving safety, training methods, mathematical analysis of methods and strategy, or in management. Perhaps then, a formal education in industrial engineering would be a desirable if not a requisite academic background for someone desiring a management position, either on the field or off, in baseball. Just as it is necessary for one to have an engineering background in order to effectively manage a company whose work is based on technology, so too if may be optimal for one to have an industrial engineering background to manage in the complex arena of baseball.

It would be naïve to think that simple knowledge of statistics, human factors engineering, and industrial engineering in general would enable someone to make good baseball decisions. Experience in baseball is obviously a necessity. In fact, several successful managers in recent years have backgrounds closely related to industrial engineering. Tony LaRussa, well known for holding a law degree, also holds an undergraduate degree in industrial management. Davey Johnson majored in mathematics and has graduate experience in operations research. Other managers and general managers have an educational background in various management programs as well. These managers are lauded for their ability to make informed scientific decisions in both the short and long-term management of their team.

It will be interesting to observe baseball management's continued adaptation of innovations that mirror industrial engineering. An opportunity to see how an industrial engineer would fare as a baseball manager may soon be at hand. Joe Girardi, currently a catcher with the Chicago

Cubs, holds a bachelor's degree in industrial engineering from North-western University. Perhaps he will move onto the ranks of baseball management and make clear some of the benefits of a background in industrial engineering.

Notes

1. Bill James, *The Bill James Historical Baseball Abstract* (New York: Villiard Books, 1986), 39.

2. Benjamin Niebel and Andris Freivalds, *Methods, Standards and Work Design*, 10th ed. (New York: WCB/McGraw-Hill, 1999), 8.

3. *Ibid.*, 9.

4. *Ibid.*, 10.

5. *Ibid.*, 11.

6. Frank B. Gilbreth and Ernestine Gilbreth Carey, *Cheaper by the Dozen* (New York: Bantam Starfire, paperback edition, 1984), passim.

7. David Quentin Voight, *American Baseball Volume I: From the Gentleman's Sport to the Commissioner System* (University Park, PA: Penn State University Press, 1983), 289-290.

8. *Ibid.*, 290.

9. James, 48.

10. Bill James, *The Bill James Guide to Baseball Managers* (New York: Scribner, 1997), 34.

11. Burt Solomon, *Where They Ain't: The Fabled Life and Untimely Death of the Original Baltimore Orioles, the Team That Gave Birth to Modern Baseball* (New York: The Free Press, 1999), 56-57.

12. D. Christopher Risker, "Frederick Taylor's Use of the Baseball Team Metaphor: A Historical Perspective on Scientific Management and Baseball," *Nine: A Journal of Baseball History and Social Policy Perspectives*, 4, no.1 (1995): 1-11.

13. Jonathan Fraser Light, *The Cultural Encyclopedia of Baseball* (Jefferson, NC: MacFarland & Company, Inc., 1997), 575-576.

14. A brief history of the evolution of relief pitching can be found in: Light, 608-610.

15. Paul Dickson, *The Dickson Baseball Dictionary* (New York: Avon Books, 1989), 15-25.

16. Jules Tygiel, *Past Time: Baseball as History* (New York: Oxford University Press, 2000), 24.

17. *Ibid.*, 22-24.

18. *Ibid.*, 21.

19. Frederick Ivor-Campbell et al., *Baseball's First Stars* (Cleveland, OH: Society for American Baseball Research, 1996), 26-27.

20. John Thorn and Pete Palmer, *The Hidden Game of Baseball: A Revolutionary Approach to Baseball and Its Statistics* (Garden City, NY: Doubleday, 1984), 17.

21. Branch Rickey, "Goodbye to Some Old Baseball Ideas," *Life*, 2 August 1954, passim.

22. Thorn and Palmer, 41.

23. See George Lindsay, "Statistical Data Useful for the Operation of a Baseball Team," *Operations Research* 7, no. 3 (1959), passim; and George Lindsay, "An Investigation of Strategies in Baseball," *Operations Research*. 11, no. 4, (1963), passim.

24. Thorn and Palmer, 43.

25. Earnshaw Cook, *Percentage Baseball* (Baltimore, MD: Waverly Press, 1964), passim.

26. For additional information on Bill James and his approach to the analysis of baseball, see: Mike Shannon, *Baseball— The Writer's Game* (South Bend, Indiana: Diamond Communications, 1992), 123-136.

27. Rob Neyer discussed the background of several general managers in his column at ESPN.com on 29 January, 2001.

28. Roger Kahn, *The Seventh Game* (New York: New American Library, 1982), passim.

29. John Monteleone, ed., *Branch Rickey's Little Blue Book: Wit and Strategy From Baseball's Last Wise Man* (New York: MacMillan, 1995), 11.

30. Mark Sanders and Ernest McCormick, *Human Factors in Engineering and Design* 6th ed. (New York:McGraw-Hill, 1987), 4-5.

31. *Ibid.*, 6.

32. Light, 85-86.

33. Syd Thrift and Barry Shapiro, *The Game According to Syd* (New York: Simon and Shuster, 1990), 26.

34. For more information on Deming, his impact on Japanese business, his fourteen points for management, and his effect on business in the United States, see: W. Edwards Deming, *Out of the Crisis* (Cambridge, MA: MIT Press, paperback edition, 2000), passim.

35. David Quentin Voight, *American Baseball Volume III: From Postwar Expansion to the Electronic Age* (University Park, PA: Penn State University Press, 1983), 277-278.

36. Thrift and Shapiro, 28.

37. Light, 562.

38. For a description of the formulas involved in measuring pitcher abuse points, see: Rany Jazeyerli, "Re-Thinking Pitcher Abuse," in *Baseball Prospectus 2001*, ed. Joseph Sheehan, Chris Kahrl, and Clay Davenport (Washington, DC: Brassey's, 2001), 491.

39. D. Christopher Risker, "Baseball and Management Theory: Similar Concerns — Different Fields," *Nine: A Journal of Baseball History and Social Policy Perspectives* 5, no. 1 (1996), 49-61.

40. James, *The Bill James Guide to Baseball Managers*, 65.

41. James, *The Bill James Guide to Baseball Managers*, 230-231.

42. Light, 174.

43. For a discussion of Torre's management methods, see: Jerry Useem, "Joe Torre: A Manager for All Seasons," *Fortune*, 30 April 2001, passim.

Youth Select Baseball
in the Midwest

David C. Ogden

When former Detroit Tiger John Young lies in bed at night, he thinks about a generation who has grown into adolescence without baseball. African-American children, said Young, "aren't playing baseball like they used to."[1]

Young created RBI, or Reviving Baseball in the Inner Cities, a program to develop youth baseball leagues in economically depressed urban areas. Young wants baseball "to regain that luster" it held for previous generations, a goal he concedes will be difficult to reach.[2]

Young noticed that few African-Americans pursued baseball in south-central Los Angeles. He started the first RBI youth league in 1989. More than 10 years later, youth coaches throughout the Midwest also wonder if African-Americans have lost interest in the sport. According to those coaches, a variety of factors have contributed to a declining interest in baseball among African-American youth. Those coaches said ethnic diversity is seldom found on the diamonds of Midwestern select youth baseball and at the highest levels of youth competition.

Background and Methods

Omaha youth baseball coach Dan Sullivan said that his team does not have any African-American players, and neither have opposing teams during the past two years. Coach Steven Rezin says he remembers several years ago when youth teams with black players frequented the Kansas City, Kansas complex where his team plays, but now the black players are "just not there anymore."

Sullivan and Rezin are among 27 coaches and officials from six Midwestern states interviewed since June 1999 about (among other things) the racial composition of their teams and the teams they played. At the time of their interviews, 18 of the 27 coached select youth baseball with players (all male) between the ages of 12 and 14. Those 18 teams with a total of 210 players were assembled via tryout, in which only the "best" players were chosen, or consisted of "all-stars" from teams in recreational leagues. Those teams were from such communities as: Omaha; Kansas City and Manhattan, Kansas; Rock Island, Moline, Springfield, McHenry, and Quincy, Illinois; Sioux City, Iowa; Evansville, Indiana; and Rapid City, South Dakota (See Table 1). The teams played an average of 53 games each summer, with some teams playing as many as 70 games.

In addition, 50 select youth teams were observed from April to July 2000. Those 50 teams consisted of 624 players. Twenty-two of the teams were from Omaha and the rest represented most of the communities previously mentioned, plus Hastings and Lincoln, Nebraska, and Chanute and Topeka, Kansas (See Table 2).

Results

In those communities represented by the teams of the 18 select coaches in this study, approximately 10.5 percent of the population under 18 years of age is African-American.[3] Of the 210 players on the coach's teams, two (or less than 1 percent) were African-American (and played on the same Kansas City team).

In the communities represented by the 50 teams surveyed during the 2000 season, approximately 14 percent of youth under 18 were African-American.[4] Of the 624 players on those teams, eight (or 1.3 percent) were African-American.

To determine the significance of the difference between the number of African-Americans on the select teams and the number of such youths in the teams' communities, t-tests were performed on the group of 18 teams and on all 50 teams.

The t-test on the 18 teams represented by the select coaches showed a significant difference between the average percentage of African-Americans on the teams and the percentage in the communities, ($\underline{M}$ = -10.7, $\underline{SD}$ = 10.94), $\underline{t}$ (18) = -4.14, $\underline{p}$ = .001 (See Table 1). The results of a t-test on the

TABLE 1.
ONE-SAMPLE T-TEST
COMPARING PERCENTAGE OF AFRICAN-AMERICANS
ON 18 SELECT YOUTH TEAMS AND
PERCENTAGE OF AFRICAN-AMERICAN YOUTH
UNDER 18 YEARS OF AGE IN THE COMMUNITY

	Team	Community
Omaha	0%	18.3%
Omaha	0%	18.3%
Papillion, Ne.	0%	2.3%
Chanute, Ks.	0%	1.0%
Manhattan, Ks.	0%	7.3%
Kansas City, Ks.	14%	35.4%
Kansas City, Ks.	0%	35.4%
Moline, Ill.	0%	4.5%
Rock Island, Ill.	0%	26.5%
Silvis, Ill.	0%	5.3%
Springfield, Ill.	0%	24.0%
Oneida, Ill.	0%	0%
McHenry, Ill.	0%	.4%
Reynolds, Ill.	0%	0%
Quincy, Ill.	0%	7.3%
Rapid City, S.D.	0%	1.0%
Sioux City, Ia.	0%	3.3%
Evansville, Ind.	0%	16.3%
Mean Difference		-10.70*

Note: All community census data taken from U.S. Census, *www.census.gov*

*p = .001

difference between the percentage of African-Americans on all 50 teams and the percentage in their communities also showed a significant difference, (M = -12.06, SD = 8.92), t (50) = -9.56, p <.001 (See Table 2).

"I don't know why we can't get the numbers [of African-American youths] to try out," said Bob Powell of Silvis, Illinois and coach of the Quad City Hitmen. "There's a lot of good athletes out there but, for whatever reason, baseball does not seem to be what they're looking for."

Several coaches, like Omaha's Dan Sullivan and Powell, not only noted the absence of African-Americans trying out for their teams, but also mentioned the absence of such players on teams against which they compete.

TABLE 2.
ONE SAMPLE T-TEST
COMPARING PERCENTAGE OF AFRICAN-AMERICANS
ON 50 SELECT YOUTH TEAMS AND
PERCENTAGE OF AFRICAN-AMERICANS
UNDER AGE 18 IN THE COMMUNITY

	Team	*Community*
Kansas City, Ks.	14.0%	35.4%
"	0%	"
Manhattan, Ks.	0%	7.3%
"	0%	"
Topeka, Ks.	7%	15.0%
"	0%	"
"	0%	"
Moline, Ill.	0%	4.5%
Rock Island, Ill.	0%	26.5%
Springfield, Ill.	0%	24.0%
McHenry, Ill.	0%	.4%
Council Bluffs, Ia.	7.7%	1.3%
Atlantic, Ia.	0%	.3%
Omaha	15.0%	18.3%
"	8.3%	"
"	0%	"
"	0%	"
"	0%	"
"	0%	"
"	0%	"
"	0%	"
"	0%	"
"	0%	"
"	0%	"
"	0%	"
"	0%	"
"	0%	"
"	0%	"
"	0%	"
"	0%	"
"	0%	"
"	0%	"

Table 2. (continued)	Team	Community
"	0%	"
"	0%	"
"	0%	"
"	0%	"
Lincoln, Ne.	0%	4.1%
"	0%	"
"	0%	"
Papillion, Ne.	0%	2.3%
"	0%	2.3%
Bellevue, Ne.	0%	6.7%
"	0%	6.7%
Hastings, Ne.	0%	1.0%
Ralston, Ne.	7.7%	1.2%
Fremont, Ne.	0%	.7%
Blair, Ne.	0%	.3%
Nebraska City, Ne.	0%	.3%
"	0%	"
Mean Difference		-12.06*

Note: All community census data taken from U.S. Census, *www.census.gov*

*$p < .001$

In Kansas City, newspaper columnist Joe Posnanski had the same impression. According to Posnanski, "kids in the inner city all over America have stopped playing baseball. There are no clean fields. There is no organization. The game is too expensive."[5]

Tom Brasuell directs community relations for Major League Baseball and serves as national coordinator of the RBI program. He echoes Posnanski in positing three reasons for the low interest among African-American youth: lack of instruction, lack of quality playing fields, and the growing popularity of other sports (especially basketball). The coaches and officials in this study cited several other reasons, but those three were the most frequently mentioned. The coaches, however, reached consensus on a fourth reason: lack of resources (time and money) and incentives.

Lack of Instruction—"African-American kids are lacking in fundamentals," said Sam Powell of the Boys & Girls Clubs in Des Moines. "A lot of kids in the inner city have not been exposed to the game of baseball."

Hubert Moss has contended with that lack of exposure during his 10 years of coaching youth baseball in North Omaha. The neighborhoods from which his team and others in his league draw their players are heavily populated by African-Americans. He said there are no T-ball programs for youngsters in his area of the city, and maintaining a youth baseball league is a struggle. He said it's difficult to find not only enough players, but also enough coaches. During one of the past seasons, he said, seven coaches quit the league.

"They just fade away," said Moss. "They don't have time or there's something else they've got to do."

According to former Omaha Parks and Recreation Department Director Jerry Parks, parents and adults in the inner city are not as involved as they used to be in youth baseball.

"We've lost a generation of dads going out to play catch with their sons," laments John Young.

Lack of parental instruction is just part of the problem, said Parks, who played much of his baseball as a youth with Omaha native and Hall of Fame pitcher Bob Gibson. He said a paucity of baseball role models also contributes to youths' lack of exposure to and interest in the game. Without such exposure, youngsters do not learn the fundamentals. As a result, most inner-city African-Americans either play very little, if any, organized ball, or they start playing ball late in childhood.

"A teen-age kid who hasn't played since he was 8 or 9 can't just come out and play, because he's lost five years, and you can't make that five years up," said James Young, a select team coach and Schlagle High School's baseball coach in Kansas City, Kansas. "I don't care how much talent you have, you can't make up for that lost time physically or mentally. There's so much to learn every year as you get older."

Sioux City, Iowa, select youth coach Mike Malenosky and former Omaha youth coach Don Benning said there is no one to teach baseball fundamentals to inner city youth. Benning said an erosion of interest in baseball among African-Americans has created a "void" in the transfer of baseball knowledge from one generation to the other. The lack of role models in professional baseball, said Benning, contributes to that erosion and "directly has something to do with the few blacks in select youth baseball."

Moss and Benning said that with fewer African-Americans in youth ball, the number of role models will continue to dwindle. Moss and Benning said one need look no further than the college and major league ranks, where the number of blacks continues to shrink. Their concerns are supported statistically.

Approximately 6.5 percent of NCAA Division I college baseball players are black. Of the 200 players in the 1999 NCAA College World Series,

10 were black.[6] According to Dennis Bonebreak, assistant coach at Lewis University, Chicago, "There's never been very many African-American college baseball players."

In Major League Baseball, 15 percent of the players are African-American, according to Tom Brasuell, director of community relations for MLB. That's compared with 18 percent in 1992, when *Ebony* expressed concern over "the rapidly decreasing number of African-American players on the field, a situation the Commissioner, players and fans are calling 'alarming.'"[7]

Lack of Playing Fields and Facilities—A lack of interest and community support has resulted in few baseball fields in the predominantly African-American neighborhoods of North Omaha, according to Benning, Moss, and Parks.

"The facilities are not there for inner-city black players, so it's harder for them to get as good as the suburban players," said University of Miami outfielder Marcus Nettles. "That's why it's harder for them to be professional players and that's why they aren't recruited by colleges like the suburban players are."[8]

In Omaha and Sioux City, city administrators have relinquished the care of inner city fields to the private sector. In those cities and others, the support from the private sector has not been there.

"Grass is overgrown on our field," said Moss, "and every time it rains, water stands for a long time.

"If we were to have some fields like everybody else has, who knows how many good ballplayers we could send out of here."

Inner-city fields and baseball programs have had similar fates in other urban areas.[9] In Chicago, the parks and recreation department provided little maintenance for fields used by Boys & Girls Clubs baseball teams, said Dennis Bonebreak, former coordinator for the clubs' baseball program. Bonebreak said the lack of city support, coupled with the exodus of middle-class families to outlying areas, has resulted in fewer Little Leagues in the inner city.

Former Omaha city administrator Jerry Parks said that without support from businesses, organizations, and individuals, inner city youth baseball will continue to languish. That lack of support could also affect the number of African-Americans following "the pipeline" into college and professional baseball, said Wayne (Nebraska) State College baseball coach John Manganaro.

"The kids don't play baseball because they can't find organizations to lend them the resources, or money, that would provide equipment and fields," Manganaro said.

Lack of Resources and Incentives— African-Americans view youth baseball as an expensive endeavor without long-term benefits, said Don Benning.

"Kids don't see a pay-off in baseball and Mother and Father don't see a pay-off in it," he said.

Parks and University of Nebraska at Omaha baseball coach Bob Herold confirms Benning's sentiments. There are few college scholarships for baseball, compared with other sports, they said.

"In football and basketball, you have more of a chance to get a full scholarship," said University of Miami pitcher Darryl Roque. "But in baseball, full scholarships are rare. I had to walk on. So I've got a lot of bills to pay."[10]

The paucity of scholarships is not the only economic barrier to baseball for African-Americans. The cost of getting a child into youth select baseball is prohibitive for many African-American families. Equipment, travel costs and other expenditures related to playing select ball can add up to several hundred dollars for each player. Such costs are beyond the budgets of many African-American families, according to 10 of the coaches and officials interviewed.

"Select sports is really geared to suburbanites," said Omaha youth baseball coach Dan Sullivan. "It takes a lot of money and requires a lot of travel, and that cuts off a certain number of kids economically."

"Even if a kid is good [at baseball], but his parents don't have the money, then he's through," said Kansas City coach James Young.

Time is another resource of which African-American families have little to spare. Hubert Moss estimated that about 90 percent of the players in his predominantly African-American youth baseball league come from one-parent families. Benning said those families "are working just to make ends meet" and have little if any time to drive children to practice or to travel with them to games.

"When your kid is on a traveling team, it takes a lot of commitment and a lot of money," said Randy Murdock, a select baseball coach from Reynolds, Illinois. "Unfortunately, I think that is a big deterrent for African-Americans."

Basketball and Other Sports—Baseball is competing with other sports for the attention of adolescents, according to the majority of those interviewed. Football's popularity continues to rise, and in Quincy, Illinois soccer has captivated youngsters because of the town's professional team, the Gems, according to Quincy youth baseball coach Rick Fesler. But basketball was most often mentioned by those interviewed for this study. Ten coaches cited basketball as one of the main detractors from baseball.

"I think basketball has taken minority kids away from baseball," said Steve Murry of Chanute, Kansas.

"Kids are used to a higher tempo game," said Anthony Dickson, who coordinates the RBI program in Kansas City and a former select team coach. "Now kids play basketball year round. Everyone aspires to go to the NBA."

"Basketball got popular on TV, and then there was Michael Jordan," said Kansas City coach James Young. "So black kids dropped the baseball bat and started playing basketball."

Dickson, Major League Baseball's Tom Brasuell, and Omaha coach Hubert Moss also cited Jordan's influence on young African-Americans. "The Michael Jordan era of basketball elevated it to a popular level. Kids felt empowered to play the game," said Brasuell.

Many of the predominant sports role models for African-Americans are basketball players, according to several coaches. Approximately 77 percent of the players in the National Basketball Association are African-American.[11] Benning said that may be one of the reasons why African-Americans see basketball as a quicker route to sports success.

"Black youngsters see stars like Michael Jordan and some of the football players, and they say, 'What's the best and shortest trip for me to get out of the situation I'm in,' and it's basketball and football," Benning said.

Miami outfielder Marcus Nettles agrees, noting that "blacks feel it's easier for them to fulfill their goals in professional basketball, that it's an easier way to get ahead." [12]

Enhancing Interest in Baseball
Among African-American Youth

While officials in Jesse Jackson's Rainbow/PUSH Coalition lament that not enough is being done to increase interest in baseball among African-Americans,[13] Major League Baseball touts large numbers of minority youths in its RBI program. Since its inception in Los Angeles in 1989, when 180 youths enrolled, the RBI program has expanded to more than 130 cities and 100,000 players.[14] In 1997, Brasuell said, Major League Baseball enlisted the Boys & Girls Clubs of America to coordinate the RBI programs in their respective cities.

Brasuell said the RBI program has produced almost 20 Major League Baseball draftees. The racial composition of RBI participants, however, has changed during the past decade. In the inaugural years of RBI, 67 percent of its participants were African-American. Last year (2000), slightly more than half were African-American.

Brasuell said the racial make-up of RBI programs varies from city to city. In Miami and New York, for example, 70 percent of the players were Latino. In Los Angeles, approximately half were Latino and the other half African-American. African-Americans comprise about half of Chicago's RBI players.

In Kansas City, more than 73 percent of the youngsters participating in RBI in 2000 were African-American, according to Anthony Dickson, RBI Baseball Director for the Boys & Girls Clubs of Greater Kansas City. Dickson said the Kansas City program has grown substantially, from 150 youths in its inaugural year of 1992 to 630 last year (2000). He said the program hopes to add more teams and accommodate another 100 youngsters during the next two years.

The keys to his RBI program's success, said Dickson, are starting children in the program as early as possible, community support, and providing baseball role models. When Dickson took charge in 1998, he expanded the program to include 8- to 12-year-olds. Major League Baseball traditionally has targeted those between 13 and 18 years of age for RBI and earmarked funds to start leagues for that age group.

Dickson said his Kansas City program was one of the first to start an RBI league for grade schoolers. Des Moines has been among several cities to follow suit. Sam Powell coordinates the Des Moines Boys & Girls RBI program. Powell sponsored teams for 8- to 12-year-olds, in addition to those for 13- to 18-year-olds, when he launched the program in summer 2000. Powell said the preponderance of African-Americans were on the younger teams. Almost 85 percent of the 8- to 12-year-old players were African-American, compared to 35 percent of the 13- to 18-year-olds. Said Powell: "Trying to get a 13-year-old involved in baseball, who's never played Peewee or Little League baseball, is like trying to pull teeth."

Michelle Matulevicz knows firsthand what Powell is saying. Matulevicz is RBI director for the Omaha Boys & Girls Clubs. Matulevicz has not been able to support a boys baseball league for 13- to 18-year-olds because of lack of interest. She said RBI needs to target younger age brackets.

"It's difficult to get a kid who's never picked up a baseball to try something new," said Matulevicz, whose program sponsors a three-team girls' softball league. "As kids get older, they're not as likely to try something that they're going to fail at."

Omaha is not the only city finding it difficult to field teams for 13- to 18-year-olds, said Tom Brasuell. Other Boys & Girls Clubs around the nation have started RBI programs, while having few concerns about making Major League Baseball's required minimum of four teams with 15 players each.

"We found that when we get their [Boys & Girls' Clubs] end-of-the-year reports, a lot of them barely have the minimum number of players and some don't make the minimum," said Brasuell. The RBI programs which start their own leagues for 8- to 12-year-olds, however, report large numbers of players on those teams.

Brasuell and former Chicago RBI Commissioner Dennis Bonebreak said that despite the lack of players in some cities, the importance of leagues for 13- to –18-year-olds should not be underestimated. Bonebreak said such leagues fill a void in his city, where high schools and neighborhoods have cut back on baseball programs for teenagers. Almost 75 percent of pre-teens who play sports stop doing so by age 13, a primary reason RBI targeted that age bracket, said Brasuell. But Bonebreak thinks RBI could benefit communities by earmarking money for leagues for pre-adolescents. He said that the earlier a youngster starts playing ball, the more likely he is to succeed at the highest level of competition. Bonebreak said that he knows 33 youth league players who went on to play pro ball, and all but one began playing in grade school.

Besides starting youngsters at an early age, RBI programs must also enlist the support of community agencies and city government. Anthony Dickson said the Kansas City Parks and Recreation Department has been a sponsor of RBI since the league's inception in the city, but in name only. Since 1998 the department has taken a more active role in developing and maintaining the RBI program's playing fields. If inner cities have baseball facilities that are comparable to those in suburban areas, numbers of players can also be comparable, he said.

"I told the sponsors, 'Give me what they got out there [in suburbia], and I'll guarantee you these kids will play baseball,'" Dickson said. "They gave it to me so I was able to take the program to another level."

Dickson said the Kansas City Royals have also been an active sponsor. He said the Royals players hold "high profile clinics," attend RBI games, make community appearances, and recognize the program through a ceremony before one of their home games.

While the RBI program appears to be exposing greater numbers of African-American youths to baseball, some coaches such as Kansas City's James Young say the quality of play and quantity of exposure is far below that of select baseball. As mentioned previously, select teams represented by the coaches in this survey played an average of 53 games during the 2000 season. The RBI teams in Kansas City played from 18 to 21 games, said Dickson. Chicago teams played 10 "regular season" games, with all-star players from the league playing another 10, according to Bone-break.

"The highest level of competition is in the suburbs or on tournament teams," Young said.

Dickson agreed that the teams from the Kansas City RBI program could not compete with suburban select teams. However, the RBI all-star team, consisting of the best players in the program, could compete with any team comparable by age, Dickson said.

"There are kids in the urban core who could play with anybody," said Dickson, but the chances of such youngsters moving to higher levels of competition and being discovered by college or professional teams are slim.

Discussion

It appears that the RBI program has been successful in giving large numbers of African-American youths in some communities opportunities to play organized baseball. The RBI program in Kansas City, for example, is attempting to remove some of the barriers to baseball for African-Americans. The program has stressed community support, provided proper instruction for young players, and improved facilities. At the same time, the number of African-American youngsters playing organized ball has increased in Kansas City.

"I'm proud to be able to go into the community and be recognized as the person who leads the charge for these kids and to bring some discipline and respect for a program that is long overdue for urban core youth," said Dickson.

Such success, however, is tempered by the limited playing opportunities for RBI youngsters, compared with their counterparts on select or traveling baseball teams, and by the failure of some RBI programs, like Omaha's, to attract youth to baseball.

Getting youths interested in baseball means introducing them to the sport as early in their lives as possible. Boys & Girls Club Directors Dickson, Matulevicz, and Powell agree that the RBI program would benefit nationally if it supported leagues for 7- and 8-year-olds. Powell noted that the $4,500 grant from Major League Baseball to start the Des Moines program was earmarked for the 13- to 18-year-olds.

"We already know kids in the inner city don't play baseball," said Powell. "RBI may be doing itself a disservice by not placing enough emphasis on feeder programs.....RBI needs to invest some of the grant money to develop those programs to start these kids out younger."

Major League Baseball's Tom Brasuell said his organization is considering sponsoring programs for 6- to 9-year-olds. He said that in some cities, major league teams have sponsored "rookie league" programs for grade schoolers and have instructed them by using concepts developed by former American League President Bobby Brown. Such programs need to be adopted by other cities, said Brasuell. "We definitely want kids exposed at a younger age," he said.

Maintaining interest in baseball through the grade school and adolescent years is also important. That is the consensus of several of the coaches and officials interviewed in this study.

Said Omaha's Don Benning: "You have to re-teach baseball to each generation.... Kids have to learn to appreciate skills that a Cone or Griffey have, and then they have to want to do it. The less exposure they have, the less chance they have to participate."

How such participation among youth will affect the future ranks of professional baseball players is conjecture. Will programs like RBI have an impact on the future number of African-American players? Does the low number of African-American youth on Midwest select teams reflect the situation nationally? Will the current composition of youth select teams, as indicated by this study, manifest itself 8 or 10 years later at the major league level?

Tracking numbers of minorities in youth baseball programs may not be enough to answer those questions. The accuracy of such tracking, as in this study, is only as good as the representation of the sample. Whether the teams in this study truly reflect the numbers of African-American youth involved in the higher levels of competition remains in question. Another weakness of this study involves data from the federal Census (2000). The percentages of minority youths in each community include male and female, since a breakdown of that information by gender was not available when statistics for this study were compiled. Also not available was a breakdown of minority youth by specific age. Therefore, it is difficult to determine the accuracy of the comparisons between the teams and their communities.

Tracking minorities in youth baseball, however, provides a foundation for determining the extent of participation by African-American youth in baseball. But an additional step must be taken: surveying grade school youth and adolescents about their leisure activities and sports participation preferences and aspirations. Together, such tracking and surveys could help to profile the future ranks of American-born college and professional baseball players.

APPENDIX: COACHES AND OFFICIALS INTERVIEWED

Scott Anderson, Oledo, Illinois
Don Benning, Omaha, Nebraska
Dennis Bonebreak, Chicago, Illinois
Thomas Brasuell, New York, New York
Anthony Dickson, Kansas City, Missouri
Jim Dice, Omaha, Nebraska
Steve Disbrow, Manhattan, Kansas
Bret Estes, Rapid City, South Dakota
Rick Fesler, Quincy, Illinois
Vernon Henricks, Manhattan, Kansas
Bob Herold, Omaha, Nebraska
Mike Malenosky, Sioux City, Iowa
John Manganaro, Wayne, Nebraska

Michelle Matulevicz, Omaha, Nebraska
Hubert Moss, Omaha, Nebraska
Randy Murdock, Reynolds, Illinois
Steve Murry, Chenoot, Kansas
Jerry Parks, Omaha, Nebraska
Bob Powell, Silvis, Illinois
Sam Powell, Des Moines, Iowa
John Ransdell, McHenry, Illinois
Steve Rezin, Kansas City, Kansas
Jamie Stash, Springfield, Illinois
Dan Sullivan, Omaha, Nebraska
Joel Thomas, Edgington, Illinois
Tom Tomanek, Papillion, Nebraska
Tom Wuertz, Evansville, Indiana
James Young, Kansas City, Kansas

Notes

1. M.C. Imbert, "Young at Heart," *Los Angeles Times*, 11 August 2000, C-28.
2. *Ibid.*
3. U.S. Census Bureau, 2001, *http://www.census.gov/index.html.*
4. *Ibid.*
5. Joe Posnanski, "More Than a Game," *Kansas City Star*, 12 June 1999, D-1
6. Colleen Kenney, "Baseball Loses to Other Sports," *Omaha World Herald*,12 June 1999, 1-CWS.
7. "What's Behind the Shrinking Number of African-American Players?" *Ebony,* June 1992, 112.
8. Kenney, 1-CWS.
9. C. Rodriguez, "In Roxbury, Paths of Hope: Red Sox Finding a New Ball Field for City Youth," *The Boston Globe*, 4 March 1999, 28. See also Posnanski, D-1.
10. Kenney, 1-CWS.
11. Richard E. Lapchick, *Racial and Gender Report Card.* (Northeastern University Center for the Study of Sport in Society), January 2000, *http://www.sportinsociety .org.*
12. Kenney, 1-CWS.
13. *Ibid.*
14. Major League Baseball, *RBI Facts Sheet*, 2000, 1.

Labor Rights and the Restructuring of Major League Baseball, 1969–1992: A Case Study of Franchise Performance and the Myth of Baseball Management

Robert H. Jackson

In the nineteenth and twentieth centuries, labor rights and labor-management relations were among the most contested arenas of public life in the United States. The organization of labor and the acquisition of the right to collective bargaining did not come without struggle. In order to gain basic rights, labor resorted to strikes that often resulted in considerable violence, repression, and the blacklisting of labor organizers. In many ways, professional sports has been a metaphor for the mythic Horatio Alger story of success based on ability and personal drive, and for being free of the divisive disputes that dominated the history of labor-management relations. However, this myth and reality differ.

In 1969, baseball players again challenged the so-called "reserve clause" that tied them to a given franchise for the duration of their careers, unless management chose to trade them or sell their contracts. Players bargained for free agency, the right to sign with any franchise once their contract expired, and went on strike several times to protect rights gained through collective bargaining agreements. The last strike began in August of 1994, as players challenged renewed efforts by management to weaken the bargaining power of the players' union. The strike ended in 1995, but only following recriminations on the part of owners about how the players had ruined the game.

The special exemption from anti-trust rules that Major League Baseball owners have enjoyed due to a 1922 Supreme Court ruling has also been challenged. The latest effort occurred in early 1995, but the Republican controlled Congress refused to take action. Responding to players' efforts to improve their contractual status, franchise owners argued that free agency would favor larger and wealthier franchises that could afford to hire the best players. However, it should also be pointed out that it is the team owners who sign the paychecks for the players and bid salaries up.[1] The hypocrisy of management's claim becomes evident when one considers the huge salary offered to Alex Rodriguez by the owner of the Texas Rangers.

This essay examines one aspect of the long-term dispute between players and management in Major League Baseball, franchise performance. Management claims regarding the distorting impact of free agency do not hold true when the performance of one franchise not located in one of the major baseball media markets is examined. Rather, despite the advent of free agency, management personnel decisions still have a greater influence over franchise performance. This essay documents the performance of the Oakland Athletics franchise located in a lesser and divided media market, the San Francisco Bay Area, shared with the San Francisco Giants.

The Oakland Athletics franchise has been chosen as the subject of this study for several reasons. Despite being located in a small and divided market, Oakland has produced winning teams, which challenges the myth of the dominance of the large market teams. Over the last three decades, Oakland has been one of the most successful franchises, despite a history of poor fan attendance, even at the height of the team's greatest success. Moreover, a discussion of the Athletics' history spans the period of transition from the reserve clause to free agency. Key players from the Oakland team of the mid-1970s did successfully challenge the reserve clause. But, even in the era of free agency, Oakland management created competitive teams in a small and divided market.

The essay examines the way in which management put together squads that dominated the American League in the early 1970s and late 1980s both under the reserve clause and then following the advent of free agency. The analysis of player-management disputes in baseball as related to franchise finances, an issue at the core of the 1994–1995 dispute, requires additional research, and is not examined in this essay.

This study consists of several sections. The first briefly outlines origins of the reserve clause, changes in labor rights, and labor-management disputes in baseball between 1969 and 1992. A discussion of the long history of the Athletics franchise follows. The final sections offer an analysis of franchise performance, focusing on the years 1971 to 1975 and again from 1988 to 1992 when the Athletics were one of the best teams in Major League Baseball.

The essay also offers a different interpretation of Charlie Finley, the controversial owner of the Oakland franchise during the first years of success between 1971 and 1975. Finley was an innovative entrepreneur who achieved financial success in a weak market. Generally perceived as an S.O.B., Finley's successful management of the team contrasts with the one-year fiasco of the expansion Seattle Pilots in 1969.

The management of the Seattle Pilots believed that the novelty of a new team was sufficient to attract fans. However, fan support fell short of expectations, and the Pilots franchise went bankrupt and was sold and moved to Milwaukee shortly before the beginning of the 1970 season. While Finley initiated special offers for fans, the Pilots management followed a more conventional marketing plan that simply offered fans games and a weak squad. Beneath the myth of the S.O.B., Finley was an innovator who deserves to have his reputation rehabilitated, highlighting how management decisions are critical to franchise success.

Labor-Management Disputes: Free Agency and the Reserve Clause

Until 1976, management maintained the reserve clause that tied players to a franchise for the duration of their careers, unless traded, sold, or given an outright release. The reserve clause of player contracts had been a part of the game since 1879, and management long sold player contracts at will. Management had sought ways to limit the movement of players from team to team. Initially, owners instituted rules that prohibited players from changing teams during the course of the season, but in 1879 National League magnates instituted a "gentleman's agreement" to recognize five players on each team that would be reserved from negotiations with other teams, and thus, through informal collusion, keep player salaries down.[2] In 1887, National League management represented by Albert Spalding agreed to a uniform contract, but included the "reserve clause" in the contract.[3] However, in 1889 disgruntled National League players issued a manifesto challenging the recent actions of management.

In 1890, the newly formed Players League augmented player rights, but Spalding orchestrated the fall of the Players League after one year.[4]

Formal exemption from anti-trust legislation in 1922 increased the ability of franchise owners to exercise a monopoly over personnel. Despite challenges, the "reserve clause" would remain in place until the early 1970s. In 1968, player representative Marvin Miller negotiated a contract with management that raised minimum player salary to $10,000, and recognized a grievance procedure and the right of players to have representatives during salary negotiations. In 1969, a dispute over pension payments resulted in players not signing their contracts, and a boycott of training camp by at least 391 players.[5]

A major legal challenge to the reserve clause came in 1969, when St. Louis Cardinals player Curt Flood attempted to block an off-season trade to the Philadelphia Phillies franchise. Flood's major league career began in 1956, and he spent eleven seasons with the Cardinals. Flood sued in federal court to overturn the reserve clause, and his lawyers argued that the restrictive contract measure violated the Thirteenth Amendment that prohibits slavery and indentured servitude. Flood's suit failed. While the suit was still pending during the 1970 season, Flood refused to play for the Phillies. Flood subsequently agreed to a trade to the Washington Senators for the 1971 season, but only with the understanding that the trade in no way would impair the pending legal action.

Federal district and appeals courts rendered negative decisions on Flood's suit, and on June 18, 1972, the United States Supreme Court also ruled against him. Flood's career ended with these legal decisions. He saw limited playing time with the Senators in 1971 (13 games), and did not play again after the 1971 season. The majority of active major league players failed to support Flood's suit, but some retired players, including Hall of Famers Hank Greenberg and Jackie Robinson, testified on his behalf.

The next challenge came in 1973 as a consequence of terms agreed upon pursuant to a new collective bargaining agreement. Salary disputes could be submitted to impartial arbitration, and after ten years with a team a player could veto a trade. In 1974, eight Oakland Athletics players submitted salary disputes to arbitration. The arbitrator rendered favorable decisions for Rollie Fingers, Ken Holtzman, Darold Knowles, Sal Bando, and Reggie Jackson, and unfavorable decisions for Gene Tenace, Joe Rudi, and Ted Kubiak.[6] Finley's behavior during these arbitration cases contributed to growing discontent among some veteran players. Finley suffered a major reverse with the loss of Jim "Catfish" Hunter. The pitcher won free agent status because Finley had failed to fulfill the terms of Hunter's contract.[7] Hunter then signed with the New York Yankees.

Two years later the reserve clause fell. The impartial arbitrator Peter Seitz ruled that at the end of a contract the team could exercise its option to retain the player for one year, but after the option year the player became a free agent. Management fired Seitz and challenged his decision in court, but the courts upheld Seitz's ruling. This decision effectively ended the reserve clause. A collective bargaining agreement negotiated in 1976 contained the provision that a player became a free agent after six years, and in 1976 24 veteran players became free agents. A number of Oakland players, embittered by what they saw as poor treatment at the hands of team owner Charlie Finley, celebrated their free agency status.[8] Free agency did not necessarily mean that the Oakland stars would leave, but Finley's treatment of his players created a climate where they celebrated their free agency and the opportunity to play elsewhere.

Over the next fourteen years, management attempted to limit the gains made by players with free agency. Players initiated a strike in 1981 in response to an effort by management to gain compensation for free agents. After seven weeks, management backed down. Arbitration decisions in 1987 and 1990 ruled that management had colluded not to hire free agents, thus violating the collective bargaining agreement. The 1987 ruling was the most serious since it ruled that there was evidence of collusion in 1985 and 1986. A strike during spring training in 1990 ended before the beginning of the season. The strike that ended the 1994 season in early August came in response to new management initiatives to limit player rights, including the imposition of a salary cap. Spring training for the 1995 season began with replacement players in camp, but management and players eventually resolved the dispute. At the same time, Congress refused to take action on the proposal to strip Major League Baseball of the anti-trust exemption. During the last dispute, management emphasized the high salaries of the minority of elite players as a public relations ploy to undermine potential public support for the player's cause.

Franchise Performance:
The Case of the Oakland Athletics

One argument given by management against free agency was that the wealthier teams in the major media markets would dominate by hiring the best players that money could buy. The long-term performance of a franchise in a shared and smaller media market suggests that this prediction was inaccurate, and that the poor performance of teams in the lesser markets could just as easily have resulted from poor personnel decisions made by management. An analysis of franchise performance would ideally be based on information concerning earnings from ticket sales and television contracts correlated to overall standings and division, league, and World Series championships. However, as was evident in the 1994–1995 labor dispute, management has generally been reluctant to release financial information while at the same time being quite willing to release salary information for selected players who earned above the minimum. Therefore, the discussion here emphasizes the long-term team record, as well as the mechanisms used to acquire quality players for a team.

The Athletics franchise has a long history, and was originally founded in 1901 in Philadelphia by Cornelius McGillicuddy ("Connie Mack"), who ran the team until 1950. Between 1902 and 1931, the Athletics won nine American League titles and five World Series championships. Subsequently, however, the team performed poorly, and in 1955 the franchise moved to Kansas City, where it remained until 1967. The franchise in Kansas City compiled a losing record of 829 victories and 1,224 losses, a .404 winning percentage, the same percentage as in the team's last five seasons in Philadelphia. In 1968, owner Charles Finley moved the Athletics franchise to Oakland, where it remains today.

In the last several years in Kansas City, the franchise developed the nucleus of the team that would win five division titles and three World Series championships between 1971 and 1975 with an overall record of 476 victories and 326 losses. The 1967 squad included future stars Sal Bando, Reggie Jackson, Joe Rudi, and pitcher Jim "Catfish" Hunter. The move to Oakland coincided with the maturing of the young and talented players developed through the Athletics farm system. This marked the first of two multiple-year periods of dominance: the first under the reserve clause system, and the second under free agency. The second period was in the years 1988–1992. The team won the American League championship in three consecutive years and the World Series in 1989, with an overall record of 306 wins and 180 losses. The team dropped to fourth place in 1991 due, in part, to injuries, but won the Western Division again in 1992 by compiling a record of 96 wins and 66 losses.

From the inception of division play through 1992, the Oakland franchise compiled one of the best records in Major League Baseball: ten division titles, six American League championships, and four World Series titles. Moreover, in fourteen of twenty-four seasons (59 percent) the Athletics finished in either first or second place within the Western Division. The team finished in fifth place or below in only four seasons (16 percent). By contrast, examine the performance of the franchise in Philadelphia and Kansas City in a similar period, twenty-four years. Between 1943 and 1954, while still in Philadelphia, the team finished no better than 4th place in the American League, and was in eighth place five times. Similarly, in 13 seasons in Kansas City the team fared no better than sixth place, and finished in eighth place or below eight times.

The Formation of a Championship Team Under the Reserve Clause System

Under the reserve clause system, roster changes occurred from trades, the sale of contracts, and release from contracts. In the 1960s, players also developed through the farm system. However, evidence from the case of the Oakland Athletics shows that there was considerable movement on rosters, even under the reserve clause system, and Finley made numerous roster moves to fine-tune his team. On the five championship teams between 1971 and 1975, there were a total of 77 roster changes, defined here as the inclusion of new players who did not appear on the roster in the previous year. This works out to an average of 15.4 changes per year. Moreover, on a number of occasions Finley reacquired players he had previously cast off, and was almost constantly wheeling and dealing. This reached a peak during the 1972 season, when Finley engineered 65 transactions involving a total of 41 players, and employed a total of 47 players.[9] Under the free agency system, there were also roster changes, but the evidence suggests that the changes were not as frequent. Altogether, there were 58 roster changes on the four squads that won the Western Division in 1988–1990 and 1992. This works out to be an average of 14.5 changes per year.

In analyzing the roster changes on the five teams in the early to mid–1970s, several conclusions can be made. First, the nucleus of the Oakland teams came from the existing farm system. Of a sample of nineteen starting and relief pitchers, nine (47 percent) came from the farm system, and the other ten (53 percent) were acquired through trades or other transactions. The core of the pitching staff, however, was from the farm system. Six starting pitchers who recorded 253 total victories (71 percent of the victories recorded by the starting pitchers in the sample) were developed through the farm system. Likewise, two relief pitchers who recorded 42 victories and 103 total saves were developed through the farm system (see Table 1). In other words, trades improved an already strong pitching staff, and between 1968 and 1977 the starting pitchers with the highest number of victories came up through the farm system.

The same can be said of the starting batters. Between 1971 and 1975, there were 17 starting batters. Of this total, 11 (65 percent) came up through

TABLE 1.
OAKLAND ATHLETICS PITCHERS, 1971–1975

Name	Years	Wins	Losses	Percentage	Saves
Starters					
Blue*	1971–1975	89	53	.627	
Hunter*	1971–1974	88	35	.716	
Dobson*	1971	15	5	.750	
Segui*@	1971–1972	10	9	.526	
Odom*	1971–1975	31	37	.456	
Holtzman@	1972–1975	77	55	.583	
Hamilton*	1972–1975	20	16	.556	
Abbott*	1974–1975	10	12	.455	
Bosman@	1975	11	4	.733	
Bahnsen@	1975	6	7	.462	
Total		357	233	.605	
Relievers					
Fingers*	1971–1975	41	34	.547	102
Klimkowski@	1971	2	2	.500	2
Grant@	1971	1	0	1.000	3
Roland*	1971	1	3	.250	1
Knowles@	1971–1974	19	14	.543	30
Locker@	1971–1972	13	3	.813	16
Horlen@	1972	3	4	.429	1
Linblad@	1971, 1974–1975	14	5	.737	13
Pina@	1973	6	3	.667	8
Todd@	1975	8	3	.727	12
Total		107	71	.601	185

*Farm System   @Through trade.

the farm system. Finley acquired the remaining six by trade or other transactions. The starting batters provided the offense for the club. Over five years, the starting batters garnered 5,699 hits (84 percent of the total) and 691 home runs (95 percent of the total) (see Table 3).

Compare the formation of the two Oakland dynasties. For analytical purposes, I selected the 1973 and 1989 squads, both World Series champions. On the 1973 squad, an equal number of players were acquired through trade or the draft and worked their way up through the farm system. Of nine principal pitchers, five came to Oakland by way of the draft and four

TABLE 2.
CAREERS OF OAKLAND ATHLETICS PITCHERS

		Career Record		
Name	Years with Oakland	Wins	Losses	Saves
Jim Hunter	1965–1974	224	166	1
John Odom	1964–1975	84	85	1
Vida Blue	1969–1977	209	161	2
Chuck Dobson	1966–1971	74	69	0
Diego Segui	1962–65, 1967–68, 1970–71	92	111	71
Ken Holtzman	1972–1975	174	150	3
Dave Hamilton	1972–75, 1979–80	38	41	31
Glenn Abbott	1973–1976	62	83	0
Dick Bosman	1975–1976	82	85	2
Stan Bahnsen	1975–1977	145	149	20
Rollie Fingers	1968–1976	114	118	341
Rom Klimkowski	1971	8	12	4
Jim Roland	1969–1972	19	17	9
Darold Knowles	1971–1974	66	74	0
Bob Locker	1970–1972	57	39	95
Joe Horlen	1972	116	117	4
Paul Linblad	1965–71, 1973–76	68	63	64
Horacio Pina	1973	23	23	38
Jim Todd	1975–1976	25	23	24

by trade. Free agency was a factor in the acquisition of players on the 1989 Athletics squad. Of 28 players, 10 came to the team by way of the amateur draft, 12 through trade, but only six through free agency. The same pattern applied to the pitching staff: two were acquired through the draft, six through trade, and three through free agency. In the first case, as argued above, the core of the 1973 team was acquired through the draft and developed in the farm system. Management put the 1989 team together through both the draft and trades, and improved the squad through free agency. The experience of four star players illustrates the patterns discussed above.

Reggie Jackson developed in the Athletics minor league system, and reached the major leagues in 1967 while the franchise was still in Kansas City. Jackson became a full-time player in 1968, and was one of the core of the team that achieved such success in the early 1970s. In eight seasons at Oakland, Jackson hit 253 home runs, and in 1973 was the American League's Most Valuable Player. In 1976, Finley traded Jackson to Baltimore because he was in the last year of his contract and might not re-sign with

TABLE 3.
OAKLAND ATHLETICS STARTING BATTERS, 1971–1975

Name	Years at Oakland	Games Played	Hits	Home Runs
Mike Epstein	1971–1972	242	200	44
Dick Green	1971–1974	403	276	17
Bert Campaneris	1971–1975	705	731	23
Sal Bando	1971–1975	773	692	105
Reggie Jackson	1971–1975	741	743	154
Rick Monday	1971	116	87	18
Joe Rudi	1971–1975	678	740	84
Dave Duncan	1971–1972	224	180	34
Tim Cullen	1972	72	37	0
Angel Mangual	1971–1974	468	298	35
Gene Tenace	1971–1975	623	461	91
Billy North	1973–1975	435	442	10
Ray Fossee	1973–1975	294	167	11
Deron Johnson	1973–1975	181	148	26
Phil Garner	1973–1975	199	125	6
Billy Williams	1975	155	127	23
C. Washington	1974–1975	221	245	10
		Total	5,699	691

Oakland, and in 1977 he became a free agent and signed with New York. Jackson later played for the California Angels, and then returned to Oakland where he finished his career in 1987.

Jim "Catfish" Hunter also came to the Athletics franchise via the minor league system, and reached the major leagues in 1965. During the championship years, Hunter was a mainstay of the Oakland pitching staff, and from 1971 to 1974 recorded 88 wins and only 35 losses. Hunter left the team after the 1974 season, and signed with the New York Yankees, where he finished his career at the end of the 1979 season.

Vida Blue also came to the Athletics through the farm system. He first pitched for Oakland at the end of the 1969 season, and became a significant force in 1971 when he tallied 24 victories as against only eight losses. At the beginning of the 1972 season, Blue held out for an adjustment in his contract, and his record dropped to 6–10. During the championship years, Blue compiled a record of 89 victories and 53 losses, and remained with the team until the end of the 1977 season. In 1978, Blue signed with the San Francisco Giants, and played with the Giants and Kansas City Royals during the rest of his career.

The final example is the pitcher Ken Holtzman, acquired by Oakland through a trade before the 1972 season. Holtzman came through the Chicago Cubs system, and pitched for the Cubs from 1965 to 1971. Holtzman spent four seasons with the Athletics, and compiled a record of 77 wins and 55 losses. Finley traded Holtzman to Baltimore in the April 1976 trade that also involved Reggie Jackson. Holtzman pitched in 13 games for Baltimore, and then spent two seasons each with the Yankees (1976–1977) and Chicago Cubs (1978–1979) before retiring at the end of the 1979 season.

Free Agency and the Break-Up of the Oakland Squad

The end of the reserve clause and the advent of free agency contributed to the break-up of the Oakland Athletics squad that had won three World Series championships. In 1974, pitcher Jim Hunter was emancipated from his contract with the Oakland Athletics, because he was able to prove that team owner Charles Finley had failed to live up to contractual obligations. Two years later, in 1976, Finley became involved in a controversy with baseball Commissioner Bowie Kuhn when he tried to sell the contracts of three star players, pitchers Vida Blue and Rollie Fingers and outfielder Joe Rudi, to the Boston Red Sox and New York Yankees for $3.5 million. Kuhn negated the deal as not being in the best interest of baseball.[10]

In 1976, 1977, and 1978, Finley traded players, and lost other players through free agency. The loss of players in the first two years, especially 1977, gutted the squad, and the team dropped from second place in the Western Division in 1976 to seventh place the following year. In 1976, the team lost two pitchers and two other players, including slugger and future Hall of Famer Reggie Jackson. In the following year, ten key players left the team, including five pitchers with a combined record in 1976 of 36 victories and 29 saves. In 1977, the team won only 63 games. In 1978, two more major players left the team, including pitcher Vida Blue who had the highest number of wins in 1977. After gutting his championship team and replacing stars with lesser quality players, Finley later sold the team.

History has not treated Finley kindly. The labor disputes of the mid-1970s as well as several imbroglios with Commissioner Kuhn during the championship years are what the controversial Finley is most remembered for. However, Finley should also be recalled as a team owner who introduced innovative ideas to Major League Baseball and was a great promoter of his team. Despite low attendance figures in a split market, Finley turned a profit with the Oakland A's. Throughout the early 1970s, league officials expressed concerns that two major league franchises could not exist in such a small market. One analysis estimated that there was only a total of some five million people in the five contiguous countries surrounding San Francisco Bay, which was about half of the population of two-franchise markets in Chicago, New York, and Los Angeles.[11] In 1974, the San Francisco Giants drew 519,987, and the Athletics drew 843,693, which was the third lowest fan attendance in the major leagues. Prior to the move of the Athletics franchise to Oakland, the lowest Giants attendance was 1,242,480.[12] Instead of creating a new fan base, the Oakland franchise siphoned off fans who otherwise would have attended Giants games. Fans abandoned the Giants because of the better performance of the Oakland Athletics, and because of the notoriously bad weather at Candlestick Park.

Finley used special promotions to attract fans, such as half-price family nights, T-Shirt Day, Ball Day, and Helmet Day to name a few. The promotions proved successful. In 1974, for example, half-price family nights accounted for about a third of all attendance in Oakland.[13] Finley did not wait for the fans to come; he aggressively marketed the team and relied on promotions to attract spectators. Finley's style differed from the management of other major league franchises. Front office executives on other teams did not always know how to effectively manage baseball as a business. Comparing Finley's management of the Athletics to that of the ill-fated Seattle Pilots franchise highlights the consequences of ineffectual leadership and a complacent attitude that fans would automatically come to the stadium without any type of promotion.

The Seattle Pilots franchise came into existence in 1969. During the one year the team remained in Seattle, games were played at Sicks Stadium. Sicks was a minor league park that seated some 28,500 fans. At the end of Seattle's 1969 campaign, season attendance totaled around 680,000.[14] Seattle attendance for 1969 fell well below the pre-season expectation of a million admissions. The Pilots franchise, owned by William Daley and administered by Dewey Soriano, the former head of the minor league Pacific League, was bankrupt at the end of the 1969 season. The team was sold to a group headed by current Commissioner Bud Selig and moved to Milwaukee just weeks before the opening of the 1970 season.[15]

The Pilots franchise failed financially in 1969 because of multiple factors beyond the scope of this paper, including the deficiencies of Sicks Stadium. Limited promotional activity was a key factor in the Pilots' travail. I have already discussed the different promotions that Finley used to attract fans. Pilots executives did not fashion effective strategies to attract fans. This can be seen in a pre-season press release package issued by the Pilots franchise in early 1969.[16] Within the package was a pre-season ticket order form for home games. There was a simple two-tier ticket price structure. Fans could either pay $4.50 for "lounge" seats or $3.50 for "reserved" seats. The form did not list a single promotion. The argument can be made that Pilots managers were complacent about fan attendance, and made little effort to attract fans to view what turned out to be a very weak expansion squad playing in a sub-standard stadium. The result was financial disaster, although the owners of the franchise did make a profit from the 1970 sale of the team.[17]

The Second Oakland Dynasty, 1988–1992

The Oakland Athletics squad could be characterized as having been mediocre at best throughout most of the 1980s, but beginning in 1986 management took steps to rebuild the team. Towards the end of the 1986 season, Tony LaRussa was hired to manage the team. LaRussa had previously managed the Chicago White Sox franchise, and had guided the team to a division title in 1983. Young, talented players developed in the farm system also began to have an impact on the team, including power hitters Mark McGwire and Jose Canseco. The pitching staff was rebuilt largely through trades and to a lesser extent through the draft and free agency.

Between 1988 and 1990, the Oakland team won three consecutive American League championships and the World Series in 1989. Injuries crippled the team in 1991. However, in the following year the team won the Western Division of the American League, posting a record of 96–66, but then lost the American League championship to the Toronto Blue Jays. During those five years, a number of Oakland players left by way of trade or free agency, but management found effective roster replacements. After the 1992 season, the Athletics lost several key players to free agency, including the core of the pitching staff. Dave Stewart, Mike Moore, and others were traded or were lost in the expansion draft. Third baseman Carney Lansford retired.

Young pitchers developing in the farm system assumed prominent responsibilities in the staff, filling slots previously occupied by more experienced veterans, as shown in Table 4. The 1993 squad had a larger percentage of rookies and players with only a few years experience than the teams fielded during the championship seasons. In 1993, 38 percent of players were rookies, as against a figure that ranged from 15–18 percent in the previous four years. Veteran players with eleven or more years in the major leagues made up only 17 percent of players, also down from previ-

TABLE 4.
YEARS IN MAJOR LEAGUES
FOR OAKLAND ATHLETICS TEAMS, 1989–1993

Years	1989	%	1990	%	1991	%	1992	%	1993	%
Rookie	4	15	4	15	5	18	4	16	9	38
1–5	6	23	7	27	4	14	4	16	6	25
6–10	10	39	5	19	11	39	9	36	5	21
11–15	5	19	9	35	5	18	6	24	3	13
16–18	1	4	1	4	3	11	2	9	1	4
Total	26		26		28		25		24	

ous years. Management decided to rebuild the team without the services of veteran free agents. In the 1993 season, the club record dropped to well below .500. In the strike-shortened 1994 season, following the realignment of divisions, the Athletics lost more games than they won, but nearly had the best record in an otherwise mediocre division.

Examine a sample of twenty pitchers and fifteen starting batters who played for Oakland on one, two, or all of the American League championship teams from 1988 to 1990. Of this total, only nine (26 percent) came to the team by way of free agency. Of the others, 11 or 31 percent were acquired through the draft, and 15 or 43 percent by way of trade. In other words, the majority of players came to Oakland by means other than free agency.

The careers of four Oakland players typify the process of the formation of the 1988–1992 squads. The first is starting pitcher Dave Stewart, who first came up in the majors with the Dodgers in 1978. In nine seasons with three clubs, Stewart posted a journeyman record of 40 wins and 35 losses. The Athletics acquired Stewart through free agency after the 1986 season, and from 1987–1992 he posted a record of 108–71. Stewart went to Toronto as a free agent after the 1992 season. The second example is pitcher Dennis Eckersly, who first entered the majors with the Cleveland Indians in 1975. He later played for the Boston Red Sox and Chicago Cubs, before coming to Oakland as the result of a trade in April 1987. Manager Tony LaRussa converted Eckersly to the role of a relief pitcher with Oakland, and through the end of the 1992 season he saved 236 games.

The final examples are Jose Canseco and Mark McGwire, the "bash brothers," both of whom developed through the Oakland farm system. Canseco first played for Oakland in 1985, and, until being traded to the Texas Rangers in 1992, he hit 231 home runs. Canseco later spent time at Boston and Toronto, and signed with the expansion Tampa Bay Devil Rays for the 1999 season.. McGwire, a native Californian, first played for Oakland in 1986, and through the end of the 1992 season hit 220 home runs. McGwire later joined LaRussa at St. Louis, and had a record-breaking season in 1998 with 70 home runs.

Conclusions

The 1995 players strike ended, but the issues at the core of the dispute remain unresolved. A New York federal judge issued an injunction against the team owners to prevent them from using replacement players, and to resume normal labor relations under the previous collective bargaining agreement. Following the issuance of the injunction, players agreed to suspend the strike, and the season, featuring the regular players, began on April 25 with a reduced schedule. The end of the strike also found a number of free agents without teams, but the bidding for their talents began immediately after the final agreement to resume the season had been worked out. The Oakland Athletics lost pitcher Bobby Witt to the Florida Marlins, but signed three former Oakland pitchers: Greg Caderet, Rick Huneycutt, and Dave Stewart. In two days after the strike, teams made 80 roster changes. Management solidarity in the face of the strike evaporated when bidding for talented players commenced.

As the case of the Oakland Athletics team performance suggests, free agency did not prevent the creation of a winning team, even in a small and divided media market. Moreover, the break-up of the early 1970s championship squad was as much a consequence of management decisions made by Charlie Finley as it was of the changes in the contractual relationship between players and management. Free agents improved the solid 1988–1992 squad initially put together though the amateur draft and trades. However, both in the 1970s and early 1990s management allowed winning teams to be dismantled through free agency and trades for motives other than individual and team performance. The perception that free agency has somehow totally transformed labor relations in baseball is a myth.

It can also be argued that team owners also benefited from free agency and the increase in player salaries. Player salaries have increased, but so has the value of major league franchises. The short-lived Seattle Pilots franchise is a case in point. The group headed by William Daley paid $5.25 million for the Seattle franchise, and reportedly received $10.8 million in 1970 from the group headed by Bud Selig. Within half a decade, some free agents were making in excess of two million dollars. The new salary realities may have strained the finances of the lesser markets, but at the same time management did not always make effective adjustments to better market baseball. It was easier to try to break the players union and emasculate free agency. Baseball franchises are not always well managed.

The issue at stake with the last players strike had more to do with finances than free agency. Nonetheless, management selectively cited the compensation of the best paid players as an excuse to criticize the current labor system. At the same time, team owners refused to provide an accounting of profits and losses to justify their claims that the labor system required modification for the sport to survive. Moreover, during the late winter of 1995, it looked increasingly as if management was refusing to bargain in good faith, and owners attempted to use the media to manipulate public opinion against players, emphasizing the high salaries of a small elite.

When viewed against the backdrop of labor-management relations over the past twenty-five years, one salient fact emerges: owners have consistently taken steps to limit the gains of labor, in an apparent effort to regain absolute control over the careers of baseball players. Team owners have not been loath to employ unfair labor practices in an attempt to break the players union. The survival of the anti-trust exemption, which constitutes an intervention by the federal government on behalf of team owners, significantly distorts labor relations and perhaps provides management with an incentive to engage in unfair practices.

The refusal of team owners to give an accurate accounting of franchise finances muddies the water, so to speak. As the 1995 attempt to collect revenues from Little League teams that use major league team names shows, franchises earn money from a variety of sources, including lucrative television contracts. Moreover, and perhaps even more significantly, it was management that had bid up the salaries of superstars, and the efforts of the union have been limited to propping up the minimum salary for rank-and-file players and protecting labor rights by trying to ensure something close to a level playing field in labor-management relations. Management clearly wants to manipulate public opinion to undermine support for players.

Despite some gains made since the 1970s, baseball players face an increasingly hostile labor environment. Management retains the anti-trust exemption, and a conservative Congress most likely will not remove the exemption in the near future. Baseball players and other organized workers have few friends in the federal government. Moreover, it appears as if labor disputes in other professional sports, such as hockey and basketball, may give greater impetus for baseball management to take an even stronger stance against players in the future. Labor has lost, and continues to lose, ground against Major League Baseball owners.

Notes

1. The primary source for this study is David Neft and Richard Cohen, *The Sports Encyclopedia: Baseball* (New York: Grosset Dunlap, 1993). The general outline of labor-management conflict in professional baseball is well known, and is repeated here to provide context for franchise performance. Benjamin G. Rader, *American Sports: From the Age of Folk Games to the Age of Televised Sports*, 4th ed. (Saddle River, NJ: Prentice Hall, 1999), 165, 248, and 325–326.

2. Benjamin G. Rader, *Baseball: A History of America's Game* (Urbana and Chicago: University of Illinois Press, 1994), 54.

3. Ibid, 58.

4. Ibid, 60–61.

5. Ibid, 190.

6. For the arbitration cases involving Oakland Athletics players, see Bruce Markusen, *Baseball's Last Dynasty: Charlie Finley's Oakland A's* (Indianapolis: Masters Press, 1998), chapter 28.

7. Ibid, chapter, chapter 27.

8. Ibid, 398–399. See *The New York Times,* December 5, 1976, Free Agency File, National Baseball Hall of Fame Library Newspaper Files (hereinafter cited as NBH-FLNF). Clippings in the NBHFLNF often do not provide full citations. This study employed materials from the Free Agency, Oakland Athletics, and Seattle Pilots files of the NBHFLNF.

9. Markkusen, 173.

10. Ibid, 393.

11. Oakland Athletics, May 11. 1974, NBHFLNF.

12. Oakland Athletics, Ron Bergman, February 5, 1975; Ron Bergman, June 7, 1975, NBHFLNF.

13. Oakland Athletics, Ron Bergman, October 19, 1974, NBHFLNF.

14. Seattle Pilots, January 11, 1969; February 13, 1970; May 15, 1970, NBHFLNF.

15. Seattle Pilots, November 1, 1969; February 13, 1970; March 15, 1970; March 26, 1970; May 15, 1970, NBHFLNF.

16. Found in Seattle Pilots, NBHFLNF.

17. Seattle Pilots, March 26, 1970, NBHFLNF.

Establishing Women's
Professional Baseball

Elizabeth Tempesta

"Baseball is by far the most intimidating sport for women to play, intimidating to the culture."[1]

Although women are part of baseball's history and present, acceptance of women in the professional component of the national pastime remains elusive. In the past decade, numerous organizations have failed to establish successful amateur and professional women's leagues due to infrastructure difficulties and the resilience of cultural bias. Due to stereotypes about women's anatomy and athletic ability, women have not received the same opportunities as men to build skills in baseball. At present, however, advocates and players of the American Women's Baseball League strive to persuade men's professional baseball organizations to implement women's baseball from the top down. Ultimately, these advocates hope to build a solid infrastructure and create a cultural context conducive to the establishment of women's professional baseball.

Over the past sixty years, several attempts to establish women's professional baseball have ultimately failed, including the All-American Girls Professional Baseball League (1943–1954), the Colorado Silver Bullets (1994–1997), and Ladies League Baseball — subsequently renamed Ladies Professional Baseball (1997–1998). Culture bias and inadequate infrastructure were the reasons for the demise of these endeavors.

At present, women's baseball consists, at the grassroots level, of independent teams and leagues across the United States; some regularly compete in national and international tournaments. Since 1997, the American Women's Baseball League (AWBL) has worked to unify these leagues and teams, garner sponsorship from male-dominated Organized Baseball, and gain legitimacy for women's professional baseball. Numerous interviews conducted with those committed to creating professional opportunities for women in baseball provide documentation for this paper. The individuals cited have compelling stories to tell.

It was not easy growing up as a girl who played baseball. I found that I was constantly trying to prove myself and demonstrate how I did not "throw like a girl." For a time, my determination prevailed. At age twelve, however, I decided to follow the traditional trajectory of female ballplayers; I switched to softball. I enjoyed competition and praise for my ability to compete with the boys, but I also wanted to play. It was apparent that I would not be given game time (or even practice time) if I played baseball. What strikes me now about this decision is that I never questioned the absence of women's baseball. It appeared that I had two choices, playing softball or warming the bench on a baseball team.

Currently, I play in the New England Women's Baseball League (NEWBL), one of the most recent efforts at establishing professionalism for women ballplayers. Entering the NEWBL (then the Women's New England Baseball League) in 1999, I met women who not only shared my love for baseball, but also shared my past experiences and struggles, trying to acquire recognition in a game that is deemed masculine by the dominant culture.

Judy O'Brien, a player for the Bay State Express in the NEWBL, remembers well her youth:

> I grew up playing softball. Now, I wish I had played Little League baseball, ...(but) I really couldn't cuz there was softball. Actually, I don't know that I couldn't. I wish now my dad had taken me to the Little League tryout as opposed to the softball one. I used to go watch my brother play Little League and when I wanted to play, my dad said, "great," and took me to the softball tryouts.[2]

Like Judy, most of the women from the NEWBL grew up playing softball It was not because they were unable to handle hardball or because they lacked playing skills, but female ballplayers were and are culturally conditioned to play softball, which is presented as the female counterpart to baseball. Several women in the NEWBL, including myself, fought to play baseball in our youth, but sooner or later met with political and bureaucratic roadblocks.

Deb Scrozynski, a former Silver Bullet who currently plays for the NEWBL, says, "When I got to high school, they would not let me try out for the baseball team. They said, 'there is an equal program. Baseball is for the boys, and softball is for the girls.'"[3] This applied distinction demonstrates how sports acquire distinct gender designations. Indeed, since its rise in the 1930s, softball has presented itself as a "girl's" game.

In 1943, the All-American Girls Professional Baseball League (AAGPBL) emerged as a modified version of softball. The league combined baseball and softball (pitcher's threw underhand, the ball was larger than a hardball but smaller than a softball, and the configurations of the diamond were a hybrid of the two games), but it eventually developed into a true hardball league. Reaching its peak in 1948, the AAGBL drew thousands of fans to each game, allowing an entire nation to witness women playing baseball. Although the women of the AAGPBL served another purpose for Americans, sustaining patriotism by acting as a distraction from WWII, the league's success illustrates that people enjoy watching women playing baseball. Unfortunately, due to the postwar pressure for women to return to the domestic realm and support their families, the idea of women playing baseball faded into the background. The AAGPBL eventually folded due to an inadequate infrastructure. The AAGPBL failed to create a farm system that would generate new talent.

Since the demise of the AAGPBL in 1954, efforts at establishing women's professional baseball have met similar obstacles, struggling to shed ongoing prejudices about girls playing "a man's game." One such effort occurred in 1984 when Bob Hope formed the Sun Sox and attempted to affiliate the co-ed team with the Class A Florida State League.[4] Beginning in the 1970's, Hope, an Atlanta Braves executive, began the effort to form a professional team for women. In the fall of '84, Hope held tryouts, and sixty women showed up. The Sun Sox, however, failed to gain admission to the FSL. Hope eventually abandoned his efforts in 1985.

After Hope's venture, formidable attempts to establish women's baseball leagues followed. Some of these organization have been primarily recreational, such as the American Women's Baseball Association (AWBA), which originated in Chicago in 1988. The Washington Metropolitan Women's Baseball League (WMWBL), after modest beginnings, established the teams that comprise the Eastern Women's Baseball Conference (EWBC).[5] And others, including those who created the Colorado Silver Bullets, have aspired to true professionalism.

In 1994, the Silver Bullets began their inaugural season, igniting one of the most substantial and comprehensive efforts to push women's baseball into the professional arena. Sponsored by the Coors Brewing Company, the Silver Bullets set off on a tour of fifty exhibition games against men's minor league, semi-professional, and college teams. "As an independent of the AA Short Season Northern League the team…(played) in the hometown of each of the six Northern League teams — Duluth, Minnesota; Sioux City, Iowa; Sioux Falls, South Dakota; Winnipeg, Manitoba; St. Paul, Minnesota; and Thunder Bay, Ontario."[6] Silver Bullet games were played in several major league ballparks, including Candlestick Park, the Seattle Kingdome, and Mile High Stadium.

Managed by ex–major leaguer, Phil Neikro, the Silver Bullets set out to prove to another generation that women can play baseball. Unfortunately, after four years the Bullets were not able to a attract sufficient fan base, and the team disbanded.

As with the AAGPBL, the fall of the Silver Bullets was largely due to an inability to generate good talent due to the lack of preparatory leagues available to girls. O'Brien, who played for the Bullets in 1997, offers her opinion on why the Silver Bullets did not obtain lasting success:

> I think the Bullets had a poor model, and that Coors did it to make a quick buck. I think Phil Neikro truly believed in it, but he should have taken the time to build it up a little more. I think the people really enjoyed it at first and thought it was a novelty, but they should have never started out playing men. I don't know what the hell they were thinking. And it is not because the women cannot hit the men, but because the [women's] pitching was not developed enough. Women have not had the opportunity to play continuously. A lot of women pitched from ages six or seven until they were fifteen and got forced out. Even if you come back at twenty, you have not had the …time to develop.[7]

Although the Silver Bullets did not catch on in the way some had hoped, their contribution to raising the awareness about women in baseball paved the way for future clubs and organizations. In the words of Jim Glennie, Commissioner of the American Women's Baseball League, "Stadiums filled almost everywhere the Silver Bullets played, and in their wake they left a residue of interest and established a benchmark for women playing baseball."[8]

Another significant development in women's baseball occurred in 1992 with the creation of the Michigan Women's Baseball League (MWBL). League founder Jim Glennie has been an important figure in organizing and supporting women in baseball. In 1997, the MWBL evolved into the American Women's Baseball League (AWBL), which presently serves as an umbrella organization, providing a network for all women's baseball leagues throughout the country.

In 1997, Ladies League Baseball (LLB) emerged with four teams from the West Coast — two teams from Los Angeles, one from San Jose, and one from Phoenix. Due to financial problems, the LLB was forced to end its season early, but in 1998 reorganized as Ladies Professional Baseball (LPB) and expanded to six teams, three on each coast. Unfortunately, the league's financial problems persisted, and it disbanded after sixteen games.[9] O'Brien, who played for the LPB in 1998, describes the reason for its inevitable demise:

> Mike Ribant [Owner of LPB] maximized cost and decreased revenue. He didn't put any money into marketing and promotions and put it all on the field. Well, what good does having the best people [do] if no one knows that you're playing? And then he had us flying back and forth [from coast to coast] and maximizing costs.[10]

Attempts to establish pro women's ball have been short-lived. In an interview, Jim Glennie argued that the nontraditional notion of women playing baseball continues to impede any efforts to establish professionalism.

The expectation that women play softball rather than baseball remains a powerful obstacle, and I experience it everyday. When I tell people I play baseball, I usually end up repeating myself, emphasizing, "Yes, BASE-BALL." O'Brien observes:

> I would like it to be seamless where kids could play Little League baseball and not get forced out at 15, and still have somewhere to go. It bothers me. Why wasn't there just boy's baseball and girl's baseball? Now it has been so deeply conditioned, so we have a tough battle. Are you going to draw kids at a young age away from softball when they don't have the opportunity to get a scholarship to college for baseball? If you are a young athlete, where are you going to go?[11]

The notion of women playing baseball defies cultural expectations. Kenesaw Mountain Landis, the federal judge who became baseball's first Commissioner, asserted, "Baseball is something more than a game to an American boy. It is a training field for his life work."[12] And Glennie's recollections are also gender specific, recalling, "as a *boy* going to bed thinking about baseball." Girls, on the other hand, have been traditionally conditioned to dream about other things. I propose creating a true *field of dreams* for women as well as men. We need to obliterate stereotypes by allowing girls the opportunity to develop baseball skills at an early age. In addition, we need to place the same emphasis on women's sports as we do on men's sports.

O'Brien's reflection on her childhood illustrates how prejudice and inequity in sports are played out:

> I remember as a kid, the biggest impression on me was walking by a baseball field, which had a nice fence, dugouts, and sponsorship signs.

> And I'm walking by what looks like a ballpark to our softball field, which is grass fields underneath the power lines, with a chicken wire backstop, and bags on the dirt. We didn't even have base lines. I remember walking by and thinking, man, I wish I could play there, cuz I would like to know what it would feel like to hit it out.[13]

Women's leagues have failed to generate new talent due to the lack of preparatory leagues. In fact, baseball is quite unique in this way since girls are not given the same opportunities in baseball as they are in other sports, such as basketball, soccer, and volleyball. Consequently, girls are not socialized in baseball. Conversely, males have the opportunity to play from early childhood until they are venerable figures on senior teams..

Justine Warren, president of the Women's Baseball League, is currently involved in creating opportunities for young girls to play baseball. She is interested in "developing youth baseball" and developing an online resource for women's baseball at MsWBL.com. Warren strives to "enhance awareness and provide the opportunity for female athletes to participate in baseball, and to promote the quality and standards of the game."[14]

As a former player, Warren describes her own experience as a female playing baseball:

> My biggest fault in playing with men was that the coaches would not give me the same training time nor the same playing time as my male teammates. It is hard to play well when coaches only let you play when you are losing or only winning by a lot. There are so many instances of my coaches killing my confidence by their actions or words, that even when they let me play on their team, I was not a real part of it. If I had received the same type of coaching and encouragement as my teammates, as a pitcher, I could have competed at a higher level with the men.[15]

Nicole Zarrett, a player for the North Shore Navigators in the NEWBL, also points to encouragement and opportunity as being at the heart of truncating women's athletic growth:

> I remember playing baseball when I was younger, and I was a home run hitter, you know? I was younger than the boys were, and if I was allowed to continue playing baseball and not forced to switch over to softball, then I probably would have been just as good as any of those guys. My physique would have been different. My skill level would have been different. It is a matter of giving me the opportunity to do it! Women have been denied the opportunity to play.[16]

Zarrett underscores the importance of giving young girls the opportunity to strengthen their skills, by allowing them to engage in the same regimen as boys. She asserts, "It is not physical...[but rather] socialization that exacerbates these differences."[17]

Physical ability and skill level are issues frequently mentioned by skeptics of women playing baseball. Specifically, it has been argued that women are not strong enough to play hardball because they lack the upper body strength. However, many feel this is a cultural issue rather than a physical one. When Bob Hope was "asked what prevents women from playing in the minors," he replied, "The level of prejudice is what stands in the way.'"[18] Hope points to prejudice, not a lack of physical ability, as the barrier that curtails women's involvement in baseball. American society has fabricated the idea that women are unable to acquire a strength comparable to that of men. The problem is girls and boys are brought up, encouraged, and trained differently. They are not taught to like and appreciate the same things, and, therefore, their minds and bodies develop differently, based on gender bias, not natural biological makeup.

Women's physical abilities are constantly being measured against men. However, one cannot adequately compare the baseball abilities of men and women because women have not been given the same opportunities to develop and enhance their bodies. One of the reasons for this is that athleticism in women is still not fully embraced. Sure, Nike ads depict women who play hard and sweat, but it seems equally important for women athletes to purposefully promote "femininity." This blatant emphasis is exemplified in advertisements for the Women's National Basketball Association, which constantly emphasize that the women of the WNBA are mothers as well as basketball players. The reason for this is that athleticism and physical strength are still designated as masculine, and the idea of women as physically aggressive individuals compromises traditional notions of femininity.

In order to obliterate the negative stereotypes about the physical aptitude of female ballplayers, we must first acknowledge that conditioning determines physical ability and that society instills the notion that boys are better athletes than girls. For example, can we honestly say that boys are biologically equipped with the motor skills to throw a baseball, and that girls somehow lack this ability? In her book, *The Frailty Myth*, Collete Dowling enlarges this discussion:

> The average person who has not been taught how to throw properly will follow an "ipsilateral pattern," which means using just one side of the body. If a person is right handed, his or her inclination is to step forward on the right foot. Most boys as well as girls will throw ipsilaterally when they start out.[19]

Dowling provides further evidence that cultural conditioning determines differences in the orientation of girls and boys to baseball. So, if a girl was throwing in an ipsilateral pattern, a parent might disregard it, since she is female and assume that she cannot throw a ball. But if a boy throws in this fashion, a parent might try harder to improve his throwing technique, for American culture asserts that he is equipped with the physical ability to throw a baseball.

As O'Brien, Zarrett, and Warren have illustrated, girls need to be given opportunities equal to boys to acquire and enhance their baseball skills. Deb Scrozynski adds, "What if Hank Aaron never had a chance to play ball or what if Nomar [Garciaparra] never grew up in an area where there was organized baseball? Would they still be the great players they are today?"[20]

Today, women's baseball is beginning to create a training infrastructure for women. Their efforts need to be augmented by the formation of a professional organization that is top solid so that it will grow down, generating opportunities for young female ballplayers, which will ultimately feed the professional clubs. Judy O'Brien elaborates on this point:

> In the short run, I would like to see a national governing body to bring these leagues together. I think that is when we will get more recognition. When USA Baseball sees the already built structure, then they are going to want to buy in. I think we should adopt playing rules across the nation, a semblance, like ASA softball (women's majors) where you have all these leagues that are regional and state structures across the nation. My hope in New England is that we [will] continue to increase the awareness and build good players to be able to come up with a pro team. And hopefully other leagues will be able to do [the same] so that we could say, 'OK there are enough talented ballplayers now across the nation so that we could form four or six pro teams.' And then have the sponsorship to pay them so that we could get the players to come to a central locale and play.[21]

O'Brien's point leads to Jim Glennie's other assertion, regarding the need to implement a solid governing body that is backed and promoted by men's professional organizations in order to pave the way for its acceptance and success. Historically, women's baseball has lacked a solid and cohesive infrastructure with scant support from men's professional (and amateur) organizations. Consequently, novice women's leagues have been forced to work from the bottom up. Due to prejudice against women playing baseball, Glennie asserts, expansion and professional recognition are unlikely to emanate from a grassroots level. In fact, what needs to happen is the opposite. Women's organizations need to work from the top down in order to establish themselves in the professional arena. This involves backing from organizations such as Major League Baseball (MLB) and USA Baseball in order to create a cultural context that will grow down, eventually establishing youth organizations and a farm system that will feed the professional league.[22] The AAGPBL and the Silver Bullets are good examples of women's professional baseball leagues that folded due to an inability to grow down. No farm system or feeder teams evolved to augment their efforts.

In an effort to create a more unified system for women's baseball, several organizational bodies promote national and international tournament play. In 1995, for example, the National Women's Baseball Association (NWBA) was formed. At present, the American Women's Baseball League advocates for local women's baseball leagues throughout the United States; it is also planning to host a World Series with teams from the United States, Canada, Australia, and Japan. NWBA officials hope to gain the support of Major League Baseball and USA Baseball.

Such backing is needed for the continued growth and success of the AWBL. Commissioner Glennie cites the National Basketball Association's support of the Women's National Basketball Association. He notes that the WNBA receives promotion and financial backing from the NBA and is considered a sister league to the NBA. The NBA has received good press from its partnership with the WNBA, and the WNBA has survived.

Judy O'Brien is another who views the NBA/WNBA partnership as a model for women's professional baseball:

> Can we get through to Major League Baseball? It is a good ol' boys system, much more than any other sport, that, I believe, does not want to see women play baseball. But the mighty dollar speaks. We [just] need to show them that there is enough talent out there now [to] make money. The WNBA won out because they had that backing. Why did they get on TV? Not because any of these stations wanted to carry them, but because the NBA said if you want the NBA games, you're gonna have to carry so many of the WNBA games too. You want to be a sponsor of the NBA, guess what? You're gonna have to sponsor the WNBA too. They had negotiating power and that is what it is going to take.[23]

O'Brien also points to the regulation and structure of women's soccer as a model for success:

> Soccer is one of the most unbelievably organized sports, developing talent and having developmental programs that are consistent across the country, and licensing for umpires at different levels to make sure you are getting the same quality no matter where you are. They are playing by the same rules and on the same size fields.[24]

Unfortunately, unification has not happened in women's baseball yet. It is still growing and currently consists of little networks across the United States. According to O'Brien, "We are trying to get in with USA Baseball and Major League Baseball to get that structure from the top down, [so that we can] take all these leagues and form a governing body and then hold a true national championship."[25] As mentioned above, one small network is the NEWBL, which continues to work on a local level, fine tuning its talent and enhancing the product. O'Brien describes the league's mission:

> Establishing the NEWBL in 1999, Jerry Dawson and Christine Lindeborg wanted to have a women's professional baseball league, and thought they could begin as semi-pro. Although they did not want to label the league semipro or pro status until they had the product to put on the field, because I think to some extent that ruins the brand name. The NEWBL wants to make sure they are promoting baseball and giving people an opportunity to play but at the same time tries to raise the competitive level by increasing the teaching, and attracting better players.[26]

In the NEWBL's early days, the league worked from a franchise model, in which each team had its own owner and sponsors, and promoted themselves. However, the NEWBL found that this created inequity amongst the teams, since some were able to promote themselves better than others were. So in 2001, the league altered its structure. The NEWBL is currently operating under one league umbrella. The purpose is to generate a solid, competitive league, and move back to a franchise/pro model after a stable infrastructure is established..

Judy O'Brien envisions a bright future for the NEWBL. She believes that women's baseball is on the road to professional recognition:

> I have definitely seen it grow from when I started playing in 1993. [It's grown] from a team at each one of these places to leagues, and the competitiveness has really taken off. I also think we are getting more exposure. A lot of softball players are coming over. A lot of women had played Little League when they were kids and then went and played softball, and are now coming back cuz they loved it and missed it. It's great![27]

Nicole Zarrett also expressed optimism about the future of women's baseball. She reflected on a NEWBL game played on Doubleday Field in Cooperstown, New York during the 2000 season:

> They [the fans/visitors to Cooperstown] were psyched that we were playing baseball. And it was a great game. Bottom of the ninth, a tied game with a runner on second, and Kate (Titus) got up and hits a bomb that bounces off the outfield wall for a double. You just heard this roar from the crowd. It was the best experience, and I thought, 'This could really happen.'[28]

Throughout its history, baseball has created a tradition and culture that disenfranchises women. Over the years, there have been several efforts to establish professional baseball for women, but a cultural tradition that depicts baseball as the exclusive domain of men has impeded those efforts. The American Women's Baseball League and hundreds of aspiring women ballplayers are currently making enormous contributions to rid American culture of gender discrimination. They are seeking to establish a professional model that will grow down, creating a new cultural context that allows girls and women to identify themselves as baseball players.

Jim Glennie hopes to attract the attention of men's professional organizations so that the infrastructure will build down, augmenting the efforts of youth organizations and other preparatory leagues. He believes this will provide the opportunity for girls to play more competitively, enabling them to enhance their skill level and strive for professionalism. According to Glennie, it is imperative to begin from the top and to have the support of men's professional baseball organizations. This, asserts Glennie, is necessary in order to eliminate bias and to successfully end disenfranchisement against women in baseball.

Notes

1. Nicole Zarrett, interview by the author, 11 November 2000.
2. Judy O'Brien, interview by the author, 13 May 2001.
3. Deb Scrozynski, interview by the author, 20 May 2001.
4. Barbara Gregorich, *Women at Play: The Story of Women in Baseball* (San Diego: A Harvest Original Brace & Company, 1993), 177.
5. James Glennie, interview by author, 5 February 2001.
6. Kathleen Christie, "From a Dream to a Reality," (Colorado Silver Bullets, *http://www.cs.berkeley.edu/~j-yen/SilverBullets/history.html*), February 2001.
7. O'Brien, interview.
8. Glennie, interview.
9. *Ibid.*
10. O'Brien, interview.
11. *Ibid.*
12. Geoffrey C. Ward and Ken Burns, *The History of Baseball* (New York: Alfred A. Knopf, 1994), 144.
13. O'Brien, interview.
14. Justine Warren, interview by author, 8 February 2001.
15. *Ibid.*
16. Zarrett, interview.
17. *Ibid.*
18. Gregorich, 182.
19. Colette Dowling, *The Frailty Myth: Women Approaching Physical Equality* (New York Random House, 2000), 162.
20. Scrozynski, interview.
21. O'Brien, interview.
22. Glennie, interview.

23. O'Brien, interview.
24. *Ibid.*
25. *Ibid.*
26. *Ibid.*
27. *Ibid.*
28. Zarrett, interview.

Index